HISTORY OF
WALKER COUNTY
ITS TOWNS AND ITS PEOPLE

By

JOHN MARTIN DOMBHART

CAYCE PUBLISHING COMPANY

THORNTON, ARKANSAS

This volume was reproduced from
an 1937 edition located in the
publisher's private library,
Greenville, South Carolina

Please Direct all Correspondence & Orders to:

**Southern Historical Press, Inc.
P.O. Box 1267
375 West Broad Street
Greenville, S.C. 29602-1267**

Originally published: Thornton, Ark., 1937
Reprinted: Southern Historical Press, Inc.
Greenville, S.C., 2002
New Material Copyright © 2002
ISBN # 0-89308-725-4

DEDICATED
TO
SYBIL AIKEN DOMBHART
who conceived and inspired this work
and to
VERA KITCHENS DOMBHART
whose sympathy and encouragement made it possible

CONTENTS

CHAPTER		PAGE
Introduction		7

PART ONE — THE COUNTY

I.	The Creation of a State	11
II.	The Rise of a New County	19
III.	The Flush Times in Walker	28
IV.	Progress and Prosperity	35
V.	War and its Aftermath	45
VI.	Recovery	54
VII.	Railroads and Prosperity	58
VIII.	Down to Earth	67
IX.	World War and World Depression	75

PART TWO — THE TOWNS

Carbon Hill	83
Cordova	84
Dora (Sharon—Horse Creek)	87
Jasper	89
Manchester	103
Oakman (York—Days Gap—Marietta)	103
Parrish (Hewitt—Jonesboro)	106
South Lowell	110
Townley (Holly Grove—Pleasant Grove)	111

PART THREE — THE PEOPLE

Early Settlers	117

INTRODUCTION

This volume contains information gathered by the author in pursuit of a "hobby." A native and resident of Washington, D. C., I did not come to Walker County to make my home until 1929. Desiring to know something of the county, its towns and its people, I began to seek this information, and was immediately struck by the fact that so little had been written about Walker County. From that fact grew the hobby of collecting historical data on the county.

However, this work could not have been completed without the aid of Prof. Albert Burton Moore's "History of Alabama and Her People," published by the American Historical Society in 1927. Prof. Moore has done a wonderful work in recording facts concerning the social and economic life of the early settlers, and his descriptions of that life have been extensively used by me. Thanks and apologies are hereby extended him for any failure to give him due credit for any material used.

A great deal of Walker County's history centers around the coal mining industry, and most of the facts regarding this industry were recorded by Ethel Armes in her "Story of Coal and Iron in Alabama," published in 1910. Thanks and apologies are extended to Miss Armes for any material from her book, that may have been inadvertently used without due credit being given.

Dr. Thomas McAdory Owen's "History of Alabama and Dictionary of Alabama Biography," published in 1921, has been the source of a great deal of information.

Thanks are also extended to those good people of Walker, too numerous to name individually, who have answered my inquisitive questioning and made available their family records, during the three years that I have been engaged on this work. The lack of early courthouse records, destroyed by fire in 1877, has been a serious handicap, which has only been overcome through many private records.

In the preparation of this work I have striven for accuracy, and I believe every statement made herein to be true. Lack of authentic information has caused the exclusion of a number of items, particularly in regard to families.

Individuals have been given the most prominent parts in this volume for the reason that it is people who make history. And whether this work is a history or merely a directory of early settlers is an open question. I did not strive for literary excellence, but rather to record facts as I found them, and to convey to my readers, through these facts, a picture of the sturdy settlers who made the county,—those hardy pioneers, who came into the "hill country," with little or no possessions, and through the work of their own hands, alone, created the county.

In so far as I have failed to present the picture of their hardships and toil; their sorrows and pleasures; and above all, their independence; I have fallen short of my goal.

THE AUTHOR.

Parrish, Alabama, October 17, 1936.

PART ONE—THE COUNTY

CHAPTER I

THE CREATION OF A STATE

Man cannot journey to and fro without engraving upon the world a record of his travels. The roads he builds are inscriptions in which later generations read of his trials and struggles. These traces which he etches upon the earth may be merely a pathway through a virgin forest, beaten deep by the padding feet of Indian warriors, or the broad expanse of some stream upon which he has floated to his destination, yet the story of these trails is the story of civilization.

The section of Alabama now called Walker County had many Indian trails. Situated in a "corner" formed by the boundaries of the Creek, the Cherokee and the Chickasaw countries, these trails not only tied up the several tribes, but also extended into other parts of the state and into Florida, Georgia and Mississippi. Several of these trails were highly important to early settlers of the state, and in a lesser degree to early settlers of Walker County.

One, known as the "High Town Path," extended from near the present site of Atlanta, through the present city of Gadsden, passed just south of Sand Mountain, and into the Chickasaw country in northwest Alabama and northern Mississippi. Another, called the "Southern Trail," led from the present site of Augusta, Georgia, through Columbus, across the Tallapoosa and Coosa Rivers to Cahaba Old Town on the Cahaba River. From thence it extended to the Warrior River, which it crossed at Squaw Shoals, where Lock Seventeen is now located, and then northwestward to the Chickasaw crossing of the Tombigbee River at Cotton Port. A third road was one that led from Greenville, South Carolina, through Saluda Gap in the Blue Ridge mountains, to Asheville, North Carolina; thence along the course of the French Broad and Tennessee Rivers to Knoxville and Chattanooga. From Chattanooga the early settler could float down the Tennessee to any point that might suit his fancy.

There was also an Indian trail extending from Ditto's Landing on the Tennessee to Mudtown on the Cahaba. During the War of 1812 General Jackson cut a military road along this Indian trail, from Huntsville, through Jones Valley by the present site of Birmingham, to Tuscaloosa. The Huntsville Road, as it came to be called, was used by many of Walker County's earliest settlers; indications being that they followed this road to its crossing of the Mulberry Fork of the Warrior River and then followed down the river to a likely point of settlement.

Before 1819 the entire country, now embraced within the boundaries of Alabama, suffered from extensive land speculation. The government enacted the first public land law in 1785, which was revised in 1796. The second general land law was enacted in 1800 and amended in 1803. Each of these acts seemed to contemplate the purchase of very large tracts by individuals or groups of individuals, and the subsequent re-sale in smaller tracts. In 1819 the act was again amended and small tracts could be purchased for one dollar and twenty-five cents per acre.

A great host of settlers thronged the roads of Alabama, seeking lands under these various acts, and as a suitable region was reached by these homeseekers, they stopped. In these cavalcades of migrants there was represented all classes and all degrees of the social scale, from the entourage of a wealthy planter with his many slaves in wagons, to those who came with all their possessions packed in a single wagon, or to those who could afford only pack horses to transport their goods. Others poorer still, perhaps owning only a pony or an ox, packed their goods in a hogshead, put trunions into the ends, attached shafts to which the pony or ox was harnessed, and completed the long journey in this way. The depths of poverty was reached however, in a description of a traveler, printed in the Augusta Chronicle of September 24, 1819, "Passed through this place from Greenville District, South Carolina, bound for Chatahouchie; a man and his wife, his son and his wife, with a cart but no horse. The man had a belt over his shoulders and he drew in the shafts; the son assisted his father to draw the cart; the son's wife rode in the cart, and the old woman was walking, carrying a rifle and driving a cow."

The rich planters and the more well to do settlers sought land on the Alabama, the Tombigbee or the lower Warrior, while those of poorer estate sought out the creek bottoms. It was a few of the poorer class who, before 1820, turned aside into the "hill country" of Walker, and settled along its creek bottoms and on its hillsides. Most of them were squatters who hoped to improve their lands and to make enough by the time of their sale to pay for them. Some succeeded, others did not, but the total number that blazed the trail into Walker, before 1820, was few.

Settlers were slow to occupy this section of the country because of its remoteness from navigable waters and the consequent difficulties of reaching the markets. Ethel Armes, in her "Story of Coal and Iron," tells us that "As late as 1816, Richard Breckenbridge made a horseback trip from some point near Columbus, Mississippi, through this region. His diary gives an account of what he saw and experienced during the two weeks of his lone passage through the wilds without meeting with a human being or discovering any signs of the habitation of white men or Indians. On August 20th he came upon some deserted Indian cabins at the site of Old Warrior Town, at the confluence of the Sipsey and Mulberry Forks. These were probably cabins that had escaped destruction at the hands of Colonel John Coffee in October 1813, when he attacked and burnt the town."

But while Breckenbridge failed to see them, there were undoubtedly some few settlers in this section at that time. Some believe that Wallace Jones, an Irish immigrant, settled on the Warrior River prior to 1800. Mathias Turner, one of General Jackson's Tennessee Volunteers, had settled on a creek in the lower part of the county, and became a noted hunter of wild animals. Because of the number of wolves found along this creek, he named it Wolf Creek. William Guttery had come down from Tennessee, in the early 1800's, with his three sons, Robert, Johnson and Isham, and settled on Lost Creek, near Holly Grove. Henry Sides had come in with several married sons and settled near Pleasant Grove.

Others followed before 1820. On September 13, 1819, two brothers, David and William Payne, entered government land in Section 17, Township 13, Range 4, and James Elliott in Section 29, Township 14, Range 5. A month later, on October 9, 1819, a blacksmith named William Butt entered land in Section 35, Township 13, Range 5, and on the same day David Murphree entered land in Section 3, Township 14, Range 5. There were no doubt many others whose names are now unknown.

What manner of living was there for these early settlers of Walker? Perhaps the most vivid description of pioneer life in Alabama is given by Albert Burton Moore in his "Alabama and Her People." He says, "The settler's first problem was to erect a cabin with the rude implements brought along. A single cabin was usually provided with just one door and one window. The window gave light and ventilation was supplied by the cracks in the walls and the floor. A shutter was put on both the window and the door, which was made of rough clapboards fastened together by wooden pegs driven into auger holes. Glass windows were unknown. The clumsy old shutters swung and creaked upon wooden hinges, for steel hinges were unknown.

"Later on when wealth was accumulated and trade developed, dwellings began to improve; hewn logs were used instead of round logs; the cabins were more carefully and more neatly plastered, and instead of the rough clapboards, they used high grade boards and shingles, sawed out at first with the old hand whipsaw, before the establishment of sawmills.

"The interior of the early cabin was as humble as the exterior. With an axe, saw, drawing knife, plane, augers and chisels, the master of the household made his rough bedsteads, stools, chairs, benches and cradles from the timber that grew on the sides of the hills. A description of the cradle, which was common to every household, will suffice to give some idea of the utter crudeness of the furniture of the household. It was simply half of a hollow log with a bit of rocker-shaped clapboard fastened on each end. In such a cradle (Walker's) first young hopefuls, wrapped in quilts or the fur skins of wild animals were lulled to sleep.

"Kitchen and table furnishings were both crude and scanty. Of course there were no cooking stoves, and the cooking utensils of the best equipped homes consisted of a skillet, an oven and a pot. Plates, bowls, dishes and spoons were made of pewter and knives of material almost as soft. Tin cups, gourds and squash rinds completed the equipment. As pewter utensils were hard to replace, every disabled piece was carefully saved until the "tinker" came around to repair it or to remodel it into some other kind of utensil.

"Clothes were hung on wooden pegs set in the walls. A water shelf and a bucket, a churn and dasher, a brush broom, a spinning wheel, a reel, a pair of cards and a loom, usually completed the household furnishings.

"Until the first crop was made, food was none too plentiful. Game could be had at the cost of a few hours stalking and an accurate shot, but bread was scarce, and coffee, tea, sugar, salt and pepper were almost unobtainable. Salt in particular, when it could be purchased, was almost prohibitive in price, selling as it did at ten dollars a bushel.

"Corn was brought along from the old settlements when possible, on pack horses, but the supply was often very, very scarce. While the corn lasted "ash cake" and "johnny cake" were very popular.

"When the cabin had been built the settler busied himself with the clearing and fencing of the fields. Trees were deadened or hacked down with dull and clumsy axes. Rails were split with mauls made out of hickory saplings and wedges of hickory or dogwood. Everything was speeded up as much as possible to get the land ready for the first crop and that crop planted, which usually consisted of corn, the various garden vegetables, tobacco, cotton and sometimes flax.

"Until the first cotton crop came in, the wearing apparel of the early settler was made largely from the skins and furs of wild animals.

"When any of these pioneers became sick they usually doctored themselves. It took something especially bad to have the doctor called. Every old woman was both a druggist and a physician. In the absence of drugs she learned how to make her own, and in the absence of a doctor she learned how to 'dose' her medicine and to administer it. The bark, roots, leaves and berries of herbs and trees furnished a great variety of teas, oozes, poultices and salves. 'Suets' were made and employed to combat all kinds of human and animal ailments.

"Even the 'conjurer' was called into service, and there were many who were patrons of his uncanny art. But the doctors, grandmothers and conjurers alike were helpless before epidemics of fevers and pneumonia, and at times the rate of mortality was frightfully high.

"Dentistry was an unknown art and there was no remedy for a decaying tooth. When one became bothersome, there was only one thing to do and that was to extract it. The sufferer had the choice of having it pulled by a professional tooth-puller, who used a pair of rough iron or steel pincers which had been made in some blacksmith shop, or by a non-professional tooth-puller who jerked it out with a piece of cord or knocked it out by setting a nail or spike against the tooth and hitting it a heavy blow with a hammer.

"The toil that was necessary for the early settler to establish himself was constant, heavy and back-breaking. Both sexes labored from early morning hours far into the dead hours of the night. Some became discouraged and disheartened, but many won through."

On July 5, 1819, a Constitutional Convention was held at Huntsville, for the purpose of adopting a State Constitution. What is now Walker County was then a part of Madison County, which was represented by John W. Walker, of Huntsville, who was also elected chairman of the convention. Congress approved the constitution submitted and a joint resolution, admitting the State into the Union was adopted and received the approval of President Monroe on December 14, 1819.

Re-arrangement of county lines had taken place and the territory embracing Walker County was included within the boundaries of Tuscaloosa County.

The establishment of statehood was to have a great beneficial effect on the "hill people" and the era of rapid settlement and prosperity was about to open.

CHAPTER II

THE RISE OF A NEW COUNTY

The success of any pioneer settlement depends in a large measure upon the means of transportation;—transportation for the settler to get into the country and transportation for him to get his products to market. Lack of roads therefore retarded the progress of settlement in Walker County, for there were no roads, prior to 1820, other than Indian trails and those that were built by the settlers themselves. It is merely a courtesy to call such thoroughfares roads, for they were little more than wide paths cut through the forest, upon high ground wherever possible; such roads as we still see today leading back to some timber cutting operation and used to haul out the logs.

The best roads in the state were constructed by private corporations, as turnpike or toll roads, and were operated as commercial enterprises, many companies also operating stages on their roads.

One such road was of extreme importance to Walker County. On December 16, 1819, an act was passed authorizing John Byler and associates to construct a turnpike from Big Shoal Creek in Lauderdale County to Tuscaloosa, and by 1822 this road was completed. The act authorizing the road also stipulated the toll rates to be charged, as follows: "On a four wheel carriage and team, seventy-five cents; on a two wheel carriage, fifty cents; on a man and horse, twelve and a half cents; on each pack horse, six and a fourth cents; for each head of cattle, one cent; for each head of hogs or sheep, half a cent."

Postmen, express messengers, Federal and state troops, footmen, persons going to or from church, and laborers on their way to or from their fields were exempted from tolls.

"Byler's Road," as it is still known today, traversed Walker County, entering the county from Fayette County, three or four miles southwest of the present town of Eldridge, passing through Eldridge, and leaving the county at the Winston County line, six or seven miles northeast of Eldridge. It not only gave an entry into the county from Tuscaloosa on the south and from the Tennessee Valley on the north, but of more importance still, it gave the early settler a highway over which to haul his products to Tuscaloosa, which was to be the main trading center for Walker County, until the advent of the railroads almost seventy years later. In wagons, drawn not infrequently by oxen, the people hauled their corn and cotton and staves and other products to town, and their supplies, particularly salt, back home. The round trip frequently took a week and the people often went in parties of two or more, camped out along the road at night, and endeavored to make a picnic trip out of the journey.

Squaw Shoals, twenty-six miles above Tuscaloosa, on the Warrior River, marked the head of navigation on that stream, and transportation of Walker County products down the Warrior was barred until some method of crossing the shoals could be devised. In the early 1820's the first flatboat was launched on the Mulberry Fork of the Warrior, loaded with staves belonging to William Dunn. William Jones carried this boat through Squaw Shoals, on the first trip ever made over the shoals, to Tuscaloosa, where the boat and its cargo were both sold. For the return trip a keel was purchased and loaded with two hundred sacks of salt and other merchandise to be carried back up the river. The trip back over the shoals was most arduous. No cable could be found strong enough to pull the loaded keel over the turbulent waters. When the rapids were reached, the salt would be taken from the keel and carried by hand to a point upstream from which the keel could be pulled with its load. The keel would be re-loaded and pulled until again checked by the rushing waters. When the most violent rapids were reached the salt men of the crew were assisted by two farmers living near, and they returned the favor by helping roll logs on the farm.

The trip was successfully completed and the markets of Tuscaloosa, Demopolis and Mobile were opened to Walker County farmers. From this time, until the advent of the railroads many years later, much merchandise was shipped by boats to the lower rivers. In the first years of flatboat transportation, hogs, beeves, poultry, piles, staves, corn and cotton were shipped and sold in South Alabama. When the market was reached and its cargo disposed of, the craft was sold for what it would bring, in preference to attempting to pole or warp it back up stream. Before 1830 steamboats were operating on the Warrior as far up as Tuscaloosa, and those who flatboated their goods to Demopolis or Mobile could return in grand style. It was good to be aboard the old "Cherokee" as her side paddles spun and her stacks belched forth black smoke from fat pine. The luxury of a trip aboard her was worth many hardships.

Settlers now began to flow into Walker, and amongst them were men who had some trade other than farming, although invariably they combined the two. And so we begin to find blacksmiths, cobblers, millers, carpenters, chimney builders or bricklayers, saddlers and many others, settling among the hill people. In 1821 and 1822 there came into the county such men as Joseph and Bailes Nations, Andrew Stockridge, John and William Hellams, John Wood, Peter Baker, Jonathan Orr, James Little, William M. Richey, William Stewart, Moses Barton, Hawkins Burdin, Benjamin Murray, Samuel Thompson, Daniel and John Townley, Young Norris and Martin Ward. By 1820 Hugh Lollar was established on his farm near Providence.

Dr. Edward G. Musgrove came in from Blount County about 1822 and settled on the present site of Jasper. The old family lot extended east from Town Creek to about the line of the present Birmingham Avenue, and from Nineteenth Street south to the limits of the old Jasper Golf Club.

Likewise John King came in with his family in 1822 and settled on Lost Creek, near the present community of Hilliard or King's Chapel, and there he erected a grist mill.

In 1823 James Cain came in from Edgefield, South Carolina, and entered government land on Lost Creek, on a small tributary that is still known as Cain Creek. Mr. Cain was a farmer and stock raiser, and operated a stave plant, a mill and a ginnery.

About this same time John Key had settled near the present site of Coal Valley, and the Davis family was established on Cain Creek near Oakman.

Settlers in the hill country had now become sufficiently numerous to justify a separate county, and in 1823 the agitation was started. In the meantime, Dr. Musgrove had laid off a town site on his property, which some claim was named Jasper, by Hugh Lollar, in honor of Sergeant Jasper, a war hero in South Carolina, who won fame at the battle of Fort Moultrie, Charleston, S. C., when he recovered the battle flag that had been shot down by the British. Steps were taken to have Jasper designated as the county seat of the new county, although the community of Holly Grove, on Lost Creek, about one mile from the present town of Townley, had also been established and presented its claims to be chosen as the seat of justice. However, in 1823 Dr. Musgrove donated the ground upon which the present courthouse stands in Jasper and the erection of the first courthouse was started in that year. This act was apparently the deciding factor and when the State Legislature, by an act approved December 20, 1824, created the county of Walker, the town of Jasper was selected as the county seat.

The territory of Walker was taken from Tuscaloosa and Marion Counties, and embraced all of the present county of Winston, which was later created from territory taken from Walker County. Walker was named in honor of the Hon. John W. Walker, of Huntsville, Ala., who was president of the Constitutional Convention which framed Alabama's first constitution and who was also the first United States Senator from Alabama.

Dr. Musgrove was the first judge of the County Court of the newly created county. Ethel Armes tells how during the trial of cases he sat on a big rock near which is another larger rock, on which sat the jury. These two rocks can be seen today, just outside the yard of the Musgrove home in Jasper, close by Town Creek.

Walker was placed in a senatorial district with Fayette and Marion Counties, and was represented in the State Senate by Jesse Van Hoose during 1825 and 1826; by James Moore during 1827 and 1828; and by John Wood during 1828 and 1829.

Jesse Van Hoose originally came from New York with his parents about 1815, when they settled in a colony established by Major William Russell in a part of the Chickasaw country, now known as Russellville in Franklin County. In 1821 young Van Hoose became the first clerk of the Circuit Court of Franklin County, but shortly afterwards he went on a trading trip to Fayette County and decided to stay there. In 1825 he was elected to the State Senate from the senatorial district that included Fayette, Marion and Walker Counties. John Wood came to Walker County in 1821 and entered government land near the confluence of Lost and Wolf Creeks.

Walker County had no representative in the legislature until 1834, and prior to that time was voted with Marion and Tuscaloosa Counties.

In this new county there were some who were college bred and who had had the advantages of a cultural environment, but many of them, in following the spirit of enterprise and adventure, forsook the ways of their old homes. They fell into the life of the backwoods, where the masses were poor and unlettered before they came, and had nothing in their new surroundings to improve their culture. A great number never learned to read and write, and they were suspicious and superstitious. The fortune teller and the magician found them gullible subjects, for many of them believed in witchcraft, and they were forever devising schemes to overcome the devilish art of the witches.

Picture the consternation then of two young men, camping out one night on Lost Creek. A fire had been built in a sort of receptacle made from two or three black stones that had been picked up on the creek bank. Their meals having been cooked and eaten, these young men stretched out on the ground to sleep. Awakened after several hours, imagine their fear and horror to find that the stones which had surrounded their fire were dully glowing and burning. No one but the devil himself could cause such a phenomenon, and needless to say these young men lost no time in departing from their camp site. Their weird tales of the burning stones caused wiser men to seek the cause, and thus the presence of coal was discovered. Numerous outcroppings were found on the land, and the bottoms of the creeks and the river seemed to be a solid bed of coal.

A new industry came into being, for coal brought high prices on the lower markets, particularly in Mobile, and it immediately rivaled cotton as a "money crop." With picks and crow bars it would be dug and prized from its beds on the land and in the bottoms of the creeks and the river, and loaded into flatboats. The streams were all too shallow for these boats during the dry summer months, but during these dry months, there was much activity all along the Warrior River and its tributary streams, not only in the working of crops, manufacturing of staves and raising of stock, but also in the building of boats and the gathering of coal. The boats were built and loaded in the dry season, and when the fall freshets came they were pushed out into the swollen stream and steered down the river.

The first boat load of coal from the Warrior field to Mobile was shipped about 1827 by Levi Reed and James Grindle, who dug it from the Locust Fork (now called the Little Warrior) of the Warrior River.

James Cain is claimed by some to have been the first coal operator in Alabama, and he secured his first coal from the beds of Lost and Cain Creeks. In any event he was active from the very beginning in the mining, handling and shipping of coal on the Warrior River and its tributaries.

The flatboats were heavy cumbersome affairs, measuring seventy feet long by twenty-five feet wide. Their cost was generally estimated at seventy dollars, being based on one dollar per foot of length, inside measurement. The average size of a keel was sixty feet by sixteen feet. These boats carried a crew of from four to ten men, in addition to the pilot, who was the most important man aboard, for it was upon his skill and knowledge that depended the safe passage over Squaw Shoals, and even with experienced pilots, one boat in every eight passing over the shoals was lost.

Daring pilots were needed and many were called into service. Many tales are related of hairbreadth escapes of boats and crews from destruction, as they passed in the swift, rushing waters over the shoals. Noted among the pilots were John Bess, James Tuggle, William Payne, James Short, James Patton, William Benson and John Ballenger. Ballenger was finally drowned in the shoals in 1861, after years of piloting boats safely through them. These men lived and farmed along the banks of the Warrior, and the sites of many of their homesteads are still designated by the names of the men themselves, such as Tuggle Bend, just above the present site of Gorgas, and Payne Bend, right at Gorgas.

With the markets of the lower rivers opened through the agency of the flatboats and the pilots; with overland routes into Tuscaloosa established; with its political identity a settled fact; Walker County was ready to exploit its "white gold" and its "black diamonds," and cotton and coal was to produce, for the hill people, the flush times of the 1830's.

CHAPTER III

THE FLUSH TIMES IN WALKER

The first government census subsequent to the establishment of Walker County was taken in 1830, and showed a population of 2,034 whites and 168 blacks. These figures were destined to almost double during the next decade, for it was during this period that the foundation for the speculative orgy of 1835–1837 was laid, and those years will ever be known in Alabama history as the "Flush Times," which ended in the financial panic of 1837.

During the early 1830's there was a condition of unrest over the entire country, and men of ambition, both young and old, had the feeling that a change would secure for them better economic advantages. Many turned their faces to Alabama, because of its virgin and productive soil, the good prices received for its products and the absence of Indians, who had been removed from the state.

Walker County attracted many because of its coal deposits, which were easily worked from surface outcroppings, and its ready sale on the lower river markets, as well as its proximity to the important trading center at Tuscaloosa, where all farm products were easily and quickly disposed of. Money and credit were plentiful, and so we see in the years 1832 to 1836, and during the first six months of 1837, what almost amounted to a stampede into Walker, and the county became the new home of hundreds of settlers.

With this influx of people and easy economic conditions, there also came a desire for some of the better things of life. Opportunities, among the poor, for education, were few and far between; yet these settlers, unlettered as most of them were, craved educational opportunities for their children. And so there came into being in the county the "meetinghouse," a combined schoolhouse and meeting place on week days and a church building on Sundays. These "meetinghouses," like the homes, were log cabins without floor or heating apparatus. Unfortunately the history of these early meetinghouses, their location and the names of the men who made them, has been lost and cannot now be ascertained.

We do know that with the earliest settlers came the itinerant preacher, calling the sinners to repentance. These preachers followed their usual vocation on week days; farming, mining, milling, etc., as the case may be; but on Sundays they devoted their time and efforts to their work for the church, for which they received no pay whatever. Preaching services were first held in the homes of settlers where small groups would come, or occasionally to larger assemblages under the boughs of trees. In this way churches were founded, and in the course of time secured regular pastors. The Methodist and the Primitive Baptist religions were the predominating ones in those early days.

One of the first records in existence of the early ministers in Walker is an inscription on a tombstone at the grave of Robert Guttery, who, while living at Holly Grove, joined the Primitive

Baptist Church in 1824 and was ordained a minister of that faith in 1826. It would therefore appear that a church existed at Holly Grove in 1824 or prior thereto.

There can be no doubt that Methodism in Walker County had its beginning a number of years before the first authentic records are available. It is very probable that Methodist missionaries and circuit riders came into the county with the early settlers, from Madison, Blount or Tuscaloosa Counties, although we know not the names of these men, nor any details of their lives or work.

The date of the founding of the Methodist Church at Jasper, conceded to be the oldest in the county, is hid in the mysteries of the past, yet the most probable date would appear to be about 1826, when a building was constructed of large hewn logs, on land donated by Dr. Edward G. Musgrove.

The earliest authentic record of Methodism in the county that has been preserved is the report of a quarterly conference for the Blount Circuit, which convened in Walker County, in the home of John Key, on June 14, 1833. The meeting was presided over by the Rev. Anthony S. Dickenson, the preacher in charge of the circuit; and there was present Theophilus Moody, junior preacher on the circuit; John Turner, Edward G. Musgrove, I. G. Deskin, and Robert Williams, local preachers; Alfred Lane and John Gurganus, exhorters; Jesse Harbin, Joseph Richey, James M. Patton and David Blanton, class leaders. Edward G. Musgrove was the secretary.

John Key, at whose home this meeting was held, was born in Amherst County, Virginia, in 1765 and came to Walker County about 1824. He lived in the vicinity of the present Antioch Church on Key Hill, northwest of Oakman.

John Turner, one of the local preachers, was the son of Mathias Turner, and lived on Wolf Creek, which was named by his father. Robert Williams, another local preacher, came from Georgia some time in the 1820's and settled near the present site of Townley.

Alfred G. Lane, exhorter, lived in Section 1, Township 13, Range 10, in 1833, but later moved to Jasper and practiced law there in 1854. John Washington Gurganus came from South Carolina in the late 1820's and settled on a farm near Oakman.

Joseph Richey, class leader, was the son of William M. Richey, who entered government land in the northwest part of the county on February 19, 1821. James M. Patton lived on Patton Hill, near the present community of Patton Junction, while David Blanton lived on Cain Creek, southeast of Oakman.

The Walker Mission, later called the Jasper Mission, of the Methodist Church was established in December, 1833, and in 1838 two Sunday schools were reported under the Jasper charge; one at Pleasant Hill meetinghouse and one at McConnell's schoolhouse. In 1837 John R. Gamble moved from Shelby County to Jasper, and on September 8, 1838, he was licensed to preach. Also in 1837 the Methodists report Thomas Whitson, William Cole and James H. Freeman as being local preachers; and William Crump, Benjamin Jones, Jonathan Shirley, Jesse Freeman, Ashby Aldridge and Robert Davis as being class leaders and exhorters.

During the 1830's many camp grounds were established and

many camp meetings were held, which oftimes would last for several days. The shed, the stand, the altar with its straw, and the group of tents, were common to every camp ground; and were usually made of raw, rough materials, in most instances the shed being built of the brush and the boughs of the forests. Tents were made of coarse cloth. There was preaching four times a day. Those who could afford it came in carriages, but others came on foot, in ox-carts or ox-wagons, on horseback, some in the saddle, some in the lap, some behind; for a horse that could not carry double, or treble, was by no means a choice animal.

With the increase in population and the prosperous times, the people began to take more interest in politics. Walker's senatorial district was represented by John M. Dupuy from 1830 to 1832; by John Brown from 1833 to 1835; by Harrison W. Goyne from 1836 to 1837; by Walker K. Baylor in 1838; and by Green P. Rice from 1839 to 1840.

In 1833 Walker County was granted representation in the legislature and Samuel B. Patton was elected the first representative for the county, serving during the sessions of 1834 and 1835. Very little is known of Samuel B. Patton, other than that he came into the county in 1824 and entered government land at two points on the Warrior River, one near Heard Shoals and the other near Snow Ferry.

Two men now became political leaders of the county— Eldridge Mallard, a Democrat of the Andrew Jackson school, and James Cain, an ardent Whig and Nullifier and a man of pronounced ability and wide popularity.

Eldridge Mallard, who came into the county in 1825, was an intelligent farmer and the keeper of a very popular house of entertainment on the Byler Road. He was a man of fine personal appearance and popular manners, but his family were much more stylish than he, and hardly in keeping with the times. This fact was used extensively by his opponent, James Cain, in their political battles. Mallard was elected representative for the sessions of 1836, 1839 and 1840, but was defeated by James Cain, who served during the sessions of 1837, 1841 and 1842. Joseph Rutherford was elected and served during the session of 1838.

The year 1837 saw the first public execution in the county. Robert N―――was convicted of the murder of his stepfather and was hung for the crime in June of that year. The gallows was erected in the woods a mile and a half from Jasper, and consisted of two upright sawed pine posts set in the ground and spanned with a cross-beam of the same material. No trap was provided and instead a common cart was used. The condemned man was put in the cart, the noose placed around his neck, and when all was ready the cart was driven from beneath the gallows. The gallows stood until 1856, when the second public execution was handled in the same manner.

As the county prospered, traffic on the Warrior River increased accordingly, with farm products and coal being flatboated to Tuscaloosa and frequently to the lower markets. The menace of Squaw Shoals was ever present and many were the boats lost in its whirling waters. In 1835 James Cain and Richard Chilton secured a government contract to clean out

Squaw Shoals and direct the current of the waters so that keels and flatboats could pass over them with less danger. The work was duly undertaken and some good was effected, but the dangers of passage were still so great that the little relief through the government contract work was scarcely reckoned in the course of business.

However, this menace could not stop the increase in coal production. In 1837 William Whitson began to dig coal out of lower sections of Wolf Creek, not far from where it empties into Lost Creek. In 1839 Gideon, Gordon and Joe Frierson, three brothers living in Tuscaloosa, sunk the first coal shaft in Walker County, on land owned by Jesse Van Hoose and James Cain, near the mouth of Lost Creek. The shaft was known as "Frierson's Shaft," and some claim that it was the first active mine and coal shaft sunk in Alabama. A hand windlass was the shaft lift. It brought up a tub of coal as an empty tub was let down to be loaded.

With an economic depression existing over the entire country and state, Walker County with its small independent farmers, raising diversified crops, and its cheaply produced coal, was affected very little as compared to other parts of the state.

CHAPTER IV

PROGRESS AND PROSPERITY

The financial panic that started in 1837 brought distress all over the country. Banks failed, commodity prices dropped and many people lost their all. All manner of relief schemes and remedies were tried, but it was to be years before the country fully recovered from the ill effects of the panic.

However, Walker County suffered less from the panic than many other parts of the state, and far less than the country as a whole. Its principal effect upon the county was to retard its settlement. The census of 1840 showed the county with 3,820 whites and 212 negroes, or about double the population in 1830, the increase occurring almost entirely during the years 1833 to 1837.

During the ten years from 1840 to 1850 the population was increased by only eleven hundred people, which increase was due largely to the birth rate, as only a few new settlers came in.

But for those who were already established in the county the times were not so bad, as compared with other sections, especially those sections that depended almost exclusively on cotton. The people of Walker had diversified their interests, and while cotton was raised, it was by no means the principal source of income. Grain was being raised; cattle, hogs and sheep roamed the hillsides; lumber came from its forests and coal was easily mined. Commodity prices dropped almost to the vanishing point, but the cost of producing Walker's products was low, and a profit could still be made.

Especially was a good deal of coal mining undertaken in the early 1840's. Jacob Gibson and others, near the present site of Cordova, raised coal out of the bottom of Warrior River, prizing it up from the bed of the river with crow bars and loading it into boats. Perhaps this is the only occasion on record of coal being mined by diving. Jacob Phillips, the Sanderses, the Burtons and the Gravlees were also engaged in mining coal. William Gravlee, the elder of the family, ran a transportation line of boats. Judge William Hewlett shipped coal from Benchfield on the Cordova side of the river. The Burdins also shipped from this neighborhood.

James Davis, William Robertson, Reuben Morgan, James Hancock, John Sullivan and others dug coal out of the bottom and banks of the Warrior River, near the present site of Dora, and also out of the banks and bottom of Horse Creek.

Other industries were also thriving. Richard Chilton operated one or more grist mills and in addition shipped many boat loads of stock to Mobile. James Cain operated a grist mill, stave plant, cotton gin, and in addition was a large stock raiser. Moses Camak operated a very popular grist mill. Thus was being laid the foundation of a satisfactory economic life for the people of Walker that lasted until the country was torn by Civil War.

The early settlers now began to think of things other than the immediate needs of the moment, and this thought found its first expression in more improved living conditions. The old one room rough log cabin gave place to fairly comfortable log houses of two or three rooms, usually set in a clump of trees by the roadside. However, the door was still made of rough planks and creaked on its wooden hinges. Windows were still scarce and the old clumsy shutter was still in existence. The interior of the house was still rough and the walls were studded with pegs or nails on which hung suspended all manner of things.

Dim roads and paths connected the sparsely settled communities, with a maze of such roads radiating out of the small village of Jasper, and along these roads a beginning was made in the social life of the community. Still uneducated and uncultured, religion was the settler's only emotional outlet, and weddings, church, burials and all day singings were the only social institutions.

Church buildings were still few and by 1842 the Methodists had possibly three, located at Jasper, Pleasant Hill and McConnell's Schoolhouse; however, preaching was conducted at Blanton's, near Marietta; Snow's, on lower Warrior River; Williams', near Townley; Turner's, on lower Wolf Creek; Tubb's, on Lost Creek, and at Cole's.

Dissension had been rife in the ranks of the Baptists for several years, due to the questions of education and missions. One element did not believe that education of its ministers was necessary, holding that God alone called the man to preach and that He would endow that man with the accomplishments necessary for His purpose; putting understandable words into his mouth; wisdom and knowledge into his speech and furnish sustenance on which to support himself and family. They further held that missions were unnecessary, and that the payment of money to any man for his services to God was commercializing an honorable calling and destroying its purpose and effectiveness.

Opposing this view was another element who held that the ministers should be men educated for their calling; devoting their entire time and talents to their work; and paid a reasonable compensation for their services by the church itself. They believed in missions and held that their ministers should go into the highways and byways to carry the Word to the unenlightened.

With such directly opposite opinions, it was inevitable that a split in the church should occur, and in the early 1840's the actual division took place.

Those holding the first mentioned opinion organized themselves into what is known as the Primitive Baptist Church, and within its folds we find such early settlers as Robert Guttery, Eli Safford, John M. Barton, James M. Kitchens, and others, following their normal pursuits on week days, but devoting their Sabbaths to the church, with no compensation other than the satisfaction from a well done job.

Those holding the second belief organized themselves into what is known as the Missionary Baptist Church, and by 1845 they had placed three missionaries at work in Walker County— D. W. Andrews, Thomas Barnes and Nathan Roberts. In 1842 the first Missionary Baptist Church in the county was constituted at Pleasant Grove, and in 1853 another was constituted at Providence, followed in 1857 by one at Liberty Grove.

While authentic records are not available, it would appear

that as early as 1840 the Primitive Baptists had established churches at Holly Grove, at Old Zion on the Jasper-Russellville road, at Old Sardis on the Warrior River below Lynn's Park, and at other places.

On July 6, 1844, the Sulphur Springs Primitive Baptist Church was constituted by Elders Eli Safford and John M. Barton, with twelve charter members, consisting of John D. Randolph and Frances Randolph, James Kitchens, William Kitchens, Christopher C. Kitchens, Sarah Kitchens, Thomas Brown and Lovey Brown, Harvey W. Hamilton and Mary Polly Hamilton, Susan Acuff and Hancy Dill. Eli Safford was chosen for the first pastor and Harvey W. Hamilton for the first deacon.

Interest in politics had grown apace and during the political campaign of 1841 a new leader appeared on the scene. About 1835 John Manasco moved in from Morgan County, and settled a few miles west of Jasper. The son of parents who were close neighbors to General Andrew Jackson, young Manasco adopted him as a model and developed into a prototype of that famous Democrat.

The Whigs, led by James Cain, had made great inroads on the Democratic party. In 1841 Manasco entered his first political campaign as a supporter of Eldridge Mallard, candidate for the Legislature, who was opposed by Cain himself. His defeat by Cain was a foregone conclusion; however, Manasco threw himself into the breach and although a comparative stranger, he developed such political sagacity and such traits as a leader that his influence was felt throughout the county. Cain, however, was elected and in 1842 again returned to the Legislature.

In 1843, with the aid and influence of Manasco, John E. Clancy was elected. Clancy was a rather eccentric young lawyer; very fond of display and with aspirations to be an orator. However, he was a Democrat, far in advance of his party on the subject of internal improvement, and made his big speech in the House in favor of internal improvement by the state. Denounced as a radical by many, Clancy was again a candidate in 1844, against John Manasco himself, and Lambert W. Baker, a young Jasper attorney. In the spirited three cornered race, the Democratic vote was split between Clancy and Manasco, thus permitting Baker to win by the skin of his teeth. In 1845 the race was between Baker and Manasco, and the latter was an easy victor. The terms of the representatives were now extended from one year to two years, and in 1847 Manasco was again the victor.

In 1849 Manasco was again a candidate and was opposed by his old political enemy, James Cain. At this time the territorial limits of Walker reached from the Tuscaloosa County line nearly to the Tennessee Valley, embracing all of the present county of Winston and portions of Lawrence, Cullman, Blount and Jefferson Counties. The issue in the campaign was the division of the county. Manasco advocated a division being made from north to south, with a re-location of the county seat from Jasper to a site near the old Cheatham place, thirteen miles west of Jasper. Cain was in favor of an east to west division, with the county seat retained at Jasper. Cain defeated Manasco on this issue, and Cain's ideas as to the division of the county were put into effect by an act of February 12, 1850, establishing the lines as they are today.

Manasco was elected to the Legislature of 1851, but was defeated for re-election in 1853, by John Irwin. Irwin had previously been clerk of the County Court and when the probate system was inaugurated he was elected the first Judge of Probate for the county. In 1852 he resigned to make his race against Manasco for the Legislature. However, he only served for one term and was defeated by Manasco in 1855.

Irwin was succeeded for Judge of Probate by Thomas M. Gabbert, who was a minister in the Baptist Church and a most excellent man. He served as Judge of Probate until 1859, when he was succeeded by F. A. Gamble.

The last judge of the County Court was a young Jasper lawyer, William A. Hewlett. He served only a short time, however, owing to the establishment of the probate system. A young man of fine personal appearance, and very prepossessing in conversation, he was universally popular. A Democrat of the old school, in 1852, he entered the race and was elected State Senator from the district composed of Lawrence, Winston and Walker Counties. He served from 1853 to 1857, having been re-elected for the second term.

William Read was elected representative for the term of 1857. Mr. Read was a very plain farmer, quite modest, but courteous and obliging to all. No man in the House was more respected.

Josiah M. Easley was elected in 1859 in contest with John Manasco. He served but the regular session and then moved from the state. His brother-in-law, Frances A. Musgrove, was elected to fill the unexpired term and served during the first called session of 1861.

During 1859 the present town of Cordova was founded by Benjamin M. Long, a veteran of the Mexican War, who moved in from Carrollton, Georgia. The community was named Cordova, after a town in Mexico where Captain Long had been stationed during his service with the army. An ardent Republican, Captain Long was destined to later become one of the economic and political leaders of the county.

In the late 1850's political victories were won largely by those who advocated no change in existing social and economic conditions, rather than by any appeal to party loyalty. Slavery was the burning question throughout the state and the secession movement was well under way.

But Walker County had very few slaves. Its people were made up largely of independent farmers, stock raisers and small business men, engaged in milling, mining, lumbering or merchandising. If they were not rich, they at least were enjoying a certain degree of prosperity, and had reached the point where they were enjoying comforts and pleasures and opportunities that had been denied them in their old settlements. With their own hands they had hewn out of this forbidding hill country homes and churches and schools.

As early as 1854 Campbell's Southern Business Directory, a publication covering all the Southern States, lists Walker as a county of 5,400 population, with thirty-one churches and one High School. It also lists James Savage, Turner and Carmichael, Gabbert and Stanley, and F. A. Musgrove as general merchants in Jasper; and Robert Guttery, A. Williams, and James Hogan as general merchants in the county. William

A. Hewlett and A. G. Lane were listed as attorneys at Jasper. Of course there were other merchants and lawyers in the county, but this is quite a remarkable showing when it is remembered that listing in this directory was in reality an advertisement paid for by the one listed.

The one high school shown for the county was the old Jasper Academy, which had been erected a few years earlier. Unfortunately, however, little is now known of the history of this academy, other than with its establishment a Superintendent of County Schools was appointed, and David Manasco was the man selected.

Another evidence of the enlarged social life is seen in the organization at Jasper, on August 7, 1854, of York Lodge, No. 211, the first Masonic lodge in the county. Organizers were G. C. Jones, John W. Warren, D. L. Stovall, Benjamin Boteler, Griffin Lamkin, James Savage, W. N. Gibson, Thomas M. Gabbert, A. B. Watson, James N. Fondren and Robert Davis. This group includes men from all parts of the county.

In 1855 a new Federal land law was enacted which made government lands available at twelve and a half cents per acre. This law caused another great migration into Walker, and almost as many new settlers came into the county in 1855 as came in during the flush times of 1836.

The community of Jasper was progressing, and in 1859 the only church there, the Methodist, found its church building too small. A new frame church building was erected with lumber dried and made ready by Lewis Stovall. The old log building that had served for so many years was continued to be used as a school.

As a people, happy, contented and moderately prosperous, with slavery a minor issue, in so far as they individually were concerned, they wanted no part in the strife that was brewing, and desired only to be let alone to work out their own destinies in their own way. But the slave owning counties of the state were preponderantly in the majority and the weight of their power was to eventually force Walker into a movement abhorrent to most of its people. War clouds were looming and Walker could not escape.

CHAPTER V

WAR AND ITS AFTERMATH

With the turn into the 1860's the state as a whole seemed headed for secession, and with the election of President Lincoln the people were ready to resist the "Abolition" administration.

Governor Moore called for an election on December 24, 1860, for delegates to a State Convention to meet at the capitol on January 7, 1861. Slavery would disappear under a Republican regime, and the people generally were determined not to submit to Republican rule.

But this did not hold true in Walker County. Her small independent farmers held very few slaves; her people were satisfied and contented with their lot; and their great and only desire was to be let alone to work out their own destinies, as they were so ably doing, without outside interference. And so when it came to the election of a delegate to the convention of 1861, now commonly known as the "Secession Convention," they would have none of the politicians. They seemed to think that the political leaders of Walker had failed them, and that they were being forced into a situation against their will. In one last tragic gesture they sought a delegate who was not a politician. Elder Robert Guttery was elected as Walker's delegate; a man of God who had been a minister of the Primitive Baptist Church for close to forty years; one of Walker's earliest settlers who had come into a virgin country and had watched its development; a man who, by intimate contact, knew the will and desires of his neighbors. And how nobly he fought for those neighbors on the floor of the convention! When the "Secession Ordinance" was brought up he voted first to submit it to the people for ratification, and when that proposition failed he not only voted against the passage of the ordinance, but refused to sign it after it was passed on January 10, 1861.

With the passage of the Secession Ordinance events moved rapidly. By the middle of March the Confederate States of America had been organized; Jefferson Davis had been elected president; Congress had met and adopted a permanent Constitution; and Alabama was now unreservedly a member of the Southern Confederacy, in honor bound to support it with all the means at its command. In early October Governor Moore reported that there were twenty-seven thousand Alabamians in the field.

These dramatic and swift moving events found the people of Walker in a daze. Many were the despairing cries of a "rich man's war and a poor man's fight." But their participation in the war was inevitable, and leaders, such as Robert Guttery, who so ardently opposed secession, threw themselves wholeheartedly into the support of the Confederacy. Isolation and neutrality was impossible, and each individual must make his own decision as to which side he would support. Some few, following the dictates of their consciences, and with the courage of their convictions, departed for the North and service with the Union Army. But the great mass cast their lot with the South.

One of the first was William A. Hewlett, a young lawyer

of Jasper, who had served as Judge of the County Court and later as State Senator. When the war broke out he organized a battalion of cavalry and was commissioned major. His battalion was finally consolidated with another and formed into a regiment, and Major Hewlett was then promoted to lieutenant colonel, the highest rank obtained by any Walker Countian during the war.

John C. Hutto also recruited a company of volunteers for service in the Confederate Army, was elected captain of Company K, Fiftieth Alabama Infantry, and was later promoted to major. Francis A. Musgrove was elected captain of Company C, Twenty-eighth Alabama Infantry, and was later promoted to major. Esom D. Kelley, B. M. Long, John B. Shepherd, Daniel H. Whatley, A. J. Gutherie, Hugh Lollar, and others recruited companies and were elected captains.

Every post office became a recruiting station. Men enlisted at Jasper, at Holly Grove, at York (now Oakman), at Liberty Hill, at Lost Creek Post Office or Steadmans. Before 1863 all the men in some families were in the army. Some idea of the wholesale recruiting and conscription can be gotten from a letter written by James Matlock Kitchens to one of his children on February 15, 1863. He says: "George Dutton was captured in the Fort Donaldson fight. George is dead. . . . . I received a letter from Matlock (his son) dated 13th January. He was in Rome, Georgia, wounded in the right foot at the Murfreesborough fight. . . . . L. W. Baker is dead; he died at Chattanooga. Four of Harvey W. Hamilton's sons are in the army. Your uncle Jesse Kitchens was captured in Kentucky and paroled. He has now gone back to the army."

From 1861 to 1865 there was no business other than the business of war. The daily life of the people could not be other than dull and drab and irksome, changed only by added sorrows as word came back from the battlefields of this or that disaster or the death of some relative, friend or neighbor. Soldiers home on furlough were the greatest source of news, because postal service was so bad and postal rates so high that letters were few and far between. When a letter was received people visited the recipient merely to hear the reading of the news from the front.

With most of the able-bodied men away to war, the work of making a living was left to the women, children, and old or crippled men. Conditions therefore were extremely hard. With the blockade that was established around the state by Union forces there was no opportunity for importations except by blockade running. Such few supplies as came through the blockade, together with the output of Alabama factories, were woefully inadequate for the needs of the army, much less for the civilian population. Clothing for the civilian population, necessities for the home, and wearing apparel for the soldiers were made largely in the homes, and was done mostly by the women. Their sacrifices and labors were perhaps as great as those of the men bearing arms. Added to all other difficulties was the depreciated currency of the Confederate States, which continued to grow less valuable throughout the war.

James Matlock Kitchens, in a letter of February 15, 1863, referred to elsewhere, states that: "Times are very distressing with us. . . . . Salt has been selling at sixty to sixty-five cents per pound; pork at twelve and a half to fifteen cents here

(Walker County), and at Tuscaloosa at from twenty to twenty-five dollars per hundred."

Although there were many hardships of life imposed upon her people, Walker County was free from hostile invasion until a few months before the close of the war. Early in 1865 General J. H. Wilson, with a force of 13,500 Federal Cavalry, set out from Lauderdale County upon a raid into Central Alabama, which finally ended at Selma. A part of this force came through Walker, entering the county along the Double Springs road, and on March 27, 1865, reached Jasper. A home guard company which had been organized, with Dr. L. C. Miller, of Holly Grove, as captain, was wholly inadequate to meet this invasion, as it was small and its main purpose was to help hunt out deserters and spies. An unverified story is told of how Wilson's raiders were opposed by only one man. Samuel Snoddy, living near Jasper, heard that the Federal forces were coming, and went out to meet them and encountered three Federal scouts just north of the present Oak Hill Cemetery. Fired upon by the scouts, he returned their fire and killed one of them. He then hurried back to Jasper to advise the people and give the home guard a chance to leave. The story goes on that another Jasper citizen, James O'Rear, refused to leave until he had finished eating his dinner. However, the Federal forces arrived before the dinner was finished, and in trying to make a belated escape he was shot through the head and killed. This happened on Nineteenth Street, just east of Birmingham Avenue.

The Federal forces burned the courthouse, the Methodist Church and some other buildings, and then continued on their way to Fayette and Tuscaloosa, burning the Sulphur Springs Primitive Baptist Church, about three miles west of Jasper, and destroying any food supplies that they could not carry with them. Many other depredations were committed. The soldiers robbed the people of anything that happened to strike their fancy, and rapine was not unknown. Fortunately, however, the column was moving fast, and their stay in the county was only for two days; yet in those two days Wilson's raiders left behind them a path of desolation.

After Lee's surrender at Appomattox, Walker's battle scarred veterans—half starved, in rags, despondent—came straggling home to behold the wreckage of war. Property had been destroyed; if not by Wilson's raiders, then by the lack of necessary care. Houses had either fallen down, or were falling down, with chimney, roof, door or window gone; fences were beyond repair; the people in want and many on the brink of starvation. Walker was again back to the conditions that existed in the old frontier days, with the people poverty stricken, farms in poor condition and lacking equipment, and frequently with planting seed not available. Roads were impassable, post offices and postal routes had practically stopped functioning, and schools and public buildings were destroyed or dilapidated.

However, neither the state or county could recover economically until its political affairs were put in order, and some arrangement made to restore Alabama into the Union. Governor Parsons ordered that an election be held on August 31, 1865, for delegates to a State Convention to provide for a permanent State Government. Walker County elected Captain B. M. Long, of

Cordova, who, before the war, had been a Whig and opposed to secession, but who was one of the first to recruit a company for service in the Confederate Army. The delegates met in Montgomery on September 12, 1865, and considered President Johnson's plan of restoration. The Secession Ordinance was declared null and void, the Confederate war debt was repudiated and slavery was abolished.

New state and county officers were elected in November, 1865, and General John Manasco, who had served as Walker's representative in the Legislature since 1863, was again elected. The new Legislature confirmed the work of the State Convention, adopted the Thirteenth Amendment and passed laws securing the negro in his person and property. However, they rejected the Fourteenth Amendment. With this rejection the Radicals in Congress passed the famous Reconstruction Act on March 2, 1867, and a military regime was established over the people. The ten Confederate States were divided into five military districts, with a general military officer in charge of each district, who had complete control over the lives of the people, their schools, churches, public meetings and their public utterances.

Alabama, with Georgia and Florida, composed the Third Military District. General John Pope was appointed commander and in the latter part of March, 1867, he set up his headquarters at Montgomery. Under the rule of General Pope the registration of voters was ordered for the purpose of electing delegates to a State Convention to put into effect Reconstruction. Negroes were registered with the whites, and, the registration complete, the election was held in October, 1867. The elected delegates were obscure native whites, immigrants from various Northern States, and eighteen negroes.

It is to the honor of Walker County that it is one of the few counties that did not demean itself by having a delegate at this convention of 1867. The constitution set forth by this convention failed of adoption when voted on by the people; however, on June 25, 1868, Congress declared that Alabama had adopted the new constitution and was entitled to representation in Congress as soon as the newly elected Legislature ratified the Fourteenth Amendment. The Legislature was inferior in every way, as the state's politics were in the hands of the carpet-baggers, the scalawags and the negroes.

Walker was one of the counties that suffered the least in this respect, due to its small negro population. It had elected as representative in this Legislature William Thomas Stubblefield, of Eldridge, who was a native of Wilkes County, Georgia, who had moved to Alabama with his parents early in life, living first in Talladega County and later in Coosa County, where he had served as Clerk of the Court for many years. He served as First Sergeant in the First Alabama Volunteer Regiment during the war with Mexico, and served as major of the Second Battalion of Hilliard's Legion during the Civil War. He moved to Walker County about 1853. It is unfortunate that other counties could not have been as well represented as Walker, but Major Stubblefield and his kind were overwhelmingly outnumbered, and there was very little good that they could accomplish. Major Stubblefield also served during the sessions of 1869 and 1870, when conditions were not much better.

During the war period, or from 1862 to 1868, Moses Camak served as Judge of Probate, and in 1868 he was succeeded by John Brown, who served until 1874.

CHAPTER VI

RECOVERY

The census of 1870 showed the population of the county to be 6,235 whites and 308 negroes. These people continued to be satisfied with their old leaders, the men who had grown up with the country, and readily followed them in their work of rehabilitation, both economically and politically.

Judge F. A. Gamble was one of these leaders. In 1872 Judge Gamble and Jobe Richardson conceived the idea of organizing a colony of northern people to come and settle in Walker County, and to this end they secured the assistance of Abner Hitchcock, of Cleveland, Ohio. Mr. Richardson made the proposition that he would deed to such a colony one hundred acres of land for the building of a town, under the condition that they would build him a home under given specifications. This was agreed to, and Mr. Richardson deeded certain of his property, which lay about six miles from Jasper.

The colony of South Lowell was then organized in Cleveland, Ohio, as the Ohio and Alabama Agricultural, Manufacturing and Mineral Company. A code of laws was adopted and an engineer employed to lay out the town, which was composed of twenty blocks with a total of 424 lots. In the fall of 1872 colonists arrived from Michigan, Ohio, New York and Maine, and thus began the town of South Lowell, which was destined to be the leading town in the county for the next fifteen years.

During the same year (1872) Anthony and Winfield Persinger established the Mountain Eagle, in Jasper, the first newspaper in the county; a courageous undertaking for a small country town in a territory that had no railroads or highways. In 1876 the Mountain Eagle was sold to Judge Gamble.

In 1873 the Louisville and Nashville Railroad Company, having previously acquired the interests in the South and North Alabama Railroad Company, completed the construction of that road, which gave through rail connections from Birmingham to all northern points through Nashville.

This indirectly helped Walker County, for the products of its farms and forests, and goods and merchandise which heretofore had to be hauled by wagons for long distances, to and from Tuscaloosa, or the then small town of Birmingham, and sometimes from as far away as Memphis, could now be handled by railroad delivery at Warrior. New markets and new interests were opened up, and the traffic over the road from Jasper through South Lowell to Warrior became quite heavy for its day and time.

There were only a few doctors in the county; however, in 1876 the Walker County Medical Society was formed, with only five or six members.

In 1877 the courthouse at Jasper was badly damaged by fire, and practically all county records were destroyed. The courthouse was repaired, but in 1878 it was again burned in another disastrous fire, which also destroyed the Mountain Eagle building, including all equipment. Soon after this Judge Gamble sold the paper again to Winfield Persinger, one of the original founders, who re-equipped the plant.

In May, 1878, the Baptist Church of Jasper was organized with twenty-four members and the Rev. J. E. Cox as the first pastor. The courthouse was used for the first meetings and for several years later.

Political conditions in the state continued to be bad from 1870 to 1874. The Radicals were still in control; however, Walker County continued to elect decent honest men to represent it in the Legislature.

From 1871 to 1872 the county was represented by Dr. L. C. Miller, of Holly Grove, a physician who came to Jasper in 1839 and who later moved to Holly Grove, and who, during the war, had acted as captain of the Home Guard company.

During 1872 and 1873 the county was represented by Captain Esom D. Kelley, of Eldridge, who had served as captain of Company K, Fourth Alabama Cavalry, during the entire period of the war. Captain Kelley was a modest unpretending member and brought to bear a native good sense on all occasions, which, together with his general courtesy, made him highly respected by all.

From 1874 to 1876 the representative was J. M. C. Wharton, who had also fought in the Confederate Army.

Better political conditions in the state started in 1875 when a new constitutional convention was called. General John Manasco was elected as Walker's delegate to this constitutional convention, and he became a conspicuous figure in that body. The convention was composed of many of the life-long friends of General Manasco, and his opinions were respected; his advice was sought, and his genius became engrafted upon its work. In 1876 and 1877 he was Walker's representative in the Legislature.

General Manasco was succeeded in the Legislature by Major John C. Hutto, another war veteran, who served during 1878 and 1879. Major Hutto was opposed in his campaign by John B. Shields, who unsuccessfully contested his election.

In 1874 Jacob Robert Shepherd was elected Probate Judge of the county. Little is known of Judge Shepherd other than that he came to Walker County about 1859 and served with distinction during the war. He served as Probate Judge until 1877, when he was succeeded by Judge F. A. Gamble.

CHAPTER VII

RAILROADS AND PROSPERITY

With the turn into the 1880's Walker County's 9,479 people started to become railroad conscious, and while Judge Gamble continued to be one of the business leaders of the county, two new leaders now came to the front.

John B. Shields, who had come in from Tennessee and established a woodworking plant at South Lowell, and L. B. Musgrove, a grandson of Dr. Musgrove, who had founded the town of Jasper, together with Judge Gamble, began to put forth every effort to secure railroad facilities for the county.

The Birmingham District was growing by leaps and bounds, as was, in fact, all of Alabama's mineral region that was served by railroads. It was very apparent that Walker could not realize on its wealth in coal and timber until railroads were available to haul these products to the markets that needed them. The report of Dr. Eugene A. Smith, State Geologist in 1876, had shown the condition of the county's soils, and its coal and timber resources invited large investments of capital. The building of railroads would naturally be followed by the erection of planing and saw mills; a large cotton mill was a possibility; mercantile business and farming interests would be placed on a better basis; and, above all, coal mines would be opened to give employment to thousands. There was no one man or group of men within the county with sufficient capital to start any of these enterprises, but men in the county joined with outside capitalists, and through their energies and vision brought about the development of industrial business.

The Georgia Pacific Railroad, now the Southern Railway, had started building its line eastward from Columbus, Mississippi, but coal operators did not wait for the rails to reach Walker County.

The Corona Coal Company was organized with General Coulter, an outside capitalist, as president and L. B. Musgrove as vice president. On August 14, 1883, the opening of the Corona mines was begun. About this same time Patton mines were begun by W. E. Leake and Dunn Brothers. Long before the railroad was in striking distance of Walker tipples had been constructed and coal was stored on the ground awaiting the coming of the first train. When, in 1884, the railroad reached Alta, in Fayette County, about five miles from Corona and Patton mines, Dunn Brothers, who were also railroad contractors, used their teams for hauling coal from Patton mines to the rail head, where it was shipped to Columbus.

Very little coal was hauled by wagons from Corona mines, but this mine was the first to receive railroad facilities. The Georgia Pacific Railroad was required, under its contract, to have rails laid in Walker County by a specified date. In order to protect its rights a temporary track was rushed into the Corona mine. On a Sunday morning in 1884 five Mobile and Ohio cars were placed on this track, which David Kirkwood, superintendent of the Corona mine, had loaded and shipped out, thereby shipping by rail the first coal ever loaded in cars within the limits of Walker County. It is said that more than five hundred people gathered to see the train. Late in 1884 a forty-ton lump of coal was sent by Evans J. Dunn from Corona to New Orleans for the 1885 exposition. It is believed to be the largest single lump of coal ever mined. As the railroad car capacity was only thirty tons, two cars were broken down enroute to New Orleans.

In November, 1884, the Georgia Pacific completed its line into Day's Gap (now Oakman) and a terminus was established at that point. Day's Gap immediately sprang into prominence as a distributing center for the entire county, and a hamlet quickly became a town of four hundred people. Freight of all kinds was now shipped from and to Day's Gap, and a great deal of the old laborious and expensive wagon haulage, outside of the county, was eliminated, although the distribution from Day's Gap to Jasper and other towns in the county was still handled by wagons. A stage line was operated from Day's Gap to Birmingham via Jasper and South Lowell.

Within a short time after the railroad was completed to Day's Gap spur tracks were laid into Coal Valley and Mountain Valley, and coal mines were in operation at both of these points.

Also in 1884 a post office was established at Cordova. Mail was received from Jasper twice a week and was carried by Tibe Johnson. It usually consisted of one newspaper and four or five letters. The first postmaster was J. A. Jones, better known as "Bud" Jones, and the office was in the general store of Captain Long.

Day's Gap and South Lowell were now the leading towns in the county, but Jasper was not progressing very fast. Very little building was being done; however, in 1882 the Baptists of

Jasper, who had been holding their meetings in the courthouse, erected a building on the west side of Fourth Avenue, between Eighteenth and Nineteenth Streets.

In 1884 a disastrous fire caused the destruction of the courthouse, and it was replaced in 1885 by a brick structure, which was again destroyed by fire before completion. The courthouse was finally completed and put into use on December 22, 1886.

It is interesting to note that the oldest issue in the files of the Mountain Eagle, that of September 10, 1884, carries advertisements of W. B. Appling, John McQueen, C. J. Cunningham, Sheriff Lacy and S. M. Gunter, all lawyers in Jasper. Merchants carrying advertisements were Musgrove Brothers and James Savage. Shields Brothers were advertising pianos and organs; E. W. Miller, the Miller Hotel; Camak Mills were advertising flour; and S. P. Smith, his steam mill, four and a half miles from Jasper on the South Lowell road. Even the doctors advertised, and the following had cards in this issue: Dr. W. M. Cunningham, at Wolf, Ala.; Dr. John Manasco, at Holly Grove, Ala.; Dr. A. M. Stovall, at Jasper; and Dr. R. P. Griffin, at Antioch Church.

By 1885 the Birmingham District was booming and several railroads were desirous of extending their lines into this fertile mineral field. Land owners in Walker gave up much valuable land as an inducement for the railroads to lay their lines through the county. The population of Jasper at this time was about two hundred people, yet the forward minded men of the community, such as L. B. Musgrove, Judge Gamble and others, finally prevailed upon the officials of the Kansas City, Memphis and Birmingham Railroad (now the Frisco), who were building a railroad from Birmingham to Memphis, to route their line through Jasper. As an inducement, the village had been laid off into a town site, streets and building lots indicated; and every third vacant lot was given to the railroad. The line was completed in 1886 and Jasper had its first railroad and a rich undeveloped portion of the county was now accessible to all markets.

However, the railroad missed South Lowell, which was Jasper's greatest competitor, and this meant the doom of that thriving town. Railroad facilities made Jasper the logical industrial and commercial center and South Lowell quickly and surely died. Today it is a deserted village; a dream that did not come true.

Likewise the railroad missed the old settlement of Holly Grove, and immediately, on the completion of the line, the town of Townley was founded on the railroad, about one mile west of Holly Grove. It was named after the Townley family, who were pioneer settlers on the site of the town, and Bob Townley was appointed the first postmaster. Holly Grove, like South Lowell, became a deserted village. T. S. Hendon had much to do with the founding of Townley, and is said to have donated the property on which each of its churches are built.

The town of Carbon Hill came into existence upon the completion of the railroad and the opening of mines at that point by the Kansas City Coal and Coke Company. This company did not undertake any extensive work, and within a short time sold out to the Galloway Coal Company. The Galloway Company entered large scale operations and is responsible for the development of the town of Carbon Hill. A post office was established there in 1887, with John T. Anderson as the first postmaster.

Cordova, which had been established as a post office in 1884, now had two railroads, for not only had the K. C. M. & B. laid its rails through the town, but the Georgia Pacific connected up its line from Day's Gap to Birmingham, and also passed through the town. A number of people were immediately attracted to the community, and the year 1887 saw the establishment of Cordova's first church, the Methodist Church of Cordova. It was organized by Rev. D. W. Ward, and the charter members were Captain B. M. Long and his wife, Amanda Long; Mr. and Mrs. W. W. Stagg; Mr. and Mrs. Henry Nation; Mr. and Mrs. M. W. Root; Mrs. C. L. Carmack; Alex Chamblee and Willoby Stagg.

About this same time an enterprising young coal operator named Walter Moore, a native of Jefferson County, organized the Magellan Coal Company and the Horse Creek Coal and Coke Company, to open mines on the K. C. M. & B. R. R. at Horse Creek, or Sharon, as it was then known, and thus founded the town that was to be later called Dora.

By the latter part of 1887 the rails of a third railroad were nearing Walker County. The Sheffield, Birmingham and Tennessee Railroad (now the Northern Alabama) was being built from Sheffield to Jasper, and on May 16, 1888, the line was completed and railroad service between Sheffield and Jasper was established. About two years later the line was extended to intersect the Georgia Pacific at Parrish.

While new towns were springing up along the railroad lines none of them, and in fact none of the old towns, had the boom that came to Jasper. The town had been platted, new streets had been laid out, and what had previously been farm land was now turned into business and building lots. The city was incorporated and at the first election, held on December 26, 1887, George H. Guttery was elected mayor; C. J. L. Cunningham, treasurer, and Captain W. S. Foster, city clerk and collector.

The county had heretofore been without banking facilities and late in 1887 the Walker County Bank, the first bank in the county, was organized in Jasper and opened for business February 20, 1888, with Hinton E. Carr, of Mississippi and Arkansas, as president, and John B. Hughes, of Jasper, as cashier.

A new process of making steel with coke was being used in Birmingham and furnaces were clamoring for coke. A number of coke ovens were being built, the first ones being those on D. L. Stovall's place, one mile southeast of the town.

The Jasper Land Company was organized by outside capitalists, with Judge F. A. Gamble, L. B. Musgrove, J. C. Musgrove, and W. L. Wallis, all of Jasper, on the Board of Directors. This company purchased four thousand acres of land in and around Jasper, including the land previously given to the railroads as an inducement to enter the town, together with practically every unimproved lot in the community, with the intention of re-selling the property for business and residence purposes on such attractive terms as would induce business enterprises and home seekers to come to Jasper. A lottery scheme was even used and a large number of business and residential lots were disposed of through a grand drawing held on July 31, 1888.

Much building was going on. The Methodists found their

old house of worship, which they erected in 1868, inadequate for the increased population. The old building was torn down and a new brick building erected in its place.

The Presbyterian Church sent an evangelist into Jasper in 1888, and the Presbyterian Church of Jasper was organized by the Rev. P. G. Morton with three members, as a result of a week's evangelistic services. J. T. Sherer was the first Ruling Elder. In October, 1888, eleven additional members were added, and W. J. Haynes was elected Ruling Elder. Meetings were held in the Baptist Church until 1889, when a church building was erected on a lot donated by L. B. Musgrove, of the Jasper Land Company. Lumber for the building and furnishings was cut at the sawmill owned by J. B. Shields and D. K. Carter.

The year 1889 also saw the organization of Jasper's second bank, the Jasper Trust Company, with F. A. Gamble, president; Judge J. B. Shields, vice president; J. A. Gravlee, cashier; and a board of directors including Dr. W. C. Rosamond, T. L. Long, J. H. Cranford, L. B. Musgrove, J. B. Chamberlin and W. G. Davis.

In the meantime the town of Carbon Hill was progressing, and by 1888 the community had grown enough to support a church. The Carbon Hill Methodist Church was organized with the following charter members: R. R. Hooker, Dora Hooker, M. P. Leith, John Leith, Elizabeth Leith, J. W. West, Emma West, J. J. Warranfeldt, Luda Ballinger and Callie Welch.

The increase in population in the county and the amount of business being done, particularly in the transfer of land titles, recording of mortgages, etc., made the office of Probate Judge far more attractive than it had been heretofore. The office was filled by Judge F. A. Gamble from 1877 to November, 1886, when John B. Shields was elected.

In the Legislature the county was represented by Captain B. M. Long during 1880 and 1881, by B. F. Tingle during 1882 and 1883, by John B. Shields during 1884 and 1885, by J. F. Files during 1886 and 1887, and by McPherson Cornelius during 1888 and 1889.

CHAPTER VIII

DOWN TO EARTH

During the ten years from 1880 to 1890 the population of Walker County had grown from 9,479 in 1880 to 16,078 in 1890. The population of Jasper had grown from about two hundred in 1886 to about three thousand in 1890, and many were predicting a town of fifteen thousand in a very short time. In any event Jasper was having the biggest boom of any town in the county, and in 1891 the Mountain Eagle listed its advantages as four hundred coke ovens in operation, six coal mines within a few miles of the town, one foundry and machine shop, one brick works, two sand stone quarries, thirty stores, four hotels, two banks, three school buildings, three churches, two railroads and twenty highways.

But while Jasper was getting the most publicity, principally through the efforts of L. B. Musgrove and the Mountain Eagle, other towns in the county were having their own little booms and were growing rapidly, and more towns were still coming into existence.

The town of Sharon, which was later changed to Horse Creek and finally became known as Dora, had reached sufficient size to justify its first church, the First Methodist Church of Dora. It was organized in 1890 and used the Davis Building for its meetings.

The advent of the railroads caused the abolishment of the old pony express for the handling of mail, and on January 1, 1891, the post office known as Hewitt, which was located near the present site of America, was moved to the intersection of the Sheffield, Birmingham and Tennessee R. R. (now the Northern Alabama) and the Georgia Pacific R. R. (now the Southern), and the name was changed to Parrish. The first home built in Parrish was erected by William Rufus Jones, the postmaster, and was used for the post office.

On February 14, 1891, the town of Carbon Hill was incorporated and a mayor and board of aldermen elected, and in the spring of that same year the town received a great deal of unfavorable publicity, due to the number of depredations and killings that occurred there. It became known as a bad town, but in a few months the desperadoes were stamped out and Carbon Hill became a normal town. Its growth was rapid, and in 1892 the second church in the town, the Baptist Church of Carbon Hill, was organized with twenty members.

On April 16, 1891, the people of Jasper and Walker County had the thrill of seeing the President of the United States, Benjamin Harrison, when he passed through Jasper, the first president to ever pass through the county. Judge Gamble was chairman of the committee that welcomed President Harrison.

The boom that was in progress all over Walker County, like all booms, must have an ending. The panic of 1893 was the thing that halted Walker's boom. Elsewhere in the state farm lands and farm products became almost valueless. Cotton would bring only four cents a pound; potatoes were selling at ten cents a bushel; and cattle and other live stock was not worth transportation charges to market. Forty cents a day was the current wage for farm hands, and those who earned their living by the sweat of their brows suffered in hunger and rags.

But while Walker's boom was stopped, the foundations of its economic advancement were too secure; the wealth of its mines and forests, served by the railroads, was too permanent to suffer more than a temporary setback; and even in the days of the panic much business was still being done; new people still came to the county; established towns continued to grow; and new communities came into being.

The panic year of 1893 brought to Jasper a young attorney, John Hollis Bankhead, Jr., who had just finished his law course, and on August first of that year started to practice law as junior member of the firm of Coleman and Bankhead. The son of an illustrious father, who, as United States Senator from Alabama, became nationally known as the "father of Federal highways," this young man was destined himself to become a United States Senator forty years later, and to win national prominence as the author of the famous Bankhead Cotton Control Act.

Before the Sheffield, Birmingham and Tennessee Railroad was built a post office was located a few miles from the present site of Nauvoo, at what was known as Ingle Mills, owned by the father of J. W. Dodd. In 1895 the post office was moved to the railroad and was given the new name of Nauvoo by a Mr. Carroll, who took it from an Indian name. Luther Lander was the first postmaster at Nauvoo.

Townley had increased in size, and on June 17, 1895, the town was incorporated and John W. Guttery was elected the first mayor.

The town of Day's Gap had changed its name to Oakman, and a telephone line was started from Oakman to Jasper. It was completed and put into service on August 28, 1895, the first telephone line in the county.

The war with Spain in 1898 had little or no effect on Walker County, and its progress went on. Captain B. M. Long was making every effort to expand the town of Cordova. After negotiations with the Indian Head Mills Company, of Boston, Mass., and the donation of several hundred acres of coal lands as an inducement, that company completed a mill and started operations in Cordova in 1898, bringing to the town several hundred employees.

The town of Oakman continued to grow, and on July 7, 1898, the Oakman Church of Christ was organized by J. T. Rose, E. Cranford and George Swindle, acting elders. The Rev. James Hill was the first pastor. A lot on Main Street was purchased from J. M. and L. J. Corry and a frame building was erected with lumber which was cut and sawed by Thomas Conwell, who had a mill located near Oakman.

A month later, during August, 1898, the First Christian Church of Jasper was organized by the Rev. F. D. Srygley with twenty members. Its first building was a small dwelling house located on Fourth Avenue, between Eighteenth and Nineteenth Streets, which was used until 1901, when the old Baptist Church building was purchased.

In politics the 1890's saw the rise and fall of the Populist party, consisting largely of the Farmers Alliance and the Knights of Labor. These organizations were both represented in Walker County, but the Populist party never attained any great numerical strength. Walker continued to vote largely the straight Democratic and Republican tickets. During the race for governor in 1890 Captain B. M. Long, of Cordova, was the Republican candidate, but he was defeated by Thomas G. Jones, the Democratic nominee. However, his son, Thomas L. Long, was Walker's representative in the Legislature in 1890-91. T. L. Sowell served in 1892-93; H. A. Gaines, in 1894-95; W. B. Appling, in 1896-97, and Sheriff Lacy, in 1898-99. T. L. Sowell was State Senator in 1898-99.

The census of 1900 showed that Walker's population had almost doubled during the previous ten years, it having grown from 16,078 in 1890 to 25,162 in 1900. This growth was spread throughout the county, but Jasper was now definitely the leading town in the county, and as such was due for further expansion. In 1901 the Central elementary school building was erected there at a cost of approximately fifty thousand dollars. During the same year the old Baptist Church building on Fourth Avenue was sold to the First Christian Church, and the lot on Fifth Avenue was purchased and a new building erected.

In 1899 John H. Cranford organized the Bank of Jasper. He rapidly became one of the leading business men of the town, and in 1904 he organized the Jasper Water, Light and Power Company, giving to the community its first water system, from a well and pump located on North Third Avenue. On June 1, 1905, Mr. Cranford organized the First National Bank of Jasper.

In May, 1906, a charter was granted for the building of the Alabama Central Railroad, which was constructed north from Jasper to serve the vast lumber holdings of the Western Electric

Company. Ed Hall and John Kilgore began the grading of the railroad from Jasper to what was to be later known as Manchester, a village six miles north of Jasper, in a bend of Blackwater Creek. In a short time many miles of logging roads had been built; a commissary and dwellings for employees and their families had been erected and the main plant and logging pond constructed. Manchester became a thriving lumber center and here came the Russells, Camps, Brittons, Mattinglys, Hubbards, Covingtons, Atwoods, Lees, Sallades, J. Metzer, Captain White, and many others. Manchester remained the center of lumber activities in Walker County until 1926, when the timber gave out. The plant was then dismantled, the hum of the saws ceased and Manchester became another deserted village.

The building of the Alabama Central Railroad and the activities of the timber operations that it served brought many new faces to the county, and naturally helped the growth of Jasper. The population of the county, as well as of Jasper, had now grown to such an extent, and its business transactions reached such a volume, that the old courthouse facilities were inadequate, and in 1907 a new courthouse was built, which cost approximately two hundred thousand dollars.

During the same year the Burton Manufacturing Company was founded in Jasper by T. C. Burton and his sons, C. L. and J. R. Burton, for the manufacture of leather goods.

Also in 1907 the Nazarene Church of Jasper was organized by the Rev. R. M. Guy. It was located in West Jasper, and had nine charter members. Meetings were held in various rental buildings until 1909, when the membership had grown to 102, and a building was erected on Ninth Avenue and Nineteenth Street.

The first automobile registered in Walker County was a little Maxwell runabout, which H. W. Cranford purchased from a Birmingham dealer on October 7, 1907, and which he drove from Birmingham to Jasper in eleven hours, which was exceptionally good time.

In 1910 the Jasper Bank and Trust Company was organized with H. W. Cranford, president; F. A. Merrell, cashier, and O. F. Cobb, assistant cashier.

A State Constitutional Convention was held in 1901, and Walker County was represented by three delegates—Thomas L. Long, E. W. Coleman and Rufus A. O'Rear. The effect of the new constitution was to hold regular sessions of the Legislature every two years instead of yearly, and also to give Walker County two representatives instead of one. In the session of 1903 Walker was represented in the Senate by Christopher Columbus Nesmith, and in the House by John H. Bankhead, Jr., and Wilson Alexander Gray. At this session of the Legislature the regular sessions were extended from every two years to every four years.

In 1905 William B. Bankhead, a lawyer prominent in politics in Huntsville, came to Jasper to engage in practice with his brother, John H. Bankhead, Jr., under the firm name of Bank, head & Bankhead. He was destined to be elected to represent Alabama in Congress in 1916 and to serve in that office for many years.

From 1907 to 1910 Walker was represented in the State Senate by M. L. Leith, and in the House by E. R. Lacy and J. H. Cranford, and from 1911 to 1914 by C. A. Beasley, Senator, and J. H. Cranford and J. D. Hollis, Representatives.

CHAPTER IX

WORLD WAR AND WORLD DEPRESSION

From 1900 to 1910 Walker County had another great increase in population, growing from 25,162 in 1900 to 37,013 in 1910. This was due largely to the opening of many coal mines and the establishment of many timber operations. Coal mining, however, was the main industry that was attracting people to the county, and this industry was to continue to grow until Walker had become the principal coal producing county in the state.

The story of the growth of this industry is too lengthy to be embodied in this work, and has been told so much better by other writers. However, Ethel Armes states that "The history of a large number of them (coal mines) is traced back to the pioneer work set afoot here mainly by Walter Moore, Enoch Ensley, Henry W. Milner, L. B. Musgrove and J. C. Musgrove. Among the county men who have been most active in the renaissance of business enterprises here are Judge F. A. Gamble, Colonel B. M. Long, Judge J. B. Shields, Judge J. J. Hayes, W. G. Gravlee, Judge James W. Shepherd, Dr. W. C. Rosamond, L. B. and J. C. Musgrove, John King, T. S. Hendon, David Kirkwood, John Ryan, A. McDonald, Bryan and Gus Whitfield, Robert Palmer, H. P. Gibson, George S. Gaines, C. C. Kelley."

The industrial growth was not confined to any one section of the county. All sections shared in the prosperity, and all communities grew to larger size and more importance. Substantial public buildings were erected. During 1912 a twelve thousand dollar brick structure was erected in Cordova by the heirs of Captain B. M. Long to replace the old Methodist Church building, and the name was changed to the Long Memorial. In 1915 the Methodists in Jasper erected a two hundred thousand dollar marble structure, one of the most beautiful in the entire state. A forty thousand dollar Walker County High School was built in Jasper in 1916, and in 1919 a one hundred thousand dollar post office building.

With America's entry into the World War in 1917 Walker County, along with the rest of the state and country, devoted all its energies to the winning of the war. Under the selective draft the county registered 4,128 men, under a county board of military registrars composed of Sheriff J. M. Phillips, County Health Officer Dr. C. A. Grote, and Circuit Clerk J. W. Crocker, which board also acted as the county board of exemption. Sheriff Lacy, of Jasper, was chairman of the district board of exemption. Physical examinations were in charge of Dr. J. L. Sowell, of Jasper, Dr. D. H. Chilton, of Patton (later of Parrish), and Dr. H. J. Sankey, of Nauvoo.

Previous to America's entry into the war one hundred and fifty-five men from Walker County had enlisted for service on the Mexican border, the majority being in Company B, First Alabama Cavalry, under Captain R. A. O'Rear and Lieutenant H. S. Long, of Jasper, which company was at San Antonio, Texas, in April, 1917. Other Walker County men were stationed at Nozales, Ariz.

Under the first draft Walker's quota was 480 men, less 155

already in service, or 325 men. This number was quickly secured, and the first detachment left Jasper on September 5, 1917, for mobilization at Camp Pike, Little Rock, Ark. It consisted of sixteen men—Enoch Miller Black, Virgil Enoch Dill, Judson O'Rear, Henry Kelley Herron, John Bernard Gallagher, Berry Barney Brown, Robert Skelton, Ed Callahan, Marcus Lester Tubbs, Asa Martin Estes, Elmer Anthony Phillips, Russell A. Thirsk, Ben Huggins, Reuben Gammons, John Joseph Elliott, Dennis Franklin Winn, and Daniel W. Pittman. A second detachment of sixty-one men left on September 21st; and a third, on October 3rd, and other detachments at regular intervals, as they were called. The first colored detachment of about 100 men left for Fort Dodge, Iowa, on October 29, 1917. Just as rapidly as they were required Walker County furnished its full quota of men.

And those that stayed at home did their full part. Food production and food conservation was very important, and Walker's farmers concentrated on the production of food, while the women of the county attended to its conservation, under the direction of L. B. Musgrove, County Food Administrator.

Coal was another essential item, and Walker's established mines worked to full capacity, while many new mines were opened. One of the largest mines in the state was opened in 1918 at Parrish, by the Railway Fuel Company, under the direction of W. E. Leake. The production and conservation of coal was under the direction of J. D. Acuff, County Fuel Administrator.

Walker's assigned quota in Liberty Loan Drives, Red Cross and Y. M. C. A. memberships, War Savings Stamps campaigns, and all other activities incident to the war, were always exceeded, and, in fact, in one of the Liberty Loan drives the county exceeded its quota one thousand per cent, the best record in the entire country. Such campaigns and drives were under the leadership of men like John H. Bankhead, Jr., John H. Cranford, J. M. Pennington, E. W. Long, Judge John B. Shields, S. R. Preston and many others.

When peace came on November 11, 1918, Walker County's industries, like all other industries in the country, were organized for a stupendous production, and this condition had again brought many new faces to the county. Its population had grown to 50,593 in 1920.

After a short depression following the war business went on a boom all over the United States. Installment buying was started on a scale never before thought of. Credit was extended to everybody, and rare indeed was the individual who was not making monthly payments on household furniture, an automobile, a radio, or some household electric appliance, such as a refrigerator, a range, or a washing machine. Real estate took on fictitious values, and mortgages were given for amounts far in excess of intrinsic worth. Banks were top-heavy with deposits which were being loaned out on collateral valued at boom prices. A great mass of the public started to gamble on the stock market, and stocks were quoted on Wall Street at prices that were in no way consistent with the earnings or opportunities of the companies issuing the stock. Farmers produced more cotton, wheat, corn and other exportable items than could be absorbed by the world markets. Factories were ever increasing their output, through the use of new and better machinery, which machinery was replacing manual labor, and thereby causing unemployment.

Spending was not confined to individuals but was indulged in by state, county and city governments through the issuance of bonds, and many public buildings were erected and roads constructed.

The orgy of spending was prevalent all over the country, and Walker as a county, and its people as individuals, were no different in this respect than others elsewhere.

In 1922 the town of Parrish was incorporated, and Walter L. Guttery was elected the first mayor. The following year the town issued bonds for the construction of a sixteen thousand dollar high school building. Prof. Ira Helms was the first principal.

Also in 1922 there was built, in Jasper, the Temple Emmanuel at a cost of fifteen thousand dollars.

During the following year, 1923, the Walker County Hospital was incorporated and construction started on the hospital building. The West Jasper school building was completed this year at a cost of thirty-five thousand dollars. An addition was built to the Walker County High School building in 1929 costing seventeen thousand five hundred dollars. Many roads were built; the Bankhead Highway having been hard-surfaced from the Jefferson County line to Jasper, as was likewise the road from Jasper to Parrish.

The wild spending throughout the country could not continue forever, and the first real break came with the collapse of the stock market in October, 1929, and from then on the depression held sway. Factories curtailed production or closed entirely. Unemployment grew by leaps and bounds. Farm products filled all warehouses, with no buyers. Commodity prices dropped. Mortgages and bonds were defaulted, and banks were closing everywhere, with frozen assets of doubtful value.

Walker's timber operations were curtailed and its mines cut down production or closed entirely. The climax came, however, in March, 1933.

At the time of President Franklin D. Roosevelt's inauguration on March 4, 1933, every bank in the country was closed by presidential decree and the country had more than ten million wage earners unemployed.

The story of the climb out of the depression after March 4, 1933, is a story for a later historian. The opening of the banks, the vast Federal expenditures for relief, the slow recovery of business, are of national interest, and Walker County was affected only as the nation was affected. The "New Deal" of President Roosevelt is too new and its permanent aspects merely in the formative stage now, but from it, Walker County will no doubt emerge with its promised "more abundant life."

PART TWO—THE TOWNS

CARBON HILL

While Carbon Hill did not come into existence until after 1886, the land upon which it is located is the site of some of Walker County's early settlements.

William M. Richey entered government land February 19, 1821, in Section 24, Township 13, Range 10, which is within the present limits of the town. It was five years later when Jeptha White entered land, on February 23, 1826, in Section 25, Township 13, Range 10. Alex Richey entered land on September 10, 1830; John Kitchens, James Hogan, James Barbee and Isaac Brown, in 1835; George Brazeal, John Phillips, Alex McDonald and Morgan Brazeal, in 1836; James Simpson, in 1837; Jason C. Alexander and Abraham Myers, in 1848; Henry Ferguson, in 1850; James McDonald, in 1851; Preston B. Phillips, in 1852; William H. Pate, in 1855; and J. B. Brasfield, in 1860. In 1865 Dr. James L. Gilder settled on the present site of the town and became one of the county's leading citizens.

All of these settlers were farmers, and no community was established until after the Kansas City, Memphis and Birmingham Railroad (now the Frisco) was built through in 1886, and coal mines were opened by the Pratt Consolidated Coal Company and the Galloway Coal Company.

In 1887 a post office was established, with John F. Anderson as the first postmaster. By 1888 the community had grown enough to support a church, and the Carbon Hill Methodist

Church was organized with the following charter members: R. R. Hooker and Dora Hooker, M. P. Leith, John Leith, Elizabeth Leith, J. W. West, Emma West, J. J. Warranfeldt, Luda Balleger, and Callie Welch.

The census of 1890 gave the town a population of 568, and on February 14, 1891, it was incorporated and a mayor and aldermen elected. The rapid growth of the community attracted a number of rough characters, and during the spring of 1891 the town suffered a number of depredations and killings. However, this was rapidly stamped out by the newly elected town officials.

The following year, in 1892, the Baptist Church of Carbon Hill was organized with twenty charter members.

By 1900 the population had grown to 830, and during the next ten years it doubled, the census of 1910 giving it as 1,627 persons.

In 1913 the Carbon Hill Journal was established, a weekly newspaper that serves the western end of the county.

CORDOVA

Government land records show that as early as February 11, 1822, Hawkins Burden (or Borden) entered government land on the present site of Cordova, while Stancil Cobb made entries on April 29, 1822, and May 12, 1823.

However, William Gravlee had come down from Tennessee in 1819 and settled on land across the river from Cordova, and in the 1820's he started a transportation line of boats on the Warrior River, freighting the products of the farmers to the markets of Tuscaloosa, Demopolis and Mobile, and bringing back the necessities they could not raise.

In the late 1830's the early settlers began to dig coal from the river and creek bottoms and in the early 1840's a great deal of coal mining was undertaken around Cordova. Jacob Gibson, who settled across the river from Cordova, raised coal out of the bottom of the river, prizing it up with crow bars and loading it into boats.

Jacob Phillips, the Sanderses, the Burtons, and the Gravlees were also engaged in mining coal, while William Gravlee, the elder, continued to run his transportation line of boats. Judge William Hewlett shipped coal from Benchfield, on the Cordova side, while the Bordens also shipped from this neighborhood.

Notwithstanding all this activity no community was established until 1859, when Benjamin M. Long came in from Carrollton, Georgia, opened a mercantile establishment and started the community, which he named Cordova, after the name of a town in Mexico in which he was stationed while a soldier during the Mexican War.

It was not until 1861 that the first church was organized in Cordova. This was the Baptist Church, which started with very few members, in a small log cabin, situated a short distance from where the present church building now stands. "Uncle" Joseph Nations was one of the first ministers.

The Civil War followed closely after the first establishment of the community, and Cordova had no opportunity to grow during the war period or the dark days of reconstruction that followed. But by 1884 it had increased sufficiently in importance to justify a post office, although for sometime thereafter mail was only received, from Jasper, twice a week, it being carried by Tibe Johnson and usually consisted of one paper and four or five letters. The first postmaster was J. A. Jones, better known as "Bud," and the office was located in the general store of B. M. Long.

However, better days came soon, for in 1886 the Georgia Pacific Railroad (now the Southern) and the Kansas City, Memphis and Birmingham Railroad (now the Frisco) both laid their rails into Cordova and gave the town direct rail connection with Birmingham, Memphis, Tennessee, and Columbus, Mississippi. This fact immediately attracted people to the struggling community.

The following year (1887) saw the establishment of the Methodist Church of Cordova. It was organized by Rev. D. W. Ward, and the charter members were Captain B. M. Long and Amanda Long (his wife), Mr. and Mrs. W. W. Stagg, Mr. and Mrs. Henry Nation, Mr. and Mrs. M. W. Root, Mrs. C. L. Carmack, Alex Chamblee, and Willoby Stagg. The first church building was a two room dwelling, with the partition torn out, and this humble structure served as a house of worship for several years, when an attractive frame building was erected.

The town did not grow as fast as it was hoped it would, and in 1895 Captain Long offered to donate a site for any industry that would locate in Cordova. The offer was accepted by the Indian Head Mills, of Boston, Mass. The mill was completed and started operations in 1898, bringing to the community several hundred employees, and causing the census of 1900 to show the town's population as 567. This was sufficient to justify the incorporation of the town, which was done in that year.

The establishment of the cotton mill had a tendency to develop the agricultural resources around Cordova, which in turn reflected better business conditions in the town. Several coal mines were opened up near by, and this also had its effect on the town, which trebled in size in a ten year period. Its population in 1910 was 1,747.

In 1912 the old frame Methodist Church building was removed and the heirs of Captain B. M. Long erected a twelve thousand dollar brick structure as a memorial to Captain Long, and the church is now known as the Long Memorial.

DORA

(SHARON—HORSE CREEK)

The earliest settlers on the present site of Dora were, no doubt, James Davis, Ezekiel Morgan and his son, Reuben Morgan, but the dates of their arrival in Walker County are unknown. Attracted by the pretty valley through which runs Horse Creek they, and others that followed them to this section, settled there for a life of farming. But coal mining soon became a thriving industry, and in the early 1840's we find James Davis, William Robertson, Ruben Morgan, James Hancock, John Sullivan and others busily engaged in digging coal out of the banks and bottoms of Horse Creek and the Warrior River, near Dora, and boating it to Tuscaloosa, Demopolis and Mobile.

No real community was built up, however, until after the

Kansas City, Memphis and Birmingham Railroad was built through in 1886, and within the next three or four years the town of Sharon, as it was then called, was established.

Closely following the railroad an enterprising young coal operator named Walter Moore, a native of Jefferson County, organized and operated the Magellan Coal Company and the Horse Creek Coal and Coke Company, which, in 1891, he merged with the Lady Ensley Coal, Iron and Railroad Company. Subsequently these mines were acquired by the Pratt Fuel Coal Corporation.

The railroad and the mines brought many people to Sharon, and in 1889 R. H. Palmer opened, here, one of the largest department stores in the county.

No church existed in Sharon until 1890, when the First Methodist Church was organized and occupied a building donated by the Davis family. About this same time the Masonic lodge was organized.

Sometime during the 1890's the name of the town was changed from Sharon to Horse Creek, and it was not until 1906 that the name was again changed to Dora.

In 1900 the old Methodist Church building was sold and the church was moved to a home on the present public school site. The population of the town at this time was 385.

Post offices had previously been established and closed, and it was not until 1902 that a permanent post office was opened, with W. E. Webb as the first postmaster. The town grew rapidly, and by 1910 almost trebled in size, having a population of 916.

The World War and the post war boom brought great prosperity to Dora, and by 1928 old facilities were inadequate. In that year the Methodist Church property was sold to the city and a school building was erected on the site at a cost of forty-five thousand dollars. The Methodists acquired a new site on the main street of the city and erected a twenty-five thousand dollar brick edifice. The Masons constructed a two story lodge building costing fourteen thousand dollars.

Churches had been established by the Baptists, the Holiness and the Nazarenes.

JASPER

Jasper, the county seat of Walker County, owes its very existence, perhaps, to the keen foresight and business judgment of its first settler, Dr. Edward G. Musgrove, who, attracted by the beautiful rolling land and gently sloping hills of the valley in which it lies, entered government land, which lay east of the present Town Creek and south of the present Nineteenth Street, and extended back through the Jasper Golf Club grounds, south of the Frisco Railroad. The exact date of Dr. Musgrove's settlement in Walker County is a matter of dispute, some claiming that it was as early as 1815, but the most authentic date seems to be 1822, as quoted by Owens in his History of Alabama.

It is extremely doubtful whether any community existed on the present site of Jasper at that time, notwithstanding local tradition that an Indian trading post had been established there a number of years before, during the days of the old Mississippi Territory.

At the time Alabama was admitted to the Union, the present territory of Walker was a part of Tuscaloosa and Marion Counties, and when the question of establishing a new county was brought before the State Legislature in 1823, the community of Jasper came into existence and made its claim to be the county seat, on account of its central location, surrounded as it was by well to do farmers.

Griffin Lamkin was established near Jasper. John Black had taken up land near the present site of Union Chapel, a few miles east of Jasper. Stancill Cobb, William Gravlee and others were farming on the present site of Cordova. Reason Courington, Hugh Lollar, Sr., and his son, John Lollar, were located near the present site of Providence, south of Jasper, while still farther south James O. Cain was at Liberty Hill, and B. Murray and John Wood were near the confluence of Lost and Wolf Creeks. Samuel Patton was on Patton Hill, and Daniel Townley and John Key were near the present site of Townley, with William Guttery and his three sons, Robert, Johnson and Isham Guttery, at Holly Grove. John King was located near what is now Hilliard, and Henry and William Sides were in the vicinity of Pleasant Grove Church. Along the Warrior River, William Butt and Jacob Phillips were near the confluence of the Mulberry and Sipsey Forks, Andrew Stockridge was near the mouth of Blackwater Creek, while William Dunn and William Jones were farther south. On the present site of Dora J. M. Davis and Ezekiel Morgan were busy tilling the soil.

Added to this decided advantage of a central location was the keen foresight and judgment of Dr. Musgrove, who, in 1823, gave the land and erected a small frame building to be used as the county courthouse. The community thus established was named Jasper, in honor of Sergeant Jasper, a Revolutionary War soldier of South Carolina, who won fame at the battle of Fort Moultrie, Charleston, S. C., June 28, 1776, when the Fort Moultrie flag, said to have been the first American battle flag, was shot down early in an attack by the British Admiral Sir Peter Parker, and was recovered and replaced on the staff by Sergeant Jasper. When the county of Walker was finally established by act of the State Legislature, approved on December 24, 1824, Jasper was designated as the county seat.

As yet no church building had been erected, but Dr. Musgrove, who was also a local preacher in the Methodist Church, donated the land, and in 1826 the first church building was constructed of large hewn logs. This humble building was used during the week days for school and on Sundays for church and Sunday school. In December, 1833, the Walker Mission of the Methodist Church was established, and later changed to Jasper Mission, and in 1838 they reported two Sunday schools under the Jasper charge—one at Pleasant Hill Meeting House and one at McConnell's Schoolhouse. John R. Gamble moved from Shelby County to Jasper in 1837, and on September 8, 1838, he was licensed to preach.

In the early 1830's the first hotel was established, and the first saw mill was built on Town Creek. The hotel was built of logs and was known as the Camak and Ryan Hotel. Isaac Ryan was the owner of the first saw mill.

Although Jasper was the seat of justice, a roll of attorneys licensed to practice at the Alabama bar in 1845 showed only four located in Jasper—Lambert J. Baker, William J. Bryan, John E. Clancy and Wade B. Taylor.

However, the town was devolping into a trading community, although the number of inhabitants was still very few. In 1854 the first volume of Campbell's Southern Business Directory was issued, and it listed the following general merchants in the town of Jasper: James Savage, Turner & Carmichael, Gabbert & Stanley, and F. A. Musgrove. Lawyers listed were William A. Hewlett, who, at that time, was State Senator; E. G. Musgrove, and A. G. Lane.

Also in 1854 a sufficient number of Masons had established themselves in and around Jasper to justify a Masonic Lodge, and on August 7, 1854, York Lodge, No. 211, the first Masonic Lodge in Walker County, was organized by G. C. Jones, John W. Warren, D. L. Stovall, Benjamin Boteler, Griffin Lamkin, James Savage, W. N. Gibson, Thomas M. Gabbert, A. B. Watson, James N. Fondren, and Robert Davis.

About 1857 the old Jasper Academy was built and upon its completion David Manasco became the first County Superintendent of Education.

Jasper continued to prosper, and in 1859 the Methodists erected a new frame church building with lumber dried and made ready by Lewis Stovall, while the old log building was continued to be used as a school.

At this time Jasper had two mails a week—one from Decatur and the other from Tuscaloosa, and W. L. Stanley was the postmaster. When the mail arrived Mr. Stanley would empty the mail sacks on the floor of his store. Each person present would pick out his own mail, and Mr. Stanley would take charge of the remainder.

A list of persons living in Jasper in 1859 included James Boteler, A. R. Carmichael, F. M. Carmichael, Thomas Childers, James Daniel, T. M. Gabbert, F. A. Gamble, L. E. Gilbert, James Gregg, G. W. Howell, Dr. W. W. Jones, H. G. Lollar, A. R. Lollar, F. A. Musgrove, Jesse O'Rear, James O'Rear, Dr. W. C. Rosamond, James Savage, W. L. Stanley, and D. L. Stovall.

With the outbreak of the Civil War, Jasper whole-heartedly gave its support to the cause of the South. Its young men, and many not so young, enlisted in the Confederate Army. Captain F. A. Gamble recruited a company of men, while Major F. A. Musgrove recruited a battalion in Jasper and Walker County.

Jasper was spared the scenes of actual conflict until March 27, 1865, when a detachment of Michigan troops under General Wilson marched through Walker County and burned the courthouse and the Methodist Church building, which were the only buildings available for public meetings. The courthouse was repaired, but the Methodist Church was a total loss and the old original log building was put back into use again.

In 1868 the Methodists, with the assistance of the Masonic Lodge, erected a new church building to replace the one burned by Wilson's raiders. The second floor of the building was used as a lodge room by the Masons.

During the dark days of reconstruction following the war Jasper, like all other southern communities, suffered greatly. Many schemes were devised to alleviate the economic distress, one of which, for a time, seriously retarded the growth of

Jasper. A colonization project resulted in the establishment, in 1872, of the town of South Lowell, six miles northeast of Jasper, which was destined to grow and rank as the leading town of the county for a number of years, overshadowing Jasper and absorbing a great portion of what would have been Jasper's growth.

However, in the same year (1872) Anthony and Winfield Persinger established, in Jasper, the Jasper Mountain Eagle, the first newspaper established in Walker County. The Persingers operated the Mountain Eagle until 1876, when it was sold to Judge F. A. Gamble.

The year 1876 saw the formation of the Walker County Medical Society, which was organized in Jasper with only five or six members.

The following year (1877) again saw the courthouse burned and repaired, and a year later, in 1878, another fire burnt out the Mountain Eagle building, completely destroying all equipment. Soon after this Judge Gamble sold the Mountain Eagle back to Winfield Persinger, one of the original founders, who re-equipped the plant and re-established the newspaper.

In May, 1878, the Baptist Church of Jasper was organized, with the Rev. J. E. Cox as the first pastor and twenty-four charter members, consisting of Col. and Mrs. W. B. Appling, Mr. and Mrs. John B. Hulsey, Mr. and Mrs. John B. Randolph, Mr. and Mrs. James W. Richardson, Mr. and Mrs. Lewis Barrentine, Dr. and Mrs. R. L. Y. Long, G. D. O'Rear, Elijah O'Rear, N. P. Gabbert, Mary Dunkin, R. L. Y. Long, Jr., Mrs. A. C. Long, Mrs. E. H. Lollar, and Mrs. Hannah O'Rear. The courthouse was used for the first meeting and for all other meetings for several years later. A Sunday school was started the first year through the efforts of John Stewart, a young student at the Jasper Academy.

About this time another county newspaper, the Walker County Times, had been established, but in 1880 both the Times and the Mountain Eagle were purchased by L. B. Musgrove and consolidated under the name of the Mountain Eagle.

The members of the Baptist Church of Jasper, who had been holding their meetings in the courthouse, erected a church building in 1882, on the west side of the present Fourth Avenue, between Eighteenth and Nineteenth Streets.

The old courthouse, originally built in 1823, and partly destroyed by fire in 1865 and again in 1877, caught fire for the third time in 1884 and was totally destroyed. A new courthouse was constructed of brick in 1885, but before it could be completed fire again razed the structure, and it was not until 1886 that it could be completed and put into use.

The old Jasper Academy, built in the 1850's, was abandoned, and a new Jasper Academy or high school was built by public subscriptions of about fifteen hundred dollars. It was completed and opened for the first session on January 18, 1886. Prof. W. K. Brown, of North Carolina, was the principal, with Mrs. J. F. Haley, of Jasper, and Miss Mae Ware, of Nashville, as his assistants. There were about fifty pupils enrolled. In addition to the Jasper Academy there was opened, on October 26, 1885, the Male and Female Institute, a private school conducted by Prof. Ira Robbins, about one-half mile north of Jasper.

Walker county, which had no railroads and no good highways, was agitated at this time by the prospects of having three railroads. The survey of the Kansas City, Memphis and Birmingham Railroad (now the Frisco) crossed Town Creek at the old gum spring, which had served the founders of Jasper for more than fifty years. The citizens of Jasper were very anxious that the rails be laid through the town, and at a mass meeting held on August 18, 1886, they agreed to incorporate Jasper, one mile square, and to donate two thousand dollars, together with every third unimproved lot, in consideration of the railroad laying its rails through the town. This offer was accepted, and in the latter part of 1886 Jasper, with a population of only two hundred, and heretofore situated thirty-two miles from a railroad, was afforded railroad facilities.

At this time all business in Jasper was centered around the courthouse, and a directory of the business houses in September, 1886, shows the following:

No. 1, Courthouse Square, James Savage, General Merchandise.

No. 2, Courthouse Square, Captain John Spears, Butcher—Meats.

No. 3, Courthouse Square, Files Brothers, Groceries.

No. 4, Courthouse Square, George, the Barber.

No. 5, Courthouse Square, Mountain Eagle Office.

No. 6, Courthouse Square, Musgrove Brothers, General Merchandise; Jack Cranford, clerk.

No. 7, Courthouse Square, D. L. Stovall, General Merchandise.

No. 8, Courthouse Square, F. A. Gamble, General Merchandise; George O'Rear, clerk.

JASPER 97

No. 10, Courthouse Square, Sides & Rosamond, General Merchandise.

No. 12, Courthouse Square, W. L. Gravlee, General Merchandise.

No. 14, Courthouse Square, W. C. Rosamond, General Merchandise.

No. 16, Courthouse Square, R. H. Smith, General Merchandise.

No. 17, Courthouse Square, G. H. Guttery, General Merchandise.

No. 21, Courthouse Square, Lowery & Long, General Merchandise.

No. 28, Courthouse Square, Elijah O'Rear, General Merchandise.

No. 5, East Street, Jasper Hotel, Sam. P. Smith, Proprietor.

No.—, East Street, James W. Richardson, Blacksmith.

No. 2, West Street, J. A. Johnson.

No. 4, West Street, G. W. Stewart, Jeweler.

No. 8, West Street, Gordoz & Parker.

No. 12, West Street, John Richardson, Blacksmith.

On May 16, 1888, the Sheffield and Birmingham Railroad (now the Northern Alabama) was built into Jasper, thus giving the town two railroads. The advent of the railroads meant the doom of Jasper's greatest competitor, the town of South Lowell. Jasper's railroad facilities made it the logical industrial and commercial center. Prohibition was in effect in Jasper, while South Lowell had three saloons, which were patronized by men from all over the county; but this, alone, could not overcome Jasper's new advantages, and South Lowell quickly and surely died, becoming, in a short time, a deserted village.

The railroads brought on a great boom for Jasper, and, like all booms, results did not come up to expectations. However, a large number of people were attracted to the town and the population grew from two hundred in 1886 to three thousand in 1890. Abnormal prosperity reigned during these years.

In 1887 the first bank in Walker County was organized—the Walker County Bank, with Hinton E. Carr, of Mississippi and Arkansas, as president and John B. Hughes, of Jasper, as cashier.

Also in the same year the Jasper Land Company was incorporated with a capital stock of three hundred thousand dollars, and with Joseph F. Johnston, president; L. B. Musgrove, vice president; and with a board of directors which included, among others, F. A. Gamble, J. C. Musgrove, L. B. Musgrove, and W. L. Wallis, of Jasper. This Company purchased four thousand acres of land in and around Jasper, including practically every unimproved lot in Jasper.

In 1888 the town of Jasper was incorporated, and G. H. Guttery was elected the first mayor. In this same year the Methodists of Jasper tore down the frame church building which had been erected in 1868 and erected a new church building. This year also saw the organization of the Presbyterian Church of Jasper, the first one of that denomination organized in the county. This church was established by the Rev. P. G. Morton, an evangelist, with only three members, as the result of a week's evangelistic service. J. T. Sherer was the first Ruling Elder. In October of the same year eleven new members were added and

W. J. Hayes was elected Ruling Elder. All the meetings were held in the Baptist Church until the following year. On December 18, 1889, a church building was completed, which cost about two thousand dollars, the lot having been donated by the Jasper Land Company. The lumber used in the building was cut at a saw mill owned by J. B. Shields and D. K. Carter.

The year 1889 also saw the organization of the Jasper Trust Company, with F. A. Gamble, president; Judge J. B. Shields, vice president; J. A. Gravlee, cashier; and a board of directors which included Dr. W. C. Rosamond, T. L. Long, J. H. Cranford, L. B. Musgrove, J. B. Chamberlain, and W. G. Davis.

By the end of 1890 the boom in Jasper was reaching its height. An English syndicate, known as the Jasper Town and Lands, Limited, with a capital of approximately one million dollars, purchased four-fifths of the stock of the Jasper Land Company, which company owned about four thousand acres in and around Jasper, including about six thousand building lots within the town. In addition, the Jasper Town and Lands purchased about eighteen thousand acres of coal lands at Corona, about ten thousand acres of coking coal lands south of Jasper, about two thousand acres of hematite brown ore lying north of Jasper, and about twenty thousand acres of long leaf yellow pine lying east of Jasper.

The advent of the railroads had caused a quick development of the coal and lumber industries along their lines in Walker County, and while this would have naturally caused Jasper to enjoy a steady and normal growth, the knowledge of the operations of the Jasper Town and Lands caused a wave of optimism

—of almost hysteria—to seize the people. The town, which had grown from two hundred people in 1886 to three thousand in 1890, now began to picture itself as a city of fifteen thousand population within a year or two. In a special edition of 1891, the Mountain Eagle lists Jasper's advantages as follows:

Four hundred coke ovens in operation; six coal mines within a few miles of the town; one foundry and machine shop; three school buildings; three churches—Methodist, Baptist and Presbyterian; two saw mills; one large brick works; two large sand stone quarries; two railroads and twenty highways; thirty stores; four hotels; two banks.

In its optimistic picture of what was to be the Mountain Eagle saw the immediate construction of furnaces, mills and foundries. "Steel Rails Will Be Manufactured In Jasper," reads one headline. "The furnaces, rolling mill and steel works are only the large industries to be built at once. A score of foundries and mills of various kinds will be erected and many of them in operation long before the larger works are completed," reads another paragraph.

Unfortunately these dreams never came true, yet Jasper continued to grow. By 1899 a third bank was thought necessary, and the Bank of Jasper was organized by J. H. Cranford. In August, 1898, the First Christian Church of Jasper was established by the Rev. F. D. Srygley, with twenty members.

By 1901 the Baptist Church building on Fourth Avenue, between Eighteenth and Nineteenth Streets, was sold to the First Christian Church, and a lot on Third Avenue, where the present Baptist Church is located, was purchased and the present building erected at a cost of about eight thousand dollars. In this same year Jasper felt the need of more adequate school facilities and the Central Elementary School Building was erected at a cost of fifty thousand dollars.

Other civic developments now came along in a normal manner. In 1904 J. H. Cranford organized the Jasper Water, Light and Power Company, to furnish residences with water and lights. The water was supplied from a well and pump located on North Third Avenue. On June 1, 1905, Mr. Cranford organized the First National Bank of Jasper.

The population of both the county and town had grown to such proportions that the volume of business transactions made the old courthouse facilities inadequate. In 1907 a new courthouse was built at a cost of two hundred thousand dollars. In this same year a new enterprise was brought to Jasper. T. C. Burton and his sons, C. L. and J. R. Burton, founded the Burton Manufacturing Company for the manufacture of leather goods.

On October 7, 1907, the first automobile came to Jasper. It was a Maxwell runabout, purchased in Birmingham by H. W. Cranford and driven by him to Jasper, in the then exceptional time of eleven hours. Citizens of the town looked on in amazement as Mr. Cranford drove his car through the streets at the bewildering speed of eight miles an hour.

In 1910 the Central Bank and Trust Company was organized with H. W. Cranford, president; F. A. Merrell, cashier; and O. F. Cobb, assistant cashier.

The start of the World War in 1914 brought new prosperity

to the county and town. Walker's cotton and coal and timber were needed by the warring nations, and the demand for these products could not be filled. Money was plentiful and was being spent.

In 1915 the Methodists erected a new marble church building costing two hundred thousand dollars, and one of the most beautiful in the state.

The Walker County High School was built in 1916 at a cost of forty thousand dollars. A new post office building was completed on July 1, 1919, at a cost of one hundred thousand dollars. The Walker County Hospital was incorporated by Dr. Albert C. Jackson on February 12, 1923, and construction started. In 1925 the Walker County Creamery was established by George H. Davis and his son, Carl Davis. The Walker County Farm Bureau was organized in 1927 with ninety members, for the co-operative buying of fertilizer, seed, feed, insecticides, etc., and the co-operative selling of cotton.

In 1929 an addition was built to the Walker County High School building, costing seventeen thousand five hundred dollars.

In 1930 The Walker County Library was opened through the efforts of J. Alex Moore, County Superintendent of Education, with the aid of the Rosenwald Fund. The Library Board consisted of Judge E. W. Long, J. Alex Moore, Mrs. James L. Sowell, Mrs. James Freeman, and Mrs. Earnest Lacy. The library was located in the old Bankhead home on Second Avenue, which was remodeled for this purpose, and the first librarian was Eunice Coston.

In 1931 the courthouse was badly damaged by fire, and the old structure was removed and a new building erected.

MANCHESTER

The Western Electric Company, a company of national prominence, purchased vast lumber holdings north of Jasper. In order to realize on these holdings it was necessary to have railroad facilites. Accordingly, in May, 1906, a charter was granted for the building of the Alabama Central Railroad, which was to run from Jasper to the site of a proposed village that was later to be called Manchester. Immediately upon the granting of the charter Ed Hall and John Kilgore began the grading of the road from Jasper to Manchester, the site of which was six miles north of Jasper, in a bend of Blackwater Creek. Here was built the main plant, the logging pond, the commissary, and dwellings for the workmen and their families. This enterprise brought to the county the Russells, Camps, Brittons, Mattinglys, Hubbards, Covingtons, Atwoods, Lees, Sallades, J. Metzger, Captain White, and others. By 1910 Manchester was a thriving, humming, lumber center.

From 1910 to 1926 Manchester remained the center of lumber activities in Walker County, but in 1926 the merchantable timber was gone. The plant was dismantled and the hum of saws ceased, and today Manchester is another deserted village.

OAKMAN

(YORK—DAY'S GAP—MARIETTA)

The present site of Oakman is in close proximity to some of the earliest settlements in the county. Thomas Davis was born on Cane Creek, near Oakman, in 1826. Tinson Shepherd settled on a near by farm in 1827. John Key settled on Lost Creek, northwest of Oakman, in 1824. At Providence Church, a few miles east, Hugh Lollar settled before 1820, and Reason Courington before 1832. John Washington Gurganus settled near Oakman about 1830. William Jones was living on Cane Creek, two miles south of Oakman, in 1838, and the Morris family were on Lost Creek before 1839. Elijah Blanton was born on Wolf Creek, near Oakman, in 1846, and in the same year Isaac Brown was born on Lost Creek. In the early 1840's William Swindle, Samuel H. Simpson, Willian Cobb and Samuel Tubb settled on near by farms. Robert T. Palmer settled on Wolf Creek in 1859, while Mortimer Corry was another early settler.

As early as 1833 a report of a Methodist quarterly conference held at the home of John Key, on Lost Creek, lists John Gurganus as an exhorter and David Blanton as a class leader. West, in his History of Methodism, lists Blanton's and Tubb's among the preaching places in Walker County in 1842.

A post office was established near the present site of Oakman before 1860 and called York Post Office. Early records of this post office are unavailable, but it is assumed that it lay on the old Jasper–Tuscaloosa highway, which ran just west of the present town. A recruiting station was established at York during the Civil War and a number of enlistments were made there.

In 1862 William Byrd Day came in and settled at a gap in the mountainous ridges that surround the town. Shortly after this the community became known as Day's Gap.

The community did not grow to any size until 1884, when,

in November of that year, the Georgia Pacific Railroad (now the Southern) was built in from Columbus, Miss., and established a terminus at Day's Gap, this being the first railroad built in the county. Freight of all kinds, which heretofore had to be transported by wagon or ox team for long distances, usually from Tuscaloosa or Warrior in Jefferson County, was now shipped by railroad, and Day's Gap sprang into immediate prominence as a distributing point for the entire county. A stage line was operated to Birmingham via Jasper and South Lowell.

In addition the work of building spur tracks into Coal Valley and Mountain Valley was speeded up by the railroads, and in a short time coal mines were in operation at both of these points. The Coal Valley mine, an enterprise inaugurated by T. J. Dunn & Company for the development of their coal properties, was the first one in operation. While the mine was some distance from the community, its effect on the business of the town was soon apparent. The boom was on, and by 1885 the town's population had grown to four hundred.

In the meantime, J. E. Cook, formerly of Columbus, Mississippi, had purchased a large body of mineral land, and while developing it endeavored to establish the town of Marietta on the opposite side of the Gap. However, Marietta could not compete with Day's Gap. By this time Wiley W. Hutto, James S. Watts, J. J. Phifer, and James I. Odom were prominent residents. Business and professional men from Jasper and other points moved in, among them being Dr. W. C. Rosamond, J. H. Cranford and Dr. J. W. Gravlee. Lee Williams and a Mr. Bean were the Gap's blacksmiths, while Joe Bush was the town marshal. James Corry, affectionately known as the "Duke of Day's Gap," was offering building lots free to any religious denomination that would erect a church.

The completion of the Kansas City, Memphis and Birmingham Railroad (now the Frisco) through Jasper, in 1886, had a tendency to stop the boom in Day's Gap. However, it still held its own, and improved some in 1888, when the Georgia Pacific completed the line from Day's Gap into Birmingham.

On August 28, 1895, the first telephone line in Walker County was completed from Oakman to Jasper.

On July 7, 1898, the Oakman Church of Christ was organized by J. T. Rose, E. Cranford and George Swindle, acting elders. A lot on Main Street was purchased from J. M. and L. J. Corry and a frame building erected with lumber that was cut and sawed by Thomas Conwell, whose mill was located near Oakman. The first minister was Rev. James Hill. This building remained in use until July 1, 1924, when a new building was started, which was completed in 1925.

PARRISH

(HEWITT—JONESBORO)

It is not known who were the original settlers on the present site of Parrish, which grew from an old post office known as Hewitt.

Hewitt was established in the year 1878, and was located on the old Baltimore Road, about two miles northeast of the present site of America, on what was then known as the Rufus Jones place, and was sometimes called Jonesboro. The first postmaster was William Rufus Jones, who served during the years 1878-79, and was then succeeded by Tram Jones. The mail at that time was handled by pony express. The route was from Jasper to Birmingham, and the service rendered was one round trip per week. In 1886 Tram Jones was succeeded by William Rufus Jones, the original postmaster. The post office was moved to what is known as America when the Georgia Pacific Railroad (now the Southern) was built in 1888, but the original name Hewitt was retained.

About the year 1890 the Sheffield, Birmingham and Tennessee Railroad (now the Northern Alabama) was completed, and it intersected the Georgia Pacific Railroad. At the point of intersection an old box car was set off on some crossties, a telegraph instrument installed and an operator employed. The first operator was named Parrish, and the telegraph station took his name and was called Parrish.

At this time there was no community whatever at Parrish, and Tom Christian was farming the land east of the present Bank Street. The land west of Bank Street was owned by William B. Appling, a lawyer in Jasper.

As the mail was now being handled by the railroads instead of by pony express, Postmaster William Rufus Jones was instructed to move the post office at Hewitt to the intersection of the railroads, and, effective January 1, 1891, the name was changed from Hewitt to Parrish.

The first home built in Parrish was erected by Postmaster

Jones, about two hundred yards east of the present depot, and was used for the post office.

The following year, in January, 1892, the Parrish Methodist Church was organized by the Rev. W. L. Miles, and six charter members, consisting of Elliott C. Tierce and his wife, Francis Tierce; Moses N. Stephenson and his wife, Mary A. (Tierce) Stephenson; and Robert Taylor and his wife, Rachel (Stephenson) Taylor. A small building was erected on the top of the first knoll on the east side of Bank Street, with rough lumber sawed and furnished by Martin T. Hendrix, who was operating a saw mill about one and one-half miles northeast of the community.

The Tierces, the Stephensons and the Taylors were farmers living west of Parrish on the old Jasper-Taylor's Ferry road.

About this time the second home was built in Parrish by A. J. White, and the third by L. V. Covin, both of whom were connected with the railroad.

In 1894 the Parrish Missionary Baptist Church was organized by a Judge Hilton and J. R. Sartain, with nine charter members, consisting of Mr. and Mrs. John H. Stephenson, Mr. and Mrs. John H. Robinson, and Mrs. Margaret Robinson, all of whom lived near old Antioch on the old Parrish-Jasper road; and Mr. and Mrs. John P. Gray, Edward W. Shepherd, and Joseph Kirkpatrick, all of whom lived near Pleasantfield.

The building used by the Methodists was also used by the Baptists, and later, still, was used as a schoolhouse.

About 1895 G. Riley Sanford came in from Good Springs and settled about one mile east of the depot, and he was followed in the next year or so by his brother, Wes Sanford, who settled just west of him. Also, in 1895, Dr. Demp Busby opened a general store, but he did not stay in business long. In 1898 a Robert Waldrop opened a store, but stayed only a short time. Others moved in during 1898-99, among them Sylvester H. Clements, who built the fourth residence in the town proper. About this time Postmaster Jones opened a store in the old Busby building, and for a number of years was the only merchant in the community.

Several years previous, both Tom Christian and W. B. Appling had had part of their land holdings platted and laid off in town lots, and while the sale of these lots was slow, a few people now began to purchase and to move in. However, while no actual census figures are available, it is thought that by 1910 there were not more than one hundred inhabitants in the town.

The Methodists had built a small church building on the present church lot, while the Baptists had built on a site at the northeast corner of White Street and Main Drive.

In 1914 Postmaster William Rufus Jones, after continuous service from 1886, was succeeded by Robert G. Waldrop, who served until 1918; and he, in turn, was succeeded by Mrs. Mattie Waldrop, who served during the year 1919. In 1920 William Lloyd Jones was appointed, and served until 1936, when he was succeeded by Jennings B. Key.

The booming of Parrish came in 1918, when ground was broken for the opening of the mine of the Railway Fuel Company, about one mile east of the town. In a year the mine was in full operation and the town and the adjoining mine camp housed almost three thousand souls.

Churches were too small for their congregations. The Methodists tore down their old building and erected a new and larger one in 1920. During the same year the Baptist Church was burned. The old lot was sold and a new one purchased, on which the present church building was erected.

It was soon apparent that the town should be incorporated, and this incorporation was effected on October 1, 1922, with Walter L. Guttery elected as first mayor.

School facilities were inadequate, but by the opening of the fall school term in 1925 a one story fire proof structure, costing approximately fifteen thousand dollars, was ready for occupancy, with Prof. Ira Helms serving as its first principal.

SOUTH LOWELL

The town of South Lowell, located about six miles northeast of Jasper, was created through a colonization scheme, fostered by Judge F. A. Gamble, of Jasper, Abner Hitchcock, of Cleveland, Ohio, and Jobe Richardson, who lived on and owned the land on which the town was laid out.

The colony was organized in Cleveland, Ohio, as the Ohio and Alabama Agricultural, Manufacturing and Mineral Company. Jobe Richardson made the proposition that he would deed one hundred acres of land to the company for the building of the town, under the condition that the company would build a home for him, under certain given specifications, which was agreed upon.

A code of laws was adopted and an engineer was employed

to lay out the town, which was composed of twenty blocks with a total of 424 lots.

In the fall of 1872 colonists arrived from Michigan, Ohio, New York and Maine, and thus began the town of South Lowell, which was destined to be the leading town in the county for the next fifteen years. The town prospered, being situated in a rich agricultural and timber section; and furthermore, with Jasper and most other towns in the county having a prohibition law, South Lowell was wet and boasted of three saloons, which were patronized by men from all over the county.

However, when the Kansas City, Memphis and Birmingham Railroad (now the Frisco) avoided South Lowell, and built its line through Jasper in 1886, it meant the doom of South Lowell, for it served to emphasize the fact that Jasper was the logical industrial and commercial center. Two years later, in 1888, the Sheffield and Birmingham Railroad (now the Northern Alabama) built its line into Jasper, and South Lowell quickly and surely died.

Today it is a deserted village, a forgotten dream of forgotten men.

TOWNLEY

(HOLLY GROVE—PLEASANT GROVE)

The building of railroads through a new country usually spells the doom of certain established communities and the birth of new communities to replace the doomed villages.

Such was the case in regard to the towns of Holly Grove and

Townley. When the Kansas City, Memphis and B:rmingham Railroad (now the Frisco) laid its rails one mile south of Holly Grove that community received its blow, and the town of Townley, one mile away and located on the railroad, came into existence.

That section of Walker County in the vicinity of Townley and Holly Grove is perhaps the scene of the earliest settlements in the county, and Holly Grove itself is perhaps the first community.

William Guttery and his sons, Robert, Johnson and Isham Guttery, were perhaps the first settlers in Holly Grove, coming there in the early 1800's. At what is now Townley Daniel Townley entered government land in 1822; Jesse Tyree, in 1823; and David and William Brown, in 1824. However, John King settled a short distance east of Townley about 1820, and Henry Sides was living in the vicinity of Pleasant Grove before 1820.

Holly Grove was the community center and post office for all these early settlers. The Bethel Primitive Baptist Church was established there before 1824, for it was during that year that Robert Guttery joined the church.

The Boshell, the Pike, the Keeton, the Cooner, the Lawson, and the Romine families were established in this section before 1835. General John Manasco came in 1836 and George Leith in 1839. The Wright and the Cheatham families settled in the vicinity about 1840. Dr. L. C. Miller moved from Jasper to Holly Grove in 1842. The Rutledge family was settled near Pleasant Grove before 1846, and Joseph Ferguson moved to Holly Grove in 1849.

Pleasant Grove came into existence as a community in 1842 when a dissension entered the Baptist Church over the matter of missions. The Bethel Church, at Holly Grove, continued to follow the Primitive Baptist beliefs, while those who subscribed to the tenets of the Missionary Baptists organized and built their church at Pleasant Grove, the first of that faith to be built in the county.

Holly Grove continued to be the trading center, and an old business directory for 1854 shows Robert Guttery as the leading merchant. However, the community never grew, and its final doom came with the building of the Frisco Railroad in 1886.

With the building of the railroad, Townley was founded and named after the Townley family, the original settlers of the land. Robert Townley was appointed the first postmaster. Efforts were made to attract people to the town, and T. S. Hendon offered to donate lots for any church that would erect a building. The town grew with the opening of several coal mines, and on June 17, 1895, it was incorporated, and John W. Guttery elected the first mayor.

PART THREE—THE PEOPLE

EARLY SETTLERS

AARON, JAMES, a native of South Carolina, was a small boy when his parents moved to Walker County, where he spent his entire life engaged in farming. He was married to Sallie Chambers.

Moore, Vol. II, page 178.

AARON, CHARLES, a pioneer settler of Walker County, who entered government land in Section 32, Township 13, Range 5, on April 11, 1836.

Walker County Tract Record.

AARON, JOHN, a pioneer settler of Walker County, who entered government land in Section 34, Township 13, Range 7, on August 17, 1836.

Walker County Tract Record.

AARON, WILLIAM, entered government land in Section 24, Township 14, Range 6, on November 28, 1854.

Walker County Tract Record.

AARON, IRA, the son of James and Sallie (Chambers) Aaron, was born in Walker County and served in the Confederate Army during the Civil War. He was married to Winnie Tubb, who was also born and reared in the county. During middle age he moved to Hanceville in Cullman County.

Moore, Vol. II, page 332.

AARON, FRANCIS MARION, the son of James and Sallie (Chambers) Aaron, was born in Walker County in 1846. He engaged in farming until 1922, when he retired to Cordova. He was married to Mary Mayberry, who was born in Walker County in 1853 and died near Boldo in 1914. Children—Joseph, who moved to Arkansas; James, a farmer in Walker County; John, a coal miner who died near Littleton at the age of twenty-nine; Monroe, a banker in Cordova; Coy Richard, who served in the U. S. Army; Leroy, moved to Arkansas; Luvena, married Isaac Downs, of Louisiana; Novella, married Allen Harris, of Walker County.

Moore, Vol. II, page 178.

AARON, MONROE, a son of Francis Marion and Mary (Mayberry) Aaron, was born near Williams' Mill, Walker County, August 2, 1878. Educated in the public schools of the county, he worked first in a sawmill, later as a coal miner, and then entered the mercantile business in Dora, which he operated until 1910. Mr. Aaron then developed and operated a successful coal mine near Cordova and subsequently became interested in the Citizens Bank and Trust Company of Cordova, and served as its first president. He was married at Cordova on January 17, 1904, to Miss Nora Reid, the daughter of Dr. William Reid, of Cullman County. Children—Gracie, Sybil, Monroe, Jr., Dewey Hobson, William Jean, and Brack.

Moore, Vol. II, page 178.

ABBOTT, HILL, born in Indiana in 1801, was married in Walker County in 1827, to Jane Mills Key, daughter of John and Belinda Key. Children—James Stanley, married Rebecca Blevins; John Wesley, married the widow of his brother, James; Elizabeth Caroline, married James Duskin; Aseneth Adeline, married Hiram Raines; Hill Copland, married Mary Polly Nelson; William Washington, married Ann Raines; Malinda J., married first to Geo. V. McNeal, second to James Motes; Pilgrim, married Sarah Ann Lay; Basheba, married Samuel Brooks; Sheran, married Dora Myers; Ira, married Meta Sandlin; Sophronia, married John Sandlin.

Key and Allied Families, page 267.

ABLES, JAMES, a pioneer settler, entered government land in Section 19, Township 14, Range 8, on November 13, 1836.
Walker County Tract Record.

ADGERTON, JAMES P., entered government land in Section 25, Township 14, Range 4, on August 13, 1855.
Walker County Tract Record.

ADKINS, WILLIAM, a Confederate veteran, living in Walker County in 1895.
Mountain Eagle, July 3, 1895.

AKINS, JOHN CALVIN, born April 25, 1832, at Carrollton, Ga. Enlisted in the Confederate Army at Jasper on September 1, 1862, and served as a private in Company H, Fifty-sixth Alabama Cavalry, under Captain Johnson. He died March 1, 1922, and is buried at Union Chapel, five miles east of Jasper. His wife, Sarah, born January 7, 1854, died January 1, 1915, and is also buried at Union Chapel.
Census of Pensioners, 1907.
Gravestones.

ALDRIDGE, ISHAM, entered government land in Section 22, Township 13, Range 10, on October 3, 1832.
Walker County Tract Record.

ALDRIDGE, ASHLEY, entered government land in Section 23, Township 13, Range 10, on February 2, 1836. He is mentioned in West's History of Methodism as a worthy Christian who helped to found the Methodist Church in Walker County.
Walker County Tract Record.

ALDRIDGE, PRINCE W., entered government land in Section 33, Township 13, Range 10, on February 2, 1836.
Walker County Tract Record.

ALDRIDGE, ALFRED, entered government land in Section 22, Township 13, Range 10, on January 14, 1846.
Walker County Tract Record.

ALDRIDGE (or ALDRICH), JAMES, entered government land in Section 30, Township 13, Range 7, on October 19, 1854.

Walker County Tract Record.

ALDRIDGE, ABNER B., operator of the Stith Coal Company mines at Aldridge and the South Eastern Fuel Company mines at Gorgas, was born in Wilcox County, Ala., September 2, 1881; son of Abner B. and Etta S. (Pharr) Aldridge, and grandson of Jefferson Aldridge, who was born in Monroe County, Ala. The son of poor parents, Abner B. Aldridge, Jr., spent his boyhood days on the farm and attended local schools. He eventually went to work in a mine at one dollar a night, but finally became superintendent. Later still he went into business for himself, leasing a coal property in the county which he later purchased. For a number of years he has been one of the leading coal operators in the county, controlling more than twenty thousand acres of coal lands. In 1906 Mr. Aldridge was married to Miss Annie Milner Burton, of Jefferson County, and they reside in Birmingham.

Moore, Vol. II, page 623.

ALEXANDER, JEREMIAH, was residing in Washington County, Va., on April 1, 1780, when he enlisted with the Virginia troops in the Continental Army, serving first under Captain Montgomery, later under Lieutenant Davidson and Captain Neil, and then transferred back to Captain Montgomery's company under Colonel Campbell. He was in an engagement with the British at Whitsitt's Mill on the Reedy Fork of the Haw River in North Carolina. After the close of the Revolutionary War Jeremiah Alexander moved from Washington County, Virginia, to the State of Tennessee. Later he moved to North Carolina, and in 1819 he came to Alabama and settled in Morgan County. He was living in Morgan County in 1832, but in

1840 he was known to have been residing in Walker County, where he is presumed to have died on January 26, 1847.

Files U. S. Veterans Bureau.

ALEXANDER, JASON C., entered government land, where Carbon Hill now stands, in 1848.

Walker County Tract Record.

ALLEN, JOHN, a pioneer settler, entered government land in Section 9, Township 13, Range 8, northeast of Townley, on October 27, 1826.

Walker County Tract Record.

ALLEN, JOSEPH, entered government land in Section 27, Township 13, Range 10, on October 8, 1833.

Walker County Tract Record.

ALLEN, ASA, entered government land in Section 8, Township 13, Range 5, on July 10, 1855.

Walker County Tract Record.

ALLISON, ZACHARIAH DEASON, who lived at Nauvoo, was born September 13, 1843, in Carroll County, Georgia. In September, 1863, he volunteered as a private and was sent to Missionary Ridge to join Company E, Twenty-eighth Alabama Infantry, under Captain Henderson. He was wounded at Tunnell Hill, Georgia, on February 25, 1864. Later he was captured by the Federal troops at Pond Springs, Alabama, and was imprisoned at Camp Chase, Ohio, until the close of the war.

Census of Pensioners, 1907.

ANDREWS, RICHARD HARRISON, who lived at Dora, was born August 18, 1844, in Monroe County, Alabama. On April 15, 1863, he enlisted at Quinton in Company L, Musgrove's Battalion of Cavalry, and served until December, 1864, when he was furloughed.

Census Confederate Soldiers, 1907.

APPLING, WILLIAM B., an attorney in Jasper, was born

in Chickasaw County, Miss., on December 18, 1841, the son of Richard and Jaily W. (Embry) Appling, and grandson of William Appling. Richard Appling was born in Georgia April 13, 1816, but at an early age was brought by his parents to Tuscaloosa County, where he was reared. He was a thrifty and industrious farmer, who also served Tuscaloosa County many years as Justice of the Peace, Tax Assessor during the Civil War, census taker in 1865, and later again as Tax Assessor. He died at the home of his son in Jasper February 15, 1888. In 1840 he was married to Jaily W. Embry, who died in Jasper in June, 1886. Children—William B., Joseph F., Elizabeth C., Salina S., Martha L.

William B. Appling studied law, was admitted to the bar and began his practice in Jasper. In 1870 he was appointed Solicitor of Walker County but resigned in 1872. He served for several years as Registrar in Chancery. Mr. Appling became a large land owner, both in the town of Jasper and in Walker County, and owned considerable of the land on which the town of Parrish is now located. He died on October 21, 1901, and is buried at Oak Hill Cemetery, Jasper. In 1861 Mr. Appling enlisted in Lumden's Battery of Light Artillery and served until the close of the Civil War. He took part in the battles at Corinth, Perryville, Murfreesboro and Chickamauga, but was never wounded or captured. In 1868 he was married to Mattie W. Cummins, of Tennessee, who was born on May 12, 1843, and died on September 15, 1900. Children—Etta, Waller, Myra (married on February 12, 1895, to Dr. Frank Hausman, of Jasper), William J., Mattie J., Newbern M., and Edmund W.

Owens' Alabama, Vol. III, page 47.
Memorial Record, Vol. II, page 1019.

APPLING, JAMES C., a member of Company K, Ninth Alabama Cavalry, C. S. A., together with his wife, Martha

Ann, born June 10, 1849; died December 6, 1915, is buried in Tubbs Graveyard.

Gravestones.

ASHCRAFT, THOMAS, was born in Chester District, South Carolina, on January 9, 1808; moved to East Alabama in 1821, and joined the Protestant Methodist Church in 1826. Soon after moving to Walker County he joined the Methodist Episcopal Church at Jasper. On October 5, 1841, he was married to Mary L. Apperson.

Mountain Eagle, November 4, 1885.

ATKINS, WILLIAM COLUMBUS, of Nauvoo, was born July 23, 1843, near Northport, Tuscaloosa County. In September, 1864, he enlisted at Jasper as a private in Company B, Tenth Alabama Cavalry, under Captain Whatley. He was captured by Federal troops at Courtland, Alabama, on December 29, 1864, and imprisoned at Camp Chase, Ohio, until the close of the war. He died April 13, 1925, and is buried at Liberty Grove.

Census of Confederate Soldiers, 1907.

AVERY, A. W., a Confederate veteran living in Walker County in 1895.

Mountain Eagle, July 3, 1895.

BACHELOR, ELISHA, entered government land in Section 24, Township 14, Range 7, on September 18, 1856.

Walker County Tract Record.

BAGBY, JOAB, entered government land in Section 3, Township 16, Range 5, on December 6, 1836.

Walker County Tract Record.

BAKER, PETER, a pioneer settler, entered government land in Sections 12 and 20, Township 14, Range 8, on November 14, 1821.

Walker County Tract Record.

BAKER, ALVIN R., thought to be a son of Peter Baker,

was brought to Walker County by his parents in 1821. Upon reaching manhood he entered government land in Section 22, Township 14, Range 8, in the vicinity of King's Chapel or Steadman's, originally Lost Creek Post Office, on November 16, 1836. Mr. Baker was a man of extraordinary mind and neighbors said of him that he was a benefactor to all. For several years he filled the office of Justice of the Peace. In later years Mr. Baker said he was present at the organization of the first Circuit Court ever held in the county, and he attended every term of that court until his death. He died on September 11, 1874. He was married twice—first to Susan Kitchens, a daughter of James Matlock and Sally (Brown) Kitchens, and after her death to Virginia J. ―――. Children, by first marriage—

James A. Baker, who moved to Blount and later to Cullman County.

John D. Baker, who moved to Granbury, Hood County, Texas.

Mary Caroline Baker, born in 1840, died in 1932; was married in 1858 to Eli A. Sparks, a son of Eli and Frances (Kitchens) Sparks, who was born January 22, 1835, and died July 28, 1872. Children—Alvin S. Sparks, Thomas E. Sparks, Rutha Susan Sparks, and John E. Sparks.

Louisa Baker, who married, first, James Williams, and, second, a Mr. Townley.

Darling P. Baker, who married M. C. Watts, a daughter of Rev. J. J. Watts.

Elijah P. Baker.

Children, by second marriage—

Sarah L. Baker, who married James F. Steadman, Cullman County.

George H. Baker and Susan J. Baker, minor children at the time of the death of their father, who were reared by their brother-in-law, James F. Steadman, in Cullman County.

Willie Baker, Minnie Baker, and Annie Baker, minor children

at the time of the death of their father, who were taken by their mother to Canton, Van Zandt County, Texas.

Walker County Tract Record.
Powell's Fifty-five Years in West Alabama.
Probate Record, Estate Alvin R. Baker.
Probate Record, Estate Eli A. Sparks.

BAKER, OBID, entered government land in Section 19, Township 15, Range 9, on January 21, 1833.

Walker County Tract Record.

BAKER, WILLIAM, entered government land in Section 11, Township 14, Range 7, on March 1, 1834. Mr. Baker was born April 20, 1818, and died December 22, 1905. His wife (Mary) was born in May, 1828, and died August 26, 1906. Both are buried in Zion Graveyard on Lockhart Hill.

Walker County Tract Record.
Gravestones.

BAKER, BETHEL, entered government land in Section 17, Township 15, Range 9, on August 19, 1836.

Walker County Tract Record.

BAKER, NATHAN, entered government land in Section 17, Township 15, Range 9, on November 28, 1836.

Walker County Tract Record.

BAKER, DEMPSEY D., entered government land in Section 22, Township 14, Range 8, on November 16, 1836.

Walker County Tract Record.

BAKER, ELIJAH, entered government land in Section 18, Township 16, Range 6, on June 18, 1836. He was married to Mary Ann Cain, the eldest daughter of James Cain, a pioneer settler of the county. Mr. Baker went to California during the gold rush and never returned, but his wife remained in Walker County. There were two children—a daughter (Guinea), who married a Boshell at Townley, and a son (Willis), who in later life also went to California.

Walker County Tract Record.
Family Records, James Cain.

BAKER, LAMBERT W., an attorney at Jasper, was elected on the Whig ticket as Representative for the 1844 session of the Legislature. He served one term and shortly after left for the West.

Powell's Fifty-five Years in West Alabama.

BALLENGER, WILLIAM, entered government land in Section 29, Township 15, Range 5, on January 22, 1855.

Walker County Tract Record.

BANKHEAD, JOHN HOLLIS. Side by side in the old burying ground at Bullock Creek Presbyterian Church, York District, South Carolina, lie James Bankhead and his wife, Elizabeth (Black) Bankhead, who were one time the principal owners of the town of Pinckneyville, the county seat of the old Camden District. They had lived on Broad River and their lands lay on the Broad and the Pacolet Rivers, in Union District, and here was born a son, George Bankhead, who, when he had grown to manhood, was married to Jane Greer. About 1818 George and Jane (Greer) Bankhead moved to Moscow, in what was then Marion, now Lamar, County, Alabama, and here reared a large family. Among their sons was one named James Greer Bankhead, who married Susan Fleming Hollis, the daughter of Colonel John Hollis, and granddaughter of Captain John Hollis, a Revolutionary soldier who died in Fairfield District, South Carolina. On September 13, 1842, there was born to James Greer and Susan Fleming Bankhead, a son whom they named John Hollis Bankhead.

On August 2, 1861, at the age of nineteen, John Hollis Bankhead entered the service of the Confederate Army as Second Lieutenant of Company K, Sixteenth Alabama Infantry, and in

1863 he was promoted to Captain, serving in that capacity until the close of the war, when he was paroled at Decatur, Ala., Captain Bankhead was wounded three times during his service with the army.

After the close of the war Captain Bankhead had various business interests and also represented Marion County in the General Assembly during 1865, 1866 and 1867; was in the State Senate in 1876-1877; was Representative from Lamar County in 1880-1881; and Warden of the Alabama Penitentiary from 1881 to 1885. He was elected to Congress from the Sixth Congressional District in November, 1886, and served successive terms from March 4, 1887, to March 4, 1907. On June 18, 1907, he was elected United States Senator and served until his death on March 1, 1920. During his service as Senator he originated legislation covering government co-operation with states in the construction of highways, and will ever be known for this work as the "father of good roads."

Captain Bankhead was married to Tallulah James Brockman, a daughter of James and Elizabeth (Stanley) Brockman, of Greenville District, S. C. Children—Louise Bankhead, who married, first, Col. William Hayne Perry, of Greenville, S. C., and, second, Andrew J. Lund, of Washington, D. C.; Marie Susan Bankhead, who married Thomas McAdory Owen, a practicing attorney and author, of Carrollton, Ala., who later became Director of Department of Archives and History, State of Alabama, and which office is now filled by his widow; John Hollis Bankhead, Jr.; William Brockman Bankhead; and Col. Henry M.

Owen, Vol. III, page 88.

BANKHEAD, JOHN HOLLIS, JR., a son of John Hollis and Tallulah (Brockman) Bankhead, was born July 8, 1872, at Moscow, Lamar County. Graduating from the University of Alabama in 1891, he attended the law school of Georgetown University, Washington, D. C., and graduated in 1893. On August 1, 1893, he began the practice of law at Jasper as junior member of the firm of Coleman and Bankhead. Mr. Coleman died in 1904, and Mr. Bankhead was joined by his younger brother, William B. Bankhead, who had been practicing law in Huntsville. John Hollis Bankhead, Jr., is the author of the Alabama election law under the constitution of 1901; in 1903 was elected to the State Legislature from Walker County, and in 1930 was elected United States Senator. On December 26, 1894, he was married to Musa, daughter of Walter Worth and Lula (Harris) Harkins, of Fayette, Ala. Children—Marion; William Walter, who married Emelil Crumpton, of Maplesville; and Louise.

Owen, Vol. III, page 92.

BANKHEAD, WILLIAM BROCKMAN, a son of John Hollis and Tallulah (Brockman) Bankhead, was born April 12, 1874, near Sulligent, Lamar County. Graduating from the University of Alabama in June, 1893, he at once entered the law school of the Georgetown University, Washington, D. C., from which he graduated in 1895. He was admitted to the bar at Fayette, Ala., in September, 1895, and entered upon the practice of law at Huntsville. In 1905 he moved to Jasper to practice with his brother, John H. Bankhead, Jr. He was City Attorney of Huntsville in 1900-1901; Circuit Solicitor, fourteenth circuit, 1900-1914. In 1916 he was elected to Congress and is still a member of that body at this writing (1935). He was married, first, to Adelaide Eugene Sledge, daughter of J. Thomas and Evelyn Eugenia (Garth) Sledge, of Memphis, and, second, to Florence, daughter of Joseph H. and Saleta (Anderson) McGuire, of Jasper. Children by first wife—Evelyn Eugenia, married Morton Hoyt; Tallulah Brockman, an actress, who has won international renown on both the legimate stage and in motion pictures.

Owen, Vol. III, page 92.

BANKS, P. L., a pioneer settler who entered government land in Section 5, Township 16, Range 7, near the confluence of Lost and Cain Creeks, on October 12, 1836.
Walker County Tract Record.

BANKS, WILLIAM, entered government land in Section 17, Township 14, Range 6, on July 5, 1855. He was born August 23, 1832, and died November 30, 1900. His wife, Elizabeth, was born July 18, 1830, and died June 20, 1901. Both are buried at Sardis Graveyard.
Walker County Tract Record.
Gravestones.

BANKS, SANFORD W., a Confederate veteran, was born April 20, 1836, and died July 27, 1920. His wife, Sallie, died May 30, 1909, at the age of 68. Both are buried at Boldo.
Mountain Eagle, July 3, 1895.
Gravestones.

BARBEE, JAMES, entered government land in Section 25, Township 13, Range 10, on August 25, 1835.
Walker County Tract Record.

BARNES, ALEXANDER H., entered government land in Section 13, Township 14, Range 4, on October 28, 1859.
Walker County Tract Record.

BARTON, MOSES, the first of that name to come to Walker County, is, according to family tradition, a descendant of David Barton, who, with his brother, Abraham, came to America from England in 1672. Abraham settled first in Maryland and later went to New England. David settled on the James River in Virginia. One of his descendants, also named David Barton, went with Daniel Boone into Kentucky and was killed by Indians at Harrodsburg in 1767. Five of his sons served in the Revolutionary War, and one of them, another David Barton, was a Colonel of Virginia troops and served with George Washington at Valley Forge. Thomas Barton, a son of the last named David

Barton, was married to Susan Keys, a daughter of John and Susan Keys, of Fairfax Courthouse, Va.

Thomas and Susan (Keys) Barton moved to Morgan County, Georgia, in 1794 and came to Alabama Territory in 1817, the first white settler to locate north of the Tallapoosa River; cleared the first plantation and built the first grist mill in that locality. It is thought that Moses Barton was a son of Thomas and Susan (Keys) Barton.

Moses Barton came to Walker County about 1822, for in that year the records show that he entered government land on the Warrior River near the mouth of Blackwater Creek, in Section 27, Township 14, Range 6. Little is known of him other than that he was a successful farmer. He died in 1840 and is buried in old Sardis Graveyard, on the Warrior River. He was the father of a large family, among his children being Hiram Barton; John Mace Barton; Nathaniel Barton; Moses Barton, Jr.; Lidia Barton, who married Samuel Morrow; Nancy Barton, who married John Robbins and moved to Texas; Rebecca Barton, who married Burgess Mullens and moved to Texas; Frances Barton, who married James Morrow and moved to Calhoun County, Miss.; James A. Barton; Louisa Barton, who married a Mr. Sanders; Mary A. Barton, who married a Mr. Nations; Milley Barton, who married a Mr. Raines.

Walker County Tract Record.
Barton Family Tradition.
Probate Records, Estate of Hiram Barton.

BARTON, JOSHUA, a pioneer settler who entered government land in Section 19, Township 14, Range 7, on November 11, 1826.

Walker County Tract Record.

BARTON, HIRAM, a son of Moses Barton, who was born April 10, 1801, and died March 25, 1876. In 1821 he was married to Sarah Willis, who was born August 5, 1803, and died April 15, 1877.

Gravestones.

BARTON, MOSES, JR., a son of Moses Barton, came to Walker County with his father about 1822. Little is known of Moses Barton, Jr., other than that he was a farmer and a member of the Methodist Church. One son, Henry Barton, Sr., entered government land in Section 27, Township 14, Range 6, on April 24, 1837.

Walker County Tract Record.

BARTON, NATHANIEL, a son of Moses Barton, Sr., came to Walker County with his father about 1822. He was married three times, his second wife being Mary Wilson, and his third a Miss Yarborough. Nathaniel Barton was the father of five sons —Moses Barton, Hiram Barton, Lize Barton, William Barton, and James Barton.

Barton Family Records.

BARTON, MOSES, a son of Nathaniel Barton, was born February 18, 1818, and was brought to Walker County by his parents about 1822. He was reared in the county and was a farmer all of his life, living near the present site of Cordova. However, he served one term as Sheriff of the county in 1885. He died on April 14, 1890, and is buried at old Sardis Graveyard on the Warrior River. His wife, Margaret A. Barton, was born in Lawrence County, Ala., on January 19, 1819, and died on October 5, 1898.

Barton Family Records.
Gravestones.

BARTON, HIRAM, a son of Nathaniel and Mary (Wilson) Barton, was born in Georgia, May 18, 1821, and was brought to Walker County by his parents while still an infant. He was reared and educated in the county and was a farmer all of his life. During the Civil War he served in the Confederate Army under Captain B. M. Long. In 1885 he served one term as a member of the County Board of Revenue. He died on July 1, 1893, and is buried at old Sardis Graveyard on the Warrior River. Hiram Barton was married twice—first to a Miss Black, and second to Rachel Daniel, who was born July 4, 1836, and died February 16, 1906. Children—first marriage, Hugh Barton, born July 1, 1846, died February 19, 1919; married Irena Stoval, born in 1854, died in 1928; Nathaniel Barton, married Barbara King; Ephraim Barton, married Sallie Brock; Margaret Barton, married Thomas Evans. Second marriage—Irena Barton, married John Roberts; Washington Barton, married Mollie Morrow; James H. Barton, married Martha Jane Kitchens, a daughter of Jesse Simeon Kitchens; Lee Barton, died single at the age of nineteen; Felix Barton, married Dovie Morrow; Martha Barton, married S. J. Kirkpatrick; Sarah Barton, married Henry Morgan; Della Barton, married James Sumner.

Barton Family Records.

BARTON, ABSALOM, entered government land in Section 8, Township 14, Range 7, on February 4, 1836.

Walker County Tract Record.

BARTON, NANCY K., entered government land in Section 11, Township 14, Range 7, on August 17, 1836.

Walker County Tract Record.

BARTON, TANEY, SR., entered government land in Section 27, Township 14, Range 6, on April 24, 1837.

Walker County Tract Record.

BARTON, JOHN M., a son of the first Moses Barton, became a prominent elder in the old Mount Zion Association of the Primitive Baptist Church and assisted in the organization of the Sulphur Springs Primitive Baptist Church on July 6, 1844. He died at his home on Warrior River on November 1, 1885.

Sulphur Springs Church Record.
Mountain Eagle, November 4, 1885.

BARTON, WILLIAM WALLACE, born February 4, 1839, near Cordova on the Warrior River; enlisted at Jasper on March 27, 1862, as Second Sergeant in Company L, Twenty-eighth Alabama Infantry, Musgrove Battalion, and was discharged from a hospital in Selma in the spring of 1864. Mr. Barton became a minister in the Primitive Baptist Church. He died on July 11, 1919, and is buried at Boldo.

Census of Confederate Soldiers, 1907.
Gravestone.

BARTON, JAMES ALLEN, born March 11, 1844, near Sanders Ferry on the Warrior River; enlisted in the spring of 1863, in Lawrence County, as a private in the Confederate Army under Captain Warren. Discharged in the spring of 1864 on account of ill health, he re-enlisted at Jasper about July, 1864, in Captain Mason's Company, Musgrove Battalion. He was captured by the Federal troops at Ten Island Shoals on the Coosa River in September, 1864, and was paroled.

Census of Confederate Soldiers, 1907.

BARTON, ELIAS, a Confederate veteran, residing in Walker County in 1895.

Mountain Eagle, July 3, 1895.

BATES, LEVI, died September 25, 1895, aged eighty-four years, nine months and one day; buried at Samaria. One of the county's oldest citizens.

Mountain Eagle, September 25, 1895.

BATES, JAMES, entered government land in Section 36, Township 12, Range 5, on December 11, 1832.

Walker County Tract Record.

BATES, JOHN, entered government land in Section 35, Township 14, Range 7, on April 17, 1836.
Walker County Tract Record.

BAYES, JOHN, entered government land in Section 9, Township 16, Range 6, on January 1, 1836.
Walker County Tract Record.

BEASLEY, ELIJAH AND ELIZABETH, entered government land in Section 34, Township 15, Range 9, on January 15, 1833.
Walker County Tract Record.

BEASLEY, JESSE, entered government land in Section 27, Township 15, Range 9, on December 20, 1832.
Walker County Tract Record.

BECKERSTAFF, M., entered government land in Section 25, Township 14, Range 9, on October 23, 1832.
Walker County Tract Record.

BECKERSTAFF, JOHNSON, entered government land in Section 16, Township 14, Range 7, within the present limits of the town of Jasper, on February 25, 1833. His daughter, Gemine Adelia, born on March 1, 1827, was married to Wash. Williams on January 16, 1843, and died on October 14, 1893. She is buried at Coal City Graveyard.
Walker County Tract Record.
Gravestones.

BEDDINGFIELD, W. H., a Confederate veteran living in Walker County in 1895.
Mountain Eagle, July 3, 1895.

BELL, ANTHONY, entered government land in Section 6, Township 17, Range 6, on March 8, 1836.
Walker County Tract Record.

BENNETT, JESSIE LIVINGSTON, who lived in the Layman's Chapel community, was born February 23, 1839, at Clear Creek Falls. In September, 1861, he enlisted as a private in

Company F, Sixteenth Alabama Infantry, and served throughout the war, until June, 1865, when he was paroled at Huntsville. He died August 28, 1912, and is buried at Layman's Chapel. He was married to Josephine L. Jones, who was born August 16, 1845, and died June 20, 1914. She is also buried at Layman's Chapel.

Census of Confederate Soldiers, 1907.
Gravestones.

BENSON, W. H., a Confederate veteran living in Walker County in 1895.

Mountain Eagle, July 3, 1895.

BIDDY, EDWARD, entered government land in Section 7, Township 14, Range 6, on September 5, 1836.

Walker County Tract Record.

BILLINGSLEY, JEPTHA, JESSE, SAMUEL, THOMAS, W. M., pioneer settlers who entered government land in Sections 20, 24, 27, 28, and 34, Township 14, Range 7, in the years 1833, 1834 and 1836.

Walker County Tract Record.

BIRDWELL, JOHN, entered government land in Section 14, Township 14, Range 9, on November 21, 1835.

Walker County Tract Record.

BLACK, SAMUEL, entered government land in Section 19, Township 14, Range 5, on November 29, 1833.

Walker County Tract Record.

BLACK, ARCHIBALD, entered government land in Section 6, Township 15, Range 6, on September 6, 1836.

Walker County Tract Record.

BLACK, HUGH, entered government land in Section 31, Township 14, Range 6, on December 31, 1836.

Walker County Tract Record.

BLACKBURN, JOHN, entered government land in Section 36, Township 15, Range 9, on March 29, 1824.
Walker County Tract Record.

BLACKSTON, JAMES, who lived at Pocahontas, was born February 27, 1828, at Augusta, Ga. In April, 1862, at Kansas, Walker County, he enlisted in Company H, Forty-third Alabama Infantry, under Captain Lawrence, and served throughout the war. He surrendered at Appomattox Court House, Va., on April 9, 1865.
Census of Confederate Soldiers, 1907.

BLACKWELL, JAMES M., entered government land in Section 4, Township 14, Range 8, on November 26, 1844.
Walker County Tract Record.

BLACKWELL, DAVIDSON, entered government land in Section 32, Township 13, Range 8, on January 28, 1846.
Walker County Tract Record.

BLACKWELL, ALEXANDER HENRY, who lived at Kansas, Walker County, was born February 10, 1834, at Carrollton, Ga. In September, 1862, he enlisted at Jasper in Company A of Hewlett's Battalion and served throughout the war. He was paroled at Decatur in May, 1865.
Census of Confederate Soldiers, 1907.

BLACKWELL, WILLIAM RALEIGH, was born December 20, 1845, at Blackwell, Walker County, and lived there all of his life. On December 25, 1863, he enlisted at Jasper as a private in Company L, Fifty-sixth Alabama Cavalry, under Captain Guttery, and served until the close of the War.
Census of Confederate Soldiers, 1907.

BLACKWELL, J. F., born February 23, 1859; died on January 24, 1934, and was buried at Flat Woods Cemetery. He was a member of the Primitive Baptist Church for forty-one years and a respected citizen of the county. He was the father of

three sons (McKinley Blackwell, Robert Blackwell and Zack Blackwell) and four daughters (Mrs. Jasper Manasco, Mrs. Joe Miller, Mrs. Troy Nix, and Miss Lavilla Blackwell).
Jasper Advertiser, April 4, 1934.

BLACKWOOD, WILLIAM, entered government land in Section 3, Township 13, Range 6, on February 14, 1855.
Walker County Tract Record.

BLANKENSHIP, CULLEN, entered government land in Section 32, Township 14, Range 9, on January 22, 1834.
Walker County Tract Record.

BLANKENSHIP, AUGUSTUS, entered government land in Section 29, Township 14, Range 9, on February 18, 1836.
Walker County Tract Record.

BLANTON, JOHN, entered government land in Section 35, Township 15, Range 9, on Wolf Creek, west of Marietta, on March 28, 1826.
Walker County Tract Record.

BLANTON, DAVID, entered government land in Section 2, Township 16, Range 8, on Cane Creek, southeast of Oakman, on August 16, 1832. He took a prominent part in the establishment of the Methodist Church in Walker County and is mentioned as a class leader as early as 1833.
West's History of Methodism, page 549.
Walker County Tract Record.

BLANTON, JAMES, entered government land in Section 31, Township 15, Range 8, on Wolf Creek, west of Marietta, on January 1, 1833.
Walker County Tract Record.

BLANTON, AARON, entered government land in Section 31, Township 15, Range 9, on Wolf Creek, west of Marietta, on February 11, 1833.
Walker County Tract Record.

BLANTON, BENJAMIN, who was born in 1807 and died August 11, 1904, entered government land in Section 18, Township 15, Range 8, northwest of Parrish, on February 10, 1836.
Walker County Tract Record.

BLANTON, ELIJAH, entered government land in Section 31, Township 15, Range 8, on Wolf Creek, west of Marietta, on September 14, 1836.
Walker County Tract Record.

BLANTON, ISAAC, born May 2, 1805, and died November 1, 1907, is buried at Pleasant Grove, as is also his wife, Millie (Cheek) Blanton, who was born October 13, 1826, and died October 17, 1920. Isaac Blanton entered government land in Section 31, Township 15, Range 8, on October 11, 1832.
Walker County Tract Record.
Gravestones.

BLANTON, ELIJAH, a son of Isaac and Martha Blanton, was born on Wolf Creek, near Marietta, on November 17, 1846. He was reared on his father's farm and educated in the county schools. In June, 1863, when less than seventeen years of age, he enlisted at Jasper as a private in Company G, Eighth Alabama Cavalry, under Captain Wharton, and was detailed as courier for General Holtzclaw. He served as courier until the close of the war and was paroled at Meridian, Miss., in May, 1865. After the close of the war Mr. Blanton returned to Walker County, where he remained until about 1883, when he moved to Haleyville, in Winston County, and engaged in the mercantile business. He died January 25, 1935, at the home of his son, Judge R. L. Blanton, at Jasper, and was buried in the Haleyville Cemetery. Mr. Blanton was married to Mary Isbell. Children—Robert L. Blanton, of Jasper; Marvin Blanton, of Florida; Ida Emily Blanton, who married C. W. Stubblefield, of Jasper; and E. M. Blanton, of Haleyville.
Census of Confederate Soldiers, 1907.
Mountain Eagle, January 30, 1935.

EARLY SETTLERS 139

BLANTON, ROBERT LEE, of Jasper, one of the Judges of the Fourteenth Judicial Circuit, was born March 18, 1874, in Beat 8, Walker County. He is the son of Elijah and Mary Ann (Isbell) Blanton, natives of Walker County, the former a farmer and business man, a Confederate soldier, for 30 years before his death in 1935 a citizen of Haleyville, Winston County. Judge Blanton's grandparents were Isaac and Mille (Cheek) Blanton, and Godfrey and Ruth (Cook) Isbell, all of Walker County. Judge Blanton was educated in Godfrey High School, in Winston County, and Southern University, Greensboro, Ala. He read law in a private office and was admitted to the bar in 1903, practicing at Haleyville and Jasper. He was appointed Probate Judge of Winston County by Governor Oates in 1895 at the age of twenty-one years, serving until December, 1904, when he was elected Solicitor of the Fourteenth Circuit, serving only two months when a decision of the Supreme Court invalidated the Circuit and abolished the office. He was elected Judge of the Fourteenth Judicial Circuit in 1922 and still holds that position. He is a Democrat, Methodist, a member of the Kappa Alpha college fraternity and Omicron Delta Kappa college honorary fraternity. Judge Blanton married January 30, 1895, at Double Springs, Ala., to Mary M., daughter of Judge Isham P. and Sarah Elizabeth Gibson, of that place. Children—Elsa, married to James S. Spinks; Robert Quinton, married to Fannie Mae Sartain; Perrine, married to Howard P. Drewry; Alton Maurice, unmarried.

Jasper Advertiser, June 5, 1936.

BLEVINS, JOHN, entered government land in Section 9, Township 13, Range 5, on December 21, 1853.

Walker County Tract Record.

BLYTHE, JAMES, entered government land in Section 34, Township 14, Range 9, on March 10, 1836.

Walker County Tract Record.

BOATNER, JOHN R., entered government land in Section 8, Township 14, Range 5, on July 14, 1836.
Walker County Tract Record.

BOLDING, MARVID, entered government land in Section 36, Township 13, Range 5, on May 31, 1822.
Walker County Tract Record.

BONNER, GEORGE M., a Confederate veteran living in Walker County in 1935.
Mountain Eagle, January 30, 1935.

BOSHELL, McMINTER, born April 22, 1811, died September 23, 1895, and is buried at Macedonia Graveyard, as is also his wife, M. C. Boshell, who was born October 16, 1814, and died October 8, 1894. Mr. Boshell was of French descent and the name was originally spelled Bouchelle. It is thought that he was born and reared in the Abbeville District, of South Carolina, to which place his grandfather came in the late 1700's after sailing from France. McMinter Boshell entered government land in Section 8, Township 14, Range 8, near Holly Grove, on December 23, 1833.
Walker County Tract Record.
Gravestones.

BOSHELL, NICHOLAS, entered government land in Section 9, Township 14, Range 8, on March 2, 1835.
Walker County Tract Record.

BOSHELL, ROBERT, entered government land in Section 15, Township 14, Range 9, on February 22, 1836.
Walker County Tract Record.

BOTELER, Wm. A., entered government land in Section 26, Township 12, Range 7, on May 29, 1855.
Walker County Tract Record.

EARLY SETTLERS

BOX, JOHN, entered government land in Section 32, Township 12, Range 8, north of Luckey, on January 20, 1827.
Walker County Tract Record.

BOYD, JAMES LEE, and wife, HANNAH, entered government land in Section 1, Township 13, Range 5, on August 1, 1833.
Walker County Tract Record.

BRADLEY, LOUIS W., entered government land in Section 20, Township 14, Range 7, on January 14, 1837.
Walker County Tract Record.

BRADLEY, THOMAS, was born April 12, 1836, three miles south of Jasper, on Cane Creek. On February 1, 1862, he enlisted at Jasper as a private in Company E, Twenty-eighth Alabama Infantry, and served until the close of the war.
Census of Confederate Soldiers, 1907.

BRADLEY, JOHN, entered government land in Section 15, Township 13, Range 8, on February 8, 1837.
Walker County Tract Record.

BRADLEY, FRANCES M., a member of Company I, Fiftieth Tennessee Infantry, is buried at Heard Shoals.
Gravestone.

BRAKE, JOHN, born February 28, 1822; died October 3, 1877, and is buried at Payne Graveyard. He entered government land in Section 32, Township 13, Range 5, on December 23, 1854.
Walker County Tract Record.
Gravestone.

BRAKEFIELD, DAVID A., entered government land in Section 5, Township 14, Range 7, on September 23, 1857.
Walker County Tract Record.

BRAKEFIELD, GEORGE, entered government land in Section 31, Township 13, Range 7, on December 17, 1859.
Walker County Tract Record.

BRAZEAL, MORGAN, entered government land in Section 29, Township 13, Range 9, on February 12, 1825.
Walker County Tract Record.

BRITTON, LLOYD C., was born September 3, 1880, in Williamsburg, Ohio, a son of William and Luceta (Beck) Britton, and a grandson of Burwell Britton, who was born in Virginia in 1824, and carried to Ohio by his parents when still a small boy. Lloyd C. Britton grew up in Williamsburg, attended the public schools there and finally graduated from the engineering school of the Ohio State University with the degree of Civil Engineer. He was engaged in railroad location and construction work in various states until 1911, when he came to Walker County as Superintendent of the Manchester Lumber Company. He left the state in 1913, but returned again in 1914 as general manager of the Alabama Central Railroad Company, with headquarters at Jasper. He also practiced as a civil and consulting engineer, and during 1920-1922 he was Highway Commissioner of Walker County. On June 4, 1907, he was married to Lida Sellers, daughter of Henry and Rachel (Rust) Sellers, of Batavia, Ohio. Children—William Henry Britton, born May 23, 1908; and Lloyd C. Britton, Jr., born November 28, 1911.
Moore's Alabama, Vol. III, page 129.

BROWN, JAMES G., entered government land in Section 1, Township 17, Range 8, on October 3, 1836.
Walker County Tract Record.

BROWN, JAMES W., entered government land in Section 17, Township 14, Range 7, west of Jasper, on November 26, 1858.
Walker County Tract Record.

BROWN, THOMAS, and his wife, Lovey Brown, came to Walker County in 1835 and settled west of Jasper. He was a brother to Sallie (Brown) Kitchens, the wife of James Matlock Kitchens, and Frances (Brown) Randolph, the wife of John D.

Randolph, all of whom were charter members of the Sulphur Springs Primitive Baptist Church when it was organized on July 6, 1844. Thomas and Lovey Brown were the parents of seven children—Elizabeth Brown, who married Elijah Sparks; Eleanor Brown, born May 12, 1837, died June 9, 1872, who was married to Jesse Kitchens; John Brown, who was married to Matilda Kitchens; Mary Brown, who was married to G. W. Dutton; A. H. Brown, a son born in 1844, died May 23, 1908, who was married to L. C. Gabbert; I. B. Brown, born September 11, 1849, died February 24, 1924; and Martha Jane Brown. Thomas Brown died in June, 1871.

> Probate Record, Estate Thomas Brown.
> Church Book.
> Gravestones.

BROWN, JOHN, a son of Thomas and Lovey Brown, was elected Probate Judge in 1868 and served until 1874. He died in the latter part of 1874 or the first part of 1875. Judge Brown was married to Matilda Kitchens, a daughter of James Matlock and Sallie (Brown) Kitchens. Children—Lucinda A. Brown, who was married about 1875 to Robert B. Meek; Mary F. Brown, who married L. W. Collison, Jr., Saline County, Ark.; and Susan M. Brown.

> Probate Record, Estate John Brown.

BROWN, ISAAC, was born March 15, 1846, near Oakman, on Lost Creek. In February, 1863, he enlisted as a private in Company D, Fourth Mississippi Cavalry, and served until the close of the war. Isaac Brown was the son of John Brown, who came to Walker County some time in the 1830's, and was married to Mary Dutton. He moved to Mississippi prior to the Civil War and died there. Isaac Brown returned to Mississippi after the war, but about 1870 came back to Walker County. He was married to Margaret Lollar, a daughter of John A. and Susan (Gillen) Lollar. Children—William Frank Brown, who married, first, Adis Walton, and, second, Carrie Reeves; Richard Lee Brown, who married Bell Robinson; Mary Susan Brown, who married Frank Raburn; Della Brown, who married Bert W. Day; Bettie Brown, who never married; John Harvey Brown, who married Mabel Crump, a daughter of Henry Crump; and Queenie Brown, who married Rome Kingsley.

Census of Confederate Soldiers, 1907.
Brown Family Records.

BROWN, JOHN, a native of Chester, South Carolina, came to Alabama about 1854, settling first near Warrior, in Blount County, where he remained about a year, before coming to Walker County in 1855 to operate a farm near Jasper. He was married in South Carolina to Martha Elizabeth Clack. Children —Ensley Lightle Brown, who married Lohamie C. Sherer; Noland Brown, who never married; Thomas Brown, who married a Miss Calvert; Julia Brown, who married Andrew Jackson Thomas; and Sarah Ann Brown, who married Isham P. Guttery.

Brown Family Record.

BROWN, REV. ENSLEY LIGHTLE, a son of John and Martha Elizabeth (Clack) Brown, was born June 5, 1846, at Chester, South Carolina. Brought to Walker County by his parents when he was about nine years of age, he was reared on his father's farm and educated in the county schools. A mere youth at the outbreak of the Civil War, yet he enlisted at Eldridge as a private in Company K, Fourth Alabama Cavalry, under Captain Kelley, and served until the close of the war. Returning to his home in Walker County after the war, he operated a farm for a number of years. He felt the call to preach the gospel and was ordained a minister in the Missionary Baptist Church. He died on April 19, 1915, and is buried at New Prospect. On December 31, 1867, he was married to Lohamie C. Sherer, a daughter of John T. Sherer, who was born February 1, 1849, and died May 19, 1915. Children—Thomas Brown, who married Emma Snoddy; Joseph Brown, who never married; Samuel Houston Brown, who married Fannie Sherer, a daughter of Madison Monroe and Martha (Kilgore) Sherer; David Lightle Brown, who married Jansie Elkins; Luther Huss Brown, who married Jessie Sherer, a daughter of Madison Monroe and Martha (Kilgore) Sherer; Lily Lutetia Brown, who married J. Morgan Malone; Callie Brown, who married Wesley C. Cooner; and Lucy Brown, who married Garnie Hudson.

Census of Confederate Soldiers, 1907.
Gravestones.
Brown Family Records.

BROWN, DAVID, entered government land in Section 7, Township 14, Range 8, east of Townley, on September 3, 1824.

Walker County Tract Record.

BROWN, HOLMAN, was born in 1813 and died October 11, 1888. He was a Methodist minister who lived in the High Hill beat from its earliest settlement.

Mountain Eagle, October 31, 1888.

BROWN, EARLY A., entered government land in Section 1, Township 13, Range 5, on December 11, 1832.

Walker County Tract Record.

BROWN, SAMUEL, entered government land in Section 13, Township 14, Range 8, west of Jasper, on December 22, 1832.

Walker County Tract Record.

BROWN, GEORGE, entered government land in Section 35, Township 14, Range 4, on October 1, 1833.

Walker County Tract Record.

BROWN, JOHN M., entered government land in Section 29, Township 14, Range 9, on January 14, 1833.

Walker County Tract Record.

BROWN, ISAAC, entered government land in Section 25, Township 13, Range 10, on December 26, 1835.

Walker County Tract Record.

BROWN, WILLIAM, entered government land in Section 18, Township 14, Range 7, west of Jasper, on December 26, 1835.

Walker County Tract Record.

BROWN, EBENEZER, was born December 25, 1837, near Liberty Hill Church, Walker County. On September 16, 1861, he enlisted at Tierce's Mill, on Lost Creek, as a private in Company K, Fiftieth Alabama Infantry. After the battle of Shiloh he came home on furlough, and was transferred to Company L, of Colonel Patterson's Regiment of Cavalry, under Captain Shepherd, and served until the close of the war. He died on February 25, 1914, and is buried at Fairview.

Census of Confederate Soldiers, 1907.
Gravestone.

BROWN, JOHN, and his wife, Hannah Brown, residents of Morgan County in 1820, came to Walker County sometime in the 1830's. Their daughter, Nancy Brown, born in Morgan County on February 2, 1820, was married on February 3, 1843, to Elijah Sides, a son of Henry Sides, Jr., and a grandson of Henry Sides, Sr. She died at her home near Lucky on April 12, 1886.

Files of the Mountain Eagle, April, 1886.

BRUCE, JOHN, entered government land in Section 31, Township 13, Range 9, on October 1, 1835.

Walker County Tract Record.

BRYAN, WILLIAM J., an attorney, practicing in Jasper in 1845.

Roll of Attorneys Alabama Bar, 1845.

BRYANT, WILLIAM, entered government land in Section 7, Township 16, Range 8, on July 24, 1827.

Walker County Tract Record.

BRYANT, JAMES, a native of Ireland, was married to

Martha (Walker) Morgan, who was born July 5, 1825, and died August 15, 1896. She was the widow of Peter A. Morgan, of Dora, who died November 5, 1857. Children—Nancy Bryant, Mary Bryant, Lurania Bryant, Suttania Bryant, J. Thomas Bryant.

Records of Walker Family.

BRYSON, ROBERT, entered government land in Section 28, Township 14, Range 6, on July 11, 1845.

Walker County Tract Record.

BRYSON, DUNLOP, a Confederate soldier who served in Company F, Fifty-sixth Alabama Cavalry.

Census of Confederate Soldiers, 1907.

BRYSON, JOSEPH T., a Confederate soldier who served in Company F, Fifty-sixth Alabama Cavalry.

Census of Confederate Soldiers, 1907.

BURDIN, HAWKINS, entered government land in Section 9, Township 15, Range 6, where Cordova is now located, on February 11, 1822.

Walker County Tract Record.

BURKE, W. H., a Confederate soldier residing in Walker County in 1895.

Mountain Eagle, July 3, 1895.

BURKETT, DANIEL, entered government land in Section 7, Township 15, Range 7, on April 11, 1859.

Walker County Tract Record.

BURKETT, BENJAMIN FRANKLIN, of Townley, was born February 11, 1844, in Pickens District, South Carolina. He enlisted at Jasper in Company E, Twenty-eighth Alabama Infantry, under Captain Hugh Lollar, and was wounded at Missionary Ridge.

Census of Confederate Soldiers, 1907.

BURNUM, JOEL, entered government land in Section 23, Township 14, Range 6, on June 11, 1855.
Walker County Tract Record.

BURRELL, ASA, entered government land in Section 33, Township 14, Range 4, on October 9, 1855.
Walker County Tract Record.

BURRELL, WM. RICHARD, of Eldridge, was born March 14, 1836, at Summitt, Blount County, Alabama. In October, 1861, he enlisted as a private in Company D, Twenty-sixth Alabama Infantry.
Census of Confederate Soldiers, 1907.

BURTON, ROBERT, entered government land in Section 19, Township 14, Range 5, on November 26, 1833.
Walker County Tract Record.

BURTON, JOHN, entered government land in Section 9, Township 14, Range 8, on February 5, 1834. Mr. Burton was born in 1800 and died on August 12, 1888. He is buried in the Dutton Graveyard, as is also his wife, Fannie, who was born September 3, 1800, and died March 4, 1904.
Walker County Tract Record.
Gravestones.

BURTON, CALLER, entered government land in Section 4, Township 14, Range 8, on September 19, 1836. Mr. Burton was born June 20, 1812; died September 23, 1907, and is buried at Macedonia Graveyard, as is also his wife, Lavina, who was born December 20, 1824, and died August 12, 1900.
Walker County Tract Record.
Gravestones.

BURTON, JOHN, who lived at Gamble mines, was born in South Carolina on December 20, 1828. In September, 1862, he enlisted at Jasper as a private in Company B, Fifty-sixth Alabama Cavalry, under Captain Johnson, and served throughout the war.

Census of Confederate Soldiers, 1907.

BUSBY, STEPHEN, a member of an old and honored family of Irish descent that settled in South Carolina during Colonial days, came to Walker County in young manhood and entered government land on Wolf Creek before 1829. During his entire lifetime he was a successful farmer and, along with James Cain, he was the first to gather coal from the bed of Lost Creek and flatboat it to Mobile. He was killed by an accidental fall from a fodder stack.

Moore's Alabama, Vol. III, page 473.

BUSBY, JOHN T., a son of Stephen Busby, was born about 1829 on his father's homestead on Wolf Creek. Reared on the farm, he purchased the homestead from his father's heirs and resided there all of his life, becoming one of the county's most progressive and extensive farmers. For many years he was a prominent minister in the Missionary Baptist Church, and throughout the Civil War he served as a soldier in the Confederate Army. He died at his home on January 25, 1894. He was married to Nancy Ann Melissa Ireland, who was born in 1843, and died in March, 1915. Children—Elizabeth, married William Handley, a farmer on Wolf Creek; Luanna, married John W. Sanford, a farmer on Wolf Creek; James Madison Busby; Elias Demson Busby, who was a physician at Good Springs; S. Levin Busby; Martha J., married Frank Lockart, a farmer south of Oakman; Jalie, married Henry Key, a farmer at Good Springs; John T. Busby; and Stephen Sampson Busby.

Moore's Alabama, Vol. III, page 473.

BUSBY, STEPHEN SAMPSON, a physician, who lived at Oakman, was born on the Busby homestead on Wolf Creek on January 2, 1879, a son of the Rev. John T. and Nancy Ann Melissa (Ireland) Busby. Reared on the farm he attended local schools and the Teacher's Training School at Jasper. He taught school in the county for two years and then entered the Birmingham Medical College, from which he graduated in 1908 with the degree of Doctor of Medicine. He began the practice of medicine at his home, but in 1914 moved to Oakman. He served as a member of the City Council of Oakman for two years and for more than ten years was the city health officer. On March 17, 1901, Doctor Busby was married near Oakman to Kennie Snow, a daughter of Rev. Francis A. and Eliza (Franklin) Snow. Children—Vance W. Busby, of Birmingham; Irvin Busby; Estelle Busby; Autress Busby; and Ernest Busby.

Moore's Alabama, Vol. III, page 473.

BUTT, WILLIAM, a pioneer settler and blacksmith, entered government land in Section 35, Township 13, Range 5, east of Gravleeton, on October 19, 1819, and five years later, on September 16, 1824, entered land in Section 22, Township 14, Range 6, near the confluence of Blackwater Creek and the Warrior River.

Walker County Tract Record.

BUTT, WILLIAM, Jr., was born February 24, 1824, near the forks of the Mulberry and Sipsey Rivers. On September 5, 1862, he enlisted at Jasper as a private in Company F, Hewlett's Thirteenth Alabama Battalion, and was later transferred to Company K, Fifty-sixth Alabama Cavalry. He served as a blacksmith for his company. On December 30, 1864, he was captured during the Jonesboro battle near Atlanta, and was imprisoned at Chicago until the close of the war.

Census of Confederate Soldiers, 1907.

BUTT, WASHINGTON McDONALD, of Cordova, was born October 19, 1847, at Gravleeton. In August, 1864, he enlisted at Jasper as a private in Company B, Musgrove's Battalion of Cavalry, and served until the close of the war.

Census of Confederate Soldiers, 1907.

BUTCHER, HENRY P., entered government land in Section 28, Township 15, Range 5, on March 29, 1842.
Walker County Tract Record.

BUZBEE, WILLIAM, entered government land in Section 29, Township 14, Range 6, on October 19, 1855.
Walker County Tract Record.

BUZBEE, HUDSON HALL, was born near Arkadelphia, August 31, 1859, a son of Hudson Hall and Sarah (Stephens) Buzbee. He was reared on his father's farm, taught rural schools in Cullman and Walker Counties, and for many years was Justice of the Peace in Beat 15, near Saragossa. He was married to Sarah M. Burton, who was born on a farm near Sipsey in 1860 and died at Bankhead in 1921. Children—John Everett Buzbee; Hubert Hudson, a minister in the Baptist Church; Samuel Sebastian Buzbee, a dentist in Jasper; Robert Buell Buzbee, of New York City; and Joshua Quinton Buzbee.
Moore's Alabama, Vol. III, page 121.

BUZBEE, JOHN EVERETT, a son of Hudson Hall and Sarah (Burton) Buzbee, was born January 9, 1884, near Sipsey. Reared on the farm, he attended rural schools and the public schools at Jasper, taught for two years, and then entered the medical department of the University of Alabama at Mobile, where he graduated in medicine in 1908. He practiced at various places until 1917, when he went to Townley as physician for the Supreme Mining Company, and later went to Bankhead as surgeon for the Bankhead Coal Company. On April 21, 1924, he was appointed postmaster at Jasper and served in that capacity for several years. On January 7, 1909, Dr. Buzbee was married to Cora Drew Morrow, a daughter of Thomas B. and Martha (Sanders) Morrow, her father having been a prosperous farmer near Dora. Children—Everett Orville Buzbee, Cora Orlane Buzbee, and Berma Armasia Buzbee.
Moore's Alabama, Vol. III, page 121.

CAIN, JAMES OSCAR, was born in Edgefield, South Carolina, a son of James Cain, a native of Wales, who set out for America about the middle of the eighteenth century, in a cheese-laden boat. After suffering the pangs of thirst, due to the shortage of water, he safely landed in South Carolina and began the pursuit of his trade of the manufacture of felt hats, in the city of Charleston. He married Joanne King, of Charleston, and James Oscar Cain was his eldest son. James Oscar Cain moved from South Carolina to Walker County territory before it was formed into a county, and settled at a place that they called Liberty Hill. Records show that he entered government land in Section 24, Township 16, Range 8, on January 18, 1827, and in Section 22, Township 16, Range 8, on October 8, 1832, both of these entries being on Wolf Creek. He was a farmer and stock raiser and operated a stave plant, a mill and a ginnery. In addition, he was active from the beginning in the mining, handling and shipping of coal on the Warrior River and its tributaries, and it is claimed that he was the first coal operator in Alabama. He and Stephen Busby were among the first to gather coal from the bottom of Lost Creek and flatboat it to Mobile. The passage over Squaw Shoals of the Warrior River was extremely hazardous and the shoals were always under discussion and study. The continuous reports of the dangers and difficulties in transporting products on the river finally secured a government contract in 1835 to Richard Chilton and James Cain to clean out Squaw Shoals and direct the current of the waters, so that keels and flatboats could pass over them with less danger. The work was duly undertaken and some good was effected, but the dangers of the passage were still so great that the little relief through the government contract work was scarcely reckoned in the course of business.

In 1839 James Cain and Jesse Van Hoose were owners of coal lands near the mouth of Lost Creek, on which was sunk in that year the first coal shaft in Walker County, and it is thought by some to be the first active mine and coal shaft sunk in Alabama. Gideon, Gordon and Joe Frierson were in charge of the work and the shaft was known as "Frierson's Shaft." A hand windlass was the shaft lift. It brought up one tub of coal as an empty one was let down to be loaded.

Mr. Cain was active in state and county politics, and was the leader of the Whig party in Walker County. He represented the county in four sessions of the Legislature—1837, 1841, 1842 and 1849. He was a leader of men and his election was solely by reason of his natural abilities and his practical services to his times. Wm. Garrett, in "Reminiscences," says of him: "He was a man of good habits, of very little pretension, and grew largely in the esteem of the public men for the probity and consistency of his character. By industry and economy he had acquired before the war a good property, and was hospitable and charitable in his relations to society. He was a favorable specimen of a class of men who have been aptly styled the bone and sinew of the country. Without the aid of books, he possessed a sound practical judgment in every-day affairs of life, doing justice to all men and requiring the same equivalent. In proportion as his character was understood, it was increased in public estimation."

Mr. Cain's most powerful political opponent was General John Manasco, the leader of the Democratic party in the county. For more than a decade their battles were fought at the polls, with first one and then the other coming out victor. Perhaps the most heated campaign was that of 1848, when the issue was the division of Walker County. The territorial bounds of Walker at this time extended from the Tuscaloosa line nearly to the Tennessee Valley, embracing all of the present county of Winston and portions of Lawrence, Cullman, Blount and Jefferson. Manasco advocated the division from north to south, while Cain was in favor of an east to west line. Cain was victor and the division was made as it is today.

An ardent Whig and Nullifier, Mr. Cain was opposed to secession, but when Alabama cast her lot with the Confederacy he gave his hearty support to the cause of the South. Like all others, he suffered great financial loss, and William Garrett speaks of meeting him in Chattanooga "a broken old man, enroute to Knoxville to seek a son lying wounded in a military hospital."

Mr. Cain died in Birmingham on January 14, 1883, and is buried near his old home at Liberty Hill.

James Cain was married to Elizabeth McAuley, of Edgefield, S. C., who was born October 30, 1803, and died at Liberty Hill on November 16, 1870. Children—William Cain, no information; Mary Ann Cain, born August 28, 1822, died August 22, 1863, was married to Elijah Baker (see Baker); Lucinda Cain, married a Ransom Wallace and moved to Oklahoma; Charlotte Cain, married Thomas W. Price, of Walker County (see Price); Elizabeth Cain, born August 18, 1835, died June 18, 1917, was married on January 6, 1853, to Francis A. Musgrove (see Musgrove); Joyce B. Cain, born January 27, 1841, died December 28, 1880, married Sylvester John Chilton (see Chilton); Armanda Cain, born April 14, 1839, died September 15, 1907, married a Mr. Boyle; Nancy Cain, born July 27, 1830, married Samuel Monroe Sanders, of Blount County (see Sanders); Renie Cain, married Napoleon Bonaparte McGlathery and lived in Arkansas; R. Wood Cain, married Georgia Ann Simpson; Adkin Cain and Robert Cain, no information; James F. Cain, born November 11, 1842, died August 28, 1901, and buried at Fairview. He was a member of Company K, Fiftieth Alabama Infantry, C. S. A.

> Garrett's Reminiscences of Public Men.
> Armes' Story of Coal and Iron.
> Mountain Eagle, March 27, 1895.
> Walker County Tract Record.
> Cain Family Records.
> Gravestones.

CAIN, RANDOLPH P., entered government land in Section 34, Township 15, Range 8, on Cane Creek, southeast of Oakman, on January 14, 1835.

> Walker County Tract Record.

CALLAHAN, JOSHUA, entered government land in Section 23, Township 12, Range 5, on September 8, 1852.

> Walker County Tract Record.

CALVERT, GEORGE F., entered government land in Section 19, Township 12, Range 5, on April 9, 1855.

> Walker County Tract Record.

CAMAK, JAMES, and his wife, Nancy (Hutchinson) Camak, Irish immigrants, settled in Fairfield District, South Carolina, where they remained for a number of years. They later moved to Greene County, Alabama, and about 1835 moved to Walker County, where, along with John Ryan, he built a log cabin in Jasper which was operated as an inn or tavern under the name of Camak and Ryan Hotel. The children of James and Nancy (Hutchinson) Camak were: Thomas Camak, born January 15, 1801, who entered government land in Section 3, Township 14, Range 7, north of Jasper, on August 8, 1835, and who, with his brother, Moses Camak, operated Camak Mills on Blackwater Creek; Margaret Camak, who was born November 15, 1804, and who married Peter Summey, of Fairfield District, S. C.; Mary Camak, who married Isaac Ryan (see Ryan); David Camak, who was born March 5, 1803, and was married to Elizabeth A. Barton on January 9, 1834; Moses Camak, who was born January, 1812; Martha Camak, who was born February 4, 1814, and was married to Thomas Elliott; and Nancy Camak.

Camak Family Records.

CAMAK, MOSES, a son of James and Nancy (Hutchinson) Camak, was born in Fairfield District, South Carolina, on January 16, 1812, and came to Walker County with his parents about 1835. A very enterprising young man, he studied medicine and was a practicing physician and merchant in Jasper before the "flush times" of the 1830's, and who, of course, did not escape the hard times that followed. He became financially embarrassed and the struggle of his life was to meet the obligations that these embarrassments put upon him. He struggled on for almost thirty years, and at the outbreak of the Civil War he had just thrown off the last load of the burden. In 1862 he was elected Judge of Probate, the third man to hold that office in the county. He died, universally respected, on June 6, 1873, and is buried in the old graveyard at Jasper. Moses Camak was the father of seven children—W. H. Camak, who married Fradonia Elliott; Sarah J. Camak, who married Wilson Shepherd; Amanda H. Camak, who married W. L. Sively; David H. Camak, who married Lavonia Catherine Miller, daughter of Dr. Lucius C. and Mary Jane (Leith) Miller; Julia A. Camak, who married David Montgomery; Alice R. Camak, who married J. L. Craig, of South Lowell, and who died on March 8, 1887; and James N. Camak.

Powell's Fifty-five Years in West Alabama.
Mountain Eagle, January 15, 1887.
Mountain Eagle, March 9, 1887.
Walker County Tract Record.
Camak Family Record.

CAMAK, DAVID H., born February 22, 1850, was a practicing physician in the county. On April 7, 1875, he was married to Lavonia Catherine Miller, daughter of Dr. Lucius C. and Mary Jane (Leith) Miller, of Holly Grove. Children—Fred. L. Camak, born January 10, 1876; Dr. Burwell L. Camak, born July 3, 1878, married Daisy Kilgore on August 7, 1904; Chas. M. Camak, born November 5, 1881; J. Newton Camak, born January 20, 1884; and Anna Mae Camak, who married Dr. J. Leon Fields on October 7, 1907.

Genealogy of the Branner Family.

CAMP, DAVID, entered government land in Section 3, Township 15, Range 6, on September 19, 1835.

Walker County Tract Record.

CAMPBELL, ADAM, entered government land in Section 1, Township 13, Range 6, on January 4, 1855.

Walker County Tract Record.

CAMPBELL, ALEXANDER, entered government land in Section 23, Township 12, Range 6, on July 25, 1855.

Walker County Tract Record.

CARAWAY, JOHN, entered government land in Section 32, Township 15, Range 9, on November 20, 1846.

Walker County Tract Record.

CANNON, ELISHA BARTON, was born September 22, 1838, near old Democrat. In September, 1861, he enlisted at Jasper in Company I, Fiftieth Alabama Infantry, under Captain B. M. Long. He re-enlisted in January, 1865, in Company G, Stewart's Cavalry, under Captain John Wharton, and served until the close of the war. He died on September 10, 1923, and is buried at Pleasantfield, as is also his wife, Zylpha, who was born March 4, 1839, and died December 10, 1920, a daughter of William Henry and Matilda Ann (Chilton) Snow.

Census of Confederate Soldiers, 1907.
Gravestones.

CARELTONS, JOHN S., entered government land in Section 27, Township 14, Range 6, on October 27, 1836.
Walker County Tract Record.

CARMICHAEL, JAMES TAYLOR, a son of Francis M. and Sarah (Hamilton) Carmichael, born in Walker County about 1849, joined the Confederate Army at the age of fifteen. Enlisting at old Houston, he was provided with a uniform by friends in Jasper. He was wounded in the battle of Vicksburg and shortly thereafter the war ended. Returning to Walker County, he followed farming for the rest of his life. Several years before his death he was made Commander of Camp Hutto of the U. C. V., but on account of the few veterans left in the county the camp ceased to function. He died January 11, 1934, and was buried in the Dutton Graveyard. He was the father of Frank Carmichael, of Oakman; Edward Carmichael, of Hillard; Mrs. Dora Lockhart, of Birmingham; and Mrs. Fannie Sherer, of Jasper.
Jasper Advertiser, January 17, 1934.

CARMICHAEL, A. L., born about 1856, died October 30, 1934, and is buried in Mt. Carmel Cemetery at Cordova. He was the father of Mrs. Robert Robinson and Mrs. J. Gurley, both of Walker County; Thomas Carmichael, who lived near Cordova; and Judge V. H. Carmichael, of Jasper.
Mountain Eagle, October 31, 1934.

CARROLL, MOSES, entered government land in Section 36, Township 14, Range 4, on January 27, 1851.
Walker County Tract Record.

CARTER, J. W., a Confederate veteran, who was born May 3, 1844, died February 23, 1927, and is buried at Layman's Chapel, as is also his wife, Laura V. Carter, who was born in 1854 and died December 11, 1927.
Gravestones.

CHANCE, GEORGE S., entered government land in Section 35, Township 13, Range 5, on February 17, 1837.
Walker County Tract Record.

CHEATHAM, JAMES, entered government land in Section 25, Township 13, Range 9, on August 11, 1827.
Walker County Tract Record.

CHEATHAM, LOUIS E., entered government land in Section 23, Township 13, Range 9, on February 22, 1836.
Walker County Tract Record.

CHEATHAM, JONATHAN EVANS, born December 29, 1841, near Holly Grove, enlisted in January, 1863, at Holly Grove as a private in Company A, Thirteenth Alabama Cavalry.
Census of Confederate Soldiers, 1907.

CHEATHAM, JAMES WAYTT, born November 3, 1837, near Nauvoo on Blackwater Creek, enlisted at Jasper in September, 1862, as a private in Company A, Thirteenth Alabama Cavalry.
Census of Confederate Soldiers, 1907.

CHILDERS, LEVI, entered government land in Section 32, Township 15, Range 5, on December 31, 1831.
Walker County Tract Record.

CHILDERS, THOMAS, was born in Walker County and was a prosperous farmer before the Civil War. His name appears on a list of Jasper citizens in 1859. He died from wounds received while serving as a soldier in the Confederate Army. He was married to a daughter of Samuel Jackson, who lived near Oakman.
Moore's Alabama, Vol. III, page 117.
Mountain Eagle, April 26, 1895.

CHILDERS, WILL AB, a son of Thomas Childers, was born near Jasper in 1863. For many years he was an extensive and successful farmer, but in 1903 he left the farm and came to

Jasper, where he engaged in dealing in live stock. He died at Carbon Hill on June 21, 1923. He was married to Maggie Etta Masters, who was born at Baldwin, Miss., in 1873 and died at Jasper in 1921. Children—William Samuel Childers, born June 27, 1890, married Annie C. Kemp, daughter of Thomas P. and Savannah (Kelly) Kemp, on November 3, 1915, at Ensley, and is the father of Doris Juanita Childers and Mildred Kemp Childers; Ida Childers, who married James T. Stanford, of Carbon Hill; Thomas H. Childers; John C. Childers; Edward Childers; and Blanche Childers.

Moore's Alabama, Vol. III, page 117.

CHILDRESS, JOHN, entered government land in Section 36, Township 14, Range 8, on November 15, 1854.

Walker County Tract Record.

CHILTON, RICHARD L. (DICK), a pioneer blacksmith, miller and farmer, came to Walker County in the early 1820's, and on September 10, 1824, entered government land in Section 3, Township 15, Range 8, which was on Lost Creek, north of Oakman. In 1840 he operated a mill at the mouth of Blackwater Creek. Later on he secured property on Lost Creek, south of Parrish, where he built and operated a grist mill and where he made his home. At his death he was buried on the old homestead.

Mr. Chilton was an industrious and shrewd business man, and in addition to operating his blacksmith shop, grist mill and farm, he undertook other enterprises. In 1835 he, with James Cain, secured a government contract to clean out the dangerous Squaw Shoals on Warrior River and divert the current of the waters so as to make the passage safer. The work was not entirely successful, and the Shoals continued to be a menace to transportation on the Warrior River.

Records show that in 1840 Mr. Chilton was shipping boat loads of stock to Mobile. It is said that during the dangerous trip over the Shoals and until the pilot had his boat in safe waters, Mr. Chilton would show his uneasiness by his perfect silence, the anxious expression on his face and by gently scratching his head. He was married to Nancy Key, a daughter of John and Belinda (Milstead) Key, of Amherst, Va., another pioneer settler of Walker County. Children—James K. Polk Chilton; William (Bud) Chilton; Belinda Chilton, married Lee Williams; Sally Chilton, married Gabriel (Gabe) Key; Mary Ann Chilton, married James Bibb; Matilda, married William Henry Snow; Sylvester John Chilton, born April 8, 1837, died November 4, 1899, buried at Liberty Hill, married to Joyce B. Cain, a daughter of James Cain. She was born in 1841 and died in 1880.

The children of Sylvester John and Joyce B. (Cain) Chilton were Richard, James, Darle, and David Houston Chilton.

David Houston Chilton graduated in medicine from Emory College in Atlanta and began his practice at Corona with Dr. W. M. Cunningham. He later practiced at Parrish and became one of the best known and best loved physicians in the county, where he died on June 2, 1935. He married Lula May Gaines, a daughter of John Strother Gaines, of Corona. Their only child, Kathleen, was married to Captain Walter Kellogg Smith, of Cape Henry, Va., on December 25, 1934.

>Armes' Story of Coal and Iron.
>Key and Allied Families, page 268.
>Walker County Tract Record.

CHRISTIAN, JOHN, entered government land in Section 17, Township 16, Range 6, on September 7, 1852.
>Walker County Tract Record.

CHRISTIAN, THOMAS ANTHONY, born April 25, 1834, about eighteen miles north of Tuscaloosa, in Tuscaloosa County, enlisted at High Hill, Walker County, on April 7, 1862, as a private in Company L, Twenty-eighth Alabama Infantry. He was wounded at Chicamauga, but served until the close of the war.

Census of Confederate Soldiers, 1907.

CLANCY, JOHN E., who represented Walker County in the Legislature of 1843, was a rather eccentric young lawyer, very fond of display, and thought himself an orator. He was a Democrat, but was far in advance of his party on the subject of internal improvement, and he made his big speech in the House in favor of internal improvement by the state. He practiced law in Jasper and is shown on the 1845 Roll of Attorneys of the Alabama Bar. Shortly after this date he mysteriously disappeared while on a trip to Tuscaloosa and was never seen or head of again.

Powell's Fifty-five Years in West Alabama.

CLARK, JAMES ALLEN, who lived at Dora, was born September 20, 1840, at Sanders Ferry, on the Warrior River. In October, 1862, he enlisted at Jasper as a private in Company F, Fifty-sixth Alabama Infantry, under Captain E. J. Rice. He was doing scout work between Charleston, S. C., and Richmond, Va., under Captain Bibb, of the Twelfth Mississippi Regiment, when the army surrendered.

Census of Confederate Soldiers, 1907.

CLARK, WILLIAM RICHARD, who lived at Dora, was born December 5, 1841, near the forks of the Sipsey and Mulberry Rivers. In February, 1862, he enlisted at Jasper as a private in Company G, Twenty-sixth Alabama Infantry, under Captain B. M. Long. In March, 1865, he was transferred to the cavalry and was cut off at Milledgeville, Ga., while in the escort party to President Jefferson Davis. He escaped and made his way home.

Census of Confederate Soldiers, 1907.

CLARK, RUFUS, who lived at Kansas, was born May 21, 1844, in Jasper County, Georgia. On January 20, 1863, he enlisted at Kansas as a private in Company B, Fifth Alabama Cavalry. From December, 1864, to the close of the war he was detailed with squad, under James Bicknell, to do scout work in Winston, Marion, Fayette and Walker Counties, looking after recruits and deserters.

Census of Confederate Soldiers, 1907.

CLARK, WYATT, a native of North Carolina, came to Walker County about 1872, and engaged in farming, near Jasper, for the balance of his life.

Moore's Alabama, Vol. II, page 97.

CLARK, JOSEPH M., a son of Wyatt Clark, was born in North Carolina in 1853. Reared and educated in his native state, he moved to Walker County about 1871, and settled on a farm near Jasper, which he operated for many years. He was married to Mary King, who was born in Walker County about 1860. Children—Ira L. Clark, Robert Clark, William Clark, Edward Clark, and John Clark.

Moore's Alabama, Vol. II, page 97.

CLARK, IRA L., a son of Joseph M. and Mary (King) Clark, was born near Jasper on November 28, 1878. He was reared on his father's farm and educated in the public schools of the county. Mr. Clark was employed in several different mercantile lines until May, 1922, when he established the Clark Lumber Company, of Jasper. Mr. Clark was married on December 24, 1907, to Mattie Palmer, a daughter of Thomas A. and Lucy (Ellis) Palmer, of Jasper. Children—Ira Louie Clark and Clyde Edward Clark.

Moore's Alabama, Vol. II, page 97.

CLEMENTS, HARDY, has the honor of being the first name recorded on the Walker County Tract Record, he having entered government land in Section 4, Township 14, Range 4, on September 7, 1819. However, he remained in this county only a few months and then moved on to Tuscaloosa County, where he was married in 1822 to Martha Hargrove, a daughter of Rev. Dudley and Mary (Coleman) Hargrove, who came to Tuscaloosa County in 1819. Mr. Clements was born October 16, 1783, in Edgefield, S. C., and died September 29, 1867, in Tuscaloosa County.

Owen's Alabama, Vol. III, page 349.

CLEMENTS, JOSEPH B., a son of Thomas Clements, an Irish immigrant who settled on the Warrior River, a few miles north of Tuscaloosa, in Tuscaloosa County, at what was known as Clements' Bend, in the early days of the state's history. Joseph B. Clements came to Walker County when still a young man and settled on Blackwater Creek, about midway between Jasper and Nauvoo. Mr. Clements was born on March 24, 1829, and died June 27, 1902, and is buried at Sardis Graveyard, near Bankhead. He was married to Louisa Caroline Chism, of Walker County, who was born April 2, 1834, and died April 24, 1911. Children—Fannie Clements, married, first, a Mr. Ferguson, and, second, John Key; Shalie Clements, married Elizabeth Ferguson; Middleton Clements, died a bachelor about 1897; Benjamin F. Clements, the oldest child, was born October 6, 1852, on Blackwater Creek. He was married about 1873 to Mary Susan Phifer, of Providence, and lived on a farm at Providence for the balance of his life. Children—Sylvester Houston Clements, born at Providence September 12, 1874, was married to Lavada Jones, a daughter of W. R. Jones, postmaster at Parrish; Victor A. Clements, married Cora Payne, of Cordova; Joseph H. Clements, married Bell Hamilton, of Jasper; Middleton C. Clements, married Alice Manuel; William O. Clements, married Madie Gabbert, of Birmingham.

Records of the Clements Family.

CLIFTON, LOUIS, entered government land in Section 12, Township 14, Range 7, on January 25, 1858.

Walker County Tract Record.

COBB, STANCIL, entered government land in Section 9, Township 15, Range 6, on the present site of Cordova, on April 29, 1822.
Walker County Tract Record.

COBB, DAVID, entered government land in Section 34, Township 14, Range 6, on Cane Creek, south of Jasper, on December 27, 1823.
Walker County Tract Record.

COBB, WILLIAM, Sr., of Day's Gap, or Oakman, was born in 1813 and died September 21, 1886, and is buried at Providence. He was a member of the Primitive Baptist Church for forty-five years and a resident of Walker County for more than forty years. His wife, Lucinda Cobb, born in 1819, died August 20, 1886, is also buried at Providence.
Files of the Mountain Eagle.
Gravestones.

COKER, L. H., a Confederate veteran living in Walker County in 1895.
Mountain Eagle, July 3, 1895.

COLBERT, JAMES, entered government land in Section 26, Township 12, Range 6, on April 11, 1855.
Walker County Tract Record.

COLE, WILLIAM, was a local Methodist preacher in Walker County prior to 1837, although he had his church membership at Zion, in Fayette County.
West's History of Methodism, page 551.

COLE, BYRD GARLAND, was born in the spring of 1803, but his birthplace is unknown. Neither is it known when he came to Walker County; however, his daughter, Rachel Cole, married Joseph Key; and his daughter, Nancy Louise Cole, born about 1828, was married about 1845 to Dock Clifton Key; both being sons of John and Belinda Key (see John Key).
Key and Allied Families.
Mountain Eagle, April 24, 1895.

COLE, JOSEPH MARION, of Dora, was born December 15, 1833, in Morgan County, Alabama. On September 20, 1862, he enlisted at Jasper as a private in Company F, Twenty-eighth Alabama Infantry, under Captain Gamble. He was captured by Federal troops at Orchard Knob, Chattanooga, while on picket duty, the evening before the main battle of Missionary Ridge on November 24, 1863. He was imprisoned at Rock Island, Illinois, until the close of the war.

Census of Confederate Soldiers, 1907.

COLE, JAMES RICHARD, of Jasper, was born January 4, 1843, on the Sipsey River in Walker County. In September, 1861, he enlisted at Jasper as a private in Company I, Fiftieth Alabama Infantry, under Captain Long. He died June 22, 1920, and is buried at Sardis, on the Warrior River. His wife, Carissa Cole, born November 9, 1847, died September 8, 1927, is also buried at Sardis.

Census of Confederate Soldiers, 1907.
Gravestones.

COLEMAN, EZRA W., was born near Akron, in Hale County, Alabama, August 10, 1861, a son of Thomas Wilkes and Frances Jane (Wilson) Coleman; grandson of James Cobb and Martha Ann (Anderson) Coleman; and a descendant of Charles Coleman, a quartermaster in the Third North Carolina Regiment during the Revolutionary War. He was born in 1744 and died in 1824. He married Mary Roundtree, and moved to Alabama in 1818. John Coleman, a son of the Revolutionary War soldier, was born September 19, 1781, and died June 9, 1852. He married Rhoda Cobb and settled near Eutaw, Alabama. James Cobb Coleman, grandfather of Ezra W. Coleman, was born November 15, 1810, and was about eight years old when the family came to Alabama. He died in 1868. He was married twice; first, to Martha Ann Anderson, and, second, to Juliet Bestor. Thomas Wilkes Coleman, the father of Ezra W. Coleman, was born near Eutaw, March 24, 1833. He graduated from Princeton University in 1853, studied law under Stephen F. Hale at Eutaw and was admitted to the bar in 1855. He was honored with many state offices and in 1891 was appointed Associate Justice of the Supreme Court of Alabama. He died in 1920. On November 1, 1860, he was married to Francis Jane Wilson, a daughter of James Wilson, a soldier in the War of 1812, and a granddaughter of Robert Wilson, a soldier with a South Carolina regiment during the Revolutionary War. She died on July 23, 1920.

Ezra W. Coleman graduated from the University of Alabama in 1879, with an M. A. degree, studied law and shortly thereafter was admitted to the bar and started to practice in Jasper, in 1887, with Thomas L. Sowell, under the firm name of Coleman and Sowell. In 1893 Mr. Sowell left the firm, and Mr. Coleman took in John H. Bankhead, Jr., and the firm continued under the name of Coleman and Bankhead until Mr. Coleman's death. Mr. Coleman was Solicitor of the Fourteenth Judicial District for several years and was a member of the Constitutional Convention of Alabama in 1901. He died October 13, 1904, at Jasper.

On September 3, 1893, he was married at Jasper to Nanette Shields, a daughter of John B. and Carrie (Long) Shields (see Shields Family). Children—John S. Coleman, Ezra W. Coleman, Ellen Coleman, Thomas Wilkes Coleman, Caroline Coleman.

>Owen's Alabama, Vol. III, page 374.
>Moore's Alabama, Vol. III, page 550.
>Memorial Record of Alabama, Vol. II, page 1020.

COLLINS, WILLIAM D., was born in Fayette County, in 1860, a son of James B. Collins, a native of North Carolina, who came to Alabama when still a young man and settled on a farm near Fayette. William D. Collins was reared on his father's farm and married in Fayette County. About 1884 he came to Oakman and opened a store, which he operated for a number of years. Later on in life he returned to Fayette. He was married to Dora Renfro, of Fayette, Ala. Children—Lula Collins, married Travis McCollum, of Carbon Hill; Pauline Collins, married Howard H. Huggins, of Winter Garden, Fla.; Bessie Mae Collins, married Philip R. Upchurch, of Atlanta, Ga.; and Richard Dean Collins, born at Oakman, August 7, 1891, married on June 18, 1920, at Oakman, to Mrs. Vera (Cannon) Jones, a daughter of Melvin F. Cannon, of Berry, Ala.

Moore's Alabama, Vol. II, page 79.

CONLEY, JOHN, entered government land in Section 36, Township 12, Range 5, on August 23, 1851.

Walker County Tract Record.

CONWAY, GEORGE, entered government land in Section 36, Township 12, Range 6, on September 9, 1837.

Walker County Tract Record.

COOK, JOHN, entered government land in Section 23, Township 16, Range 7, on March 26, 1836.

Walker County Tract Record.

COONER, JAMES P., came to Walker County from the Abbeville District, of South Carolina, in the early 1830's, and entered government land in Section 34, Township 14, Range 8, near Pleasant Grove, on September 23, 1833. He lived on a farm near Pleasant Grove all of his life and is buried in a little graveyard south of the Frisco Railroad, about one mile west of Lost Creek. He was the father of James Carroll Cooner; Samuel Ellison Cooner; and Polly Cooner, who married, first, a Mr. Harrison Sides, and, second, a Mr. Townley.

Walker County Tract Record.
Records of Cooner Family.

COONER, SAMUEL ELLISON, was born October 12, 1819,

in the Abbeville District, South Carolina, a son of James P. Cooner. He was brought to Walker County by his parents when he was about fourteen years of age, and was reared on a farm near Pleasant Grove. After reaching manhood he settled on a farm about two miles west of Jasper. He served one term as Sheriff before the Civil War, and later served as Tax Collector and County Treasurer. He died August 27, 1884, and is buried in the Cooner Graveyard at Coal City. Mr. Cooner was married three times; first, to Lusinda Dill, who was born June 20, 1821, and died December 31, 1851; second, to Diana H. Burton, who was born October 12, 1835, and died October 10, 1876; and, third, to Mary Ann Bennett, born August 31, 1826, died about 1885, and the widow of a Mr. Wilson. Children by first wife—William James Cooner, born February 25, 1841, married Anice Lollar; Martha Jane Cooner, born Feburary 14, 1847, married Jacob Hamilton, a son of Harvey W. Hamilton; Lusinda Elizabeth Cooner, born December 6, 1851, married William T. Davis, of Nauvoo. Children by second wife—John Ellison Cooner, born October 7, 1855, married Isabella Odom; Samuel Green Cooner, born September 18, 1857, died April 24, 1929, married Roxey Ann Randolph, born April 11, 1860, died January 28, 1933; both buried at New Prospect; Wesley Carroll Cooner, born August 19, 1859, died June 13, 1881, at Paris, Texas; Sarah Margaret died in infancy; Francis Marion Cooner, born October 27, 1862, married Annie Pierce.

Family Bible Record.

COONER, JAMES CARROLL, a son of James P. Cooner, was born December 25, 1835, near Pleasant Grove on Lost Creek. On September 6, 1862, he enlisted at Jasper as a private in Company G, Thirteenth Alabama Cavalry, under Captain Shepherd.

Census of Confederate Soldiers, 1907.

COPELAND, WASH, entered government land in Section

19, Township 16, Range 6, at what is now known as Copeland Ford, on the Warrior River, on September 5, 1832.
Walker County Tract Record.

CORLEY, CLEMENT, entered government land in Section 4, Township 16, Range 8, on November 2, 1836.
Walker County Tract Record.

CORNELIUS, ABNER, entered government land in Section 10, Township 13, Range 6, on Feburary 13, 1855.
Walker County Tract Record.

CORNELIUS, BRADFORD, entered government land in Section 6, Township 13, Range 5, on June 25, 1855.
Walker County Tract Record.

CORRY, JOSEPH MORTIMER, born October 14, 1829, settled near the present site of Oakman about 1852. He was a public spirited citizen who had much to do with the building up of that community, and in its early days he donated property for the erection of churches. He was affectionately known as the "Duke of Day's Gap." He died on July 27, 1910, and is buried in the Key Graveyard at Old Antioch. Mr. Corry was married twice; first, to Elizabeth Manervy McGarnes, who was born May 16, 1828, and died April 18, 1867; and, second, to Martha A. Guttery, who was born December 24, 1834, and died April 18, 1872. His daughter, Editha Isabella Corry, born November 30, 1855, died in August, 1888, was married, first, to a Mr. Gaines, and, second, to Wiley Davis.
Files of the Mountain Eagle.
Gravestones.

COURINGTON, REASON, born in 1795, died August 15, 1878, and is buried in Providence Graveyard. On October 1, 1832, he entered government land in Section 36, Township 15, Range 8, near Gayoso. He spent his entire life on a farm in this locality. His wife, Susie Courington, was born February

EARLY SETTLERS 171

27, 1802, died October 19, 1889, and is also buried at Providence. Two of his sons were Robert Courington and Randolph Courington.

Family Records.
Gravestones.

COURINGTON, ROBERT, a son of Reason Courington, was born near Pleasantfield on December 23, 1832. In February, 1862, he enlisted at York Post Office (now Oakman) as a private in Company K, Fiftieth Alabama Infantry, under Captain Hutto. In the fall of 1864 he was transferred to Captain W. H. Shepherd's company of cavalry and served until the close of the war. He died on February 24, 1925, and is buried at Providence. He was married to Mary Sumner, who was born August 4, 1844, and died October 3, 1918. Children—Martha Courington, married William Sartain; Belle Courington, married, first, Sim Thomas, and, second, F. P. Reed; John D. Courington, married Maud Earnest; Emily Courington, married James J. Phifer; Margaret Courington, married Bud Savage; Josephine Courington, married Sid McMillan; and Rufus M. Courington, married, first, Katie Savage, and, second, Ella Kimball, their children being Morris Luther Courington, Lester Courington, and James Courington, all of Parrish; John Courington, of Kentucky, and Vera Courington, who married Wiley Randolph.

Census of Confederate Soldiers, 1907.
Gravestones.
Family Records.

COURINGTON, RANDOLPH, a son of Reason Courington, was born September 27, 1839, near what is now Gorgas. In February, 1862, he enlisted at York Post Office (now Oakman) as a private in Company K, Fiftieth Alabama Infantry, under Captain Hutto. In the fall of 1864 he was captured by Federal troops at Leighton, Ala., and imprisoned at Camp Chase, Ohio, until the close of the war. He died January 25, 1911, and is buried at

Providence. He was married to Caroline Sumner, who was born September 15, 1847, and died August 27, 1931. Children—James Reuben Courington; Jane Courington, married Bud Robinson; Martha Courington, married Felix Swindle; Radie Courington, married, first, Rufus Sartain, and, second, James Carmichael; Leithie Courington, married, first, Arthur Shaw, and, second, G. D. McKenzie; G. A. (Ab) Courington, married Nedie Gray; and Alice Courington, married Charles Sartain.

Census of Confederate Soldiers, 1907.
Gravestones.
Family Records.

COURINGTON, JAMES BENJAMIN, was born near Providence on March 21, 1847. In July, 1864, he enlisted at Jasper as a private in Company I, Sixty-second Alabama Infantry, under Captain George B. Shorteridge, and served until the close of the war. He died May 14, 1931, and is buried at Sardis, near Bankhead.

Census of Confederate Soldiers, 1907.
Gravestones.

COVIN, LAZARUS, who entered government land in Section 31, Township 16, Range 7, and Section 36, Township 16, Range 8, on August 29, 1836, was a grandson of Lazarus and Marie Annie (Le Roy) Covin, French Huguenots, who came from Marseilles, France, and Hainault, French Flanders, respectively, in 1763, and died in Abbeville, S. C. Lazarus Covin, of this article, was born and reared in South Carolina, where he was married to Scotty Kilgore. The family came to Walker County in the 1830's. One of their sons, Simeon S. Covin, born in South Carolina about 1822, was married in Walker County to Mary Elizabeth Morris, daughter of John Harvey and Catherine (Hubbard) Morris. One of the sons of Simeon S. and Mary Elizabeth (Morris) Covin, was Lewis Vann Covin, who was Justice of the Peace and Mayor of Parrish for several years.

Lewis Vann Covin married Mariah Agnes Plylar, a daughter of James B. Plylar. She died in 1935. Children—Louis Emmett Covin; James Walter Covin; Rose Lee Covin, who married Fayette Jones, of Parrish; and Daisy Elizabeth Covin, who married S. Raymond Walker, of Parrish.

> Walker County Tract Record.
> Owen's Alabama, Vol. IV, page 1665.
> Family Records.

CRANFORD, JOHN, a native of Virginia, who served in the war of 1812, and was in the final battle at New Orleans, came to Alabama in the early days of the state's history, and in the early 1830's was living near Falkville, in Morgan County. Sometime prior to 1838 he moved to Walker County. He was married to Elizabeth Wilkes, of Virginia. Children—Abner Cranford, born in 1803; entered government land in Section 6, Township 14, Range 9, on April 16, 1838; died July 18, 1888; William Cranford; John Cranford; Chesley Hardy Cranford; Polly Cranford, who married William Stringer; Minerva Cranford, who married Jack Childress; Patsy Cranford, who married a Mr. Speagle; Winnie Cranford, who married David Speagle; Celia Cranford, who married Arm Blevins; Charlot Cranford, who married Thomas Gibson; Lydia Cranford, who married Mattie Randolph; Nancy Emily Cranford, born October 7, 1827, died September 20, 1919, married Daniel Lee Tubbs; Malinda Cranford, born April 18, 1825, married Samuel Tubbs.

> Owen's Alabama, Vol. III, page 418.
> Owen's Alabama, Vol. IV, page 1687.
> Cranford Family Records.

CRANFORD, JOHN E., a son of Abner Cranford, was born February 11, 1837, on Cranford Creek, about two miles west of Carbon Hill. In September, 1862, he enlisted at Jasper as a private in Company A, Thirteenth Alabama Cavalry; trans-

ferred in August, 1863, to Company B, Tenth Alabama Cavalry, and served until the close of the war.
Census of Confederate Soldiers, 1907.

CRANFORD, CHESLEY HARDY, a son of John and Elizabeth (Wilkes) Cranford, was born February 5, 1833, at Falkville, Morgan County, Alabama. It is not known just when he came to Walker County. In October, 1862, he enlisted as orderly sergeant, in Company G, Fifty-sixth Alabama Cavalry, and in July, 1863, he was transferred to Company E, Tenth Alabama Cavalry, and served until the close of the war. After the close of the war he served the county for a number of years as Tax Assessor. He died May 9, 1911, and is buried at New Hope. He was married to Elmartha Morris, who was born March 16, 1838, and died June 26, 1910. She was the daughter of John Harvey and Catherine (Hubbard) Morris, the latter a sister of Hon. David Hubbard, of Lawrence County, the first Confederate Commissioner of Indian Affairs. Among the children of Chesley Hardy and Elmartha (Morris) Cranford were John Harvey Cranford and W. Lafayette Cranford, born February 7, 1860; married to Etta Swindle on October 23, 1881; died May 27, 1896, and buried in Swindle Graveyard.

Owen's Alabama, Vol. III, page 418.
Owen's Alabama, Vol. IV, page 1687.
Memorial Record, Vol. II, page 1021.
Census of Confederate Soldiers, 1907.
Gravestones.

CRANFORD, JOHN HARVEY, affectionately known as "Captain Jack Cranford," of Jasper, was born March 12, 1855, a son of Chesley Hardy and Elmartha (Morris) Cranford. Reared on his father's farm near the present town of Oakman, his educational opportunities were limited, and he attended the country schools for a mere total of eighteen months. Yet by self application he had acquired sufficient education at the age of twenty

EARLY SETTLERS

to teach in the county schools, and farmed between school terms. At the age of twenty-five he secured a job in the store of B. M. Long, in Jasper, and worked there until 1882, when he went into business with Dr. W. C. Rosamond. In 1883 Mr. Cranford bought out the business. In 1887 he shipped the first cotton to be moved out of Jasper by rail. From 1892 to 1894 and from 1904 to 1906 he was mayor of Jasper, and during the interim was a member of the city council almost every year. From 1907 to 1909 he represented Walker County in the Legislature. During his administration as mayor several additions and developments to the city of Jasper carry credit to his courage and foresight. The city was without water supply and electric lights until he organized the Jasper Water, Light and Power Company. He was president of this company for seventeen years. In 1899 he organized the Bank of Jasper, out of which grew the First National Bank, and for twenty-five years from its opening served as the president of the bank. On October 18, 1892, he was married at San Antonio, Texas, to Annis Eleanor Lyon, a daughter of John and Elizabeth (Morris) Lyon, of Barnesville, Ga. Mr. Cranford died in 1934.

> Owen's Alabama, Vol. III, page 418.
> Memorial Record, Vol. II, page 1021.
> Files of Birmingham News-Age-Herald.

CROCKER, MOSES, entered government land in Section 32, Township 13, Range 7, on October 5, 1855.

> Walker County Tract Record.

CROFT, JAMES, entered government land in Section 3, Township 14, Range 5, on November 10, 1836.

> Walker County Tract Record.

CROWNOVER, WILLIAM F., Sr., of Oakman, was born in Evansville, Ind., in 1863, but was reared in Lawrence County, Alabama, where he was brought by his parents at an early age. In 1887 Mr. Crownover, who was a building contractor, came to the new town of Oakman, and was successful in his calling until 1915, when he retired. For a number of years he served as a member of the city council of Oakman. He was married in Lawrence County to Ursula A. Pool, who was born in Lawrence County, a granddaughter of James A. Poole, a native of South Carolina, who came to Alabama in young manhood, first settling at Mount Hope, in Lawrence County, and subsequently moving to Oakman, where he died. Children—J. Files Crownover, a building contractor at Oakman; Joseph B. Crownover; William F. Crownover, Jr., married Belma Wright, daughter of William M. Wright, of Parrish; Uless A. Crownover; Lila Crownover, who married L. F. Lelievere, of Oakman; and Annie Crownover, who married Grafton Dutton, of Madisonville, Ky.

Moore's Alabama, Vol. II, page 71.

CROWNOVER, JOSEPH BERRY, of Patton, was born May 16, 1846, at Moulton, Lawrence County, Alabama. During the Civil War he served in Company B, Thirty-eighth Tennessee Infantry, and later in Company B, Tenth Alabama Cavalry. He died April 24, 1919, and is buried at Patton Hill, as is also his wife, S. C. Crownover, who was born in May, 1846, and died June 14, 1908.

Census of Confederate Soldiers, 1907.
Gravestones.

CROWSON, RICHARD T., entered government land in Section 8, Township 14, Range 6, on November 28, 1836.

Walker County Tract Record.

CROWSON, THOMAS, entered government land in Section 6, Township 14, Range 6, on November 28, 1836.

Walker County Tract Record.

CROWSON, WILLIAM, entered government land in Section 8, Township 14, Range 6, on November 28, 1836.

Walker County Tract Record.

CRUMP, HENRY CLAY, was born January 7, 1845, near

Lexington, Tuscaloosa County. In September, 1861, he enlisted at Jasper as a private in Company E, Twenty-eighth Alabama Infantry, under Captain Henderson. On July 28, 1864, he was wounded at Atlanta and sent home. He died March 10, 1928, and is buried at Sardis, near Bankhead. He was married to Missouri Posey, a daughter of N. B. and Effie (Dailey) Posey.

Census of Confederate Soldiers, 1907.
Gravestones.

CUMMINGS, JOHN M., entered government land in Section 3, Township 14, Range 7, on August 7, 1835.

Walker County Tract Record.

CUNNINGHAM, JOHN, a pioneer settler, moved from Seneca, South Carolina, in 1848, and entered a tract of land eleven miles northwest of Jasper on what was known as Paul's Creek and extending westward and including practically all of the so-called "Piney Woods." Only three other settlers were his neighbors at that time—Carter Scott, Abner Shirley and Davidson Blackwell. He resided there, a farmer, mechanic and justice of the peace until 1871, when he removed to Morgan County. He was married in Walker County to Margaret Leonard, a daughter of David Leonard, who lived near Jasper. He was the father of Dr. W. M. Cunningham, who was at one time postmaster at Wolf, Alabama, located on Wolf Creek, where the Cheatham Road crosses it, about one mile south of the present site of Corona, before Corona was established. He became the best beloved physician in that section of the county.

DuBose, Notable Men of Alabama, page 184.
Files of the Mountain Eagle.

CUNNINGHAM, ELIAS, entered government land in Section 26, Township 13, Range 9, on November 16, 1836.

Walker County Tract Record.

CUNNINGHAM, WILLIAM CARTER, was born in Anderson County, South Carolina, on June 12, 1842. In September, 1862, he enlisted at Jasper as a private in Company A, Thirteenth Alabama Cavalry.

Census of Confederate Soldiers, 1907.

CUNNINGHAM, JUDGE C. J. L., owned and edited a Jasper newspaper, the True Citizen, in 1886; was elected the first town treasurer of Jasper in 1887, and was president of the Confederate Veterans' Association of Walker County in 1890.

Files of the Mountain Eagle.

DANIEL, JAMES, a pioneer settler of Jasper, entered government land on the corner of Nineteenth Street and the west bank of Town Creek on November 19, 1833. He is shown on a list of Jasper residents published in 1859.

Walker County Tract Record.

DAVIS, WILLIAM, a pioneer settler of the county, was born about 1781, died about 1867, and is buried in the Davis Graveyard at Coal Valley. His wife, Martha, was born about 1776, and died December 29, 1858. William Davis came to Walker County in the early 1830's and settled on Cane Creek, near the present site of Coal Valley.

Gravestones.

DAVIS, ROBERT, a son of William and Martha Davis, was born June 12, 1806, died August 13, 1883, and is buried in the Davis Graveyard at Coal Valley. He came to Walker County in the early 1830's, and on January 10, 1834, entered government land in Section 18, Township 15, Range 8, on Cane Creek, near Coal Valley. Robert Davis was a member of the Masonic fraternity and a minister in the Methodist Church. He was numbered among the first preachers of the Methodist Church in Walker County. West speaks of him as a man of little education but a worthy Christian. He was married twice; his first wife, Zilpha, was born in 1810 and died March 31, 1849, and is buried in the Davis Graveyard. His second wife, Jane

D. Davis, was born in 1810; died in 1881, and is buried at Pleasant Grove.

> Walker County Tract Record.
> West's History of Methodism, page 551.
> Mountain Eagle, January 24, 1912.
> Gravestones.

DAVIS, THOMAS, was born May 28, 1826, on Cane Creek, near Coal Valley. In September, 1862, he enlisted at Jasper as a private in Company G, Fifty-sixth Alabama Cavalry, under Captain Shepherd, and on November 30, 1863, he re-enlisted in Company G, Eighth Alabama Cavalry, under Captain Wharton. He served throughout the war as a wagoner.

> Census of Confederate Soldiers, 1907.

DAVIS, WILEY, was born near Coal Valley on March 22, 1842; died June 15, 1905, and is buried in the Key Graveyard. He was married twice. His first wife, Elizabeth, was born in August, 1836, and died October 25, 1882. His second marriage was to Mrs. Editha Isabella (Corry) Gaines, a daughter of J. M. Corry and a widow of a Mr. Gaines. She was born November 30, 1855, and died in August, 1888.

> Gravestone.

DAVIS, JESSE TYRA, of Oakman, was born June 16, 1844, on Cane Creek, near Coal Valley. On October 20, 1862, he enlisted at Tuscaloosa as a private in Company F, Fifth Mississippi Cavalry. He was part of the escort to President Jefferson Davis, and was captured with President Davis in Georgia.

> Census of Confederate Soldiers, 1907.

DAVIS, JAMES M., was born about 1790; died August 26, 1865, and is buried at Dora, as is also his wife, Lydia Davis, who was born in 1781 and died July 23, 1851. James Davis was a pioneer settler of Walker County, and entered government land in Section 18, Township 15, Range 5, on Horse Creek, near Dora, on February 13, 1830. In the early forties he dug coal out of the bottom and the banks of the Warrior River, near Dora, and also out of the banks and the bottom of Horse Creek and Barton's Creek and boated it to the lower river markets. Among his children were, J. T. Davis, born in Feburary, 1813; died March 13, 1861; and Daniel Davis, born January 12, 1816; died August 2, 1874.

Walker County Tract Record.
Armes' History of Coal and Iron.
Gravestones.

DAVIS, THOMAS W., of Dora, was born April 7, 1837, and died August 24, 1904. He was married twice; first, to Malissa Morgan, daughter of Ezekiel Morgan, of Dora, and upon her death he married her sister, Narcissus, who was born February 12, 1841, and died November 11, 1900. Children by first wife—Newton Davis, William Davis, and Patsie Davis. By his second wife there were four children, but their names are unknown to the author.

Gravestones.

DAVIS, JAMES WESLEY, of Dora, was born September 21, 1841, on Horse Creek. In September, 1861, he enlisted at Jasper as a private in Company I, Fiftieth Alabama Infantry, under Captain B. M. Long. He was wounded at Atlanta on May 12, 1864, and after recovering from this wound he re-enlisted in Company G, Fifty-sixth Alabama Cavalry, and served until the close of the war. He died February 11, 1918, and is buried at Dora. His wife, Sarah E. Davis, was born March 1, 1846, and died April 16, 1906. She was a daughter of William Henry and Matilda Ann (Chilton) Snow.

Census of Confederate Soldiers, 1907.
Gravestones.

DAVIS, BENJAMIN, entered government land in Section 22, Township 13, Range 10, near Nauvoo, on August 12, 1835.

Walker County Tract Record.

DAVIS, JOHN, entered government land in Section 22, Township 13, Range 10, near Nauvoo, on February 17, 1836.
Walker County Tract Record.

DAVIS, WILLIAM LEAS, of Nauvoo, was born November 18, 1835, near New Lexington, in Tuscaloosa County. In September, 1862, he enlisted at Jasper as a private in Company A, Fifty-sixth Alabama Cavalry, under Captain Guttery, and served until the close of the war.
Census of Confederate Soldiers, 1907.

DAVIS, WILLIAM COLUMBUS, was born August 5, 1867, in Iuka, Miss., a son of Samuel McGee and Emily J. (Lacy) Davis. Mr. Davis was educated in the public schools of Mississippi, studied law with Col. Harvey Murphy, of Aberdeen, and began to practice in Fulton, Miss. He later moved to Marion County, Alabama, and held numerous public offices in that county. In 1899 he moved to Jasper, and in 1904 served as Presidential Elector for the Sixth Congressional District. In 1915 he was elected Representative in the State Legislature from Walker County. From 1927 to 1931 he served as Lieutenant Governor of the state, and was an unsuccessful candidate for governor in 1930 against B. M. Miller. As a legislator and as a private citizen Mr. Davis rendered Alabama invaluable services in inaugurating a prison reform movement in this state which, after many weary years, finally succeeded, under his leadership, in abolishing the notorious convict lease system. In 1930 he retired to Jasper and formed a law partnership with J. J. Curtis. On July 4, 1895, he was married to Mard Elizabeth Gray, a daughter of Alanson J. and Elizabeth J. (Nethery) Gray, of Choctaw County. Children—William C. Davis, Jr., of Washington, D. C., and Elizabeth Gray Davis, of Birmingham. Mr. Davis died on October 4, 1934, and is buried at Jasper.
Owens' Alabama, Vol. III, page 469.
Mountain Eagle, October 10, 1934.

DAY, WILLIAM BYRD, born March 8, 1817, entered government land in Section 24, Township 12, Range 6, on February 13, 1854. This entry was in the northern part of the county, but in 1862 he settled at the lowest point in the mountainous ridges that surround the present town of Oakman, and this point became known as "Day's Gap." He was a successful farmer who eventually owned more than a thousand acres of land at Day's Gap. He died on July 16, 1901, and is buried in the Day Graveyard at Oakman. Mr. Day was married twice; his first wife, Nancy Day, born in Tennessee on October 22, 1817, died January 15, 1853. His second marriage was to the widow of William A. Morris.

Genealogy of the Branner Family.
Walker County Tract Record.
Gravestones.

DEASON, ABSALOM, entered government land in Section 5, Township 15, Range 6, on August 29, 1855.

Walker County Tract Record.

DEASON, MERRICK M., born October 20, 1816, died July 21, 1903, and is buried at Zion, near Parrish, as is likewise his wife, Rebecca Deason, who was born July 3, 1823, and died June 8, 1885. Merrick Deason entered government land in Section 11, Township 15, Range 7, northeast of Parrish, on March 22, 1855.

Walker County Tract Record.
Gravestones.

DEES, J. A., a Confederate veteran who was living in Walker County in 1895.

Mountain Eagle, July 3, 1895.

DESKIN, I. G., a local Methodist preacher in Walker County in the 1830's.

West's History of Methodism, page 549.

EARLY SETTLERS

DICKERSON, THOMAS, entered government land in Section 36, Township 13, Range 5, on September 16, 1831.
Walker County Tract Record.

DICKINSON, ROBERT, entered government land in Section 3, Township 14, Range 4, on February 17, 1855.
Walker County Tract Record.

DILL, ABNER, entered government land in Section 13, Township 14, Range 8, west of Jasper, on November 6, 1833.
Walker County Tract Record.

DILL, ENOCH, entered government land in Section 12, Township 15, Range 8, northwest of Parrish, on December 21, 1835.
Walker County Tract Record.

DILL, EZEKIEL, entered government land in Section 36, Township 15, Range 8, on Cane Creek, south of Gayoso, on October 23, 1835.
Walker County Tract Record.

DILL, WILLIAM, entered government land in Section 28, Township 14, Range 7, on January 4, 1837.
Walker County Tract Record.

DODSON, E. K., born December 15, 1831, at North River, Tuscaloosa County, went to California during the gold rush of 1849, and stayed eight years. Returning to Tuscaloosa County, he engaged in farming until the outbreak of the Civil War, when he enlisted and served throughout the four years of the war. Shortly after the close of the war he came to Walker County.
Mountain Eagle, October 8, 1930.

DOUGLAS, GEORGE, entered government land in Section 7, Township 15, Range 7, on December 21, 1858.
Walker County Tract Record.

DOWDY, WILLIAM, entered government land in Section 29, Township 13, Range 5, on January 12, 1836.
Walker County Tract Record.

DOWNEY, THOMAS JOHNSON, was born February 17, 1851, near the present site of Galloway Mines. When only thirteen years old, in September, 1864, he enlisted at Eldridge in Company E, Tenth Alabama Cavalry, under Captain T. J. White. On account of his youth he was detached from his command and served with the home guard. He guarded mails from Eldridge to Littleville and Leighton, Ala.

Census of Confederate Soldiers, 1907.

DOYLE, SIMON C., entered government land in Section 33, Township 13, Range 5, on May 16, 1855.

Walker County Tract Record.

DRENNEN, CHARLES, physician, a son of Rev. Walter B. and Matilda H. (Cornwell) Drennen, was born at Arkadelphia on September 6, 1842. Educated in the county schools, he entered the University of Alabama, but left in 1861 to enter the Confederate Army. He enlisted and was elected First Lieutenant of Company F, Twenty-eighth Alabama Infantry under Captain Gamble. This company served during the siege of Corinth, and took part in Bragg's invasion of Kentucky in 1862, participating in the battles of Munfordville and Perryville. He commanded the company after Captain Gamble resigned to accept the office of Probate Judge of Walker County, and at the battle of Murfreesboro, on December 31, 1862, he was promoted to Captain for gallant and meritorious service. He was in the battle of Chickamauga; was captured at Missionary Ridge on November 25, 1863, and was held prisoner at Johnson's Island until the close of the war. He commenced to study medicine in 1867; graduated in 1873, and organized the Walker County Medical Society in 1874. Later he moved to Birmingham.

Owens' Alabama, Vol. II, page 508.

DUNCAN, WILLIAM D., entered government land in Section 33, Township 15, Range 7, on April 27, 1855.

Walker County Tract Record.

EARLY SETTLERS

DUNN, WILLIAM, made the first shipment of Walker County products by flatboat over the Squaw Shoals of the Warrior River.

Armes' Story of Coal and Iron.

DUNN, NATHANIEL O., a member of Fowler's Company, Alabama Light Artillery, C. S. A., is buried at Fairview.

Gravestone.

DUPREY, JOHN M., entered government land in Section 34, Township 13, Range 7, on August 17, 1836.

Walker County Tract Record.

DUTTON, JAMES, entered government land in Section 24, Township 14, Range 8, southwest of Jasper, on January 25, 1845. When and where he was born is unknown; however, he died in Walker County on April 30, 1883. Children—Mary Jane Dutton, who married Reuben Keeton; William Dutton; Thomas F. Dutton, who married Louisa Carmichael; Elizabeth A. Dutton, who married C. C. Hamilton; S. M. Dutton, who was the father of John Dutton; and George W. Dutton, who was the father of Toney Dutton, Peter Dutton, Alvin H. Dutton, and Dollie Dutton.

Walker County Tract Record.
Probate Record, Estate of James Dutton.

DUVALL, ALEXANDER C., entered government land in Section 10, Township 16, Range 8, on Wolf Creek, south of Oakman, on February 11, 1833.

Walker County Tract Record.

DUVALL, ELISHA, entered government land in Section 16, Township 14, Range 7, on April 4, 1835.

Walker County Tract Record.

EARNEST, RICHARD, entered government land in Section 29, Township 15, Range 8, on December 6, 1833.

Walker County Tract Record.

EARNEST, ROBERT, entered government land in Section 7, Township 15, Range 8, on January 10, 1834.

Walker County Tract Record.

EASLEY, ALBERT G., entered government land in Section 8, Township 14, Range 8, on June 18, 1836.

Walker County Tract Record.

EASLEY, JOSIAH M., was elected Representative in the Legislature in 1859 in contest with General John Manasco. He served but the regular session and then moved from the state. His brother-in-law, Frances A. Musgrove, was elected to fill the vacancy.

Mountain Eagle, January 5, 1887.

ELLIOTT, JAMES, entered government land in Section 29, Township 14, Range 5, near Burton Bend, on the Warrior River, on September 13, 1819.

Walker County Tract Record.

ELLIS, RICHARD, a son of George and Peggy (Nelson) Ellis, and a descendant of Andrew Nelson, a Revolutionary War soldier, was born February 9, 1831, near Double Springs, in Winston County, and lived near Clear Creek Falls all of his life. He died in 1898 and is buried at Bennett Graveyard, near Clear Creek Falls. He was married to Ellen Eliza Bennett, born June 22, 1832, a daughter of Michael and Phoebe Head (Livingston) Bennett, of Clear Creek Falls, one of the first settlers in this section. She died in 1924 and is buried at Oak Hill Cemetery in Jasper. Children—Betty Ellis, died in Winston County, about 1876; Emma Jane Ellis, married George King, at South Lowell; George Washington Ellis, moved to Texas; Mary Susan Ellis, married Thomas G. Estes, near Mary Lee; Christiana Haynes Ellis, married W. M. Swindle, at Manchester; John Lemuel Ellis, moved to Texas; Leonia Ellis, moved to Texas;

and Richard Martin Ellis, married Martha Adeline Williams, at Clear Creek Falls, but lived at Jasper.

Ellis Family Records.

EMBRY, ANDREW H., entered government land in Section 20, Township 15, Range 9, on December 10, 1832.

Walker County Tract Record.

EVANS, JONATHAN, entered government land in Section 9, Township 14, Range 7, within the present corporate limits of Jasper, on January 7, 1834.

Walker County Tract Record.

EVANS, JOHN W., entered government land in Section 36, Township 14, Range 7, on Cane Creek, near Cordova, on February 15, 1836.

Walker County Tract Record.

EVANS, THOMAS HAMPTON, was born February 2, 1842, on Cane Creek, near Cordova. On September 1, 1861, he enlisted at Jasper as a private in Company I, Twenty-sixth Alabama Infantry, under Captain Long. In December, 1864, he re-enlisted in Captain Mason's company of Musgrove's Battalion and served until the close of the war. He died April 25, 1917, and is buried at Samaria, as is also his wife, Massie Ann Evans, born October 20, 1845; died July 10, 1916.

Census of Confederate Soldiers, 1907.
Gravestones.

FAUGHT, JOSEPH INMAN, was born November 2, 1836, on the Sipsey River, in Walker County. On March 22, 1862, he enlisted as a private in Company A, Twenty-second Alabama Infantry, but was discharged by the medical board in May, 1862. In September, 1862, he re-enlisted in Company B, Thirty-sixth Alabama Infantry. He was captured at Missionary Ridge on November 25, 1863, and imprisoned at Rock Island, Ill. He died in 1929, and is buried at old Zion. On December 24, 1867, he was married to Elizabeth ———, who was born July 22, 1848, and died June 21, 1899. She was a member of the Primitive Baptist Church for thirty-two years.

Census of Confederate Soldiers, 1907.
Gravestones.

FAVER, WILLIAM, entered government land in Section 2, Township 14, Range 5, on April 29, 1835.

Walker County Tract Record.

FERGUSON, HENRY, born October 16, 1783, died February 24, 1874, and is buried at old Sardis, on the Warrior River. He entered government land in Section 15, Township 13, Range 8, on February 23, 1846.

Walker County Tract Record.
Gravestone.

FERGUSON, JOSEPH, was born at Chester, South Carolina, on December 25, 1794. He lived in South Carolina until early in 1848, when he moved to Giles County, Tennessee, and in the latter part of the same year he came to Walker County and settled near Holly Grove. He was a devout member of the Primitive Baptist Church, having joined that church at Hopewell, Chester District, South Carolina, in March, 1831. After coming to Walker County he joined the Bethel Primitive Baptist Church at Holly Grove in 1849, and remained a member until his death on September 21, 1886. In 1817 he was married to Ruth Woods, who died in South Carolina in 1829. On June 7, 1831, he was married to Lurania Walston.

Mountain Eagle, September 29, 1886.

FERGUSON, HENRY, of Blackwell, was born September 9, 1832, in Chester District, South Carolina. In September, 1862, he enlisted at Jasper in Company L, Hewlett's Thirteenth Battalion, under Captain Gutherie; was transferred to Company B, Tenth Alabama Cavalry, and served until the close of the war.

Census of Confederate Soldiers, 1907.

FERGUSON, JOSEPH WALSTON, a son of Joseph and Lurania (Walston) Ferguson, was born June 4, 1834, in Chester District, South Carolina. He was brought to Walker County by his parents in 1849, and was reared on his father's farm near Holly Grove. On March 13, 1862, he enlisted at Zion Church as a private in Company A, Twenty-second Alabama Infantry, and served until the close of the war. He was wounded at Shiloh and at Peach Tree Creek, near Atlanta. During the 1880's he served for one term as County Treasurer.
Census of Confederate Soldiers, 1907.

FERGUSON, ELIJAH A., was born at Rock Hill, S. C., on November 17, 1843. In June, 1861, he enlisted at Holly Grove as a private in Company A, Twenty-second Alabama Infantry; was transferred to Company B, Tenth Alabama Cavalry, and served until the close of the war.
Census of Confederate Soldiers, 1907.

FERGUSON, JOHNSON, a son of Joseph Walston Ferguson and a grandson of Joseph and Lurania (Walston) Ferguson, was born near Saragossa, August 24, 1862. Reared on his father's farm and educated in the rural schools, he remained in Walker County all of his life. He joined the Primitive Baptist Church at Zion, near Saragossa, in 1886, and remained a devout member until his death on May 31, 1934. In 1883 he was married to Malinda Edgil. Children—Mrs. C. Burt, Mrs. J. E. Monteith, Mrs. J. D. Tingle, Mrs. Mattie West, Mrs. Green Haynes, Edward H. Ferguson, Walter Ferguson, Pearl Ferguson, Ernest Ferguson, Paul Ferguson, and Albert Ferguson.
Mountain Eagle, June 6, 1934.

FETERSON, JAMES M., entered government land in Section 5, Township 14, Range 7, on January 18, 1859.
Walker County Tract Record.

FIELDS, HAMPTON, entered government land in Section 29, Township 15, Range 5, on November 27, 1845.

Walker County Tract Record.

FIKE, WILLIAM P., married Martha A. Townley, who was born February 14, 1828, and died February 8, 1894, and is buried in the Fike Graveyard. A son, W. A. Fike, was born February 6, 1855, and died April 28, 1917, together with his wife, Sarah J. Fike, born September 15, 1857, and died January 21, 1929, is also buried in the Fike Graveyard.

Gravestones.

FILES, RICHARD, Sr., born in South Carolina on September 27, 1804, was the son of Abner Files, a native of South Carolina, who came to Alabama and was a pioneer settler of Tuscaloosa County, where he lived and died. About 1835 Richard Files came to Walker County and entered government land east of Jasper, near the present site of Samaria Church. He died on November 2, 1891, and was buried at Samaria Church. He filled the office of County Commissioner for a number of years, and was a most pleasant gentleman and universally respected. He was married to Mary Lindsey, who was born April 8, 1810, the daughter of a Scotch school teacher, who settled in Georgia. She died on November 11, 1890, and is buried at Samaria. Children:

John W. Files, who married and lived at Mantachie, Itawamba County, Miss., and was the father of Richard; Mack; Oliver; Cornelia; Mary; and Lou, who married J. M. Little.

Catherine Files, who married, first, a Mr. Andleton, and, second, John Stephenson (see Stephenson).

Martha Files, born December 10, 1838, died August 12, 1918; married Robert Garner. Children—Wash; Thomas; Frank; and Larandy, who married a Mr. Ivey.

Abner Files, born July 12, 1842, died June 6, 1904, who served for several years as State Auditor of Arkansas and acted as private secretary to Governor Eagles, of Arkansas. He was married to Angeline Stanley, but died without heirs.

Thomas Files, who never married.

Mary Files, born May 3, 1835, died November 5, 1921; married James Matlock Kitchens (see Kitchens).

Mildred Files, born April 27, 1846, died September 18, 1895; married J. Henry Hayes (see Hayes).

Frances Files, born January 16, 1851, died July 10, 1890; married Isom Boshell (Bouchelle), who was born May 27, 1853, and died January 28, 1924. Children—Mae Boshell, who married a Mr. Knight; Cornelia Boshell, who married a Mr. Morgan; Edgar Boshell; and Ada Boshell, who married Bascom Wright.

Cornelia Files, who married Manly Rice, of Tuscaloosa, her first cousin.

David Jasper Files, born May 9, 1840, died October 19, 1897; married Mary Barton, born October 14, 1845, died October 29, 1895. There was only one child, Florence, who married W. H. Moore.

Richard Manly Files, whose sketch is given below.

    Files of the Mountain Eagle.
    Files Family Record.
    Gravestones.
    Powell's Fifty-five Years in West Alabama.

FILES, RICHARD MANLY, a son of Richard and Mary (Lindsey) Files, was born in Walker County on January 10, 1844. He was reared on his father's farm near Samaria Church. On September 3, 1861, when but seventeen years of age, he enlisted at Jasper as a private in Company G, Fiftieth Alabama Infantry, under Captain B. M. Long. He was severely wounded at the battle of Chickamauga, and was discharged on account of being physically unable to perform military duty. He was married to Margaret Angie Carr, who was born September 6, 1846, and died March 26, 1926. Children—Mary; Belle, who married a Mr. Biochi; Thomas, who never married; Donie, who married a Mr. Henley; Lora, who married Bud Jackson; and Fannie, who married Thomas Sherer.

        Census of Confederate Soldiers, 1907.
        Files Family Records.
        Gravestones.

 FORD, JAMES, entered government land in Section 14, Township 14, Range 7, east of Jasper, on December 3, 1855.
        Walker County Tract Record.

 FORD, JOHN L., entered government land in Section 11, Township 14, Range 7, on April 14, 1857.
        Walker County Tract Record.

 FOREST, J. S. D., entered government land in Section 6, Township 16, Range 8, on February 8, 1837.
        Walker County Tract Record.

 FOWLER, JAMES B., entered government land in Section 24, Township 14, Range 9, on December 30, 1835.
        Walker County Tract Record.

 FRANKLIN, LOTT M., entered government land in Section 22, Township 16, Range 8, on August 27, 1836.
        Walker County Tract Record.

 FRANKLIN, JOHN GURGANUS, of Drifton, was born January 24, 1834, on Cedar Creek, near the Warrior River. In April, 1862, he enlisted at Jasper as a private in Company L, Twenty-eighth Alabama Infantry, under Captain Musgrove. He was captured while on picket duty at Orchard Knob, Missionary Ridge, in November, 1863, and was imprisoned at Rock Island, Ill., until the close of the war.
        Census of Confederate Soldiers, 1907.

 FREEMAN, JAMES H., was a local Methodist preacher prior to 1837. While his membership was at Zion, in the southeast part of Fayette County, he is numbered among the first preachers of the Jasper Methodist Church. He was married to Martha B. Cole. A daughter, Jerusha A. Freeman, was married to F. A. Gamble. Another daughter, Madorah F. Freeman, was married to Dr. W. C. Rosamond.

West's History of Methodism, page 551.
Mountain Eagle, January 24, 1912.

FREEMAN, DR. LUCIUS G., a son of James H. Freeman, was born October 9, 1847, in Tuscaloosa. Educated in the public schools of Tuscaloosa he also attended the Louisiana Medical College, from which he graduated about 1868. Soon after his graduation he moved to Walker County and became associated with Dr. W. C. Rosamond at Jasper. Dr. Freeman, like his father before him, was always prominent in the Methodist Church. He died on February 16, 1878, and is buried in the old cemetery at Jasper. He was married to Fatima Stanley, who was born December 2, 1850, died November 3, 1876, and is buried in the old cemetery at Jasper. Children—James S. Freeman; Birda G. Freeman, who was married on May 17, 1890, to D. A. McGregor, of Town Creek, Ala.

Mountain Eagle, February 22, 1922.

FROST, EDWARD, came to Walker County, from Morgan County, between 1840 and 1845, and settled near Corona.

Frost Family Record.

FROST, EDWARD BENTON, a son of Edward Frost, was born January 29, 1840, near Somerville, Morgan County, and was brought to Walker County by his father when still a baby. On September 20, 1862, he enlisted at Holly Grove as a private in Company L, Fifty-sixth Alabama Cavalry, and served until the close of the war. He died on June 11, 1894, and is buried at Mount Zion, on Lockhart Hill. His wife, M. V. Frost, born

November 17, 1840, died December 10, 1880, and is buried in the Frost Graveyard at West Corona.
Census of Confederate Soldiers, 1907.
Gravestones.

FROST, STEPHEN ORR, a son of Edward Frost, was born October 17, 1845, near Corona. In the summer of 1864 he enlisted at Studdard Crossroads, Fayette County, as a private in Company K, Tenth Alabama Cavalry, and served until the close of the war.
Census of Confederate Soldiers, 1907.

FROST, C. S., was a member of Company H, First Alabama Cavalry, and is buried in the Frost Graveyard at West Corona.
Gravestone.

FULTON, HORATIO S., entered government land in Section 12, Township 13, Range 5, on October 25, 1833.
Walker County Tract Record.

GABBERT, THOMAS M., a native of South Carolina, came to Walker County before 1851, as the records show that he entered government land in Section 28, Township 14, Range 7, near Calumet, on October 17, 1851. He was a minister in the Baptist Church and a most excellent man. As a Christian he was liberal towards all other denominations. He was elected the second Probate Judge of the county and served from 1853 to 1859. After retiring from office he engaged in mercantile business in Jasper, and but for the war would no doubt have been highly successful. He died some years after the war, highly respected by all that knew him. Among his children were Thomas L. Gabbert and a daughter, L. C. Gabbert, born April 30, 1838, died March 3, 1908, married A. H. Brown. She is buried in the Kitchens Graveyard.
Mountain Eagle, January 5, 1887.

GABBERT, THOMAS LEANDER, a son of Thomas M. Gabbert, was born February 3, 1834, at Union Court House,

South Carolina. In young manhood he came to Walker County with his parents, and was a farmer until the outbreak of the Civil War. On September 6, 1862, he enlisted at Jasper as a private in Company G, Fifty-sixth Alabama Cavalry, and served until the close of the war. For some years after the war he lived at and operated Camak Mills, on Blackwater Creek. He died on April 19, 1911, and is buried in the Cooner Graveyard at Coal City. His wife, Louisa Jane Gabbert, born December 20, 1838, died February 3, 1917, and is also buried in the Cooner Graveyard.

Census of Confederate Soldiers, 1907.
Mountain Eagle, January 30, 1895.
Gravestones.

GAINES, H. P., born in North Carolina on March 30, 1779, died January 1, 1865, and is buried in the Gaines Graveyard at Corona, with his wife, Nancy Gaines, who was born in North Carolina November 8, 1790, and died February 23, 1862. Henry P. Gaines entered government land in Section 27, Township 15, Range 9, near Corona, on December 9, 1833.

Walker County Tract Record.
Gravestones.

GAINES, JAMES P., entered government land in Section 27, Township 15, Range 9, on January 5, 1833.

Walker County Tract Record.

GAINES, WILLIAM M., born January 15, 1826, on the Tombigbee River, in Greene County, Alabama; entered government land in Section 22, Township 15, Range 9, near Corona, on February 17, 1845. On May 18, 1863, he enlisted at Wolf Creek as a private in Company K, Fiftieth Alabama Infantry, under Captain Hutto, and served until the close of the war. He later moved to Crosscut, Texas.

Census of Confederate Soldiers, 1907.
Walker County Tract Record.

GAINES, GEORGE SHIP, born December 8, 1828, at Old

Erie, Greene County, Alabama; enlisted at Corona, in Colonel Ball's Regiment of Cavalry, and served until the close of the war. He died December 22, 1910, and is buried in the Gaines Graveyard at Corona. His wife, Frances (Jones) Gaines, born April 9, 1832, died May 10, 1891, and is also buried at Corona. Among the children of George Ship and Frances (Jones) Gaines were Lavina J., born Febuary 12, 1854, died January 14, 1888, married to J. W. Lunn; William R., born 1865, died 1895; and Lewis, born May 15, 1858, died March 15, 1891.

Census of Confederate Soldiers, 1907.
Gravestones.

GAINES, JOHN S., entered government land in Section 27, Township 15, Range 9, on February 15, 1836.

Walker County Tract Record.

GAINES, EDMOND THOMAS, entered government land in Section 35, Township 15, Range 9, near Corona, on May 26, 1834. Mr. Gaines was married twice; first, to Ann McDowell, and second to ———. Children by the first marriage—Bartley; H. P. (Dick) Gaines, who married Callie Day, of Oakman; Elizabeth, who married Leonard Jones, of Corona; Susan, who married a Captain Smith and moved to Texas; Mary, who married Jack Gibson and moved to Texas; Nancy, who married Daniel Gibson, of Corona; Eliza, who married Frank Stanley, of Berry; James P., who married Ann Tierce; Eugenie, who died in her early twenties and never married; John Strother, who married Jennie Swindle; and by the second marriage, Mattie, who married a Mr. Thompson and moved west.

Walker County Tract Record.
Family Records.

GAINES, JOHN STROTHER, a son of Edmond Thomas and Ann (McDowell) Gaines, died at his home near Corona on December 10, 1887. He was married to Jennie Swindle. Children—Margaret Ann, who mrrried William Perry, of Electoria,

Va.; Susan Frances, who married J. E. DeLoach, of Birmingham; Eugene Pendleton, deceased, never married; Elizabeth, never married; and Lula May, who married Dr. David Houston Chilton, of Parrish.

Mountain Eagle, December 14, 1887.
Family Record.

GAINEY, LUKE R., entered government land in Section 25, Township 12, Range 7, on September 13, 1859.

Walker County Tract Record.

GALLAGHER, DAVID E., a native of South Carolina, came to Walker County about 1850. He became a very prominent citizen of the county and was elected to the office of County Treasurer for two terms. He died February 10, 1886, at the age of seventy-four.

True Citizen, Feburary 11, 1886.

GALLAGHER, JOHN WRIGHT, a son of David E. Gallagher, was born July 29, 1842, at Sandersville, S. C. On April 21, 1861, he enlisted at Eldridge as a private in Company H, Forty-third Alabama Infantry, under Captain W. H. Lawrence. He was severely wounded at Chickamauga on October 28, 1863, and sent home. Upon his recovery he re-enlisted in Company K, Fourth Alabama Cavalry, under Captain E. D. Kelley, and served until the close of the war.

Census of Confederate Soldiers, 1907.

GAMBLE, JOHN R., was the son of Robert and Margaret Gamble. Robert Gamble was a native of Ireland and a soldier in the American Revolution, and was present at the surrender of Lord Cornwallis at Yorktown, Va. John R. Gamble, following in his father's footsteps, served under General Andrew Jackson during the War of 1812 and the Indian campaigns of 1813. He was mustered out of service shortly after Weatherford's surrender and settled in the wilds of Shelby County, near the present site of Calera. When that place began to show signs of settlement he moved himself and family to Walker County and entered government land in Section 7, Township 14, Range 6, on November 28, 1836. He was a minister in the Methodist Church for many years, having been licensed to preach in Jasper, at a quarterly conference held at Gold Mine Camp Ground, in Marion County, on September 8, 1838. Mr. Gamble died in 1863, after holding several county offices. He was married in Shelby County to Jane Mills, a daughter of James and Margaret Mills, of Virginia, the former a Revolutionary War soldier. She died on July 18, 1886, and is buried at the Harrel Burying Ground in Blount County. Among their children were Dr. J. W. Gamble, of Jefferson County, and F. A. Gamble, of Jasper.

                        Owens' Alabama, Vol. III, page 630.
                        Armes' Story of Coal and Iron.
                        Northern Alabama, page 176.
                        West's History of Methodism.
                        Walker County Tract Record.

GAMBLE, FRANKLIN ASBURY, a son of John R. and Jane (Mills) Gamble, was born September 23, 1830, in Shelby County, near the present site of Calera. His father moved to Walker County with his family and goods in a wagon in 1836, and settled a few miles east of Jasper. Mr. Gamble was reared on his father's farm and educated in the common schools of Walker County. In 1855 he left the farm and entered the mercantile business in Jasper. He was elected Probate Judge in May, 1859, and served until March, 1862, when he was commissioned as Captain of Company F, Twenty-eighth Alabama Infantry. He was with Bragg's campaign in Kentucky, but the hardships were too severe, his health failed, and he was sent home in the latter part of 1862. From 1865 to 1868 he was County Administrator, and in 1869 he again entered the mercantile business in Jasper. Judge Gamble, together with Abner Hitchcock, of Cleveland, Ohio, and Jobe Richardson, of Walker

County, organized the Ohio and Alabama Agricultural, Manufacturing and Mineral Company, which company was instrumental in bringing to Walker County, in the fall of 1872, a large number of colonists who established the town of South Lowell. In 1874 he purchased and became editor of the Jasper Mountain Eagle, but in July, 1877, the Eagle office, together with the courthouse and other buildings, was destroyed by fire. Soon after this he was appointed Probate Judge, by Governor Houston, to succeed Judge Jacob R. Shepherd, and was retained in office until November, 1886. For two years he was president of the Walker County Bank; he was a stockholder and director of the Jasper Land Company, and was owner of the Gamble Mines, coal property, a mine at Carbon Hill, and much real estate and other property in the county. He was a local preacher, and took a prominent part in the affairs of the Methodist Church. On November 3, 1857, he was married to Jerusha A. Freeman, a daughter of James H. Freeman, who was a Methodist minister for sixty-two years and widely known in Walker, Tuscaloosa and Fayette Counties. She died on March 14, 1875, and is buried in the old graveyard at Jasper. In April, 1877, Judge Gamble was married the second time to Mary A. Owen, a daughter of Judge Thomas and Dolly (Williams) Owen. She was born January 6, 1846, and died February 24, 1920, and is buried in Oak Hill Cemetery in Jasper. Judge Gamble died October 5, 1895, and is buried in the old graveyard at Jasper. Children by first marriage—Leila K., who was married to John B. Carrington on December 10, 1890; by the second marriage, Frank Gamble, Foster K. Gamble, Thomas Owen Gamble.

       Owens' Alabama, Vol. III, page 630.
       Armes' Story of Coal and Iron.
       Northern Alabama, page 176.
       Gravestones.
       Memorial Record, Vol. II, page 1021.

GARRETT, EDWARD, entered government land in Section 4, Township 14, Range 5, on March 4, 1824.

Walker County Tract Record.

GARRISON, STEPHEN, born in 1764, was a soldier in the Revolutionary War, having seen service as a private in the regular North Carolina Line. In 1830 he was a resident of Lawrence County, but on June 1, 1840, he was living in Walker County and resided with Silas Garrison.

U. S. Census of Pensioners, June 1, 1840.

GARRISON, DAVID, a descendant of Stephen Garrison, came to Walker County, it is thought, some time between 1830 and 1840 and settled on Cane Creek, about three miles south of Jasper. He married Sarah Lollar, daughter of Hugh Lollar, who was born January 20, 1801, and died June 30, 1886, and is buried at the Zion Graveyard at Parrish.

Gravestone.
Garrison Family Record.

GARRISON, DAVID WILLIAM, a descendant of Stephen Garrison, was born in Walker County on December 26, 1856. He was married to Martha Caroline Robison, who was born April 27, 1856. Mr. Garrison died on January 12, 1890, leaving five children—Sallie, who married J. A. Tubb; Cora, who married W. M. Dalton; David, who married Margaret Sides, daughter of David Sides; Margaret, who married G. W. Short; and Lloyd, who married Edith Anderson.

Garrison Family Records.

GARRISON, JACOB, entered government land in Section 15, Township 14, Range 7, on June 3, 1857.

Walker County Tract Record.

GASH, LEANDER S., entered government land in Section 21, Township 15, Range 9, on May 20, 1834.

Walker County Tract Record.

GIBSON, JACOB, Sr., entered government land in Section 15, Township 15, Range 6, on the Warrior River, near Cordova, on December 17, 1832. His son, Jacob Gibson, Jr., entered government land in Section 4, Township 15, Range 6, on November 26, 1833. In the early 1840's Jacob Gibson was actively engaged in mining coal, raising it out of the bottom of the river after prizing it up with crow bars, and loading it into boats.
Walker County Tract Record.
Armes' Story of Coal and Iron, page 54.

GIBSON, GEORGE W., entered government land in Section 4, Township 15, Range 6, on December 21, 1835.
Walker County Tract Record.

GIBSON, WILLIAM N., entered government land in Section 4, Township 15, Range 6, on December 14, 1835.
Walker County Tract Record.

GIBSON, JOHN A., entered government land in Section 15, Township 13, Range 8, on January 14, 1837.
Walker County Tract Record.

GIBSON, DANIEL JAMES, was born October 26, 1836, on the Warrior River, near Cordova. On April 10, 1862, he enlisted as a private in Company K, Fiftieth Alabama Infantry, under Captain Hutto. In September, 1862, he was discharged by a medical board at Farmington, Miss. He was married to Nancy Gaines, a daughter of Edmond Thomas and Ann (McDowell) Gaines. Children—H. P. Gibson, of Jasper, and Ann Gibson, who married B. F. Jeffries, of Fayette, Ala.
Census of Confederate Soldiers, 1907.
Gaines Family Records.

GILCREASE, EDMOND, a pioneer settler in the southern part of the county, entered government land in Section 22, Township 16, Range 8, on March 16, 1825. Little is known of him, other than that he was a farmer all of his life. He was married twice, the first wife's name being unknown, while the second wife was Mary E. Gilcrease. Children, by first marriage —Frances Gilcrease, who married Jacob R. Shepherd, who served as a Captain during the Civil War and later was Probate Judge of the county; July Gilcrease, who married Thomas N. Rose; Jane Gilcrease, who married John Humber and moved to Texas; John M. Gilcrease. Children by second marriage— Edmond Gilcrease, Adaline Gilcrease, Clarinda Gilcrease, Missouri B. Gilcrease, Robert Gilcrease, Susan Gilcrease, and Martha Gilcrease. Edmond Gilcrease died on July 8, 1875.

Walker County Tract Record.
Probate Record, Estate Edmond Gilcrease.

GILDER, Dr. JAMES L., was born at Lafayette, Chambers County, Ala., and died at Eldridge in 1890. Reared at Lafayette, he graduated from the De Graffenberry Medical College at Tuskegee, and subsequently from the Emory Medical College at Atlanta, with the degree of Doctor of Medicine. In 1853 he was given a license to practice in Macon County, but later moved to Coosa County, and, finally, in 1865, came to Walker County and settled on the present site of Carbon Hill. He became a distinguished physician, a prominent man active in the Democratic party, and Superintendent of Education in 1870. He was also an eloquent preacher in the Missionary Baptist Church. During the Civil War he served as First Lieutenant in Company H, Thirteenth Alabama Infantry. He was married to Mary Ann Suttle, who was born in Rockford, Coosa County, in 1835, and died at Carbon Hill in 1910. She was a daughter of Judge Isaac W. Suttle, for twenty-five years the Judge of Probate of Coosa County.

Moore's Alabama, Vol. III, page 89.

GILDER, Dr. GEORGE SUTTLE, a son of Dr. James L. and Mary Ann (Suttle) Gilder, was born August 20, 1870, on a farm three miles south of Carbon Hill. He graduated from the medical department of the University of Alabama in 1893, with the degree of Doctor of Medicine, and began his practice at Carbon Hill, and in 1897 became surgeon for the Galloway Coal Company. He became very active in the Democratic party, and was elected mayor of Carbon Hill for four consecutive terms. In 1922 he was defeated for the office of Probate Judge by a very few votes. He was married to Martha Catherine Kelley, who was born at Eldridge on October 6, 1872. Children— Clarence Kelley Gilder, who married Clyda Brotherton, daughter of Clyde B. and Lima (Patterson) Brotherton, of Jasper; Everette, who married John M. Malone, of Birmingham; Bessie, who married Dr. Lucius L. Terry, of Dora; and Charles Haddon Gilder.

Moore's Alabama, Vol. III, page 89.

GLAZE, WILLIAM, entered government land in Section 33, Township 16, Range 6, on November 26, 1834.

Walker County Tract Record.

GLOVER, LOUIS A., entered government land in Section 5, Township 16, Range 5, on January 29, 1855.

Walker County Tract Record.

GOODWIN, WILLIAM H., entered government land in Section 8, Township 16, Range 6, on May 28, 1860.

Walker County Tract Record.

GORD, WILLIAM A., entered government land in Section 1, Township 14, Range 7, on November 14, 1859.

Walker County Tract Record.

GORE, GEORGE W., entered government land in Section 10, Township 14, Range 6, on October 21, 1846.

Walker County Tract Record.

GRACE, JOHN, a native of Zebulon, Pike County, Georgia, was born on February 14, 1789. Reared in Georgia, he spent most of his life in that state. When seventy years old he came to Walker County and entered government land in Section 30,

Township 14, Range 7, near Jasper, on April 1, 1859. He died on November 7, 1889, and is buried in the Tubb Graveyard. He was married in Georgia to Mary Polly Caldwell, who was born in 1792, and died in 1890, and is buried in the Tubb Graveyard. Children:

Daniel Grace, who married Salina Hill. Children—Vonie Grace, who married Thomas Jones; and Lucinda Grace, who married John H. Swindle.

William Grace, who never came to Walker County.

John Grace, who lived in Pickens County, and came to Walker County shortly after the Civil War. He was married in Georgia to Hannah Culpepper, who was born November 15, 1835, and died May 17, 1887, and is buried in the Pleasant Grove Graveyard. Children—Sarah J. Grace, who married Dr. John Manasco, a son of General John and Lucinda (Lester) Manasco; Rosa Grace, who married Reuben Dutton; Nancy Grace, who married Robert Bonner; John T. Grace, who married Martha Ashcraft; Joseph J. Grace, who married Abagail Kitchens; Nathan Grace, who married a Miss Boshell; Rebecca Grace; and Mollie Grace.

Joshua B. Grace, born in 1832, died May 16, 1875, and buried in the Davis Graveyard at Coal Valley. He was married to Mary Adcock, who was born December 16, 1838, and died October 21, 1923, and is buried in the Pleasant Grove Graveyard. Children—William, who married Susan Banks; John E. Grace, who married Annie Sparks; Joshua, who married, first, Martha Banks, a sister to Susan Banks, and second, Sarah Jane Dutton; Elizabeth Grace, who never married; Ellen Grace, who married Isaac Davis; Martha Jane Grace, who married Noah Banks; Margaret Grace, who married Will Banks; Salina Grace, who married John W. Myers; and Belle Grace, who married a Mr. Bonner.

Young Grace, who married Mrs. Jane (Randolph) Myers, the

widow of Richard Myers and a sister to Martha Randolph, who married his brother, Nathan Grace. Children—Malissa Grace, who married a Mr. Murph; Viola Grace, who never married; Maude, who never married; William Grace, who married Alzah Roberts; Elizabeth Grace, who married a Mr. Swanson; Blanche Grace, who married Alonzo Cain; and Leroy Grace.

Salina Grace, who married John Knight. Children—Polly Knight, who married O. C. Miller; Lila Knight, who married George McLain; Eliza Knight, who married David Thomas; Emily Knight, who married James E. Sparks; Susan Knight, who married Giles Baker; and John Knight, who never married.

James Andrew Grace and Nathan Pennington Grace, whose sketches are given below.

Owens' Alabama, Vol. IV, page 1151.
Grace Family Records.
Gravestones.

GRACE, JAMES ANDREW, a son of John and Mary Polly (Caldwell) Grace, was born February 11, 1833, in Zebulon, Pike County, Georgia. He came to Walker County about 1859 and settled near Jasper. In the fall of 1862 he enlisted at Jasper as a private in Company B, Tenth Alabama Cavalry, under Captain Whatley, and served until the close of the war. Returning to Walker County, he farmed until his death. He died on August 2, 1914, and is buried in the Tubb Graveyard. He was a Free Will Baptist preacher and desired to be buried in a homemade coffin and that his Bible be buried with him. He was married to Emily Odom, a daughter of James and Mary E. (Odom) Odom, who was born in Georgia on March 5, 1840, and died July 9, 1925, and is buried in the Tubb Graveyard. Children—James T. Grace, who married, first, Mattie Minor, second, Susan Minor, his sister-in-law; third, Phoeba Jane Handley; Mary A. Grace, who married James M. Chism; Nathan A. Grace, who married Menta Wethington; Martha E.

Grace, who married George S. Randolph; Sarah C. Grace, who married Erastus Lollar; William H. Grace, who married Julia Tubb; Ronie Grace, never married; and Chester Victor Grace, who married Maude Carpenter.

Census of Confederate Soldiers, 1907.
Mountain Eagle, 1914.
Grace Family Records.
Gravestones.

GRACE, NATHAN PENNINGTON, a son of John and Mary Polly (Caldwell) Grace, was born May 7, 1842, at Zebulon, Pike County, Georgia. He came to Walker County about 1859 and settled near Jasper. On August 20, 1861, he enlisted at Jasper as second corporal in Company I, Fiftieth Alabama Infantry, under Captain Long, and on December 20, 1863, re-enlisted in Company E, Fifth Alabama Cavalry, under Captain T. J. White. He died on January 7, 1913, and is buried in the Tubb Graveyard. He was married to Martha E. Randolph, who was born September 19, 1840, and died June 8, 1888, and is buried in the Tubb Graveyard. Upon the death of his first wife, Mr. Grace married Mrs. Missouri (Odom) Bonner, the widow of James Bonner. Children, all from first marriage—James Campbell Grace, who married after leaving the county; Mary Jane Grace, who married John E. Hooker; John L. Grace, who married Hassie Davidson; MaNelle Grace, who married a Miss Knight; Minnie Grace, who married John F. Randolph.

Census of Confederate Soldiers, 1907.
Grace Family Records.
Gravestones.

GRACE, JOHN EDMOND, a son of Joshua B. and Mary (Adcock) Grace, was born in Georgia on September 14, 1858. Brought to Alabama by his parents while still an infant, he spent his entire life in Walker County. He was a farmer, but spent some time in public office, serving as deputy sheriff and as county commissioner for two terms. He died on February 4, 1934, and is buried in the Pleasant Grove Graveyard. He was married to Annie Sparks. Children—Eula Grace, who married Robert Steadman; Ada Grace, who married a Mr. Anderson, of Chicago; Thomas Grace; Fred Grace; and Jesse Grace.

Mountain Eagle, September 7, 1934.
Jasper Advertiser, September 7, 1934.

GRAVLEE, WILLIAM, a son of Labam Gravlee, of Virginia, was born in Tennessee about 1801. William Gravlee came to Walker County about 1819, and in 1837 he entered government land in Section 2, Township 14, Range 5. In the early 1840's he was engaged in mining coal near Cordova and ran a transportation line of boats on the Warrior River. In 1861 he was elected to represent Walker County in the state Legislature. He died in 1892 at the age of ninety-one. He was married to Martha K. Fowler, a native of South Carolina. Children— Walter G. Gravlee, John David Gravlee, Harvey Jackson Gravlee.

Memorial Record, Vol. II, page 1022.
Armes' Story of Coal and Iron.

GRAVLEE, WALTER G., a son of William and Martha K. (Fowler) Gravlee, was born in Walker County on March 31, 1838. Reared on his father's farm and educated in the county schools, he became a prominent merchant and owner of considerable real estate. During the period of the Civil War he was the owner of a grist mill, and, as it was necessary that grain be ground into flour, he was exempted from military service and detailed to remain at home and operate the mill. In 1858 he was married to Sarah A. E. Roberts, a daughter of Abraham M. Roberts, of Georgia. Children—John A. Gravlee, who was cashier of the Jasper Trust Company; Walter F. Gravlee, who was a merchant in Jasper; Joseph M. Gravlee, who was a lawyer in Jasper; and W. L. Gravlee, who was a physician at Marietta.

Memorial Record, Vol. II, page 1022.

GRAVLEE, JOHN DAVID, a son of William and Martha K. (Fowler) Gravlee, was born on the Mulberry River on December 15, 1841. On September 10, 1862, he enlisted at Jasper as a private in Company F, Fifty-sixth Alabama Cavalry. In August, 1863, he was sent home on unlimited sick leave and never returned to service.

Census of Confederate Soldiers, 1907.

GRAVLEE, HARVEY JACKSON, a son of William and Martha K. (Fowler) Gravlee, was born at Gravleeton on February 18, 1847. On June 10, 1864, he enlisted at Jasper as a private in Captain Reed's company, Musgrove's Battalion of Cavalry, and served until the close of the war.

Census of Confederate Soldiers, 1907.

GRAY, WILSON ALEXANDER, a son of Merrill and Minerva (Cooper) Gray, was born in Henry County, Georgia, on March 20, 1852. Receiving only a limited education he was a farmer and miner all of his life. He came to Walker County in the early 1880's and lived at Cordova. In 1903 he was one of the representatives in the Legislature from Walker County. On January 17, 1871, he was married to Amelia Wise, daughter of John and Elizabeth Morgan (Jackson) Wise, of Henry County, Georgia.

Owens' Alabama, Vol. III, page 695.

GREEN, BENJAMIN M., entered government land in Section 28, Township 14, Range 9, on February 18, 1836.

Walker County Tract Record.

GREGORY, SAMUEL S., entered government land in Section 10, Township 15, Range 9, on February 14, 1837.

Walker County Tract Record.

GUIN, WILLIAM C., entered government land in Section 5, Township 16, Range 8, on December 26, 1835.

Walker County Tract Record.

GUNTER, SAMUEL M., born on March 8, 1828, in Cannon County, Tennessee, moved to Pickens County, Alabama, when quite young. He was educated at Irwin College, McMinnville, Tennessee. During the Civil War he served as Colonel commanding a Tennessee Regiment in the celebrated Pat Cleburn Division, and won distinction as a gallant and efficient soldier. Soon after the close of the war he moved from Pickens County to Jasper and engaged in the practice of law. On July 4, 1878, he started the Walker County Times, a weekly newspaper, owned by L. B. Musgrove, but edited by Mr. Gunter, who was a most scholarly gentleman, facile, and a ready and strong writer. The Times, under Mr. Gunter's able guidance, soon became a power, but the venture demonstrated that Jasper could not support two newspapers. The Times and its competitor, the Mountain Eagle, were neither a financial success. Mr. Musgrove then purchased the Mountain Eagle, consolidated it with the Times, and called the new paper the Mountain Eagle. Mr. Gunter continued as editor of the Mountain Eagle until 1884, when he severed his connection and became publisher and proprietor of the True Citizen, which survived for only a few years. Mr. Gunter then returned as editor of the Mountain Eagle, and continued with it until his death in 1890. He was an able lawyer, a Jacksonian Democrat, and was prominent in political affairs, although he never held public office. He died at his home in East Jasper on October 25, 1890. He was the father of four sons—P. B. Gunter, W. W. Gunter, J. R. Gunter, and P. M. Gunter; and of three daughters—Fannie Gunter, who married H. S. Argo; Pernia Gunter, who married J. D. O'Rear; and Hatton Gunter, who married Martin O'Rear.

Mountain Eagle, October 2, 1895.
Jasper Headlight, October 27, 1890.

GURGANUS, JOHN WASHINGTON, Sr., a native of South Carolina, came to Walker County in the late 1820's or early 1830's and settled on a farm near the present site of Oakman. He was also active in the mining of coal and the transportation of products on the Warrior River. In 1850 he, together with Robert Cain, a son of James Cain, secured a government contract to dam the waters on the south side of Black Rock Shoals, throw the waters to the north bank, and thereby make a safer channel. Mr. Gurganus was active in Walker County for many years, but finally moved to Texas and died near Dallas. In 1827 he was married to Sarah Earnest, a native of Alabama, who was born in 1806 and died in 1852, and is buried at Liberty Hill. Mr. Gurganus was connected with the early Methodist Church in Walker County, and in a report of a quarterly conference, held on June 4, 1833, he is listed as an exhorter.

West's History of Methodism, page 549.
Moore's Alabama, Vol. III, page 189.
Armes' Story of Coal and Iron, page 54.

GURGANUS, JOHN WASHINGTON, JR., a son of John Washington and Sarah (Earnest) Gurganus, was born April 27, 1831, on Indian Creek, near Liberty Hill Church, Walker County. In early manhood he located on a farm nine miles south of Oakman, where he was a prosperous farmer and a good citizen. On September 15, 1861, he enlisted at Tierce's Store, on Lost Creek, as a private in Company K, Fiftieth Alabama Infantry, under Captain Hutto, and served until the close of the war. Returning to his farm, the village of Gurganus grew up on his homestead and he served as its postmaster for many years. He was also a justice of the peace, a notary public, and took active part in the Democratic party, and in the support of the Methodist Church. He died on September 7, 1919, and is buried in the Fairview Graveyard. He was married to Melissa Waller, who was born in Hale County, Alabama, on April 11, 1833, and died November 13, 1894, and is buried in Fairview Graveyard. Children—Sarah Gurganus, who married B. Thacker, a farmer at

Patton, Ala.; James F. Gurganus, who never married; Jane Gurganus, who never married; Elizabeth Gurganus, who married Erastus Hutto; Martha Frances Gurganus, who never married; Joseph Gurganus, a rural mail carrier; William Gurganus, a physician, who married Susan I. Whitney, a daughter of William T. and Amelia Whitney, of Paragould, Arkansas; Windham Gurganus; and Robert Gurganus.

Census of Confederate Soldiers, 1907.
Moore's Alabama, Vol. III, page 139.
Gravestones.

GURGANUS, ISAAC, born September 16, 1840, at Longhee, Arkansas, enlisted in Company A, Sixth Louisiana Infantry, and served throughout the Civil War. After the close of the war he came to Walker County, where he lived until his death, when he was buried in Fairview Graveyard. His daughter, Viola A. Gurganus, was married on May 30, 1887, to Thomas N. Gabbert, of Jasper.

Census of Confederate Soldiers, 1907.
Mountain Eagle, June 2, 1887.

GURLEY, NATHANIEL W., entered government land in Section 8, Township 14, Range 6, on July 9, 1855.

Walker County Tract Record.

GUTTERY, WILLIAM, a descendant of an old pioneer family that settled near Charleston, South Carolina, moved with his wife, Hannah Guttery, from his home in Georgia to Lincoln County, Tennessee, and later came to Walker County, shortly before 1820, settling near the present site of Holly Grove. Little is known of William Guttery, he having died on July 7, 1825, just a few years after coming to the county. He is believed to have been among the very first settlers, if not the first, in this section of the county. That he was a farmer is a self-evident fact. The later accomplishments of his sons would indicate that their parents were exceptional people for their day and time and environment, and afforded their children the education and training that permitted them to become outstanding citizens, and leaders in the religious, political and economic life of the county.

Northern Alabama.
Armes' Story of Coal and Iron.
Owens' Alabama, Vol. III, page 717.

GUTTERY, ROBERT, the eldest son of William and Hannah Guttery, was born in Georgia on February 26, 1801, and was brought by his parents, first, to Lincoln County, Tennessee, and later to Walker County, in his young manhood, his father having settled near Holly Grove shortly before 1820. He was reared on a wilderness farm, where opportunities for education and other advantages were sadly lacking. However, through training and precept Robert Guttery was deeply religious. In 1824 he joined the Primitive Baptist Church at Holly Grove, and in 1826 he was ordained a minister of that faith, serving as such for fifty-one years. Col. E. A. Powell, in his Fifty-five Years in West Alabama, says of him: "Robert Guttery may be justly considered the father of the Primitive Baptist denomination in Walker County. He and his brothers were the first settlers on Wolf and Lost Creeks. There were three of them preachers in that denomination. They were all true and upright men—good citizens. Robert Guttery was considered the leading character in his neighborhood. No man occupied a higher position in the community than he did. He never sought public office, but in 1860 he was brought out by the Conservative Party to represent Walker County in the convention of that year, known as the Secession Convention, which assembled early in January, 1861. In that convention he sided with the anti-secession party and voted first to submit the ordinace to the people for ratification. That proposition failing, he voted against the passage of the ordinance and refused to sign the same after it was passed. (A total of twenty-four representatives refused to sign the ordinance.) But after the thing was done and resulted in the war, no one was truer to the South than he was. After the close of the war he took the true conservative ground, and his entire influence was on the side of a restoration of civil authority and the peace and quiet of the country." Robert Guttery was too old for military service, but several of his sons fought valiantly for the Confederacy. Aside from his religious and political activities, Robert Guttery was a successful farmer and merchant, and engaged in the mercantile business both at Holly Grove and Jasper. He spent his entire life in the vicinity of Holly Grove. He died on April 6, 1877, and is buried in the Boshell Graveyard, near Townley. On November 11, 1821, he was married to Sarah Ann Williams, the daughter of Robert Williams, a pioneer settler near Townley. She was born May 8, 1804, and died February 8, 1881, and is buried in the Boshell Graveyard, near Townley. Children—

John Guttery, born August 30, 1822, died January 30, 1883, and buried in the Guttery Graveyard at Townley.

Catherine Guttery, born March 22, 1824.

William Guttery, born December 12, 1825, died in Texas on April 6, 1890.

Isham Guttery, born September 30, 1827, and was married to Nancy Romine on October 29, 1848.

B. F. Guttery, born December 8, 1829, died in infancy.

Elizabeth Guttery, married and moved to Luling, Texas.

J. Russell Guttery, born December 12, 1833.

Martha Ann Guttery, born December 24, 1834.

A. J. Guttery, born May 19, 1837, died August 4, 1889. He married Araminta Ann Miller, the daughter of Dr. L. C. Miller, on October 10, 1861.

L. J. Guttery, born March 27, 1839, died a soldier at Okolona, Miss., on August 13, 1862, and is buried in the Boshell Graveyard at Townley.

Robert M. Guttery, born March 29, 1842, died April 25, 1903. He was married to Lucinda King, daughter of John and Lucinda King, who was born August 6, 1849, and died June 4, 1881.

Newton W. Guttery, born March 6, 1844.

Sarah Guttery, born April 6, 1846, died in infancy.

George Houston Guttery, born September 15, 1847, died December 5, 1911. Sketch given below.

Johnson Guttery, born July 15, 1850, died October 16, 1881.

> Northern Alabama.
> Armes' Story of Coal and Iron.
> Mountain Eagle, October 14, 1887.
> Robert Guttery's Bible.
> Gravestones.

GUTTERY, JOHNSON, a son of William and Hannah Guttery, was born in Georgia on March 12, 1806, and was brought to Walker County by his parents when he was still a young boy. Reared on his father's farm near Holly Grove, he underwent all the hardships of a pioneer life. Coming from a deeply religious family, he followed in the footsteps of his older brother, Robert, and joined the Primitive Baptist Church in 1826. In 1839 he was ordained a minister of that denomination, and faithfully served as such for thirty-seven years. He never sought and was never elected to public office, but he wielded considerable influence and was ever supporting his brother, Robert, in his public utterances. He was a successful farmer and spent his entire life in the vicinity of Holly Grove. He died May 23, 1876, and is buried in the Boshell Graveyard at Townley. On November 24, 1824, he was married to Mary Wilson, who was born July 22, 1807, and died October 13, 1885.

> Mountain Eagle, December 9, 1885.
> Gravestones.

GUTTERY, ISHAM, a son of William and Hannah Guttery, was born in Georgia on January 6, 1813. Brought to Walker

County by his parents while still a boy, he was reared on his father's farm near Holly Grove. He was a prominent minister in the Primitive Baptist Church, and along with his brothers, Robert and Johnson, had much to do with the establishment of that denomination in Walker County. He died on August 17, 1882, and is buried at New Prospect. He was married to Sarah Ann Brown, a daughter of John and Martha (Clack) Brown, who was born at Chester, S. C., on April 27, 1832, and died October 1, 1896.

Gravestones.

GUTTERY, JOSEPH G., was born near Holly Grove on May 14, 1836. On September 6, 1862, he enlisted at Holly Grove as a private in Company A, Fifty-sixth Alabama Cavalry, under Captain A. J. Guttery.

Census of Confederate Soldiers, 1907.

GUTTERY, CAPTAIN A. J., a son of Robert and Sarah Ann (Williams) Guttery, was born at Holly Grove on May 19, 1837. In 1862 he enlisted and was elected captain of Company A, Fifty-sixth Alabama Cavalry, which was a part of Hewlett's Battalion of Cavalry. Captain Guttery was captured at Resaca, Georgia, and was imprisoned at Johnson's Island for the balance of the war. After the close of hostilities he returned to Walker County, and lived at Townley until his death on August 4, 1889. He is buried at Holly Grove. On October 10, 1861, he was married to Araminta Ann Miller, a daughter of Dr. Lucius C. and Mary Jane (Leith) Miller, who was born November 18, 1844, and died October 19, 1900. Children—Alabama Guttery, who married W. H. Garrison, of Carbon Hill; Mary Lula Guttery; Alica Aurora Guttery; Lucius Curtis Guttery; John T. Morgan Guttery; and Mae Guttery.

Genealogy of the Branner Family.

GUTTERY, JOHN WILLIS, was born at Pontotoc, Miss., on February 24, 1838. He served throughout the Civil War as a private in Company H, Twenty-second Alabama Infantry. He died on June 20, 1926, and is buried in the Guttery Graveyard, near Townley. His wife, Sarah Elizabeth Guttery, was born June 2, 1844, and died February 5, 1921.

Census of Confederate Soldiers, 1907.
Gravestones.

GUTTERY, MARTIN VAN BUREN, was born at Holly Grove on September 6, 1842. On September 6, 1862, he enlisted at Holly Grove as a private in Company A, Fifty-sixth Alabama Cavalry, under Captain A. J. Guttery. He died on October 22, 1916, and is buried in the Guttery Graveyard at Townley. His wife, Mary E. Guttery, was born February 8, 1844, and died October 22, 1916.

Census of Confederate Soldiers, 1907.
Gravestones.

GUTTERY, GEORGE HOUSTON, a son of Robert and Sarah Ann (Williams) Guttery, was born on a farm on Lost Creek, near Holly Grove, on September 15, 1847. He was reared on the farm, educated at Holly Grove and Jasper, and farmed until the outbreak of the Civil War. In April, 1863, he enlisted at Jasper as a private in Company A, Fifty-sixth Alabama Cavalry, under his brother, Captain A. J. Guttery. He served with Forrest's command in Mississippi, with Johnson's army from Dalton to Atlanta, and was engaged in all the battles in which it participated until and including Peach Tree Creek. In 1866 Mr. Guttery moved from Holly Grove to Jasper and opened a mercantile business which he conducted until 1874, when he was elected sheriff of the county, and served as such until 1877. In the following year Mr. Guttery re-entered the mercantile business. The town of Jasper was incorporated on December 22, 1887, and Mr. Guttery was elected the first mayor, which office he held for several terms. He died in 1911 and is buried in Oak Hill Cemetery at Jasper. He was married to Alice C. Stanley, a daughter of W. L. and Mary P. Stanley. Children—Claud Guttery, Pearl Guttery, and John McQueen Guttery.

> Census of Confederate Soldiers, 1907.
> Northern Alabama, page 177.
> Owens' Alabama, Vol. III, page 717.
> Gravestones.

HALEY, JAMES FRANKLIN, was born February 18, 1832, in Carnesville, Franklin County, Georgia, a son of Joel and Frances (Jones) Haley, who also lived in Madison and Cherokee Counties, Georgia. James Franklin Haley served as First Lieutenant in the Thirty-seventh Georgia Infantry. He was captured at Missionary Ridge just before the battle of Chickamauga, and was imprisoned at Johnson's Island for eighteen months. In 1883 he moved from Marietta, Cherokee County, Georgia, to Jasper, and served as postmaster during the administration of President Cleveland. He died July 10, 1911, and is buried in Oak Hill Cemetery, Jasper. He was maried to Priscilla Joanne Shields, who was born in 1845 and died in 1934; a daughter of Milton and Priscilla (Brabson) Shields, of Marshall's Ferry, Grainger County, Tennessee, and a sister to John Brabson Shields, of Jasper (see sketch on John B. Shields). Children—Curtis B. Haley, of Nashville, Tennessee; Paul S. Haley, of Oakman; Elizabeth Maud Haley, who married Prof. J. Alex Moore.

> Census of Confederate Soldiers, 1907.
> Owens' Alabama, Vol. III, page 1223.

HAMILTON, JOHN B., entered government land in Section 32, Township 15, Range 7, near Bankhead Mines, on September 24, 1835, and in Section 2, Township 16, Range 8, on Cane Creek, west of Jasper, on November 22, 1838.

> Walker County Tract Record.

HAMILTON, HENRY, entered government land in Section 32, Township 13, Range 9, on December 14, 1835.
Walker County Tract Record.

HAMILTON, HARVEY W., born October 26, 1813, came to Walker County with his wife in 1838, and settled on a farm west of Jasper. He and his wife were charter members and helped to organize the Sulphur Springs Primitive Baptist Church on July 6, 1844. He was chosen as the first deacon and was elected clerk, and in August, 1871, was ordained a minister by Elders Robert Guttery and Hiram Barton. In September, 1879, on account of age and deafness, he resigned as clerk, after thirty-five years of service. Too old for military service himself, he had four sons in the Confederate Army. He died on January 28, 1888, and is buried in the Coal City Graveyard. He was married to Mary Polly Kitchens, a daughter of James Matlock and Sallie (Brown) Kitchens, who was born October 20, 1814, and died March 5, 1887. Children—

Sarah Hamilton, who married Francis M. Carmichael. Children—James Taylor Carmichael; July A. R. Carmichael, who married James McLain; Louisa Carmichael, who married Thomas F. Dutton, a son of James Dutton. Their children were William Dutton, James M. Dutton, Josephine Dutton, Malta Dutton, Joseph Dutton, Queen Dutton, and Sarah J. Dutton, who married Joshua Grace.

Barton Hamilton, who was the father of John T. Hamilton; May S. Hamilton, who married James I. McCrary; Mary B. Hamilton, who married Willis M. Jackson; and Sarah E. Hamilton, who married Robert G. Williams.

James J. Hamilton, who was born march 25, 1837, and died January 20, 1891.

Andrew J. Hamilton, who was born February 24, 1839, and died July 15, 1902. His wife, Sarah E. Hamilton, was born December 16, 1837, and died November 8, 1917.

Rebecca Hamilton, who was born May 15, 1840, and died January 18, 1908. She was married to Augustus Alexander Williams.

Jacob B. Hamilton, who was born November 18, 1843.

William P. Hamilton, who moved to Fayette County, Ala. He was the father of William Hamilton, James B. Hamilton, and Harry P. Hamilton.

Isaac Hamilton.

Christopher C. Hamilton, who married Elizabeth A. Dutton, a daughter of James Dutton.

Frances A. Hamilton, who married W. A. Jackson.

Susan M. Hamilton, who married, first, Mack Romine, and, second, James Kilgore. Children—Robert Romine, John Kilgore, Mosella Kilgore, and Etta Kilgore.

May E. Hamilton, born September 14, 1855, died May 12, 1881. She was married to John A. Williams, who was born January 16, 1851, and died February 18, 1914. Children—Cordelia Williams, who married Elijah Dutton; Ida Williams and Sarah Williams.

Sulphur Springs Church Book.
Probate Record, Estate Harvey W. Hamilton.
Gravestones.

HAMILTON, JACOB B., a son of Harvey W. Hamilton, was born November 8, 1843, on Cane Creek, west of Jasper. On February 1, 1862, he enlisted at Jasper as a private in Company E, Twenty-eighth Alabama Infantry, under Captain Henderson. On July 28, 1864, he was severely wounded in the head at Atlanta. Left on the battlefield, he was picked up by the Federals the next day, sent to a hospital and later imprisoned at Camp Douglas, Chicago, Ill., until 1865, when he was sent to Richmond and exchanged through the lines just before Lee's surrender.

Census of Confederate Soldiers, 1907.

HANCOCK, JAMES R., entered government land in Section 10, Township 16, Range 5, on December 10, 1851.
Walker County Tract Record.

HARBIN, JESSE, was a prominent class leader in the Methodist Church in Walker County in 1833.
West's History of Methodism, page 549.

HARBIN, REV. L. B., born in 1812, was a Baptist minister in the High Hill beat, and lived to be more than eighty-three years old.
Mountain Eagle, April 10, 1895.

HARBIN, JAMES LOUIS, born March 3, 1836, on Cedar Creek, in Fayette County; enlisted in April, 1862, at Fayette Courthouse, as Fourth Sergeant in Company A, Twenty-sixth Alabama Infantry. He was captured at Atlanta, Georgia, on July 1, 1864, and imprisoned at Camp Douglas, Ohio, for the balance of the war.
Census of Confederate Soldiers, 1907.

HARRIS, PHILLIP ARCHIBALD, born December 3, 1831, at Blountsville, in Blount County, enlisted at Jasper in Company E, Twenty-eighth Alabama Infantry. He was captured at Missionary Ridge and imprisoned at Rock Island, Illinois, for the balance of the war.
Census of Confederate Soldiers, 1907.

HAWKINS, JOSIAH, born October 1, 1835, in Greenville, South Carolina; enlisted in the Confederate Army at the outbreak of the Civil War, but was detailed as a mechanic at Oxmoor and Irondale, making and repairing wagons for the army. He served on this detail until Wilson's Raiders destroyed the plants in the spring of 1865.
Census of Confederate Soldiers, 1907.

HAYES, DR. JOHN S., born February 9, 1819; came to Walker County from Bibb County sometime subsequent to 1843, and settled in the vicinity of Wyatt. He became one of the county's best known physicians and one of its most respected citizens. He died on August 4, 1895, and is buried in the Wyatt Graveyard. His wife, Roseana Hayes, was born August 10, 1839, and died December 3, 1893. Children—John Henry Hayes and Jeremiah M. Hayes.

Gravestones.

HAYES, JOHN HENRY, a son of Dr. John S. and Roseana Hayes, was born October 3, 1843, at Woodstock, in Bibb County, Alabama. In July, 1861, he enlisted at Tuscaloosa as a private, later promoted to corporal of Company F, Twenty-sixth Alabama Infantry, under Captain Clements. He was captured at Resaca, Georgia, in 1864, and was imprisoned at Camp Douglas, Chicago, Illinois, for the balance of the war. He died on November 21, 1908, and is buried in Oak Hill Cemetery at Jasper. He was married to Mildred Files, a daughter of Richard and Mary (Lindsay) Files, who was born April 27, 1846, and died September 18, 1895. Children—Edgar Hayes; Oscar Hayes; Mollie L. Hayes, who married John E. Lacy (see Lacy); and Alma Hayes, who married Howard Lamar (see Lamar).

Census of Confederate Soldiers, 1907.
Files Family Records.
Gravestones.

HEARD, JOHN KEYS, entered government land in Section 6, Township 16, Range 6, on November 29, 1834.

Walker County Tract Record.

HEARD, THOMAS, entered government land in Section 6, Township 16, Range 6, on November 29, 1834.

Walker County Tract Record.

HELLAMS, WILLIAM, entered government land in Section 29, Township 15, Range 7, on Lost Creek, south of Parrish, on October 10, 1821.

Walker County Tract Record.

HELLUMS, JOHN, entered government land in Section 23, Township 13, Range 10, on August 9, 1822.
Walker County Tract Record.

HENDON, JAMES A., entered government land in Section 7, Township 14, Range 8, near Townley, on November 16, 1833.
Walker County Tract Record.

HENDON, JOHNSON, entered government land in Section 31, Township 13, Range 9, on March 13, 1835.
Walker County Tract Record.

HENDON, JAMES R., entered government land in Section 29, Township 13, Range 9, on January 8, 1840.
Walker County Tract Record.

HENDON, JAMES HARVEY, was born October 19, 1834, near Danville, in Morgan County. On September 1, 1863, he enlisted at Lost Creek as a private in Company B, Tenth Alabama Cavalry. He was captured at High Bridge, on the Appomattox River, in Virginia, on April 6, 1865, and was imprisoned at Newport News until the close of the war. Among his children were Perdie L. Hendon, who was married to L. A. Tierce on February 10, 1895; Sallie R. Hendon, who was married to Thomas J. Scott on February 10, 1895; and T. S. Hendon.
Census of Confederate Soldiers, 1907.
Mountain Eagle, October 8, 1930.

HENDON, T. S., a son of James Harvey Hendon, was born in Walker County in 1853. He was reared on his father's farm and educated in the county schools. He farmed until he was twenty years old and then became a school teacher and rural mail carrier. About 1878 he opened a store at Warrior, in Jefferson County, which he operated for a short time and then returned to Townley and entered business. He was instrumental in the opening of several coal mines near Townley. Mr. Hendon was a public spirited citizen and was ever ready to assist in any enterprise for the betterment of the community. He donated the lots on which the churches in Townley are built and contributed liberally to their support. He also built the baseball park in Townley.

Mountain Eagle, October 8, 1930.

HENDRIX, THOMAS MARTIN, was born December 25, 1841, at Marion, Perry County, Alabama. On April 9, 1861, he enlisted at Marion as a private, and later promoted to corporal and sergeant of Company G, Fourth Alabama Infantry, and served throughout the war. He was wounded at Seven Pines, Knoxville and Gettysburg. He died on June 24, 1913, and is buried in the Zion Graveyard at Parrish. His wife, A. B. Hendrix, was born June 5, 1848, and died March 9, 1925, and is also buried in the Zion Graveyard.

Census of Confederate Soldiers, 1907.
Gravestones.

HENSON, ELI, was born February 14, 1828, in Giles County, Tennessee. In November, 1862, he enlisted at Jasper as a private in Company F, Fifty-sixth Alabama Cavalry, under Captain Rice. He was discharged from a hospital at Macon, Miss., in the fall of 1864, and was physically unable to perform any further military service.

Census of Confederate Soldiers, 1907.

HENSON, JOHN, was born August 22, 1833, in Jefferson County, Illinois. On February 15, 1862, he enlisted at Jasper as a private in Company F, Twenty-eighth Alabama Infantry, under Captain Gamble, and served until the close of the war.

Census of Confederate Soldiers, 1907.

HERRON, AARON, a resident of Walker County in 1907, was born May 15, 1835, at Columbus, Georgia. In August, 1862, he enlisted at Montgomery as a private in Company G, Second Alabama Cavalry, and served until the close of the war.

Census of Confederate Soldiers, 1907.

HERRON, JOSEPH, was born May 13, 1844, near Chilton's Mill, on Lost Creek. In February, 1862, he enlisted at York Post Office (now Oakman) as a private in Company K, Fiftieth Alabama Infantry, under Captain Hutto, and served until the close of the war. He died several years ago and is buried in Fairview Graveyard.

Census of Confederate Soldiers, 1907.
Gravestone.

HERRON, WILLIAM, a member of Company G, Fourth Alabama Infantry, is buried in the Fairview Graveyard.

Gravestone.

HESTER, CHAPMAN, entered government land in Section 3, Township 14, Range 7, near Jasper, on August 17, 1836.

Walker County Tract Record.

HEWLETT, WILLIAM A., a nephew of the Hon. David Hubbard, entered government land in Section 28, Township 14, Range 5, on January 5, 1846. He took a great deal of interest in politics and was elected Judge of the County Court, but owing to the establishment of the Probate system, he served but a short time. He opened a law office in Jasper, and in 1853 he was elected Senator from the district composed of the counties of Lawrence, Winston and Walker, and served for four years. He was the first State Senator elected from Walker County. He was a young man of fine personal appearance, very prepossessing in conversation. He took a good stand in the Senate and was universally popular. Judge Hewlett was a Democrat of the old school, and in 1860 he supported the Breckenridge wing of the Democratic party. After the election of President Lincoln he was an ardent Secessionist, and when the war broke out he organized a battalion of cavalry, the Thirteenth Alabama Partisan Rangers, and was commissioned a major. His battalion was finally consolidated with another and formed into the Fifty-sixth Alabama Partisan Rangers, and Major Hewlett was promoted to the rank of Lieutenant Colonel, the highest rank obtained by any resident of Walker County during the war. After the close of the war Colonel Hewlett moved to Texas.

Walker County Tract Record.
Powell's Fifty-five Years in West Alabama.

HICKS, DANIEL, was born February 18, 1842, on Horse Creek, near Dora. He enlisted in Company G, Twenty-eighth Alabama Infantry, but in October, 1863, he was captured at Chickamauga and imprisoned in a northern prison. He died January 14, 1918, and is buried at Union Chapel.

Census of Confederate Soldiers, 1907.
Gravestone.

HILL, LARKIN, entered government land in Section 8, Township 16, Range 8, on August 24, 1836.

Walker County Tract Record.

HILL, JACOB A., entered government land in Section 12, Township 14, Range 7, on November 10, 1858.

Walker County Tract Record.

HILL, SILAS W., entered government land in Section 1, Township 14, Range 7, on August 26, 1859.

Walker County Tract Record.

HILL, WILLIAM L., entered government land in Section 2, Township 14, Range 7, on October 28, 1859.

Walker County Tract Record.

HILL, REV. JAMES A., was elected to the Senate in 1861 from the district comprising Lawrence, Winston and Walker Counties. Mr. Hill resided in Walker County, and it is believed that he came from Georgia. He was a minister in the Missionary Baptist Church and was considered as being above the average in intellect. His church looked upon him as a man of rather superior ability. In the Senate he was extremely radical. He was in favor of all measures to put everybody, from grandfathers to babes, in the militia. He opposed all measures intended for the protection of the citizens against the illegal assumption of authority over them by military officers. After the war he never returned to Walker County. There was considerable opposition to him, growing out of some hard things that transpired during the war, resulting in the loss of life, which was to some extent charged against him. He moved to Mississippi and became connected with the Orphan's Home at Lauderdale Springs. Later he went farther west.

Powell's Fifty-five Years in West Alabama.

HINSON, JOSHUA, entered government land in Section 19, Township 14, Range 5, on October 6, 1833.

Walker County Tract Record.

HINSON, JOHN, entered government land in Section 15, Township 14, Range 5, on July 12, 1833.

Walker County Tract Record.

HINSON, JOHN, Jr., entered government land in Section 25, Township 14, Range 5, on July 22, 1836.

Walker County Tract Record.

HOLBROOK, JACOB, was born April 5, 1818, and died February 17, 1904. His wife, Fatima E. Holbrook, was born October 17, 1833, and died June 14, 1912. Both are buried in the Day Graveyard at Oakman.

Gravestones.

HOLBROOK, JACOB ELIJAH, was born February 9, 1848, at Eutaw, Greene County, Alabama. On March 18, 1863, he enlisted at Brooksville, Miss., as a private in Company D, Twentieth Mississippi Infantry.

Census of Confederate Soldiers, 1907.

HOLLAND, HENRY, entered government land in Section 20, Township 15, Range 9, on December 24, 1832.

Walker County Tract Record.

HOLLAND, JAMES B., entered government land in Section 20, Township 14, Range 9, on December 21, 1835.
Walker County Tract Record.

HOLLOWAY, ARMISTEAD M., entered government land in Section 22, Township 12, Range 5, on July 18, 1855.
Walker County Tract Record.

HOLLY, JOHN C., entered government land in Section 35, Township 15, Range 8, on Cane Creek, southeast of Oakman, on November 17, 1831.
Walker County Tract Record.

HOLLY, BENJAMIN, entered government land in Section 27, Township 15, Range 8, on December 1, 1836.
Walker County Tract Record.

HOLLY, DAVID, entered government land in Section 28, Township 15, Range 8, on August 11, 1836.
Walker County Tract Record.

HOLT, A. J., a private in Company M, First Alabama Cavalry, was born December 8, 1844; died September 9, 1927, and is buried at Union Chapel, north of Eldridge. His wife, Julia Ann Holt, was born August 20, 1846, and died January 15, 1922, and is buried at Union Chapel.
Gravestones.

HOOD, DAVID, entered government land in Section 36, Township 16, Range 6, on November 21, 1836.
Walker County Tract Record.

HOOD, WILLIAM P., entered government land in Section 17, Township 16, Range 5, on October 29, 1855.
Walker County Tract Record.

HOOD, ANDREW JACKSON WILLIS, was born August 6, 1844, at Village Creek, on Little Warrior River, Jefferson County, Alabama. In September, 1862, he enlisted at Jasper as a private in Company F, Fifty-sixth Alabama Cavalry, under Captain Rice, and served until the close of the war.

Census of Confederate Soldiers, 1907.

HOPKINS, ISAAC F., entered government land in Section 28, Township 14, Range 7, on December 19, 1835.

Walker County Tract Record.

HOPKINS, ROBERT, entered government land in Section 27, Township 17, Range 7, on December 22, 1838.

Walker County Tract Record.

HOPSON, A., was born January 5, 1847, at Flat Shoals, Meriwether County, Georgia. In January, 1862, he enlisted at Dadeville, Ala., as a private in Company G, Thirty-fourth Alabama Infantry, and served until the close of the war.

Census of Confederate Soldiers, 1907.

HUBBARD, DAVID, entered government land in Section 22, Township 14, Range 5, on July 14, 1820.

Walker County Tract Record.

HUDSON, ELIJAH H., entered government land in Section 9, Township 14, Range 8, west of Jasper, on March 10, 1826.

Walker County Tract Record.

HUDSON, DANIEL G., entered government land in Section 31, Township 14, Range 9, on March 7, 1836.

Walker County Tract Record.

HUDSON, LEONARD, entered government land in Section 29, Township 13, Range 7, on November 24, 1860. He was married to Martha E. Brown, who was born September 19, 1825, and died October 17, 1906, and is buried at New Prospect.

Walker County Tract Record.
Gravestones.

HUGHES, JOHN B., was born in Tuscaloosa County, February 6, 1838. He was reared on a farm and received his early education from the county schools and the academy at Taylors-

EARLY SETTLERS

ville. He worked for some time in a tannery, but at the outbreak of the Civil War he joined Company G, Eleventh Alabama Regiment. In 1861 he was made Lieutenant and in 1862 was promoted to Captain. He was in the first battle of Manassas and all other important battles of the army of Northern Virginia, and was present at the surrender at Appomattox. He was once captured and imprisoned at Washington and Fort Delaware and was wounded at Sharpsburg and Gettysburg. In 1881 Captain Hughes was appointed Clerk of the Circuit Court in Jasper, and at the organization of the Walker County Bank, in 1887, was made cashier of that institution.

Northern Alabama, page 175.

HULSEY, JOHN BAYLESS, was born March 8, 1839, on Cane Creek, near Cordova. In February, 1862, he enlisted at Jasper as a private in Company I, Fiftieth Alabama Infantry, under Captain Long. He was wounded at Shiloh on April 6, 1862. After recovering from this wound he re-enlisted in September, 1862, as a private in Company G, Fifty-sixth Alabama Cavalry, under Captain Shepherd, but was discharged by Dr. W. C. Rosamond, the company surgeon, at Columbus, Miss., in December, 1863. In January, 1864, he again re-enlisted at Jasper as third lieutenant in Company G, Eighth Alabama Cavalry, and served until the close of the war.

Census of Confederate Soldiers, 1907.

HUTTO, JOHN C., was born in the Abbeville District, S. C., on August 25, 1830, and came to Walker County with his parents while still a young man. Reared on the farm, he followed that profession until the outbreak of the Civil War, when he recruited a company of volunteers for service with the Confederate Army and was elected captain of Company K, Fiftieth Alabama Infantry. He was later promoted to the rank of major in the Thirtieth Alabama Infantry. At the conclusion of the war Major Hutto returned to his farm in Walker County and later entered the mercantile business at Marietta. In 1878 he was elected a Representative in the Legislature and served for one term, during the sessions of 1878-1879. He was a Mason and a member of the Primitive Baptist Church. He died on May 15, 1887, and is buried at Liberty Hill. His wife, Elizabeth Hutto, born September 21, 1837, died February 10, 1903, and is also buried at Liberty Hill. She was a daughter of Tinson and Minerva (Raburn) Shepherd.

Mountain Eagle, June 12, 1887, and January 11, 1888.
Gravestones.

HUTTO, CHARLES, was born September 25, 1825, near Jackson, on Yellow Water, Butts County, Georgia. On February 14, 1862, he enlisted at Jasper as a private in Company E, Twenty-eighth Alabama Infantry, under Captain Hutto, and served until the close of the war. He died on August 30, 1911, and is buried at Samaria. His wife, Amanda Hutto, born August 16, 1828, died September 9, 1911, and is also buried at Samaria. She was a daughter of Richard and Elizabeth McDuff. Children—Richard Hutto and Louise Hutto.

Census of Confederate Soldiers, 1907.
Gravestones.

HYCHE, THOMAS BAYNES, was born August 6, 1835, at Northport, Tuscaloosa County. In September, 1862, he enlisted at Jasper as a private in Company G, Fifty-sixth Alabama Cavalry, under Captain Shepherd, and served until the close of the war.

Census of Confederate Soldiers, 1907.

HYCHE, JOSEPH CLAYTON, was born December 15, 1842, at Northport, Tuscaloosa County. In August, 1861, he enlisted at Liberty Church, on the line between Jefferson and Tuscaloosa Counties, as a private in Company G, Twenty-sixth Alabama Infantry, and served until the close of the war.

Census of Confederate Soldiers, 1907.

HYCHE, HARMON LIPSCOMB, was born January 3, 1843, at Northport, Tuscaloosa County. On September 10, 1861, he enlisted at Jasper as a private in Company G, Twenty-sixth Alabama Infantry, under Captain Long. He was wounded at Atlanta on August 2, 1864, and sent to a hospital. The surrender occurred before his recovery.
Census of Confederate Soldiers, 1907.

HYCHE, JACKSON ELI, was born June 6, 1848, near Northport, Tuscaloosa County. On March 1, 1864, he enlisted at Selma as a private in Company G, Twenty-sixth Alabama Infantry, and served until the close of the war. He died on March 31, 1928, and is buried at Union Chapel. His wife, N. L. Hyche, was born May 6, 1852, and died June 12, 1923, and is also buried at Union Chapel.
Census of Confederate Soldiers, 1907.

INGLE, ANDREW L., entered government land in Section 28, Township 12, Range 9, on November 28, 1849.
Walker County Tract Record.

INGRAM, SOLOMON, entered government land in Section 36, Township 14, Range 4, on April 5, 1851.
Walker County Tract Record.

INMAN, HENRY, entered government land in Section 9, Township 13, Range 5, on December 22, 1853.
Walker County Tract Record.

IRWIN, JOHN, entered government land in Section 7, Township 14, Range 8, near Jasper, on January 24, 1837. He became Clerk of the County Court, but when the Probate system was inaugurated he was elected the first Judge of Probate. However, in 1852 he resigned and ran for the Legislature against General John Manasco, whom he defeated, but he only served for one term, during the sessions of 1853–1854, and was defeated by Manasco in 1855. Later in life he moved to Chickasaw County, Mississippi.

Powell's Fifty-five Years in West Alabama.
Mountain Eagle, November 2, 1887.

IVY, WARREN HILL, was born October 17, 1841, in Walton County, Georgia. On September 20, 1862, he enlisted at Jasper as a private in Company F, Fifty-sixth Alabama Cavalry, under Captain Rice, and served until the close of the war.

Census of Confederate Soldiers, 1907.

IVY, YOUNG MARION, was born April 10, 1844, twelve miles north of Jasper. In the fall of 1863 he enlisted at Jasper as a private in the Fifty-sixth Alabama Cavalry, under Captain Bibb, and served until the close of the war.

Census of Confederate Soldiers, 1907.

JACKSON, WASHINGTON, entered government land in Section 5, Township 14, Range 8, on April 9, 1835.

Walker County Tract Record.

JACKSON, SAMUEL, born in 1799, entered government land in Walker County in 1836. He died on April 21, 1895, and is buried at Sardis, five miles south of Jasper. A daughter, Nancy Jackson, born July, 1820, died March 1, 1900, is buried in the Dutton Graveyard. She married Thomas Childers.

Walker County Tract Record.
Mountain Eagle, April 24, 1895.

JACKSON, SAMUEL, born in Walker County on February 14, 1849, was reared on his father's farm until the outbreak of the Civil War, when he entered the Confederate Army as a private soldier, and served throughout the struggle. After the close of the war he returned to his farm, but was elected and served one term as Sheriff of the county. He died on September 18, 1879, and is buried in the Dutton Graveyard.

Moore's Alabama, Vol. III, page 147.
Gravestones.

JACKSON, SAMUEL, Jr., a son of Samuel and Elizabeth Jackson, was born in Walker County about 1865, and was a successful farmer all of his life on his farm two miles west of Calumet. Mr. Jackson was married twice—first to Josephine Thomas, who was born in Walker County in 1865 and died near Hillard in 1895. His second marriage was to Mattie Nelson, who was born near Corona. Children by first marriage —Newbern J. Jackson; Andrew Jackson; Samuel Walter Jackson, who married Mollie Sides; and Etta Jackson, who married William Miller. By the second marriage, Colie Jackson; Robert Jackson; Meladine Jackson; Magdeline Jackson, who married Hewitt Kilgore; and Tempie Jackson, who married William Robinson.

Moore's Alabama, Vol. III, page 147.

JACOBS, DAVID, entered government land in Section 3, Township 14, Range 4, on February 21, 1855.

Walker County Tract Record.

JAMES, WILLIAM, entered government land in Section 26, Township 14, Range 5, on December 11, 1855.

Walker County Tract Record.

JELTON, EPHRAIM, entered government land in Section 32, Township 14, Range 6, on March 12, 1836.

Walker County Tract Record.

JELTON, JOSEPH SYLVESTER, was born March 17, 1830, at Quincy, Gadsden County, Florida. On March 3, 1863, he enlisted as a private in Company G, Fifty-sixth Alabama Cavalry, under Captain Shepherd. He was captured in Walker County by Wilson's Raiders in the spring of 1865 and was imprisoned at Selma until the close of the war.

Census of Confederate Soldiers, 1907.

JENKINS, WILLIAM, entered government land in Section 32, Township 15, Range 9, on August 15, 1836.

Walker County Tract Record.

JENKINS, RUFUS HENRY, was born December 27, 1826, near Tuscaloosa, Alabama. In April, 1861, he enlisted at Tuscaloosa as a private in Company F, Forty-first Alabama Infantry. He was captured near Knoxville in January, 1864, and was imprisoned at Rock Island, Ill., for the balance of the war.
Census of Confederate Soldiers, 1907.

JOHNSON, MOSES, entered government land in Section 4, Township 15, Range 6, on Cane Creek, near Cordova, on August 19, 1824.
Walker County Tract Record.

JOHNSON, NEHEMIAH, entered government land in Section 31, Township 14, Range 9, on December 31, 1834.
Walker County Tract Record.

JOHNSON, WILLIAM B., entered government land in Section 31, Township 14, Range 9, on February 18, 1836.
Walker County Tract Record.

JOHNSON, JAMES ALLEN, was born October 23, 1825, two miles north of Savannah, Georgia. On November 2, 1862, he enlisted at Eldridge as a private in Company K, Fourth Alabama Cavalry, under Captain Kelley, and served until the close of the war. He died on May 18, 1911, and is buried in the Cooner Graveyard at Coal City.
Census of Confederate Soldiers, 1907.
Gravestones.

JOHNSTON, JESSE, a pioneer settler of Walker County, was born in South Carolina of Scotch parents. While still a young man he moved to Lincoln County, Tennessee, and in the 1820's moved to Perryville, Alabama. In 1833 he moved to Walker County and settled near Wilmington, where he engaged in farming for the rest of his life. He was married to Barbara Le Crone, a native of Holland, who died in Walker County.
Moore's Alabama, Vol. III, page 439.

JOHNSTON, ALLEN H., a son of Jesse and Barbara Johnston, was born February 1, 1830, at Perryville, Perry County, Alabama, but was brought to Walker County by his parents in 1833, when but three years of age. He was reared on his father's farm near Wilmington, and in his younger days taught school. At the outbreak of the Civil War he enlisted in the Confederate Army and served until the close of hostilities, when he returned to his home in Walker County and engaged in farming. He retired from the farm in 1904 and moved to Oakman, where he died on November 3, 1906, and is buried in the Day Graveyard at that place. He was married twice and from his first marriage he was the father of four daughters— Mrs. W. B. Patton, Mrs. A. P. Waldrop, Mrs. S. A. Mullinax, and Mrs. Melissa Goins. His second marriage was to Mary Louisa Thompson, a daughter of Fleming R. and Elizabeth Thompson, who was born in Walker County on October 23, 1836, and died October 28, 1924, and is buried in the Day Graveyard at Oakman. Children—Powell Johnston, Fleming A. Johnston, Archevi Johnston, Hewitt Johnston, Noah A. Johnston, Ira J. Johnston, and Manly H. Johnston.

Moore's Alabama, Vol. III, page 439.

JONES, WALLACE, according to family tradition, settled along the Warrior River, in Walker County, prior to 1800. He was born in England about 1775, where he learned the trade of millwright and cooper. He was a suitor for the hand of Susan Beavert, and upon meeting parental objections, the couple eloped from an English tavern at night and boarded a ship for America. They made their home in North Carolina for a short time before coming to Walker County, where Wallace Jones died in 1856. After settling in Walker County, Susan (Beavert) Jones made two trips, alone and on horseback, to North Carolina to secure her bounty from the government. At that time the country through which she passed was infested with Indians, but they aided her on her way. She died in Walker County in 1870 at the age of ninety. Wallace and Susan (Beavert) Jones were the parents of four children—Giles C. Jones; William Wallace Jones; James Ausborn Jones; and Minerva Jones, who married a Mr. Whitney and moved to Fayette County; and, upon his death, married Thomas Reed. Children by the first marriage—Marion Whitney, Toney Whitney, and Susanna Whitney. Children by the second marriage—Reuben Reed, Polk Reed, Dallas Reed, and Pierce Reed.

Jones Family Records.

JONES, GILES C., a son of Wallace and Susan (Beavert) Jones, was born in Walker County in 1799, twenty years before Alabama was admitted to the Union. Reared in a wild and unsettled country, he somehow managed to secure a very good education, and became a physician and surgeon. He practiced his profession in Jasper and its vicinity all of his life. He was one of the organizers of York Lodge No. 211 of the Masonic fraternity in 1854, and served as its first Worshipful Master. Dr. Jones died in Jasper in 1859. He was married to Mary A. Brooks, who was born in Marshall County, Alabama, in 1809, and died at Newtonville, Fayette County, in 1880. Children— William W. Jones, Tobe Jones, Warren Jones, Henry Jones, Ras. Jones and Marion Jones.

Moore's Alabama, Vol. II, page 79.
Jones Family Records.

JONES, WILLIAM W., a son of Dr. Giles C. and Mary (Brooks) Jones, was born near Jasper on August 3, 1827. He was reared in Walker County but attended the old Memphis Medical College at Memphis, Tenn., where he graduated with the degree of Doctor of Medicine. From 1856 to 1866 he practiced medicine in Jasper, and during the period of the Civil War he was stationed at Jasper as a Confederate surgeon. In 1866 he moved to Newtonville, Fayette County, where he died on

August 3, 1910. Dr. Jones was married twice—first, to a Miss Stovall, who was born and died in Jasper; and, second, to Mrs. Elizabeth (Wommack) Bell, who was born and died in Newtonville, Fayette County. Children by first marriage—James J. Jones, a physician and surgeon, who died at Newtonville in 1884; Benjamin Giles Jones, who moved to San Benito, Texas. Children by the second marriage—William Warren Jones, who died in 1880 at the age of sixteen; Ida Jones, who married Judge James J. Ray, of Jasper; Dora Jones, who married Dr. William A. Graham, of Fayette; Tarley W. Jones, a physician, of Fayette; and Wilmetta Jones, who married P. P. Mayfield, of Newtonville.

Moore's Alabama, Vol. II, page 79.

JONES, WILLIAM WALLACE, a son of Wallace and Susan (Beavert) Jones, was born on the Warrior River in Walker County in 1804, fifteen years before Alabama was admitted to the Union. He became a carpenter by trade and had much to do with the building of the first flatboats that were launched on the Warrior River. In the early 1820's he went through Squaw Shoals, of the Warrior River, on the first flatboat that ever crossed them, with a load of staves that were sold at Tuscaloosa. This feat proved that the dangerous shoals could be crossed successfully, and thereby the markets of Tuscaloosa, Demopolis and Mobile were opened to Walker County products. William Wallace Jones was married twice—first, to a Miss Files; and, second, to Polly Tubb, a daughter of Daniel Tubb. Children by first marriage—

William Wallace Jones, Jr.

Abner Jones.

James W. Jones, who married Samanthia Odom.

Jasper Riley Jones, who was born near New Lexington, Walker County, on April 3, 1825. On September 15, 1863, he enlisted at Jasper as a private in Company G, Fifty-sixth Alabama Cavalry, and served until the close of the war. He was married to Bathsheba Cain, who was born August 26, 1829, and died February 10, 1864, and is buried at Providence.

Mary Ann Jones, who was married to William Cranford.
Sally Jones, who was married to Henry Evans.
Cecila Jones, who was married to Richard Carmichael.
Caroline Jones, who was married to John Minter Sherer.
Children by the second marriage—
Giles O. Jones, who was married to Jane Gray.

Paul Pinkston Jones, who was born April 15, 1844, near Oakman. On April 22, 1861, he enlisted at Jasper as a private in Company I, Fiftieth Alabama Infantry. He was wounded at Atlanta on July 28, 1864, and was sent home; but in September, 1864, he re-enlisted as first sergeant in Company H, Musgrove's Battalion, and served until the close of the war. He was a lawyer by profession and specialized in the handling of land and pension claims. He died on February 6, 1911, and is buried in the Zion Graveyard at Parrish. He was married to Evaline Covin.

Daniel Lee Jones, who was born near New Lexington, Walker County, on March 6, 1845. On June 14, 1862, he enlisted at Jasper as a private in Company G, Fifty-sixth Alabama Cavalry, under Captain Shepherd, and served until the close of the war. He was married to Millie Garner.

Thomas A. Jones, who was married to Lavonia Grace.
John J. Jones, who was married to Edna Bailey.
Samuel H. Jones, who died a bachelor.

> Census of Confederate Soldiers, 1907.
> Jones Family Records.
> Armes' Story of Coal and Iron.
> Gravestones.

JONES, JAMES AUSBORN, a son of Wallace and Susan (Beavert) Jones, was born on the Warrior River in Walker

County on February 14, 1809. Reared on a wilderness farm, he followed that profession all of his life, although at one time he was Prosecuting Attorney for the county. He died on September 24, 1892, and is buried in the Zion Graveyard at Parrish. Mr. Jones was married twice; first, to Eliza Files, and, second, to Artamissa Garrison, who was born March 6, 1825, and died April 5, 1895, and is buried in the Zion Graveyard at Parrish. Children by the first marriage—

William Jefferson Jones, who was born in 1836, and died near America in 1907, having spent his entire life in this locality. In early life he was a civil engineer, but in later years devoted himself exclusively to farming. He was a soldier in the Confederate Army and served throughout the war. He was married to Edith Garrison. Children—James Jones, William R. (Tudge) Jones, Kirg Jones, Jacob Jones, Ausborn Jones, Sarah Jones, Elzia Jones, Eady Jones, Bessie Jones, and Dorenda Jones.

Rufus Loyd Jones, who was born February 23, 1838, on Cain Creek, two miles south of Oakman. On July 13, 1861, he enlisted at Fort Jackson, Arkansas, as a private, later second lieutenant in Company B, Sixth Arkansas Infantry. After the battle of Corinth, all other officers being sick or wounded, he commanded the company at the battle of Shiloh. About May 1, 1862, the command was reorganized and Mr. Jones was discharged. However, in September, 1862, he re-enlisted at Jasper as first lieutenant in Company G, Tenth Alabama Cavalry, and served until the close of the war. In the early days of its history Mr. Jones served as mayor of Day's Gap, now Oakman. He died on September 5, 1912, and is buried at Providence. Mr. Jones was married to Mary E. Kirkpatrick, who was born October 16, 1846, and died May 4, 1897, and is buried at Providence. Children—

Sarah Delila Jones, who was married to James I. Laird.

Samariamus Jones, who married John Minter Sherer.

Jacob A. (Bud) Jones, who married a Miss Hyche.
Giles W. (Biss) Jones, who married Annie Banks.
Leighton Tramuel Jones, who married, first, Dolly Deason, and, second, Victoria Lawson.
Pernie Jones, who married John Davidson.
Susan Jones, who married William Blackwood.
Martha Ann Jones, who married a Mr. Copeland.

> Mooe's Alabama, Vol. III, page 234.
> Census of Confederate Soldiers, 1907.
> Jones Family Records.
> Gravestones.

JONES, WILLIAM R. (TUDGE), a son of William Jefferson and Edith (Garrison) Jones, was born in Walker County in 1856. In the year 1878 a new post office was established with Mr. Jones as the first postmaster. This post office was known as Hewitt and was located on the old Baltimore Road about two miles northeast of the present site of America, on what was then known as the Rufus Jones place, and was sometimes called Jonesboro. Mr. Jones served as postmaster during the years 1878 and 1879, when he was succeeded by his half-brother, Tram Jones. In 1886 William R. Jones was again appointed postmaster. In 1888 the Hewitt post office was moved to the present site of America, and on January 1, 1891, was again moved to the present site of Parrish and the name changed to Parrish. Mr. Jones built the first home erected in Parrish and used part of his residence for the post office. He served as postmaster until 1914. In addition to his work as postmaster Mr. Jones engaged in farming, operated a mercantile business and also served as justice of the peace for many years. He was married twice; first, to Amanda Robinson, and, second, to Cordelia Ann Jackson. Children by the first marriage—Gilman Jones and Vada Jones. Children by the second marriage— Temperance Ersula Jones, who married Authur T. Cole; Egbert

Ferdinand Jones, who married Hester Gray; William Loyd Jones, who married Rilla Livingston, and served as postmaster at Parrish for many years; Mattie Zula Jones, who married Lewis H. Nelson; Amanda Ethel Jones, who married Irvin Woodfin; Arthur Cecil Jones, who married Tessie Derrick; Newton Everett Jones, who married Belva Fite; Rufus Fred Jones; and Robert Lewis Jones.

Moore's Alabama, Vol. III, page 234.
Jones Family Records.

JONES, THOMAS, entered government land in Section 28, Township 15, Range 9, on December 21, 1832.

Walker County Tract Record.

JONES, SAMUEL C., entered government land in Section 4, Township 14, Range 5, on February 28, 1836.

Walker County Tract Record.

JONES, WILLIAM H., entered government land in Section 10, Township 16, Range 6, on February 4, 1851.

Walker County Tract Record.

JONES, ELIAS A., entered government land in Section 8, Township 14, Range 4, on September 8, 1855.

Walker County Tract Record.

JONES LEROY, entered government land in Section 36, Township 13, Range 7, on September 28, 1860.

Walker County Tract Record.

JONES, JEPTHA C., a Confederate soldier in Company A, Twenty-fourth Alabama Infantry, is buried in the Swindle Graveyard.

Gravestone.

JORDAN, MATTHEW M., entered government land in Section 35, Township 15, Range 8, on October 29, 1835.

Walker County Tract Record.

KARRH, SAMUEL A., born in 1811, died at his home near

Oakman on ———, 1891. He entered government land in Section 27, Township 14, Range 8, on November 26, 1836.

Walker County Tract Record.
The Headlight, February 8, 1891.

KEETON, WILLIAM, a pioneer settler of Walker County, was born in 1812. He joined the Primitive Baptist Church at Pleasant Grove in 1844. In 1857 he moved to Blackwater Creek and there joined the Liberty Grove Primitive Baptist Church, remaining a member until his death on October 24, 1886.

Mountain Eagle, November 17, 1886.

KEETON, REUBEN, was born April 26, 1832, on Lost Creek, near Pleasant Grove Church. In September, 1862, he enlisted at Jasper as a private in Company E, Twenty-eighth Alabama Infantry, under Captain Lollar, and served until the close of the war. He died on January 24, 1911, and is buried in the Guttery Graveyard at Townley. His wife, Mary Jane Keeton, was born January 2, 1834, and died December 26, 1903, and is also buried at Townley.

Census of Confederate Soldiers, 1907.
Gravestones.

KEETON, JOHN, was born January 19, 1841, on Lost Creek, near Pleasant Grove Church. On September 6, 1862, he enlisted at Jasper as a private in Company H, Fifty-sixth Alabama Cavalry, under Captain Johnson, and served until the close of the war. He is buried in Liberty Grove Graveyard. His wife, Catherine Keeton, born April 6, 1838, and died June 30, 1899, is also buried at Liberty Grove.

Census of Confederate Soldiers, 1907.
Gravestones.

KELLEY, BARNEY, born in 1810, died near Eldridge on June 26, 1887. He was a well known citizen of Walker County for many years.

Mountain Eagle, July 6, 1887.

KELLEY, JOHN, was born in South Carolina in 1811, a descendant of an Irish immigrant. When still a young man he located at Rockford, Coosa County, Alabama, where he operated a large tannery and a shoe factory. In 1853 he moved to Walker County and entered the mercantile business at Eldridge, where he died in 1883. He was married to Martha Franklin, also a native of South Carolina. Among their children were Elizabeth Kelley, who married William Thomas Stubblefield; Esom D. Kelley and Benjamin D. Kelley.

Moore's Alabama, Vol. II, page 405.
Moore's Alabama, Vol. III, page 602.

KELLEY, ESOM D., a son of John and Martha (Franklin) Kelley, was born at Rockford, Coosa County, Alabama, in 1836. He grew up in Coosa County, but in 1853 he moved with his parents to Eldridge. At the outbreak of the Civil War he enlisted as third lieutenant in Company K, Fourth Alabama Cavalry. During the first year of the war the company was badly cut up in engagements in Northwest Tennessee, and, with the loss of its ranking officers, Mr. Kelley was promoted to Captain early in 1862, which rank he held until the close of the war. He was in command at the battle of Shiloh and other subsequent engagements.

After the close of the war Captain Kelley returned to Eldridge, and engaged in a mercantile business for the next ten years, when he retired and devoted his time to his farm. Captain Kelley was a staunch Democrat and was elected Representative in the Legislature for the sessions of 1871 and 1872. He was a modest, unpretending member, bringing to bear a native good sense on all occasions, which, together with his native courtesy, made him highly respected by all. Captain Kelley died at Eldridge in 1900. He was married to Martha E. Walker, who was born in Fayette County in 1848 and died at Eldridge in 1910. Children—Gussie Kelley, who married James R.

West, of Memphis; James A. Kelley; John T. Kelley; Mattie L. Kelley, who married Dr. John L. Gallagher, of Eldridge; D. M. Kelley; and Wilson Kelley.

Moore's Alabama, Vol. II, page 405.
Mountain Eagle, January 5, 1887.

KELLEY, BENJAMIN D., a son of John and Martha (Franklin) Kelley, was born at Traveler's Rest, Coosa County, Alabama, on December 16, 1843. When but ten years of age he was brought to Walker County by his parents, and he was reared and educated at Eldridge. In September, 1861, he enlisted as a private in Company K, Fourth Alabama Cavalry, under his brother, Captain Kelley, and served until the close of the war.

Census of Confederate Soldiers, 1907.

KEMP, PRESLEY, entered government land in Section 34, Township 15, Range 6, on November 26, 1833.

Walker County Tract Record.

KEMP, JAMES, entered government land in Section 10, Township 15, Range 6, on December 17, 1833.

Walker County Tract Record.

KENNEDY, JAMES, entered government land in Section 17, Township 13, Range 5, on October 17, 1837.

Walker County Tract Record.

KERR, JOHN B., entered government land in Section 13, Township 14, Range 7, on December 14, 1859.

Walker County Tract Record.

KEY, JOHN, born in Amherst County, Virginia, in 1765, was one of Walker County's earliest settlers. He lived in Amherst County until 1797 or later, and then moved to North Carolina, from which state he came to Alabama. Some believe that he reached Walker County not later than 1816, but the first authentic record is a government land entry made in Section 10, Township 15, Range 8, on December 25, 1824. This entry was on Lost Creek, north of Oakman. He was one of the pioneers of the Methodist Church in Walker County, and the earliest record of that church in the county is a report of a quarterly conference held at his home on Lost Creek on June 14, 1833. Mr. Key spent his entire life on the farm. He died in 1861, at the age of ninety-six, and is buried near Sipsey. On July 15, 1797, he was married in Amherst County, to Belinda Milstead. They were the parents of eleven children—

William S. Washington Key, who was born in Virginia about 1802, and came to Walker County with his parents, where he was reared. He was a farmer all of his life, and died near Manchester about 1904. He was married to Cynthia Aseneth Abbott. Children—James Key; John Key; William Key, who moved to Cherokee County, Texas; Belinda Key; Nancy Key; Howell Key; and Elizabeth Key, who married W. W. Snow.

John Martin Key, who was born about 1805, and was brought to Walker County with his parents. He devoted his entire life to farming, and died at the old home place near Coal Valley in 1854. He is buried in the old Davis Graveyard at Coal Valley. He was married twice; first to Mary Snow, who died, and later, in 1841, to Lucy Allen Woods, who was born in Walker County February 23, 1827, the daughter of Samuel Woods. Children by first marriage—Thomas Key, who married, first, a Kilgore, second, a Logan, and third, a Burton; Mary Polly Key, who married, first, a Kilgore, and second, her cousin, William Key, the son of Washington Key; John Key, who married, first, Charity Elizabeth Wood, and second, a widow, Mrs. Fannie (Clements) Ferguson. Children by the second marriage— Samuel Key, who married, first, a Courington, and second, a Bevill; Rice Key, who never married, and died during the Civil War; Lucy Key, who married Jasper Voyles in 1865; Bertha Key, who married a Voyles; Lindy Key, who married a Voyles;

Zilphia Key, who married Hugh Lollar; and Nancy J. Key, who married a Hamilton.

Joseph Garland Key, who was brought to Walker County by his parents, where he was married to Rachel Cole, daughter of Byrd Garland Cole. Children—Sarah Belinda Key, who married Clayton White; John Byrd Key, who married a Williams; William Key, who died young; Jodie Key, who married a Garner; Buck Key, who married a Jones; Liza Jane Key, who never married; and Nancy Key, who married Joseph Weembs.

Dock Clifton Key, who was born in Walker County about 1825. He was a farmer until the outbreak of the Civil War, when he enlisted in Company L, Twenty-eighth Alabama Infantry, under Captain Musgrove, and died in Tennessee in 1865, while still in the service. About 1845 he was married to Nancy Louise Cole, who was born in Walker County in 1828, a daughter of Byrd Cole. She died in 1908 and is buried in the Zion Graveyard at Parrish. Children—John Clifton Key, who married Julia Key; Byrd Garland Key, who married Polly Garner; Joseph Martin Key, who married Polka Williams; Nicholas Rice Key, who married Frankie Bailey; James Buchanan Key, who married Samanthia Williams; Robert Key, who married Eaddie Jones; William Key, who married Mary Key; and Nancy Key, who never married.

Charles Rice Key, who married Dorcia Cole, and then moved to Cullman County.

Lindsay Key, who was married to Rebecca Winters.

Nancy Key, who was married to Richard Chilton.

Elizabeth Key, who was married to William Busby.

James Hezekiah Key, who was married to Elizabeth Herring.

Jane Mills Key, who was married to Hill Abbott.

Key and Allied Families.
Gravestones.

KEY, JOHN, a son of John Martin and Mary (Snow) Key,

and grandson of John and Belinda (Milstead) Key, was born near Pleasant Hill on March 13, 1836. He spent his entire life on the farm, where he died on May 29, 1900, and is buried in the Pleasant Hill Graveyard. He was married twice—first, to Charity Elizabeth Wood, who was born December 31, 1839, a daughter of Edward Thomas and Minerva Wood. She died on March 9, 1890, and is buried in the Davis Graveyard at Coal Valley. His second marriage was to a widow, Mrs. Fannie (Clements) Ferguson, who is still living (1935). Children, by the first marriage—Mary Key, who married W. H. McClain; Minerva Key, who married A. A. Rutledge; Samuel L. Key, who married Berthina Nelson; Eliza Key, who married George H. Myers; Edward Thomas Key, who married Minnie Sides; Prudy Key, who married Rufus Bell; John Martin Key, who married, first, Minter Swindle, and second, Ida Kilgore; Susan Key, who married, first, Mud Ferguson, and second, J. M. Files; Mita Key, who married John MacDonald; and Robert Powers Key, who was born September 26, 1859, and was married to Mary Ann Rutledge, who was born January 12, 1882, a daughter of James Rutledge. The children of Robert Powers and Mary Ann (Rutledge) Key are John R. Key, James D. Key, Talmage D. Key, Henry Grady Key, Ada Key, Bedford Thomas Key, Jennings D. Key, Annie Key, Bessie Key, and Aubrey Key. From the second marriage of John Key, to Mrs. Fannie (Clements) Ferguson, there were two children—Lula Key, who married Holly Johnson; and Benjamin Key, who married Emma Jenkins.

Key and Allied Families.
Key Family Records.

KEY, NICHOLAS RICE, a son of Dock Clifton and Nancy Louise (Cole) Key, and grandson of John and Belinda (Milstead) Key, was born in 1853 and died in 1934. In 1871 he was married to Frankie Bailey, who was born October 30, 1853, a daughter of William and Sarah Jane (Holden) Bailey. She died on January 5, 1922, and is buried in the Zion Graveyard at Parrish. Children—Joseph Martin Key, Julius Lorenza Key, Mandy Verlin Key, Rhoda Key, Newton Edward Key, Donie Key, Fronie Key, Floyd G. Key, Robert Clarence Key, Nancy Key, Fletcher Key, and Jacob Clifton Key, who was born July 11, 1873, and died May 27, 1920. He was married to Mintie Ann Wade, who was born December 27, 1873, a daughter of John Landon and Sarah Ann (Blanton) Wade. She died October 24, 1924. Children—Octavius Winifred Key, Shay Benjamin Key, Paul Landon Key, Clara Ann Frankie Key, Marvin Scott Key, Claudine Key, Mamie Irene Key, and Aileen Key.

Key and Allied Families.

KILGORE, WILLIAM, entered government land in Section 36, Township 15, Range 9, near Corona, on March 12, 1836.

Walker County Tract Record.

KILGORE, GEORGE, a native of South Carolina, came to Walker County in young manhood and settled near Corona. He acquired large farming interests and developed into one of the county's most prosperous farmers. He was married to Hattie Clements, a native of Alabama. They both died on the home farm near Corona. Among their children were James Kilgore and Robert Kilgore.

Moore's Alabama, Vol. III, page 123.

KILGORE, ROBERT, a son of George and Hattie (Clements) Kilgore, was born near Corona in 1848, and died in the same locality in 1878. A successful farmer, he became a leading citizen of the county and very prominent in the Republican party. He was married to Dida David, who was born near Corona in 1848. Children—Sarah Kilgore, who married John Handley; James Kilgore, who died at the age of twenty-six; Ruth Kilgore, who married John Willcutt; and Samuel D. Kilgore, who was born June 30, 1876. He was reared on his father's farm, edu-

EARLY SETTLERS 249

cated in the public schools of the county, and worked in various coal mines, later serving as convict warden on the county roads of Walker. In October, 1924, he was appointed Sheriff to serve the unexpired term of Guy V. O'Rear, and was later elected for a second term. He died in 1931. On September 16, 1904, he was married to H. Polly Garner, of Drifton.

Moore's Alabama, Vol. III, page 123.

KILGORE, JOHN M., entered government land in Section 31, Township 13, Range 9, in the northern part of the county, on November 19, 1838.

Walker County Tract Record.

KILGORE, ELZIE, came into Walker County from Georgia, presumably about 1843 or earlier. He died about 1860. He was married to Nancy Larrimore. Children—Mitchell Kilgore, who never married, and was killed in the Civil War; Charles C. Kilgore, who moved to Tuscaloosa; Thomas Kilgore, who married Matilda Busby, and lived in Jefferson County; James Kilgore; and Wiley Kilgore.

Kilgore Family Records.

KILGORE, JAMES, a son of Elzie and Nancy (Larrimore) Kilgore, was brought into Walker County by his parents while still quite young. He lived on a farm near Pleasantfield all of his life. He was married to Mary Hutto. Children—Isaac Kilgore, who married Adeline Wade; Wiley Kilgore, who was killed in the Civil War; Martha Kilgore, who married Tobe Minor; John Kilgore, who married Rodie Smith; Nancy Kilgore, who married William Odom.

Kilgore Family Records.

KILGORE, ISAAC K., a son of James and Mary (Hutto) Kilgore, was born on Wolf Creek on August 18, 1844. On January 4, 1862, he enlisted at Tierce's Mill as a private in Company K, Fiftieth Alabama Infantry, under Captain Hutto, and served until the close of the war. He died on June 8, 1920, and is buried at Liberty Hill. He was married to Adeline Wade. Children—William D. Kilgore; Wiley L. Kilgore; Sarah Kilgore, who married P. F. Knight; James M. Kilgore; Robert F. Kilgore; John R. Kilgore; Thomas Allen Kilgore; Ira Kilgore; Charles E. Kilgore; Ross M. Kilgore; Joseph O. Kilgore; Lilly B. Kilgore.

Kilgore Family Records.

KILGORE, WILEY E., a son of Elzie and Nancy (Larrimore) Kilgore, was born September 19, 1824. He was brought to Walker County by his parents while still a young man. At the outbreak of the Civil War he enlisted in the Confederate Army, and was killed in action on May 5, 1864. He is buried in the old cemetery in Jasper. In 1847 he was married to Nancy Caroline Sides, who was born in Walker County on September 11, 1831, a daughter of Levi Sides. She died on November 21, 1911, and is buried at New Prospect. Children—

Mary Kilgore, who was born in 1848, married Dock Sides and moved to Texas.

J. Thomas Kilgore, who was born August 31, 1850, and died December 5, 1911, and is buried at New Prospect. He was married to Nancy Ann Conn, who was born March 3, 1859, a daughter of James and Mahula Conn. She died November 4, 1905, and is buried at New Prospect.

Nancy Kilgore, who was born in 1852, married Benjamin Gabbert, and moved to Texas.

J. Robert Kilgore, who was born in 1855. He became a very well known farmer and stock raiser. Before the railroads were built he was a successful teamster, and on his weekly trips, to Tuscaloosa first and later to Birmingham, he and his sturdy team were conspicuous figures on the thoroughfares of the county. He bore the reputation of being the most accommodating wagoner in the service. In a few years he found himself possessed of a small stock of goods and he entered the mercantile business in Jasper. His business grew steadily, and judicious investments during boom days brought success. However, in the fire of 1893 he lost two store houses and a large hotel building, which left him practically penniless. He started over again and soon regained his losses. He was married to Mary Sherer.

Martha Kilgore, who was born in 1857, and was married to Madison Monroe Sherer.

Dorenda Kilgore, who was born in 1860, and was married to Amsi Sherer.

Mountain Eagle, July 24, 1895.
Kilgore Family Records.
Gravestones.

KILGORE, WILLIAM PARKER, was born February 10, 1843, in Randolph County, Alabama. In February, 1862, he enlisted at Elyton as a private in Company H, Twenty-fourth Alabama Infantry. He was captured at Atlanta on August 13, 1864, and imprisoned at Camp Chase, Ohio, until the close of the war.

Census of Confederate Soldiers, 1907.

KING, JOHN, a descendant of William and Mary (Woodson) King, of North Carolina, and a member of General Andrew Jackson's staff during the War of 1812, received a soldier's grant of land, which he took up in 1822, on Lost Creek, in Walker County, near the community now known as King's, where he erected a grist mill. He was a cousin to William Rufus King, who was vice president of the United States during the administration of President Pierce. Mr. King was married to Lucy Jordan, of Virginia and Georgia. Among their children were William R. King, Thomas Jordan King, and John King.

Moore's Alabama, Vol. II, page 392.
Owens' Alabama, Vol. III, page 982.

KING, THOMAS JORDAN, a son of John and Lucy (Jordan) King, was born November 2, 1820, near Ashland, St.

Clair County, Alabama, and was brought to Walker County by his parents in 1822, when they settled on Lost Creek, at the community now known as King's. His father was a miller, and Thomas Jordan King entered his father's business and remained with it until June 11, 1864, when he entered the service of the Confederate Army as a private in Company L, Fifty-sixth Alabama Cavalry, under Captain Guttery. He was captured at Atlanta in July, 1864, and was imprisoned at Rock Island, Illinois, until the close of the war. In the Reconstruction Days, after the war, Mr. King and his father, John King, had much to do with the development of the coal industry in Walker County, and he became very well to do. Mr. King took a lively interest in the government and affairs of the county, although in politics he was a staunch Republican. He enjoyed the reputation of being one of the most original characters in the county and was a little proud of the distinction. He died on April 24, 1912. He was married to Eliazbeth Wilson and was the father of several children, among them being Mrs. Martha King Lang, Mrs. Sally King Cunningham, and Mrs. Mary King Mulford.

Moore's Alabama, Vol. II, page 392.
Armes' Story of Coal and Iron, page 501.
Census of Confederate Soldiers, 1907.
Mountain Eagle, 1891.

KING, JOHN W., a son of William R. King and a grandson of John King, was born August 6, 1855. He was reared and educated in Walker County. Operating a mercantile business in Carbon Hill, and also being largely interested in coal mining, he was a self-made man who accumulated considerable property.

Memorial Record of Alabama, Vol. II, page 10.

KINSEY, THOMAS, entered government land in Section 3, Township 15, Range 7, south of Jasper, on October 3, 1833.

Walker County Tract Record.

KIRKPATRICK, WILLIAM R., a native of South Carolina,

entered government land in Section 5, Township 14, Range 7, northwest of Jasper, on July 23, 1856. He was married to Permelia E. Meek, who was born May 3, 1823, and died March 22, 1892, and is buried at Samaria. Children—Mary Kirkpatrick, who married Rufus Jones; Monre Kirkpatrick, who married, first, Emily McDuff, and second, Mrs. Sis Stephenson, a widow; Lucinda Kirkpatrick, who married Eli Hyche; Jencie Ann Kirkpatrick, who married John H. Stephenson; Narcissa Kirkpatrick, who married Daniel Price; Joseph Kirkpatrick, who married Eliza Blackwood; Nora Kirkpatrick, who married William Copeland; Benie Kirkpatrick, who married Solomon Littleton; Jacob Kirkpatrick, who married Martha Barton; and Moses M. Kirkpatrick, who was born May 6, 1866, and died February 23, 1930, and is buried at Providence. Moses Kirkpatrick was married to Mahaley Lurenz (Cricket) Kitchens, daughter of Jesse Simeon Kitchens. Their children were Earl Kirkpatrick, Fannie Kirkpatrick, August Kirkpatrick, Roscoe Kirkpatrick, and Bessie Kirkpatrick.

Walker County Tract Record.
Kirkpatrick Family Records.
Kitchens Family Records.
Gravestones.

KITCHENS, JAMES MATLOCK, born in Tennessee on August 7, 1796, was, according to family tradition, a descendant of Henry Kitchens, of Virginia, who sat in the first House of Burgesses, which met in 1619. In 1812 James Matlock Kitchens, then but sixteen years of age, came to Alabama with a brother, George Kitchens, and an uncle, James Acuff, and settled in what is now Lawrence County. About 1836 he came to Walker County and on September 26, 1836, he entered government land in Section 12, Township 14, Range 8, about two miles west of Jasper. Mr. Kitchens was a well educated man for his day and time, a successful farmer, and, in addition, was a prominent and well known Primitive Baptist minister. On July 6, 1844, he helped to constitute the Sulphur Springs Primitive Baptist Church, and in May, 1845, he was ordained a regular minister of that church by Elders Robert Guttery and John M. Barton. He served as pastor of the church for twenty-two years, until December, 1867, when ill health caused his resignation. He died on March 23, 1868, after an honorable and well spent life. James Matlock Kitchens was married to Sally Brown, evidently in Lawrence County, about 1813. Sally Brown was born September 16, 1796, and died December 16, 1842. She was a sister to Thomas Brown and also a sister to Francis Brown, the wife of J. D. Randolph, all of whom were charter members of the Sulphur Springs Primitive Baptist Church. The following children were born to James Matlock and Sally (Brown) Kitchens:

John Kitchens, who lived in Lawrence County, and died there prior to 1870. He was the father of Martha Kitchens, who married J. D. Lindsay; Frances Kitchens, who married a Mr. Lindsay; Sarah E. Kitchens; Dr. John M. Kitchens, who lived in Hartsell, Alabama; and W. C. (Buck) Kitchens.

Mary Susan Polly Kitchens, who was born October 20, 1814, and died May 5, 1887. She was married to Harvey W. Hamilton.

Christopher Columbus Kitchens, who was born November 18, 1827, and died January 15, 1861. He was married on January 10, 1847, to Sarah Ann Taylor, who was born in January, 1831, and died June 12, 1914. Mr. Kitchens made his home on the old Jasper-Taylor's Ferry Road, about two miles west of Parrish, where he spent his life as a farmer and operator of a cotton gin. With his father, he was a charter member of the Sulphur Springs Primitive Baptist Church, and in July, 1849, he was elected and ordained a deacon of that church. He was the father of eight children—William Taylor Kitchens, born October 22, 1848; James Lafayette Kitchens, born October 8, 1847;

Robert Franklin Kitchens, who was born September 11, 1849, and was married to Martha Clemantine Phifer, a daughter of John Phifer; Jesse Simeon Kitchens, who was born June 7, 1851, and was married to Mary Odom on February 9, 1868; John Matlock Kitchens, who was born March 8, 1854; Isaac Stanley Kitchens, who was born February 24, 1857, and moved to Dickens County, Texas, in 1894; Mary Elizabeth Kitchens, born January 2, 1860, died October 25, 1875. After the death of Christopher C. Kitchens, his widow married Hugh Gaunt Lollar.

William Kitchens, who died while on his way back from the Mexican War, and is buried in Mississippi.

Samuel Kitchens, who died in Lafayette County, Ark.

James Matlock Kitchens, Jr., who was born May 13, 1830. He spent his entire life in and around Jasper, with the exception of the period of the Civil War, when he was in the service of the Confederate Army. Little is known of his war record other than a letter he wrote to his father in January, 1863, when he was in Rome, Ga., recovering from a wound in his right foot, which he received in the Murfreesboro fight, while with the Twenty-second Alabama Infantry. As late as 1895 he attended the Confederate Veterans' Reunion in Houston, Texas. He died on December 11, 1896. He was married to Mary D. Files, a daughter of Richard Manly and Mary (Lindsay) Files, who was born May 13, 1835, and died November 6, 1921, and is buried at Samaria. Children—William Files Kitchens, who married Belle Sanders; Mary C. Kitchens, who married William J. Hocutt; Ida M. Kitchens, who married Clinton Inman; and Gilbert Lee Kitchens, who married, first, Anne Banks, and, second, Anne Kelley.

Jesse Kitchens, who was born December 27, 1837, and died in Birmingham on June 12, 1898. He operated the Kitchens Coal Mine at Coal City, one of the first mines to be opened on the Frisco Railroad after it was built through in the late 1880's.

He was married twice—first, to Eleanor Brown, a daughter of Thomas and Lovey Brown, who was born May 12, 1837, and died June 9, 1872; and, second, to Sally Mary Ashcraft, a daughter of Thomas Ashcraft. After the death of Jesse Kitchens, his widow married Hiram B. Chandler. Jesse Kitchens was the father of five children—by the first marriage, William Calvin Kitchens; Nancy Ann Kitchens, who married Sylvester Bell on November 16, 1887, and moved to Oklahoma; and, by the second marriage, Mary Ellen Kitchens, who married G. T. Ellis; Abagail Kitchens, who married Joseph J. Grace; and Hubert Taylor Kitchens.

Matilda Kitchens, who married, first, Judge John (Jack) Brown, a son of Thomas and Lovey Brown and one time Probate Judge of Walker County; and, second, Abner Carmichael, of Saline County, Ark.

Nancy Kitchens, who was born November 28, 1813, and died March 31, 1889. She was married to James F. Robinson. Children—James F. Robinson; Elizabeth Robinson, who married N. R. Romine; Martha R. Robinson, who married S. W. Copeland, Crossville, DeKalb County; Mary S. Robinson, who married T. J. Nicholson, DeKalb County; and Nancy J. Robinson, who married W. F. Dobbs, DeKalb County.

Elizabeth Kitchens, who married a Mr. Dutton, and lived at Graham's Gap, Morgan County, Ala. Children—Sarah J. Dutton, who married a Mr. Turrentine; Mary F. Dutton, who married a Mr. Dutton; Stephen T. Dutton; James H. Dutton; Luvina T. Dutton, who married James A. Hogan; W. C. Dutton, of Sebastian County, Ark.; John F. Dutton; Frances Dutton, and Alex Dutton.

Frances Kitchens, who married Eli Sparks. Children—Eli A. Sparks, born January 22, 1835, died July 28, 1872, married to his cousin, Mary Caroline Baker, a daughter of Alvin Baker; Louisa C. Sparks, who married J. B. Boshell; Richard Thomas

Sparks; James M. Sparks; John W. Sparks; Rutha Sparks, who married Isaac Roberts; Samuel E. Sparks; and Elizabeth Sparks. Susan Kitchens, who married Alvin Baker (see Baker).

Kitchens Family Records.
Bible of C. C. Kitchens.
Sulphur Springs Church Book.
Walker County Tract Record.
Walker County Will Record.

KITCHENS, JESSE SIMEON, a son of Christopher Columbus Kitchens and a grandson of James Matlock Kitchens, was born on his father's farm, near Parrish, on June 7, 1851. Following in the footsteps of his father and grandfather, he was a successful farmer, and a minister of the Sulphur Springs Primitive Baptist Church for twenty-five years, until his death. He was elected Treasurer of Walker County, and was filling that office at the time of his death on February 17, 1911. On February 9, 1868, he was married to Mary Odom, a daughter of James and Mehaley Elinor (Plyler) Odom, who was born May 25, 1850, and died December 29, 1918. Both Mr. and Mrs. Kitchens are buried on their old homestead. Children—Martha Jane Kitchens, who married James H. Barton, of Cordova; Mahaly Lurenz Kitchens, who married Moses M. Kirkpatrick, of Providence; Mary Susan Kitchens, who married Robbin Nations, of Cordova; James Christopher Kitchens, who married Sarah Douglas, of Parrish; Sarah Ann Kitchens, who married Patillo Deason, of Pleasantfield; Etta Artasas Kitchens, who married Sylvester Thompson, of Parrish; Wiley Leander Kitchens, who married Birdie Posey, and has followed the family tradition by becoming a minister of the Sulphur Springs Primitive Baptist Church; Jesse Andrew Kitchens, who married Mrs. Dorothy (Burger) Tandy, of Amarillo, Texas; and William Henry Kitchens, who married Bertha Smith, of Kansas City, Mo.

Kitchens Family Records.

KITCHENS, JOHN, thought to be a brother of James Matlock, Kitchens, entered government land in Section 30, Township 13, Range 9, on the present site of Carbon Hill, on December 26, 1835. Very little is known of John Kitchens or of his wife, Sarah J. Kitchens. Among their children were Sarah E. Kitchens, born March 6, 1841, died August 7, 1886, and who was married to Madison Sherer; Martha Kitchens, who married, first, a Mr. Stagg, and, second, William F. Sides, a son of William Sides; Frances Kitchens, who married Frank Sides, a son of William Sides; John H. Kitchens, who lived in Fayette County; and George Kitchens, who married Mary Ann Bennett, and was the father of five sons—William Kitchens, Joseph Kitchens, James Kitchens, George Kitchens; and John Kitchens, who was born near Jasper in 1852 and was married to Eliza Jane Sides, a daughter of Hugh Robert Sides.

Kitchens Family Records.

KITCHENS, GEORGE, thought to be a brother of James Matlock Kitchens, entered government land in Section 23, Township 13, Range 10, in the northwest part of the county, on September 14, 1836.

Walker County Tract Record.

KNIGHT, ABNER, Sr., a member of Company K, Forty-third Alabama Infantry, was born December 21, 1830; died October 28, 1902, and is buried at Liberty Hill. His wife, Nancy Knight, was born September 25, 1832; died June 2, 1916, and is also buried at Liberty Hill.

Gravestones.

KNIGHT, RICHARD TOWNLEY, was born May 12, 1845, near Gamble Mines, Walker County. On August 3, 1863, he enlisted as a private in Company B, Tenth Alabama Cavalry, under Captain Whatley, and served until the close of the war. He died February 19, 1919, and is buried in Oak Hill Cemetery,

Jasper. His wife, E. A. Knight, was born December 21, 1844, and died March 1, 1919.

Census of Confederate Soldiers, 1907.
Gravestones.

LACY, SHERIFF, was born in Randolph County, May 7, 1853, a son of Abner Wise and Martha (Brewster) Lacy. Abner Wise Lacy was a native of Maury County, Tennessee, who settled in St. Clair County, Alabama; a son of William and Mary (Wise) Lacy, of Virginia. Martha (Brewster) Lacy was the daughter of Sheriff and Malinda (Wortham) Brewster, of South Carolina. Sheriff Lacy received a common school education in St. Clair and Talladega Counties and read law in Talladega from 1879 to 1881, when he was licensed to practice his profession. In 1882 he located in Jasper, and in the following year was appointed Register in Chancery, which office he filled for a number of years. He was elected to the Legislature for the sessions of 1898-1899; was County Solicitor from 1886 to 1888, and for several years served on the board of aldermen and the city board of education for Jasper. He died in 1933. On December 24, 1876, he was married to Mary Ella McCollough, of Macon County, a daughter of John Martin and Ruth (Skinner) McCollough. John Martin McCollough was a native of Anderson District, South Carolina, who was killed in the battle of Peach Tree Creek, near Atlanta, while serving as a soldier in the Confederate Army. The children of Sheriff and Mary Ella (McCollough) Lacy were: Cecil Justus Lacy, Pauline Lacy, Ruth Lacy, Lorene Lacy; and Ernest Renfroe Lacy, who was born in Talladega County, October 11, 1877, graduated from Howard College in 1895, graduated from the law school of the University of Alabama in 1900, and began the practice of law in Jasper in January, 1902. On November 3, 1903, he was married to Gaye Musgrove Long, a daughter of John B. and Zou (Musgrove) Long.

Owens' Alabama, Vol. IV, page 1002.

LACY, JOHN E., a native of Virginia, settled in Jasper in 1883. On November 23, 1887, he was married to Mollie L. Hayes, a daughter of John Henry and Mildred (Files) Hayes (see Hayes). Children—Maud, who married a Mr. Webb; Louise, who married Boice Bailey; Alberta, who married Coleman Shepherd; and Alma, who married Cliff Herzberg, of Gadsden.

Mountain Eagle, November 30, 1887.
Files Family Records.

LAMAR, WILLIAM HARMONG, was born in Augusta, Georgia, July 13, 1827, a son of Col. Harmong and Martha Anne (Young) Lamar, and a descendant of Thomas Lamar, Sr., an early French emigrant to Virginia, who was naturalized in Maryland. William Harmong Lamar was a graduate of the Southern Botanical Medical College at Macon, Ga., and began his practice as a physician at Auburn, Ala., in 1854. He moved to Jasper in 1894, and died there a few years later. On January 7, 1847, he was married at Glenville, Barbour County, to Ann Maria Glenn, a daughter of Rev. John Bowles and Maria (Allen) Glenn. Children:

Theodore Jemison Lamar, graduate of the Agricultural and Mechanical College; President of the Auburn Female College; founder of the Lamar Training School, for young men, of Jasper, in 1894; and one time Superintendent of Education for Walker County. He was married to Orlena Augusta Cleveland.

Charles R. Lamar, a minister in the Methodist Church, who married Laura Cain.

Glennie C. Lamar, who married T. S. Phillips.

William Harmong Lamar, Jr., who married Virginia Longstreet Lamar.

Howard Lamar, who was born in Lee County December 25, 1861. He graduated from Auburn in 1889, was admitted to the bar in the same year and began his practice in Jasper. He was married to Alma Hayes, a daughter of John Henry and Mildred

(Files) Hayes (see Hayes). Children—Henry, Howard, Alma, Glenn, and Mildred.

George Holt Lamar, who married Edith Stonestreet.

Annie Lamar, unmarried.

Owens' Alabama, Vol. IV, page 1004.
Memorial Record of Alabama, Vol. II, page 1023.
Files Family Records.

LAMBERT, WASHINGTON, entered government land in Section 35, Township 16, Range 6, on October 4, 1836.

Walker County Tract Record.

LAMKIN, GRIFFIN, was born in Virginia, June 1, 1781, a son of Peter and Winifred (Dockins) Lamkin, both natives of that state. He was a well educated man, who entered the War of 1812 as a Captain and was promoted to Lieutenant Colonel. About 1800 Griffin Lamkin moved from Virginia to Madison County, Alabama, where he became a very substantial planter and slave owner, possessing at one time as many as one hundred slaves. He was elected Representative from Madison County to the first Legislature held in the state and served during the sessions of 1819 and 1820. Shortly after this he lost the greater part of his fortune by going security on a note which was defaulted, and about 1830 moved to Walker County and settled on Wolf Creek. In 1844 he was appointed Clerk of the Circuit Court of Tuscaloosa County, and served for several years. He died on June 10, 1856, and is buried in the old cemetery at Jasper. Griffin Lamkin was married twice. On December 24, 1800, he was married in Madison County to Betsy Clark, a daughter of James and Susanna Clark, and on March 24, 1831, he was married in Walker County to Sarah Thacker, a daughter of Samuel and Sally Thacker, who was born June 11, 1800, and died September 8, 1867, and is buried in the old cemetery at Jasper. Children from the first marriage—Susanna Bibb Lamkin, Peter Sharp Lamkin, John James Lamkin, Betsy Clark Lamkin,

Mary Booker Lamkin, Griffin Lamkin, Jr., Petronella Lamkin, George Griffin Lamkin, Eliza Bibb Lamkin, Lucy Clark Lamkin, and Thomas Richard Lamkin. Children by the second marriage —Petronilla Lamkin, who married Elias Right; Mariah Jane Lamkin; Peter Lamkin; Hannah Lamkin, who married William B. O'Rear; Sarah E. Lamkin, who married John C. Ryan, Thomas Peter Lamkin; Martha Jane Lamkin, who married W. L. Sides.

Owens' Alabama, Vol. IV, page 1004.
Walker County Tract Record.
Gravestones.

LAMKIN, THOMAS PETER, a son of Griffin and Sarah (Thacker) Lamkin, was born on Wolf Creek, March 2, 1844. He was reared on his father's farm and educated in the county schools. In July, 1861, he enlisted at Jasper as a private in Company F, Sixteenth Alabama Infantry, and served until the close of the war. Returning to Walker County after the war he became a successful merchant and farmer. He was very prominent in the affairs of the United Confederate Veterans and held the rank of Major General, commanding the Alabama division of the Veterans. He died in 1928 and is buried in the Oak Hill Cemetery at Jasper. He was married to Nannie M. Gravlee, who was born January 1, 1854.

Moore's Alabama, Vol. III, page 443.
Census of Confederate Soldiers, 1907.
Gravestones.

LAYMON, JAMES WASHINGTON, was born April 21, 1844, at Decatur, Morgan County, Alabama. On January 18, 1862, he enlisted at Jasper as a private in Company K, Fifty-sixth Alabama Cavalry, under Captain Johnson. In May, 1864, he was detached from his command and detailed under Lieutenant Thomas Willes, of Walker County, to do scout work for Johnson's army. He died a number of years after the war and is buried at Laymon's Chapel. His wife, Nancy E. Laymon, born

November 25, 1843, died August 21, 1924, and is also buried at Laymon's Chapel.

Census of Confederate Soldiers, 1907.
Gravestones.

LANDERS, NATHANIEL, entered government land in Section 23, Township 14, Range 6, on December 3, 1855.

Walker County Tract Record.

LANE, ALFRED G., entered government land in Section 1, Township 13, Range 10, on October 29, 1833. He took an active part in the early Methodist Church and is listed as an exhorter in a report of a quarterly conference held in 1833. Mr. Lane was also a lawyer and was practicing his profession in Jasper in 1854.

Walker County Tract Record.
West's History of Methodism, page 549.
Campbell's Southern Business Directory.

LANE, JOSEPH L., entered government land in Section 21, Township 13, Range 10, on September 28, 1833.

Walker County Tract Record.

LANGLEY, NATHAN B., a member of Company G, Eighth Alabama Cavalry, was born January 21, 1849, died January 20, 1929, and is buried at Union Chapel.

Gravestone.

LATHAM, JAMES LEANDER, was born February 14, 1845, at Blount Springs, Blount County, Alabama. On October 16, 1861, he enlisted at Blount Springs as a private in Company F, Twenty-ninth Alabama Infantry, under Captain Sapp, and served until the close of the war. He was married to Nancy Sides, a daughter of Andy Allen and Mary (Staggs) Sides.

Census of Confederate Soldiers, 1907.

LATHAM, THOMAS MARION, was born in 1845 at Blount Springs, Blount County, Alabama. In September, 1862, he enlisted at Eldridge as a private in Company K, Fourth

Alabama Cavalry, under Captain Kelley, and served until the close of the war.

Census of Confederate Soldiers, 1907.

LAWRENCE, BENJAMIN, entered government land in Section 28, Township 14, Range 9, on January 14, 1833.

Walker County Tract Record.

LAWSON, ALBERT GALLATIN, was born May 15, 1834, near Pleasant Grove Church on Lost Creek. In August, 1862, he enlisted at Jasper as a private in Company G, Fifty-sixth Alabama Cavalry, under Captain Shepherd, and served until the close of the war.

Census of Confederate Soldiers, 1907.

LEITH, CORTEZ, entered government land in Section 18, Township 16, Range 7, on November 17, 1836.

Walker County Tract Record.

LEITH, GEORGE, was born in Jefferson County, Tennessee, a son of Ebenezer Leith, a Baptist preacher. In November, 1817, George Leith was married to Elizabeth Branner at Dandridge, Jefferson County, Tennessee. Soon after this marriage the couple moved to Bibb County, Alabama, and lived on Six Mile Creek, seven miles from Centerville. In 1838 they lost much of their money through being security on a defaulted note, and shortly after this loss, on or about January 18, 1839, they moved to Walker County and settled near Jasper. Mr. Leith served for nine months as a volunteer in the Seminole War in Florida. He died at his home in Walker County on October 7, 1844. After his death his wife remained on the homestead until the outbreak of the Civil War. She died on September 20, 1864, and is buried at Liberty Hill.

Genealogy of the Branner Family.

LEITH, FRANCIS MARION, a son of George and Elizabeth (Branner) Leith, was born February 8, 1838, near Centerville,

Bibb County, Alabama, but was brought to Walker County by his parents in 1839. He received a good common school education and farmed until the outbreak of the Civil War. On December 25, 1862, he enlisted at Jasper as a private in Hubbard's Company of Roddy's Cavalry, and in September, 1863, he re-enlisted in Company B, Tenth Alabama Cavalry, under Captain Whatley, and served until the close of the war. Returning to his home in Walker County he farmed for two years and then, for the following three years, studied medicine under his brother-in-law, Dr. L. C. Miller. On October 22, 1888, he was married to a widow, Mrs. Sarah Whitson, and for some years the couple lived about three and a half miles from Lynn Station in Jefferson County, but later they moved to Oakman, where he was a physician and druggist.

Genealogy of the Branner Family.

LEITH, MITCHELL PORTER, a son of George and Elizabeth (Branner) Leith, was born at Briarfield, Bibb County, Alabama, on December 26, 1826, but came to Walker County with his parents in 1839. On May 11, 1841, he was married to Siciline Elizabeth Chilton. Mr. Leith volunteered for service during the Mexican War, but was ill with fever when the troops departed, so that he did not accompany them. In 1862 he enlisted in Company E, Twenty-second Alabama Infantry, and was in the battles of Buzzard's Roost and of Resaca. He was never wounded, but was captured at Resaca and sent prisoner to Alton, Ill. After the war he returned to his farm on Lost Creek, one mile east of the Carbon Hill mines, where he became a very successful farmer and a man generally esteemed as an excellent citizen. After his wife's death in 1873, he married Jane Lyle, of Walker County. He died on his farm near Carbon Hill on July 18, 1905. Mr. Leith had ten children by his first wife and five by his second.

Genealogy of the Branner Family.

LEITH, MARTIN LUTHER, was born near Corona on February 19, 1868, a son of Mitchell Porter and Siciline Elizabeth (Chilton) Leith, and a grandson of George and Elizabeth (Branner) Leith and Richard and Nancy (Key) Chilton, all of whom originally came from Virginia. Martin Luther Leith was educated in the public schools of Walker County. He worked on a farm until nineteen years old, after which he spent six years working in coal mines. He studied law under Thomas L. Sowell, of Jasper, and was admitted to the bar in December, 1897. He was elected to the State Senate from the twelfth district and served from 1907 to 1911, and was re-elected in 1919. On October 18, 1891, he was married to Clelia Guthrie, a daughter of John K. and Mary (Johnson) Guthrie, of Townley, a planter and a Sheriff of Walker County during the Civil War. Children—Vera Leith, who married David Erskin Moore; Quinnie Leith, who married Ralph Root; and Willie Leith, who married Leo Edwards.

Owens' Alabama, Vol. IV, page 1036.

LEONARD, DAVID, a native of South Carolina, entered government land in Section 8, Township 14, Range 8, on June 18, 1836.

Walker County Tract Record.

LEONARD, JAMES LOUIS, was born August 21, 1845, on Polls Creek, near Holly Grove. In April, 1863, he enlisted at Jasper as a private in Company H, of Musgrove's Battalion, under Captain John D. Mason, and served until the close of the war. He died on July 29, 1911, and is buried at Pleasantfield. Mr. Leonard was married to Caroline Brown. His daughter, Martelia, was married to Dr. J. Newton Odom, of Oakman.

Census of Confederate Soldiers, 1907.
Moore's Alabama, Vol. III, page 621.
Gravestone.

EARLY SETTLERS 267

LESLIE, AARON, entered government land in Section 8, Township 13, Range 6, on December 19, 1855.
Walker County Tract Record.

LESTER, JAMES, entered government land in Section 32, Township 12, Range 6, on January 23, 1850.
Walker County Tract Record.

LINDSEY, WILLIAM, entered government land in Section 4, Township 14, Range 7, on February 8, 1837.
Walker County Tract Record.

LITTLE, JAMES, entered government land in Section 23, Township 13, Range 10, on January 17, 1821.
Walker County Tract Record.

LITTLE, PETER, entered government land in Section 3, Township 15, Range 9, on March 4, 1823.
Walker County Tract Record.

LIVINGSTON, JESSE, entered government land in Section 32, Township 12, Range 7, on December 16, 1854.
Walker County Tract Record.

LOCKHART, THOMAS, a native of Georgia, came to Walker County in the early days and settled on Wolf Creek, where he died during the Civil War. His wife, Dorcas Lockhart, born July 11, 1818, died March 23, 1906, and is buried in the Fike Graveyard, on the Patton-Townley Road. Two of their children were: Samuel Lockhart, who was born August 8, 1853, and died August 4, 1919, and buried in the Fike Graveyard; and Charles Lockhart, who was born in Walker County and died of measles while with the Confederate Army at Talladega, where he is buried. S. M. Lockhart, born in 1861, a son of Charles Lockhart, is an old and respected citizen of the county.
Lockhart Family Records.

LOGGAMS, JOHN C., entered government land in Section 12, Township 13, Range 5, on February 12, 1855.

Walker County Tract Record.

LOLLAR, HUGH, Sr., entered government land in Section 34, Township 14, Range 8, on Lost Creek, on January 15, 1822. Two of his sons were Hugh Lollar, Jr., and John A. Lollar, who married Susan Gillen.

Walker County Tract Record.
Owens' Alabama, Vol. IV, page 1062.
Northern Alabama, page 177.

LOLLAR, JOHN A., a son of Hugh Lollar, was born January 30, 1810, and was brought to Walker County by his father about 1822. He engaged in farming on Lost Creek, near Providence, all of his life. He died on May 11, 1888, and is buried at Providence. He was married to Susan Gillen, who was born in September, 1811, and died January 4, 1874, and is buried at Providence.

Northern Alabama, page 177.
Gravestone.

LOLLAR, HUGH GAUNT, a son of John A. and Susan (Gillen) Lollar, was born on a farm on Lost Creek, near Providence, in November, 1829. He was a successful farmer and merchant and served for two years as Sherff of Walker County before the Civil War. He was a Lieutenant in the Confederate Army during the war, and was killed in action in the battle of Reasca, Georgia, on May 14, 1864. On November 3, 1854, Mr. Lollar was married to Sarah Catherine Leith, who was born May 6, 1829, a daughter of George and Elizabeth (Branner) Leith; granddaughter of Ebenezer Leith, a Baptist minister of Jefferson County, Tenn., who fought with John Roper's company of East Tennessee Volunteers during 1813-1814, and of J. Michael Branner and Christina (Arey) Branner, natives of Virginia, who settled near Dandridge, Tennessee, about 1800; great-granddaughter of Carl and Catherine Branner, German immigrants who settled in the Shenandoah Valley, of Virginia, near Staunton, about 1750. The children of Hugh Gaunt and Sarah Catherine (Leith) Lollar were: Cicero Lollar, who married Lizzie Cornett, and later moved to Texas; Sebastian Napoleon Lollar; Zephronia Elizabeth Lollar, who married William Oliver, and later moved to Mississippi; Lucius R. Lollar.

Genealogy of the Branner Family.

LOLLAR, JOHN BERRY, a son of John A. and Susan (Gillen) Lollar, was born near Providence on November 30, 1835. Reared on a farm, he followed that calling until September, 1862, when he enlisted as Second Lieutenant of Company G, Fifty-sixth Alabama Cavalry, under Captain Shepherd. Returning to his home in Walker County after the war, Mr. Lollar became a large raiser of corn and cotton on Lost Creek. In 1877 he was elected Sheriff of the county; in 1880 he was elected Tax Collector; in 1885 he was appointed postmaster at Jasper, and in 1886 was elected Clerk of Circuit Court. Mr. Lollar died on August 29, 1914, and is buried in the Oak Hill Cemetery at Jasper. In 1857 he was married to Elizabeth Taylor, a daughter of Isaac Taylor, of Poplar Cove, who was born February 11, 1835, and died March 10, 1915. Children—William R. Lollar; Fannie E. Lollar, who married G. W. McFall; Meta J. Lollar, who married J. M. Cranford; Queen Victoria; Margaret Eleanor, who married T. L. Sowell; Isaac H. Lollar; Andrew J. Lollar; and Joseph Lollar.

Owens' Alabama, Vol. IV, page 1062.
Census of Confederate Soldiers, 1907.
Gravestone.

LONG, BENJAMIN McFARLAND, was born November 5, 1827, at Carrollton, Georgia, a son of John and Nancy Davis (Long) Long, natives of Marshall's Ferry, Grainger County, Tenn., who settled in Carrollton in 1826; grandson of Robert and Isabel (Leeper) Long, of Marshall's Ferry, Tenn., and of James and Jane (Walker) Long, of Carter's Valley, Hawkins County, Tenn. The Long family came from Belfast, Ireland, and settled in Rockbridge County, Virginia, in 1750. Benjamin M. Long grew to manhood at Carrollton and entered the United States army during the war with Mexico, and served throughout that war under the command of Robert E. Lee. After the Mexican War he returned to Georgia and became a merchant at Carrollton, until 1859, when he came to Walker County and located at what is now Cordova, the present town being named by Mr. Long after a town of similar name in Mexico where he was stationed during the Mexican War. Mr. Long was an old line Whig and opposed secession, but at the outbreak of the Civil War he recruited Company I, Fiftieth Alabama Infantry, and served the Confederate cause until the end. After the close of the war he returned to his mercantile business in Cordova, but changed several times, alternating between his old home and Cordova, until 1876, when he finally settled in Jasper and became its leading merchant. However, he later returned to Cordova and spent the balance of his life in developing the mineral resources of the county, as he was one of its largest owners of mineral lands. It was through his efforts that the Indian Head Mills were located in Cordova. Prior to the war he was a Whig, but he allied himself with the Republican party at the time of its organization, and thereafter took an active part in politics. He was elected delegate to the Constitutional Convention of 1865, and was Representative in the Legislature in 1880-1881, the only Republican in that body at that time. He was Presidential Elector from the Sixth Alabama District in 1884, an unsuccessful candidate for governor on the Republican ticket in 1890, and was a candidate for Congress in 1894. He died on June 17, 1903, and is buried in the Mt. Carmel Cemetery at Cordova. On October 17, 1854, he was married near

Carrollton to Amanda Caroline Wooten, a daughter of Henry Pope and Melissa Carolina (Hinton) Wooten, natives of Wilkes County, Ga. Children:

Henry Whitfield Long, who married Lula Mandeville, of Carrollton, and was a merchant at that place.

John Benjamin Long, who was born in 1857 and died in 1907. He married Missouri Katherine Musgrove, a daughter of Major F. A. Musgrove, of Jasper. John B. Long was a prominent merchant in Jasper.

Carrie Gertrude Long, who married, first, Newton Camak, and, second, Lero Garner, a farmer and merchant at Phil Campbell, Franklin County, Ala.

Thomas Leeper Long, who was born at Carrollton, Ga., May 18, 1860. He moved to Jasper with his father, entered the mercantile business, and also took an active part in politics. He was elected Presidential Elector in 1892, Representative in the Legislature, 1890 and 1900; and member of the Constitutional Convention of 1901. On May 29, 1889, he was married to Augusta M. Sprott, of Livingston, Ala. Children—Henry M. Long, Carrie Long, and Fred Long.

Robert Wooten Long, who was a merchant, and died at Cordova in 1908.

Ida Long, who was born September 19, 1866, and died December 13, 1915. She was married to Dr. John M. Miller, who moved from Coketon, Ala., to Cordova.

Lou Long, who married C. Harvey Stewart, a merchant of Carrollton, Ga.

Ada Clare Long, who married Sidney Holderness, an attorney at Carrollton, Ga.

Pope McFarland Long, a real estate operator in Cordova. He married Bertie Ellis, of Cordova.

Jesse Orville Long, who married Nona Bell Sprott, of Jasper.

Edgar William Long, who was born in Jasper July 30, 1876.

He was a successful merchant; Clerk of the Circuit Court from 1904 to 1916; Judge of Probate from 1917 to 1934. On June 12, 1900, he was married to Kathleen Phifer, of Ripley, Miss. She died in Jasper in 1908. On October 18, 1918, he was married to Mrs. Ruth (Lacy) Long, a daughter of Sheriff Lacy, of Jasper.

Owens' Alabama, Vol. IV, page 1064-68.
Moore's Alabama, Vol. II, page 5.
Memorial Record of Alabama, Vol. II, page 1024.

LOONEY, MADISON W., was born May 23, 1835, in Lawrence County, Alabama. At the outbreak of the Civil War he enlisted at Hamilton, Miss., in Company B, Twentieth Mississippi Cavalry, and served until the close of the war. Some years later he moved to Walker County, where he died on August 20, 1915, and is buried at New Prospect. His wife, Annie Liza Looney, born October 15, 1848, died March 22, 1930, and is buried at New Prospect.

Census of Confederate Soldiers, 1907.
Gravestones.

LOWERMORE, SAMUEL, entered government land in Section 34, Township 14, Range 9, on April 4, 1837.

Walker County Tract Record.

McCLAIN, JOHN M., born about 1811, entered government land in Section 19, Township 15, Range 9, on January 21, 1833. He died on November 10, 1864, and is buried in the Steedman Graveyard. His wife, Eliza McClain, born October 12, 1818, died January 22, 1897, and is buried in the Steedman Graveyard.

Walker County Tract Record.
Gravestones.

McCLAIN, GEORGE W., entered government land in Section 3, Township 15, Range 6, on February 18, 1836.

Walker County Tract Record.

McCOLLUM, JOSEPH, entered government land in Section 34, Township 14, Range 9, on January 28, 1833.

Walker County Tract Record.

McCRORY, HUGH H., entered government land in Section 17, Township 14, Range 6, on December 14, 1855.
Walker County Tract Record.

McCULLAR, ANDREW MARBELL, was born at Oakfuskee, Cleburn County, Alabama, in 1839. In June, 1862, he enlisted in Cleburn County as third sergeant in Company G, Thirtieth Alabama Infantry. His right leg was shot off and he was captured at Missionary Ridge and later exchanged at Richmond. He died on July 30, 1921, and is buried at Liberty Grove.
Census of Confederate Soldiers, 1907.
Gravestone.

McCULLAR, WILLIAM HENRY HARRISON, was born August 31, 1840, at Opelika, Lee County, Alabama. On July 4, 1861, he enlisted in Fayette County as a private in Company I, Twenty-sixth Alabama Infantry, under Captain Bryson. He was captured at Fort Donaldson and was imprisoned at Camp Douglas for seven months before he was exchanged. He was wounded at Gettysburg.
Census of Confederate Soldiers, 1907.

McCORMACK, W. J., of Dora, Alabama, was born in Randolph County December 23, 1847. He joined the Primitive Baptist Church at Old Sardis in 1880 and was ordained a minister in 1882.
Pittman, History of Primitive Baptist Ministers, page 189.

McDANIEL, BENJAMIN B., entered government land in Section 35, Township 13, Range 7, on November 14, 1860.
Walker County Tract Record.

McDONALD, GEORGE W., entered government land in Section 18, Township 13, Range 10, on February 5, 1847.
Walker County Tract Record.

McDONALD, WILLIAM K., entered government land in Section 23, Township 13, Range 10, on January 18, 1847.
Walker County Tract Record.

McDUFF, ISAAC, entered government land in Section 24, Township 16, Range 8, on March 28, 1836.
Walker County Tract Record.

McELROY, JOHN, entered government land in Section 19, Township 17, Range 6, on March 18, 1837.
Walker County Tract Record.

McFINN, JAMES, entered government land in Section 10, Township 14, Range 5, on December 21, 1835.
Walker County Tract Record.

McFINN, JOHN, entered government land in Section 32, Township 15, Range 5, on November 4, 1836.
Walker County Tract Record.

McGLATHNEY, DAVID, entered government land in Section 31, Township 14, Range 6, on November 8, 1834.
Walker County Tract Record.

McGOUGH, JOHN, was born February 9, 1839, in Coosa County, Alabama. On April 10, 1862, he enlisted at Kansas, Walker County, as a private in Company H, Forty-third Alabama Infantry, under Captain Lawrence. He was wounded at Petersburg, Va., on July 26, 1864, and after recovering from his wound, joined Company K, Fourth Alabama Cavalry, and served until the close of the war.
Census of Confederate Soldiers, 1907.

McKEY, WILLIAM A., entered government land in Section 10, Township 14, Range 5, on May 12, 1852.
Walker County Tract Record.

McMILLAN, ALLEN, entered government land in Section 31, Township 15, Range 9, on September 30, 1836.
Walker County Tract Record.

McMILLAN, FRANK MARION, was born in 1836 in Jackson County, Georgia. In March, 1862, he enlisted at Tuscaloosa as a private in Fowler's Battery. He was wounded at

Chickamauga and was discharged. He died in 1931, and is buried in the Day Graveyard at Oakman. He was married to Sarah A. Whitson, who was born in 1846, and died in 1930, and is buried at Oakman.

Census of Confederate Soldiers, 1907.
Gravestones.

McMURRAY, ANDREW J., entered government land in Section 22, Township 12, Range 5, on February 12, 1855.

Walker County Tract Record.

McNEER, DANIEL, entered government land in Section 18, Township 15, Range 8, on February 1, 1837.

Walker County Tract Record.

McNEIL, MICHAEL, entered government land in Section 3, Township 14, Range 4, on February 22, 1855.

Walker County Tract Record.

McNUTT, JAMES, entered government land in Section 34, Township 15, Range 8, on September 27, 1834.

Walker County Tract Record.

MACKEREL, JAMES, entered government land in Section 26, Township 14, Range 5, on September 21, 1835.

Walker County Tract Record.

MAGBY, VARDRY, a soldier of the Revolutionary War, age 102, resided in Walker County, with Robert Magby, on June 1, 1840.

Census of Pensioners, June 1, 1840.

MAGBY, ROBERT, entered government land in Section 25, Township 13, Range 5, on February 18, 1837.

Walker County Tract Record.

MALLARD, ELDRIDGE, entered government land in Section 8, Township 13, Range 10, on March 10, 1825. He was an intelligent farmer and the keeper of a very popular house of entertainment on the Byler Road. Of fine personal appearance and popular manners, a Democrat of the Andrew Jackson school, he was the second man to represent Walker County in the Legislature, serving in the session of 1836, and also in the sessions of 1839 and 1840. His family were fond of stylish display, hardly in keeping with the times, and this fact was used by his political opponent, James Cain, in defeating him in 1841 and 1842. Shortly after 1842 Mr. Mallard moved to Texas, where he died.

> Walker County Tract Record.
> Powell's Fifty-five Years in West Alabama.

MANASCO, GENERAL JOHN, was born at Nickajack Cave, Franklin County, Georgia, on March 28, 1800, a son of John and Vicy (Odum) Manasco; and a grandson of Jeremiah Manasco, a native of Wales, who came to Virginia during Colonial times; was a Captain in the Revolutionary Army, and subsequently lived in North and South Carolina and in Alabama; and of Abraham Odum, of South Carolina. The grandfather of General Manasco achieved enviable distinction during the Revolutionary War, and his father, in turn, was also a soldier and followed the fortunes of General Jackson, participating in the famous battle of New Orleans on January 8, 1815. Early in his infancy the parents of General Manasco moved to Tennessee, where they were close neighbors to General Jackson, whom the ambitious young pioneer evidently adopted as a model and whose prototype he was in a marked degree. In his boyhood the educational institutions of the frontier sections were few and far between, and it is doubtful that General Manasco ever attended a school of any character. He was thrown upon his own resources long before maturity, and it was as a hired farm hand that he first began the study of politics. His employer was a Federalist, but found pleasure in instructing the young man in the principles of the then existing parties—Federalist, Whig and Democrat. After a thorough investigation he allied himself with the Democrats, and through all its vicissitudes, alternate triumphs and defeats, he remained steadfast in the faith. General Manasco came to Alabama in 1816, and resided for several years in Madison and afterwards in Morgan County. Accompanied by his wife and three small children he came to Walker County, entered government land in Section 19, Township 14, Range 8, on October 20, 1835, and settled here, an absolute stranger. He very quickly established himself as a successful farmer, and then began to take an active interest in politics, and for a period of more than forty years he exercised, perhaps, a more extended influence in shaping the destinies of the Democratic party in Walker County and this section of the state than any public man of his times. He was elected to the State Legislature for the first time in 1845, and for the last time in 1876, serving, in all, through fourteen sessions of the Legislature. While his official career ended in 1876, for ten or twelve years later he was at the head and front of the Democratic organization in Walker County, and actively participated in the presidential canvass of 1888. Self educated, General Manasco was, in his prime, an impressive talker, blunt and impetuous on the hustings, but engaging and prepossessing in conversation and debate. His will was inflexible. Disdaining to temporize, he was superlatively emphatic—speaking his sentiments in plain and unmistakable language, and never receding an inch from his position. Just previous to the Civil War General Manasco enjoyed a remarkable influence over the people of Walker, a veritable patriarch, to whom all looked for counsel, and whose views commanded involuntary acquiescence. An ardent states rights Democrat, he yet opposed secession, and with all the impetuosity in him, fought this blasting issue. He actively supported Robert Guttery, Walker's delegate to the Secession Convention. When Alabama seceded, however, Manasco accepted the situation and remained true to his beloved state and county. Too old then for active military duty, he fought her enemies as best he could with such means as he had at his disposal. His military title of General had been previously obtained through service as Brigadier General of the Alabama state militia. In private life General Manasco was an equally unique and attractive personage. His hospitable home was ever open and his interesting and instructive reminiscences of his career were truly a feast, coming from a man who enjoyed the personal acquaintance of such men as Andrew Jackson, Van Buren, Clay, Calhoun, Bagby, Martin, Terry, Yancy, Leroy P. Walker, and hundreds of the other patriots and statesmen of antebellum days. In 1888, while feeding his horse, General Manasco fell and dislocated his hip, which caused him to be permanently crippled and to move about on crutches with great pain and difficulty. He died on November 23, 1895, at Townley. On February 4, 1829, in Limestone County, General Manasco was married to Lucinda Luster, a member of a distinguished Kentucky family then residing in Limestone County. She died about 1893. Children:

Carlton W. Manasco moved to California in early life and became a successful mine operator, at Smartsville, in that state.

Jeremiah Manasco became a physician, but enlisted in the Confederate Army and was killed at the battle of Shiloh.

David Manasco became a minister of the Baptist faith and was a most zealous and untiring Christian. He was appointed the first County Superintendent of Education in 1857, and also edited a denominational newspaper in Jasper. He died in 1884.

Sarah Manasco, who became the wife of the Rev. J. E. Cox, who organized the First Baptist Church of Jasper in May, 1878.

James K. Polk Manasco, who was born near Holly Grove on February 27, 1845. On September 6, 1862, he enlisted at Jasper as a private in Company G, Fifty-sixth Alabama Cavalry, under Captain Shepherd. He was promoted to Second Lieutenant for gallantry at the battle of Missionary Ridge. He served until the close of the war, when he returned to Walker County and became a prominent citizen of Townley.

Dr. John Manasco, who became a prominent physician in Townley. He was married to Sarah J. Grace, a daughter of John and Hannah Grace, of Pickens County, Ala. Among their children was Dr. Orizaba Manasco, who was born at Townley January 28, 1882, and died there in 1919. He was married to Hodie Boshell, a daughter of W. R. and Martha (King) Boshell, granddaughter of William R. King, of Walker County.

Owens' Alabama, Vol. IV, page 1150.
Mountain Eagle, March 27, 1895.
Census of Confederate Soldiers, 1907.

MANASCO, JOHN C., a grandson of General John Manasco, was born in 1869 and died in 1933. He was a life-long resident of Townley, and enjoyed the esteem and confidence of the entire community. A great lover of fox-hunting, he was known to all the leading fox hunters of Alabama and adjoining states. He was the father of Carter Manasco, of Jasper, and of Lucile and Christine Manasco, of Townley.

Mountain Eagle, May 24, 1933.

MARTIN, CHARLES R., entered government land in Section 23, Township 13, Range 5, on July 9, 1855.

Walker County Tract Record.

MARTIN, JAMES B., entered government land in Section 17, Township 14, Range 4, on August 20, 1855.

Walker County Tract Record.

MARTIN, JOHN, entered government land in Section 23, Township 12, Range 7, on November 2, 1858.

Walker County Tract Record.

MASTERSON, JAMES NEWTON, was born in Tennessee October 15, 1814, a son of Thomas Masterson, who was born in Ireland in 1776 and was married there to a Miss Stenson. Shortly after his marriage he came to America, settled in Lawrence County, Alabama, and developed a farm on which he lived until his death in 1865. James Newton Masterson married in Lawrence County, where, for a long period, he was a prominent farmer. About 1887 he moved to Oakman, where he died on July 30, 1899. His wife, Mahala Masterson, born August 20, 1825, died January 3, 1897, and is buried at Oakman. They were the parents of W. T. Masterson, who was born in Lawrence County February 5, 1855, and came to Oakman about 1887 and died there on March 17, 1911; and of Sallie Masterson, who married Dr. H. W. Stephenson (see Stephenson).

Moore's Alabama, Vol. II, pages 245 and 460.

MAY, WILLIAM, entered government land in Section 36, Township 13, Range 7, on September 10, 1860.

Walker County Tract Record.

MEHARG, LEWIS, entered government land in Section 8, Township 14, Range 5, on February 14, 1839.

Walker County Tract Record.

MILLER, Dr. LUCIUS CARL, was born in Charleston, South Carolina, on December 19, 1814, and lived there until he was six years of age, when his parents moved to Forsyth County, Georgia, where he remained until reaching manhood. In 1834 he began the study of medicine, studying under a private tutor for some time before attending medical lectures. While studying he volunteered and served for one year as a hospital steward in the Seminole Indian War. In 1836 he attended a course of lectures at the Transylvania Medical College, Lexington, Ky. Returning to his home in Georgia in the early part of 1837, he practiced medicine there during that year. In 1838 he moved to Columbiana, Alabama, and in 1839 moved to Jasper. Again, in 1842 he moved from Jasper to Holly Grove, which place he made his home for the remainder of his life. Dr. Miller was an eminently successful farmer and physician, and an honorable and useful citizen, active in all works for the welfare of his family and the advancement and prosperity of his county. During the Civil War he was captain of the Home Guard Company for Walker County. He lost much property during the war, including about thirty slaves. Dr. Miller was elected Representative from Walker County and served during the legislative sessions of 1871 and 1872. He died on February 12, 1886, and is buried at Holly Grove. On January 16, 1842, he was married to Mary Jane Leith, who was born near Centerville, Bibb County, Alabama, on May 1, 1823, a daughter of George and Elizabeth (Branner) Leith (see Leith). She died on October 20, 1903, and is buried at Holly Grove. Children:

Erastus Washington Miller, who was born at Holly Grove March 10, 1843. In January, 1862, he enlisted at Jasper as Second Lieutenant in Company L, Twenty-eighth Alabama Infantry, under Captain Musgrove, having served as a cadet at La Grange College until the fall of 1861. He was captured at Missionary Ridge on the third day of the battle, after having received seven wounds, and was imprisoned at Johnson's Island, near Sandusky, Ohio, until the close of the war. He died on March 29, 1919. He was married to a widow, Mrs. E. T. Little, but there were no children.

Araminta Ann Miller, who was born November 18, 1844, and married Captain A. J. Guthrie.

John Dudley Miller, who was born April 17, 1847. He was in the Confederate Army for three months, and participated in the battle of Missionary Ridge, but on account of his age his father secured his discharge. He died November 12, 1879. Never married.

Lavonia Catherine Miller, who was born January 1, 1850, and married Dr. D. H. Camak.

Dr. Virgil Maronis Miller, who was born April 26, 1852.

He was a prominent physician at Townley for a number of years. He died September 17, 1897. He never married.

> Genealogy of the Branner Family.
> Jasper True Citizen, March 11, 1886.
> Census of Confederate Soldiers, 1907.
> Gravestones.

MINOR, ROLAND W., entered government land in Section 26, Township 16, Range 8, on November 23, 1835.

> Walker County Tract Record.

MINTER, WILLIAM E., entered government land in Section 35, Township 14, Range 4, on February 12, 1856.

> Walker County Tract Record.

MOODY, JONATHAN P., entered government land in Section 5, Township 14, Range 7, on December 12, 1855.

> Walker County Tract Record.

MOON, MOSES, entered government land in Section 9, Township 14, Range 7, on February 16, 1842.

> Walker County Tract Record.

MOONEY, JONATHAN PAUL, was born in Knucklesville, Cobb County, Georgia, on December 28, 1833. It is thought that he came to Walker County about 1855. In December, 1861, he enlisted at Jasper as fifth sergeant in Company G, Fiftieth Alabama Infantry, under Captain Long, and served until the close of the war. He died on January 6, 1915, and is buried at New Prospect. His wife, Annie C. Mooney, was born February 8, 1833, and died March 13, 1906.

> Census of Confederate Soldiers, 1907.
> Gravestones.

MOORE, SAMUEL H., entered government land in Section 31, Township 13, Range 9, on August 11, 1848.

> Walker County Tract Record.

MORGAN, EZEKIEL, was born August 21, 1797, near Raleigh, North Carolina. His opportunities were few, and his early life was spent on his father's farm, with no chance of education other than that afforded by the community. About 1820 he was married to Linnie Brantley, who was born at Raleigh February 29, 1802, a daughter of Riley Brantley, who is thought to have emigrated from Holland with his parents at an early age. Immediately after his marriage Ezekiel Morgan put his bride on a blind mule, together with their entire household equipment, consisting of one tin cup and one bottle, and walked and led the way from Raleigh to a new home in Alabama, settling first near Blount Springs, in Blount County. They later moved to a point in Jefferson County, north of Birmingham, and finally sometime during the early 1840's, came to Walker County and settled on Horse Creek, about two miles west of Dora, where they established a permanent home and spent the rest of their days. About this time coal mining became a thriving industry in Walker County, and Ezekiel Morgan's family, particularly his son, Reuben, were pioneers in the digging of coal from the banks and beds of Horse Creek and the Warrior River, near Dora. Through industry and thrift Ezekiel Morgan became a prosperous farmer and coal operator, and an outstanding and respected citizen of the county. His wife, Linnie (Brantley) Morgan, died on December 27, 1874, and is buried in the old cemetery at Dora. Shortly after this Ezekiel Morgan was married the second time to a widow, a Mrs. Rogers, but he only survived a few years. He died on November 26, 1881, and is also buried in the old graveyard at Dora. There were no children from the second marriage, but there were eleven from the first marriage:

John Morgan, who moved to, and spent his life in, Fulton, Miss.

William Morgan, who spent his life near Birmingham.

Reuben Morgan, who came to Walker County with his father and became a pioneer coal operator. He was married to

Martha Holley. Children—Ida Morgan, Etta Morgan, Octavia Morgan, John Perry Morgan, Della Morgan, Reuban (Boss) Morgan.

Peter A. Morgan, who was born December 31, 1831, died November 5, 1857, and is buried at Friendship, near Dora. He was married to Martha Walker, who was born July 5, 1825, and died August 5, 1896. She was a daughter of Samuel and Nancy Taylor (Brackett) Walker. Children—Anderson Morgan, Ezekiel Morgan, and Riley Morgan.

Eliza Morgan, who was born January 28, 1833, and was married to Amos B. Walker, a son of Samuel and Nancy Taylor (Brackett) Walker.

Robert J Morgan, who was born May 6, 1834, at Blount Springs, Blount County, Alabama. In August, 1862, he enlisted at Jasper as a private in Company F, Fifty-sixth Alabama Cavalry, under Captain Rice. He was captured in Walker County by Wilson's Raiders in March, 1865. He died on August 16, 1916, and is buried at Dora. Robert Jasper Morgan was married to Sarah Amanda Ballenger, who was born December 16, 1831, and died February 15, 1902. Children—John R. Morgan, William R. Morgan, James I. Morgan, Rachel Morgan, Sarah Ann Morgan, Martha Morgan, Hulda (Babe) Morgan, Rosa Morgan, Mary Morgan, and Dolly Morgan.

Maston C. Morgan, who was born near Baltimore Ford on the Mulberry Fork, September 10, 1837. On September 2, 1862, he enlisted at Jasper as a private in Company F, Twenty-eighth Alabama Infantry, and served until March, 1863, when he was sent home on account of physical disability. In July, 1863, he re-enlisted in Company G, Eighth Alabama Cavalry, under Captain Wharton, and served until the close of the war. He died on December 15, 1923, and is buried at Dora. He was married to Georgianna Elmore, who was born November 17, 1844, and died August 5, 1896. Children—Dock Morgan, who moved to Texas; Augustus Morgan, who moved to Texas; Henry Morgan; Louise Morgan; and Bama Morgan.

Malissa Morgan, who married Thomas W. Davis.

Narcissus Morgan, who was born February 12, 1841, and who married Thomas W. Davis, the widower of her sister, Malissa.

Henry Terrell Morgan, who was born in Jefferson County, sixteen miles north of Birmingham, on October 22, 1843. In 1862 he enlisted at Sanders' Ferry as a private in Company F, Fifty-sixth Alabama Cavalry, under Captain Rice, and served until the close of the war. He was married to a widow, a Mrs. Tompson.

Melvin W. Morgan, who was born May 24, 1846, and died December 15, 1906. He was married to Sophronia C. Elmore, who was born May 27, 1847, and died March 13, 1932.

Family Records, J. D. Walker.
Census of Confederate Soldiers, 1907.
Gravestones.

MORGAN, REUBEN MARDIS, was born at Blountsville, Blount County, March 8, 1837. In January, 1862, he enlisted at Jasper as a private in Company F, Twenty-eighth Alabama Infantry, under Captain Gamble, and served until the close of the war.

Census of Confederate Soldiers, 1907.

MORRIS, JOHN H., entered government land in Section 10, Township 15, Range 8, on February 9, 1836.

Walker County Tract Record.

MORRIS, ROBERT, entered government land in Section 11, Township 15, Range 8, on March 20, 1837.

Walker County Tract Record.

MORRIS, WILLIAM A., was born December 22, 1827. After reaching manhood, he taught school until the outbreak of the Civil War. On August 28, 1862, he enlisted in the Thirty-eighth Alabama Regiment under Captain J. R. Jenkins and died in the service at Kingston, Georgia, in 1863. On October 5, 1852, he was married to Margaret Christian Leith, a daughter of George and Elizabeth (Branner) Leith. Children—Eliza Jane Morris, who was born May 10, 1854, and was married to John John M. Guthrie; Sarah Elizabeth Morris, who was born March 29, 1856, and was married to E. W. Shepherd; Lavonia Ann Morris, who was born July 16, 1858, and was married to W. L. Phillips; Sebastian N. Morris; and Louisa Virginia Morris.

Genealogy of the Branner Family.

MORRIS, JAMES LARRY, was born January 22, 1839, near Watts' Mill on Lost Creek. In September, 1862, he enlisted at Jasper as a private in Company G, Fifty-sixth Alabama Cavalry, under Captain Shepherd, and served until the close of the war. He died on May 1, 1916, and is buried at Old Zion. His wife, Elizabeth Morris, was born February 26, 1843, and died June 25, 1918, and is buried at Old Zion.

Census of Confederate Soldiers, 1907.
Gravestones.

MORRIS, DAVID, was born August 29, 1843, near Odom's Mill on Lost Creek. In the spring of 1861 he enlisted at Day's Gap as a private in Company K, Fiftieth Alabama Infantry, under Captain Hutto. He was discharged by a medical board in 1863, and in January, 1864, re-enlisted as a private in Company E, Twenty-eighth Alabama Infantry, under Captain Lollar, and served until the close of the war.

Census of Confederate Soldiers, 1907.

MORRIS, JAMES HARVEY, was born March 11, 1845, eight miles southwest of Jasper on Lost Creek. In September, 1861, he enlisted at Tierce's Mill, as a private in Company K, Fiftieth Alabama Infantry, under Captain Hutto. He was captured at the battle of Missionary Ridge and was imprisoned at

Rock Island, Ill., until the close of the war. He died March 4, 1914.

Census of Confederate Soldiers, 1907.

MORROW, SAMUEL, entered government land in Section 4, Township 14, Range 7, on August 14, 1852, north of Jasper. He was married to Lidia Barton, a daughter of Moses Barton I.

Walker County Tract Record.

MORROW, JAMES, entered government land in Section 9, Township 14, Range 6, on March 5, 1855. He was married to Frances Barton, a daughter of Moses Barton I.

Walker County Tract Record.

MORROW, JOHN QUINCY, was born at Moulton, Lawrence County, on July 23, 1824. He came to Walker County in 1855 and entered government land in Section 9, Township 14, Range 6, on September 4, 1855. In January, 1862, he enlisted at Jasper as a private in Company H, of Musgrove's Battalion, under Captain Mason, and served until the close of the war. He died on March 14, 1918, and is buried at Old Sardis on the Warrior River. He was married to Margaret Black, who was born in 1840 and died January 18, 1901, and is buried at Old Sardis. Children—Hugh Morrow, who married Mary Ann Sanders; Archibald Morrow, who married Alta Deason; Mollie Morrow, who married Washington Barton; and Catherine Morrow, who married Burl Felkins.

Census of Confederate Soldiers, 1907.
Morrow Family Records.
Gravestones.

MULLINAX, RICHARD, born in 1813, was among the first settlers of the county and a prominent Methodist in the High Hill beat. He died on October 19, 1888.

Mountain Eagle, October 31, 1888.

MULLINS, BUDDY E., entered government land in Section 25, Township 13, Range 5, on February 3, 1851.

Walker County Tract Record.

MURPHEE, DAVID, entered government land in Section 3, Township 14, Range 5, on October 9, 1819.
Walker County Tract Record.

MURPHEE, MARTIN, entered government land in Section 34, Township 13, Range 5, on March 15, 1822, and also in Section 7, Township 14, Range 8, on June 8, 1822.
Walker County Tract Record.

MURRAY, BENJAMIN, entered government land in Section 21, Township 16, Range 7, on April 12, 1822.
Walker County Tract Record.

MURRAY, RICHARD HENRY, born August 7, 1834, at Monticello, Jasper County, Georgia, enlisted at Greenville Ala., as a private in Company C, Thirty-third Alabama Infantry, and served throughout the war.
Census of Confederate Soldiers, 1907.

MUSGROVE, Dr. EDWARD GORDON, was born about 1795 in Georgia, a son of John William and Nancy (Tate) Musgrove, who removed to Edgefield District, South Carolina, in 1797, and to Cocke County, Tennessee, in 1807. In 1822 Edward Gordon Musgrove came to Alabama and settled in Blount County, and about one year later came to Walker County and settled on the present site of the town of Jasper. He was one of the first practicing physicians to settle in the county, and was known to treat patients as far as eighty miles from Jasper, traveling over almost impassable roads in the very worst kinds of weather. Dr. Musgrove had much to do with the establishment of the county and the selection of Jasper as the county seat. He gave the land on which stands the Walker County courthouse and may be justly called the founder of Jasper. He was the first judge of the county court. Dr. Musgrove was also a local preacher in the Methodist Church and was instrumental in the establishment of that church in the county. He donated the land on which the first Methodist Church was built in Jasper.

The earliest authentic record of Methodism in Walker County is a report of a quarterly conference held on June 14, 1833, when Dr. Musgrove acted as secretary. He was married to Rachel Hychlin, of Saluda, S. C.

> Owens' Alabama, Vol. IV, page 1264.
> Armes' Story of Coal and Iron.
> West's History of Methodism.

MUSGROVE, FRANCES ASBURY, a son of Dr. Edward G. and Rachel (Hychlin) Musgrove, was born in Jasper August 22, 1827. He was fitted for college by his father, but never obtained his degree, due to the pressure of business affairs. He engaged in the mercantile business in Jasper and was one of the early coal operators of the county. In 1850 he mined coal in Bull Bottom, about a mile from Cane Creek, in partnership with Rufus Jones. The coal had to be hauled to the water to be loaded for boating to the lower river markets. At the outbreak of the Civil War he was elected captain of Company C, Twenty-eighth Alabama Infantry, and was afterwards promoted to major. Judge A. A. Coleman said of Major Musgrove that "he was one of the handsomest men he ever saw, and he made a gallant soldier. He was severely wounded at Murfreesboro and was sent home with orders to enlist men who had not entered the Confederate Army. The dominant sentiment of the county was in sympathy with the Confederate cause, but there was considerable Union element among the people. A large number of men were not enlisted for war. Drastic measures were committed to Major Musgrove, and he managed so tactfully and so persuasively that he secured, without arresting men, two battalions for active service at the front. One of these battalions was sent to the armies in Virginia and Georgia; the other, Musgrove's Battalion, Major Musgrove led under Forest to the close of the war. Major Musgrove was not only a strong business man, but he was also a genial, joyous, companionable associate with his fellow men." He died at Jasper on July 22, 1865. On January 6, 1853, he was married to Elizabeth Cain, who was born August 18, 1835, and died June 18, 1917, a daughter of James and Elizabeth (McAuley) Cain, of Liberty Hill. Children— Missouri Katherine Musgrove, who married John B. Long; Lycurgus Breckenbridge Musgrove, never married; Judge Coleman Musgrove, who married Susan Findley Neal; and Calpernia Rachel Musgrove, who never married.

Armes' Story of Coal and Iron.
Owens' Alabama, Vol. IV, page 1264.

MUSGROVE, LYCURGUS BRECKENBRIDGE, a son of Major Frances Asbury and Elizabeth (Cain) Musgrove, was born in Jasper on December 13, 1859. Reared in Jasper, his education was limited to the public schools of that community, but he was a student all of his life and was better informed than many college graduates. At an early age he served as a mail carrier and as a page in the Alabama Legislature. Acquiring a little money by his own efforts, he purchased the Mountain Eagle, a weekly newspaper in Jasper, while still a young man, and became a successful publisher. Later he became a successful merchant, real estate dealer and coal operator and accumulated a great deal of wealth. He was one of the leading business men of the county for many years. Mr. Musgrove took part in state wide political activities, and as a Democrat frequently managed campaigns, but never held public office, other than serving as Chairman of the Walker County Board of Education, as a member of the State Board of Education, and as a trustee of the University of Alabama. He was a strong Prohibitionist and was appointed, by the Anti-Saloon League of America, national chairman for the ratification of the Eighteenth Amendment. He devoted a great deal of time and money to this movement. Mr. Musgrove never married and died in Jasper in 1931.

Owens' Alabama, Vol. IV, page 1264.
Files of the Mountain Eagle.

EARLY SETTLERS 291

MYERS, JACOB, entered government land in Section 33, Township 13, Range 5, on December 20, 1826.
Walker County Tract Record.

MYERS, WILLIAM JAMES, was born May 2, 1814, a son of John James Myers, who was born in South Carolina in 1776 and died in Autauga County, Ala., in 1836, and of Elizabeth (Jumper) Myers, who was born in 1786 and died about 1834; and, according to family tradition, a grandson of Jacob Myers, who was a major in the Revolutionary War and was present at the surrender of Lord Cornwallis; and a great-grandson of Rudolph Myers, a native of Germany, who emigrated from Zurich, Switzerland, in the early 1700's and settled in New York state, but who moved to Richland District, South Carolina, about 1740. William James Myers lived for a time in Coosa County, above Wetumpka, but in 1857 he came to Walker County and settled on a farm near Pleasant Grove Church, where he spent the balance of his life. He died on October 6, 1900, and is buried in the Pleasant Grove Graveyard. He was married in Coosa County to Sarah James (or Jeems), and was the father of fifteen children—

William Dickson Myers, who was born January 6, 1837, and died November 14, 1865. He was married to Jane Randolph.

Sarah Myers, who was born November 17, 1839. She was married to James Edward Windham.

George A. Myers, who was born November 27, 1840. He was married to Sallie Lawson and moved to Oklahoma.

Jane Myers, who was born February 12, 1842, and died May 5, 1871. She was married to James Findle.

Nan Myers, who was born September 27, 1843. She was married to Melton Williams.

John Henry Myers, who was born May 20, 1845, at Bikeville, Coosa County, Ala. In October, 1863, he enlisted at Jasper as a private in Company B, Tenth Alabama Cavalry, under Captain Whatley, and served until the close of the war. He died May 9, 1921, and is buried at Pleasant Grove. He was married to Mehaley C. Swindle, who was born March 11, 1845, and died July 6, 1926.

Howell Arnold Myers, who was born December 24, 1846, and died August 3, 1919. He was married to Mandy Johnson.

Phillip Jefferson Myers, who was born July 11, 1848. He was married to Mary Ann (Polly) Tubbs, who was born May 3, 1846, a daughter of Daniel Lee and Nancy Emily (Cranford) Tubbs.

Amanda Silvera Myers, who was born April 16, 1850. She was married to Dennis Swindle, a son of Daniel Swindle.

James Augustus Myers, who was born July 15, 1851, and died September 7, 1922. He was married to Lucy B. Key.

Wake Asbury Myers, who was born June 4, 1853. He was married to Pattie Johnson.

Martha Helen Myers, who was born November 24, 1854. She was married to Lucius C. Swindle, a son of William and Susan (Hogue) Swindle.

Ellen A. Kinsey Myers, who was born July 26, 1856. She was married on July 2, 1882, to Lavator Miller, who was born May 1, 1860.

Susan Francis Myers, who was born September 21, 1858. She was married to Napoleon Colorado Posey, a son of Napoleon Bonapart Posey.

Josephine Myers, who was born April 29, 1862. She died young and never married.

> Records of the Myers Family.
> Census of Confederate Soldiers, 1907.
> Mountain Eagle, July 4, 1934.
> Gravestones.

NATIONS, JOSEPH, entered government land in Sections 21

and 22, Township 14, Range 5, near the confluence of the Sipsey and Mulberry Forks, on May 18, 1821.
Walker County Tract Record.

NATIONS, BAILES, entered government land in Section 2, Township 15, Range 7, on Bull Barn Creek, west of Cordova, on February 27, 1822.
Walker County Tract Record.

NATIONS, JOSEPH, was born August 19, 1831, near Dora. In the spring of 1862 he enlisted in the Confederate Army, but was detailed to get out saltpeter. In March, 1863, he enlisted at Jasper as a private in Company G, Fifty-sixth Alabama Infantry, under Captain Shepherd, and served until the close of the war. He died on June 19, 1913, and is buried in Mt. Carmel Cemetery at Cordova. His wife, Francis E. Nations, was born April 27, 1828, and died July 11, 1902.
Census of Confederate Soldiers, 1907.
Gravestones.

NEAL, SAMUEL, entered government land in Section 23, Township 14, Range 9, on September 24, 1836.
Walker County Tract Record.

NELSON, ANDREW, was born in York County, Pennsylvania, in 1762, but later he or his family moved to Virginia. While residing in Augusta County, Virginia, on June 15, 1779, he volunteered and served as a private in Captain John Cunningham's company of the Virginia troops, until September 15, 1779. On May 11, 1780, he again enlisted with the Virginia troops and served in Captain John McKitterick's company. He was out against the Indians in Northwestern Virginia until August 15, 1780. From December 15, 1780, until May 1, 1781, he served in Captain James Tate's company, under Colonel Campbell. He marched to North Carolina and was in the battle of Guilford. In 1832 Andrew Nelson was residing in Morgan County, Alabama, and in 1840 he was living in Walker County.

He died on November 1, 1850, while living with his son-in-law, George Ellis, near Houston, Winston County, and is buried in Winston County, in a small graveyard on the east side of the Sipsey River, between Double Springs and Addison. He is known to have been the father of at least two children—Peggy Nelson, who married George Ellis, of Winston County, and later moved to Lawrence County; and L. S. Nelson, who was born December 15, 1797, and died November 2, 1874, and is buried in the Fike Graveyard.

Records of U. S. Veterans Bureau.
Gravestones.

NELSON, JOHN N., a grandson of the Revolutionary soldier, Andrew Nelson, was born in Morgan County January 22, 1818. When nineteen years of age he moved to Walker County and entered government land in Section 30, Township 14, Range 8, near Pleasant Hill. He died on May 20, 1926, and is buried in the Pleasant Hill Graveyard. His wife, Catherine Nelson, was born December 24, 1827, and died November 11, 1891.

Gravestones.
Walker County Tract Record.

NELSON, ANDREW JACKSON, a son of L. S. Nelson and a grandson of the Revolutionary soldier, Andrew Nelson, was born in Morgan County on August 3, 1820. It is thought that he came to Walker County about 1837. In the spring of 1863 he enlisted at the old Baker Place, now Steedman's Bridge, as a second sergeant in Company B, Tenth Alabama Cavalry, under Captain Whatley. He was captured by Wilson's Raiders on March 27, 1865, while passing through Walker County, and was carried to Montgomery, where he was paroled a short time later. He died on April 6, 1915, and is buried in the Fike Graveyard.

Census of Confederate Soldiers, 1907.
Gravestones.

NELSON, JOHN MARTIN, was born near Holly Grove on

December 16, 1844. In the spring of 1863 he enlisted at the old Baker Place, now Steedman's Bridge, as a private in Company B, Tenth Alabama Cavalry, under Captain Whatley, and served until the close of the war. He died on January 10, 1934, and is buried in the old Guttery Graveyard at Townley. His wife, Laura A. Nelson, was born January 27, 1840, and died November 22, 1918.

Census of Confederate Soldiers, 1907.
Gravestones.

NOLES, JOSEPH, entered government land in Section 23, Township 12, Range 6, on October 10, 1855.

Walker County Tract Record.

NORRIS, YOUNG, entered government land in Section 18, Township 14, Range 8, near Townley, on September 3, 1822.

Walker County Tract Record.

NORRIS, JOSEPH ZACHARIAH, was born March 16, 1827, at Indian Ford on Lost Creek. In September, 1862, he enlisted at Holly Grove as a private in Company A, Fifty-sixth Alabama Cavalry, under Captain Guttery, and served until the close of the war.

Census of Confederate Soldiers, 1907.

NORVELL, PEYTON, a son of Lucien Bonaparte and Clara (Hawes) Norvell, and a grandson of William Peyton, of Dumfries, Va., and of Aylette Hawes, was born at Waverly, Prince William County, Virginia, on August 7, 1861. Educated in the public schools of Lynchburg, Va., and at Tulane University, New Orleans, he was admitted to the bar in Alabama in 1894 and started his practice in that year at Jasper. He was judge of law and equity in 1901-02. He died on July 21, 1917, and is buried in the Oak Hill Cemetery at Jasper. On March 4, 1886, he was married to Mary Leech, a daughter of Elbert C. Leech, of Mississippi. Children—Mary Hawes Norvell; Clara Davis Norvell; Kathleen Norvell; Peyton Norvell, Jr., of Abilene, Texas; and Sally Nelson Norvell, who married Charles R. Wiggins, of Jasper.

Owens' Alabama, Vol. IV, page 1287.

ODOM, WILLIAM, SR., a native of Coweta County, Georgia, was born July 8, 1777. It is thought that he came to Walker County prior to 1840; however, he entered government land in Section 20, Township 15, Range 7, south of Parrish, on October 26, 1848, and engaged in farming for the balance of his life. He died on February 15, 1856, and is buried in the Gray Graveyard near Parrish. His wife, Jansie Odom, born May 6, 1778, died March 1, 1855. Children—

James Odom, born in Georgia, September 9, 1811, and died in Walker County, April 1, 1906. He was married twice—first, in Georgia, to Mary E. Odom; and, second, in Walker County, to Mahaley Elinor Plylan. Children by first marriage: Emily, who married James A. Grace; Oliver, who married Jane Eastman, but died in the Civil War; James Odom, who never married, and died in the Civil War; Samuel Odom, who married Catherine Sanford; Annette Odom, who married James Jones. Children by second marriage: Dalton Odom, who married Elizabeth Sedberry; Mary Odom, who married Jesse Simeon Kitchens; and Isabelle Odom, who married John E. Cooner.

William Odom, Jr., who married a Miss Winkle. Children: Asbury Odom, who married Jane Plylar; Thomas Odom; James Ira Odom, who married Paralee Thompson; and Catherine Odom, who married William Chappell.

John J. Odom, who married Nancy Wilson. Children: William Odom, who married Irene Woods, and moved to Oklahoma; Basil Odom, who married a Miss Sanford; John Odom, who married Jennie Ann Love; James Odom, who married Julia Jones; Thomas Odom, who married a Miss Key; Mary Odom, who never married; and Cansada Odom, who married, first, John Bates, and, second, Virgil Jones.

Jacob Odom, who married Elizabeth Adcock. Children: Dock Odom, who married, first, a Miss Swindle, and, second, Gerusha Tenia Sartain; Noah Odom, who married a Miss Davis; and James Odom, who married a Miss Nelson.

David Odom, who lived and died in Georgia.

Lucy Odom, who married a Mr. Adcock.

Honor Odom, who married Warren Adcock.

Lidia Odom, who married a Mr. Dill.

Nancy Odom, who married Lewis Barrentine.

Odom Family Records.
Gravestones.

ODOM, JAMES IRA, a son of William Odom, Jr., and a grandson of William and Jansie Odom, was born at Newnan, Georgia, on October 1, 1841. It is thought that he came to Walker County about 1858, and later built a grist mill on Lost Creek at Cannon Bridge. On September 26, 1861, he enlisted at Jasper as a private in Company I, Fiftieth Alabama Infantry, under Captain B. M. Long. He participated in many of the major battles, including Chickamauga, Missionary Ridge and others. He was wounded at Shiloh, but after a few weeks in the hospital he rejoined his regiment and served until July 28, 1864, when he was captured west of Atlanta and imprisoned at Camp Chase, Ohio, until March 4, 1865, when he was paroled until exchanged. However, he was not exchanged before the final surrender. Returning to Walker County after the war he continued his occupation of farming until his death on May 5, 1913. He is buried in the Pleasantfield Graveyard. He was married to Caroline Paralee Thompson, a daughter of Fleming R. Thompson. Children: Jeremiah Newton Odom; James Ivan Odom; Augustus Adolphus Odom; Elvin Ray Odom; John Berry Odom; Alpha Odom, who married, first, Clarence Vines, and, second, Minter McMahan; Pearl Odom, who married Benjamin Long Evans; Minard Odom; and Hugh David Odom.

>   Moore's Alabama, Vol. III, page 621.
>   Census of Confederate Soldiers, 1907.
>   Gravestones.

ODOM, Dr. JEREMIAH NEWTON, a son of James Ira and Paralee (Thompson) Odom, grandson of William Odom, Jr., and great-grandson of William and Jansie Odom, was born near Oakman; attended the public schools of that place and then entered the College of Physicians and Surgeons, Atlanta, Georgia, from which he graduated with the degree of Doctor of Medicine. He practiced medicine at Oakman until his death in 1917. He was married to Martelia Leonard, a daughter of James Lewis and Caroline (Brown) Leonard, of Oakman. Children:

Allan Thurman Odom, who was born August 10, 1889. On December 20, 1908, he was married to Alice Leith, a daughter of Dr. F. M. and Sarah F. (Whitson) Leith, a granddaughter of George and Elizabeth (Branner) Leith. No children.

Dr. Henry G. Odom, who was born January 3, 1892. On July 23, 1915, he was married to Gaye Walton, a daughter of Samuel and Martha (Beasley) Walton, and a granddaughter of Samuel Walton. Children—Elsie Ruth Odom, Corely Odom, and Hubert Odom.

Lewis Odom.

J. Avery Odom.

Dr. Graham N. Odom.

Mrs. W. H. Utley.

Mrs. Otis Holliday.

>   Moore's Alabama, Vol. III, page 621.
>   Genealogy of the Branner Family.
>   Mountain Eagle, May 9, 1935.

O'REAR, MARTIN, a descendant of William O'Rear, an Irish immigrant, who settled in the Carolinas during Colonial times, was born in Tennessee; moved to northern Alabama, and finally settled in Walker County before 1840. He acquired extensive farming interests and served for two years as tax assessor. He died in Jasper in 1864. He was married to a Miss Alexander, of Tennessee, who died in Jasper in 1876. Children—William J., Daniel, Elijah, Jefferson, Samuel, Anderson, Joseph, Jeremiah, and William B.

Walker County Tract Record.
Moore's Alabama, Vol. II, page 481.

O'REAR, ELIJAH, a son of Martin O'Rear, was born in Tennessee in 1829, and was still a small boy when his parents settled in Walker County. He followed the trade of carpenter and farmer until the outbreak of the Civil War, when he enlisted as a member of the Twenty-eighth Alabama Infantry. After the close of the war he returned to his home and followed his old occupations until 1880, when he was elected Sheriff of the county and served for four years. From 1888 to 1896 he served as County Treasurer. He died in Jasper on September 26, 1907. He was married to Sarah Melissa Feltman, who was born in Fayette County in 1835 and died in Jasper in 1915. Children—

Martin O'Rear, who married Hatton Gunter, a daughter of Colonel S. M. Gunter.

Jefferson D. O'Rear, who married a daughter of Col. S. M. Gunter, and was the father of Edward O'Rear, Mrs. Neal Lawhorn, Mrs. Mack Chandler, and Gunter O'Rear.

George Daniel O'Rear, who was born in Tuscaloosa County on November 13, 1854, but who was reared on his father's farm in Walker County, and became a citizen of Jasper in 1880. For five years he was clerk in the office of the Probate Judge, following which he engaged in the mercantile business until 1912. In 1917 he was County Treasurer. He was largely interested in the development of the mining industry in the county. A charter member of the Baptist Church of Jasper, founded in 1878, he was treasurer of that church for forty years. On January 18, 1880, he was married to Venila Lucretia Sanders, a daughter of Samuel Monroe and Nancy (Cain) Sanders, who was born in January, 1858, and died March 16, 1934. Children—Guy V. O'Rear, who married Vesta Briggs, of Birmingham; Caine O'Rear, who married Lulu Dodd, of Oxford, Alabama; Ethel O'Rear, who married Dr. Wm. W. Wood, of Jasper; Judson O'Rear, who married Odessa Henley, of Prairie, Mississippi; Maynard O'Rear, who married Adele Brown, of Oakman; and Mabel O'Rear.

Rufus Allen O'Rear, who was born at Jasper January 29, 1869, and educated in the public schools of Jasper, the University of Alabama, the University of Nashville and the Peabody Normal College. He was Tax Commissioner of Walker County and a member of the Constitutional Convention of 1901; Captain of Troop B, First Alabama Cavalry, and served on the Mexican border and in training camps, 1916–1918; Mayor of Jasper, 1919–1920. Never married.

Moore's Alabama, Vol. II, page 481.
Owens' Alabama, Vol. IV, page 1303.
Mountain Eagle, March 21, 1934.

O'REAR, JOHN, a brother of Martin O'Rear, came to Walker County before 1840 and settled north of Jasper.

Mountain Eagle, June 28, 1935.

O'REAR, FIELDS, a brother of Martin O'Rear, came to Walker County before 1840 and settled north of Jasper.

Mountain Eagle, June 28, 1935.

O'REAR, WILLIAM BYRD, was born near Jasper on September 3, 1839. On February 20, 1862, he enlisted at Jasper as a private in Company I, Fiftieth Alabama Infantry, under Captain Long. He was wounded at Chickamauga and discharged but re-enlisted on October 20, 1863, in Company B, Tenth Alabama Cavalry, under Captain Whatley, and served until the close of the war. He was married to Hannah Lamkin, a daughter of Griffin and Sarah (Thacker) Lamkin.

Census of Confederate Soldiers, 1907.

O'REAR, JOHN, was born at Holly Grove, May 7, 1846. In September, 1864, he enlisted at Jasper as a private in Company B, Tenth Alabama Cavalry, under Captain Whatley. While detailed for service in Walker County in March, 1865, he was captured by Wilson's Raiders and was imprisoned at Selma until the close of the war.

Census of Confederate Soldiers, 1907.

O'REAR, ANDERSON, was a member of Company H, Thirty-eighth Tennessee Infantry, during the Civil War.

Gravestone.

ORR, JONATHAN, entered government land in Section 27, Township 15, Range 9, on October 17, 1821.

Walker County Tract Record.

OWEN, WILLIAM MONTREVILLE, a son of Charles Coatsworth Pinckney and Mary Catherine (Cooper) Owen, of Athens, Tennessee, was born at Calhoun, McMinn County, Tennessee, on November 27, 1827. He came to Walker County about 1860 and later moved to Birmingham, where he died on July 2, 1889. On February 26, 1862, he was married to Susanna Ryan, a daughter of Isaac and Mary (Camak) Ryan, who was born in Jasper February 13, 1837, and died in Birmingham on December 22, 1888. Children—Ida Owen, born March 5, 1866, and died August 28, 1910, was married to W. L. Barrington; Rufus Owen, born December 18, 1869, and died September 4, 1919, was married to Nora Lemons; Ella Owen, born April 16, 1868, and married to William Parker; Julia Owen, born July 16, 1871, and married to Robert Johnson; Elizabeth Owen, born February 8, 1873, and married to Dalton Robertson; Charles Coatsworth Pinckney Owen, born September 6, 1875, and married to Sadie Eason; Isaac Owen, born October 11, 1877; and Hubert Carlos Owen, born April 20, 1879.

Owen Family Records.

PALMER, ROBERT T., was born in South Carolina, a son of Jesse Palmer, a native of Virginia who died in South Carolina. Robert T. Palmer grew up in Marshall County, Alabama, where he engaged in farming until 1859, when he moved to Walker County and developed a plantation on Wolf Creek, fourteen miles southwest of Jasper. He was elected County Commissioner for 1860-61, and at the outbreak of the Civil War he enlisted in the Confederate Army and died, while in service, of typhoid fever in 1863. He was married to Elizabeth Ann White, who was born in Marshall County in 1815, a daughter of General Zack White. She died at her home on Wolf Creek in 1881. Children—

Lovenia Palmer, who, in 1866, was married to Captain James Polk Little, of Jasper. She died in Amory, Miss., in 1908.

Asbury Thomas Palmer, a merchant in Jasper, who died there in 1890.

Eustatia Palmer, who married J. W. Shepherd, former Judge of Probate at Jasper.

Robert Henry Palmer, who was born in Marshall County in 1856, but grew up on his father's plantation on Wolf Creek. He remained on the farm until 1889, when he moved to Dora and opened the largest department store in the county at that time. He became a very successful business man and one of the large property owners of the county. He served from 1887 to 1891 as Tax Collector of the county, was a member of the Jasper City Council for eight years, and was mayor of Dora for eight years. He was married at Corona on January 2, 1882, to Dora Kate Linn, who was born in Marshall County in March, 1861, and died in Walker County on October 30, 1885. Mr. Palmer was again married on October 13, 1892, at Eclectic, in Elmore

County, to Miss Gertrude Jackson, a native of Elmore County. By the first marriage there was one child, Linn Palmer; and by the second marriage there were five children—Robert T. Palmer, Jesse Dawson Palmer, Edna Palmer, Joseph Henry Palmer, and Ruth Palmer.

Moore's Alabama, Vol. II, page 491.

PARKER, WILLIAM, was born February 23, 1801. He entered government land in Section 28, Township 15, Range 9, on December 16, 1834. He died on April 2, 1885, and is buried at Wyatt.

Walker County Tract Record.
Gravestone.

PARNELL, JAMES ALLEN, was born October 11, 1843, in Abbeville District, South Carolina. On February 22, 1861, he enlisted at Oxford, Alabama, as a private in Avery's Company of sharpshooters. He was captured at Nashville on December 16, 1864, and imprisoned at Camp Chase, Ohio, until the close of the war.

Census of Confederate Soldiers, 1907.

PARSONS, THOMAS, entered government land in Section 2, Township 14, Range 6, on February 22, 1855.

Walker County Tract Record.

PARVIN, J. L., was born December 25, 1837, at Huntsville, Alabama. In March, 1861, he enlisted at Guntersville as a private in Company K, Ninth Alabama Infantry, under Captain Sheffield. He was wounded and captured at Gettysburg, and was later exchanged at Richmond as unfit for further military service.

Census of Confederate Soldiers, 1907.

PATE, ISHAM, entered government land in Section 18, Township 15, Range 6, on February 5, 1856.

Walker County Tract Record.

PATTERSON, GEORGE W., entered government land in Section 34, Township 14, Range 9, on September 14, 1836.
Walker County Tract Record.

PATTERSON, JOHN, entered government land in Section 20, Township 14, Range 9, on October 3, 1838.
Walker County Tract Record.

PATTERSON, WILLIAM B., entered government land in Section 28, Township 14, Range 9, on January 14, 1837.
Walker County Tract Record.

PATTON, SAMUEL B., the first Representative from Walker County to sit in the State Legislature, was a Methodist minister who served on the Tuscaloosa Circuit in 1822-23. On November 27, 1823, he was married in Sullivan County, Tennessee, to Nancy Morrison, and in 1824 he was a minister at Washington in Autauga County. He was ordained elder at Tuscaloosa on December 22, 1824, and served on the Tuscaloosa Circuit in 1825. On December 11, 1824, he entered government land in Section 25, Township 17, Range 7, near Heard Shoals on the Warrior River, and also in Section 17, Township 17, Range 6, near Snow Ferry on the Warrior River. He was elected as Walker County's Representative in the Legislature for the sessions of 1834 to 1836.
West's History of Methodism, page 191.
Walker County Tract Record.

PATTON, JAMES M., a noted river pilot, was also a prominent class leader in the Methodist Church in 1833.
West's History of Methodism, page 549.
Armes' Story of Coal and Iron.

PATTON, GEORGE W., entered government land in Section 21, Township 14, Range 7, on January 22, 1836.
Walker County Tract Record.

EARLY SETTLERS

PATTON, DORAN, entered government land in Section 29, Township 15, Range 9, on September 25, 1834.

Walker County Tract Record.

PATTON, WILLIAM, was born November 18, 1846, on Wolf Creek. On December 1, 1864, he enlisted at Wolf Creek as a private in Company B, Musgrove's Battalion, and served until the close of the war. He died on October 13, 1931, and is buried at Patton Hill.

Census of Confederate Soldiers, 1907.
Gravestone.

PAYNE, MATHEY, a Revolutionary soldier who resided in Walker County on June 1, 1840.

Census of Pensioners, June 1, 1840.

PAYNE, DAVID, entered government land in Section 17, Township 13, Range 5, on September 13, 1819.

Walker County Tract Record.

PAYNE, WILLIAM, a noted river pilot, entered government land in Section 17, Township 13, Range 5, on September 13, 1819.

Walker County Tract Record.

PEAKE, DANIEL B., entered government land in Section 8, Township 13, Range 5, on March 26, 1836.

Walker County Tract Record.

PENDLEY, WILLIAM M., a Confederate soldier who was a member of Company A, Fifth Alabama Cavalry, is buried in the Frost Graveyard at West Corona.

Gravestone.

PETERSON, W. F., whose parents were natives of Newberry District, South Carolina, moved from Tallapoosa County shortly after the Civil War and settled near Wyatt in Walker County. On February 20, 1855, he was married to Sarah M. Lovelady, who was born in Henry County,

Georgia, on January 28, 1829; moved with her parents to Tallapoosa County, Alabama, in 1841, and died at Wyatt on March 28, 1895. Among their children were Sarah G. Peterson, born in Tallapoosa County, November 29, 1865, and died at Wyatt, December 8, 1883, the wife of a Mr. Hayes; and the Rev. W. H. Peterson, born April 9, 1860, and died July 5, 1905.

Gravestones.

PHIFER, JOHN, a son of Martin Phifer, of Tuscaloosa, came to Walker County about 1840 and settled on a farm near Providence Church. He farmed until the outbreak of the Civil War, when he entered the Confederate Army and was either killed or died during the war. He was married in Tuscaloosa to Mary E. Cook, who was born September 19, 1820, and died at Providence December 13, 1907. Children—

Rebecca Phifer, who married Neil Summer and lived in Tuscaloosa.

Martha Clemantine Phifer, who was born December 26, 1847, and who was married to Robert F. Kitchens on October 16, 1867.

Sarah Ann Phifer, who was born October 18, 1842. She was married to David Marion Day, of Oakman, and died there April 18, 1918.

Harriett Phifer, who married Samuel Walton, of Oakman.

Thenia Phifer, who married Dr. Tubb, of Providence.

Julia Phifer, who married Daniel Lee Tubb, of Jasper.

James J. Phifer, who married Emily Courington, a daughter of Robert Courington. Children—Queenis Phifer, who married Pearl Lollar; Clyde Phifer, who married Olla Jones; Ida Phifer, who married J. W. Underwood; Sally Phifer, who married James Carroll; and Carl Phifer, who married Ostrea Simpson.

John Worth Phifer, who married Martha Rose, a daughter of Newton Rose. Children—Stalie Phifer, who married Joseph Sherer, of Jasper; Henry Phifer, who married Belle Odom, a daughter of Dalton Odom; Loyd Phifer, who married Bertie Swindle, of Oakman; and Clayton O. Phifer, who married Ethel Key, a daughter of T. D. Key, of Parrish.

William Phifer, who was killed while a soldier in the Confederate Army. Among his children were Mary Susan Phifer, who was married about 1873 to Benjamin F. Clements; Mary Jane Phifer, who was married to John R. Sartain. After the death of William Phifer his widow married John B. Sumner.

Phifer Family Records.

PHILLIPS, JACOB, was born in Virginia about 1806 and was brought to Walker County about 1810. He is thought to have had four brothers who later entered government land—Robert Phillips, who entered land in Section 19, Township 14, Range 5, on July 19, 1833; George W. Phillips, who entered land in Section 30, Township 14, Range 5, on September 22, 1835; John Phillips, who entered land in Section 24, Township 13, Range 10, on January 7, 1836; and Jefferson Phillips, who entered land in Section 8, Township 15, Range 5, on November 5, 1836. Jacob Phillips remained in Walker County until his death, and was not only a farmer and planter, but in the early 1840's was engaged in mining coal near Cordova. He was married to a Miss Henson.

Moore's Alabama, Vol. III, page 143.
Walker County Tract Record.

PHILLIPS, MARTIN MARION, a son of Jacob Phillips, was born in Walker County in 1828. Reared on a farm, he was for many years a Justice of the Peace, and served as a Confederate soldier throughout the war. He died at Dora on February 5, 1902. He was married to Elizabeth Fields, who was born near old Elyton, Jefferson County, and died near old Democrat in Walker County. Children—Alford Byrd Phillips, who was born November 23, 1861, and was married to Margaret

Terry, of Bessemer; John B. Phillips; and Marietta Phillips, who married Herbert B. Gravlee, of Dora.

Moore's Alabama, Vol. III, page 143.

PHILLIPS, JOHN WASHINGTON, was born January 31, 1840, near the confluence of the Sipsey and Mulberry Forks. In September, 1861, he enlisted at Jasper as a private in Company I, Fiftieth Alabama Infantry, under Captain Long. In December, 1861, he was discharged on account of physical disability, and in November, 1862, he re-enlisted in Company F, Fifty-sixth Alabama Cavalry, under Captain Rice, and served until the close of the war.

Census of Confederate Soldiers, 1907.

PHILLIPS, WILLIAM, was born July 27, 1840, near Dora. In August, 1862, he enlisted at Jasper as a private in Company F, Fifty-sixth Alabama Cavalry, under Captain Rice. He was severely wounded near Jackson, Miss., on February 9, 1863, and was on sick furlough for the balance of the war.

Census of Confederate Soldiers, 1907.

PHILLIPS, JEFFERSON L., was born near Dora in 1844. In August, 1862, he enlisted at Jasper as a private in Company F, Fifty-sixth Alabama Cavalry, under Captain Rice, and served until the close of the war. He died July 28, 1887, at his home near Mulberry Fork, an esteemed and highly respected citizen, who was Tax Collector of the county at the time of his death.

Census of Confederate Soldiers, 1907.
Mountain Eagle, August 3, 1887.

PIKE, JOSEPH, entered government land in Section 11, Township 14, Range 9, on October 20, 1832.

Walker County Tract Record.

PIKE, PHILLIP, entered government land in Section 22, Township 14, Range 8, on December 7, 1833.

Walker County Tract Record.

PIKE, WILLIAM, entered government land in Section 11, Township 14, Range 9, on December 12, 1835.
Walker County Tract Record.

PIKE, REUBEN, entered government land in Section 9, Township 13, Range 8, on December 7, 1844.
Walker County Tract Record.

PIKE, JOSEPH CARROLL, was born December 8, 1833, at Holly Grove. In September, 1861, he enlisted at Jasper as a private in Company A, Twenty-second Alabama Infantry, and served until the close of the war. He was wounded at Chickamauga. He was married to Martha Sides, a daughter of Andy Allen and Mary (Staggs) Sides.
Census of Confederate Soldiers, 1907.

PITT, WILLIAM, entered government land in Section 24, Township 13, Range 5, on October 5, 1859.
Walker County Tract Record.

PLYLAR, JAMES BURTON, was born December 27, 1843, near America. On September 23, 1861, he enlisted at Jasper as a private in Company I, Fiftieth Alabama Infantry, under Captain Long, and served until the close of the war. He was wounded at Chickamauga.
Census of Confederate Soldiers, 1907.

PONDER, JAMES N., entered government land in Section 5, Township 14, Range 7, on March 17, 1856.
Walker County Tract Record.

POOL, JAMES H., a veteran of the Confederate Army, was born in 1819, and died on May 30, 1901, and is buried in the Day Graveyard at Oakman. His wife, Mary A. Pool, was born in 1828 and died September 19, 1903.
Gravestones.

POSEY, NAPOLEON BONAPARTE, was born near Blountsville, Blount County, Alabama, on June 11, 1824, a son of Washington and Elizabeth (Latham) Posey; and according to family tradition, a grandson of Joseph H. Posey, a member of General Jackson's army of Tennessee Volunteers in 1812, who settled near Blount Springs and opened a blacksmith shop, and who, in 1827, had a shop on Turkey Creek, Jefferson County, one and one-half miles west of Haygood's Crossing; and a great-grandson of Jesse N. and Eleanor (Brooks) Posey, who moved to Madison County in early days from Pendleton District, South Carolina. About 1852 Napoleon Bonaparte Posey moved to Texas, but in 1854 he came to Walker County and entered government land in Section 36, Township 14, Range 8, a short distance west of the present community of Bankhead, where he became prominently known as a wheelwright and blacksmith. During the Civil War he served in the Confederate Army and was the horseshoer and blacksmith for his regiment. After the close of the war he returned to his home in Walker County, and during the balance of his life acquired rather extensive land holdings. During the days that the railroads were being built through the county, he served on a number of commissions having to do with the acquiring of right of way for the railroads. He died on August 26, 1904, and is buried at Sardis, near Bankhead. He was married to Emily Effie Dailey, who was born on Sand Mountain, Blount County, Alabama, May 21, 1826, and died in Walker County May 21, 1906; a daughter of George and Barbara (Ratcliffe) Dailey. Children—

Modine Posey, who married Bud Atkins, of Walker County.

Trissey Posey, who married James Vincent, of Winston County.

Columbus Posey, who married Sadie Cranford, of Walker County.

Missouri Posey, who married Henry C. Crump, of Walker County.

Adolphus Posey, who died in young manhood.

Augustus Posey, born May 27, 1859, died December 24, 1925. He was married to Eliza Ann Cates, a daughter of W. E. and Emily (Lovett) Cates, of Haleyville. She was born April 27, 1858, and died in Walker County April 13, 1931.

Barbara Posey, who married Seburn Posey, a son of Francis Marion Posey, of Coosa and Winston Counties.

Napoleon Colorado Posey, who was born March 24, 1855, and died in Walker County in 1930. He was married to Susan Frances Myers, who was born September 21, 1858, and died October 9, 1924, a daughter of William J. and Sarah (James) Myers. Children—Laura Ellen Posey, who married George Washington Posey, Walker County's Representative in the State Legislature in 1935 and 1936, a son of Frances Marion and Emily (Lovett) Cates Posey, of Winston County, and a grandson of 'Squire Posey, who moved from South Carolina to Coosa County and later settled in Winston County; Martha Helen Posey, who married John Davidson, who served for two terms as Mayor of Parrish; Della Posey, who married James Noble, of Birmingham; Effie Posey, who married W. Houston Stocks, of Texas; Eula Ann Posey, who married J. C. Fikes, of Birmingham; Emily Birdie Posey, who married Wiley L. Kitchens, of Parrish; Clinton Posey, who married Mary Swindle; Gilbert Posey, who married Helen Lindsay, of Birmingham; Rufus Posey, who married Minnie Sherer; Cora Posey, who married Grady Larrimore; Anice Ellen Posey, who married John Copeland; Louis Posey, who married Grace Pike; and Minnie B. Posey, who married Porter Ferguson.

Owens' Alabama, Vol. IV, page 1380.
Armes' Story of Coal and Iron, page 21.
Posey Family Records.
Gravestones.
Mountain Eagle, July 31, 1895.

POSEY, LEWIS HOLMES, was born January 10, 1843, in Edgefield District, South Carolina. In September, 1861, he enlisted at Demopolis as a private in Company A, Forty-third Alabama Infantry, and served until the close of the war. On April 6, 1877, he entered government land in Section 28, Township 6, Range 9, in Lawrence County, but later moved to Walker County, where he died on June 16, 1926. His wife, Martha E. Posey, was born in 1849 and died in 1920.

Census of Confederate Soldiers, 1907.
Lawrence County Tract Record.
Gravestones.

PRESCOTT, JOHN, entered government land in Section 13, Township 16, Range 7, on February 13, 1832.

Walker County Tract Record.

PRICE, THOMAS W., a pioneer settler, was born August 24, 1811, and died in 1860. He was married to Charlotte Cain, a daughter of James Cain.

Cain Family Records.
Gravestone.

PRICE, JAMES MONROE, was born February 18, 1844, at Pontotoc, Pontotoc County, Mississippi. On September 2, 1861, he enlisted at Corinth as a private in Company F, Twenty-sixth Mississippi Infantry, and served until the close of the war. He was wounded at Petersburg, Va., on November 28, 1864.

Census of Confederate Soldiers, 1907.

PRUITT, MAJOR, entered government land in Section 29, Township 13, Range 5, on July 4, 1836.

Walker County Tract Record.

QUEEN, HIRAM, entered government land in Section 20, Township 14, Range 8, on October 23, 1832.

Walker County Tract Record.

RABURN, JOHN B., entered government land in Section 9, Township 16, Range 8, on February 25, 1824.

Walker County Tract Record.

EARLY SETTLERS

RABURN, F. G., a lieutenant in Company K, Fiftieth Alabama Infantry, is buried at Liberty Hill.
Gravestone.

RAINS, ROBERT, entered government land in Section 24, Township 13, Range 7, on May 23, 1834.
Walker County Tract Record.

RAINS, JAMES, entered government land in Section 31, Township 14, Range 6, on December 17, 1835.
Walker County Tract Record.

RANDOLPH, ELISHA, entered government land in Section 20, Township 13, Range 5, on September 17, 1832.
Walker County Tract Record.

RANDOLPH, JEREMIAH, entered government land in Section 17, Township 13, Range 5, on September 26, 1833.
Walker County Tract Record.

RANDOLPH, LORENZO D., entered government land in Section 19, Township 13, Range 5, on June 20, 1836.
Walker County Tract Record.

RANDOLPH, JOHN D., born in 1798, was a charter member of the Sulphur Springs Primitive Baptist Church, which was organized on July 6, 1844. He was married to Francis Brown, a sister to Thomas Brown and to Sallie (Brown) Kitchens, the wife of J. M. Kitchens, all of whom were also charter members of the Sulphur Springs Church. On December 16, 1854, John D. Randolph entered government land in Section 19, Township 15, Range 7, about two miles west of Parrish. He died February 28, 1870, and is buried in the Kitchens Graveyard.
Sulphur Springs Church Book.
Walker County Tract Record.

RANDOLPH, JOHN BROWN, a son of John D. and Francis (Brown) Randolph, was born March 5, 1840, on Cane Creek, two miles south of Jasper. In August, 1862, he enlisted at

Jasper as a corporal in Company F, Twenty-eighth Alabama Infantry, under Captain Gamble. He was captured at Orchard Knob and imprisoned at Rock Island, Ill., until March, 1865, when he was carried to Akins Landing, near Richmond, Virginia, and exchanged. He died on May 20, 1915, and is buried in the Cooner Cemetery at Coal City. His first wife, Susan Jane Randolph, was born September 19, 1839, and died July 12, 1879. His second wife, Sarah E. Randolph, was born January 20, 1855, and died December 13, 1907.

Census of Confederate Soldiers, 1907.
Gravestones.

RANDOLPH, THOMAS BROWN, a son of John D. and Francis (Brown) Randolph, was born November 10, 1842, on Cane Creek, two miles south of Jasper. On February 22, 1862, he enlisted at Jasper as a private in Company F, Twenty-eighth Alabama Infantry, under Captain Gamble. On July 3, 1862, he was discharged at camp near Tupelo, Miss., on account of physical disability, and was unfit for further service. His wife, Malissa Randolph, was born in 1836, and died April 29, 1876.

Census of Confederate Soldiers, 1907.
Gravestone.

RANDOLPH, JAMES, a Civil War veteran and farmer, was the son of John D. and Francis (Brown) Randolph. He was married to a Miss Poe, of Boley Springs, Fayette County. Children—William Randolph, who married Sally Williams; Thomas Randolph, who married Roxie ———; Tillman Randolph, who married Ada Williams; Timie Randolph, who married Benjamin Banks; Nancy Randolph, who married Frank James; Ellen Randolph, who married, first, Joseph Reed, and, second, a Mr. Stocks; and George S. Randolph, who married Martha Ellen Grace, a daughter of James A. and Emily (Odom) Grace. Children—James David Randolph; Hewitt Clay Randolph, who married Flossie Russell; Queenie Randolph, who married Earl Keeton; Wiley Griffin Randolph, who married Vera Myrtle Courington; and Fannie Randolph, who married David Hyatt.

Randolph Family Records.

RAY, ALFRED, entered government land in Section 14, Township 15, Range 8, on December 28, 1836.

Walker County Tract Record.

RAY, SILAS B., was born in Meriwether County, Georgia, on April 18, 1831. He was carried by his parents to Tallapoosa County, Ala., where he grew to manhood and married Caudace Martin. In 1854 he moved to Walker County, and on March 21, 1857, entered government land in Section 23, Township 12, Range 7. He joined the Baptist Church in 1857, and was a charter member of Hermon Church when it was organized in 1858. He was ordained a deacon and served as such until his death on March 30, 1885.

Mountain Eagle, March 30, 1885.

RAY, JAMES JASPER, was born July 31, 1857, near Pilgrim Post Office, Fayette County; a son of Elijah and Lucy Ann (Wright) Ray, both of whom were natives of Virginia; and a grandson of Jesse and Elizabeth Wright, of Virginia. He was educated in the public schools of Fayette County and at the University of Alabama, from which he graduated with the degree of LL. B. in 1881. He was admitted to the bar in that year and began his practice at Fayette, but shortly after moved to Jasper. He was Register in Chancery from July 16, 1883, to November 10, 1900; State Senator 1900 and 1901; and was appointed judge of the newly created Fourteenth Judicial District on February 25, 1907. He died on November 1, 1933. He was married at Newtonville, Fayette County, on October 14, 1884, to Ida J. Jones, a daughter of Dr. W. W. Jones. She died on August 31, 1887, and on May 1, 1890, he married Ella E. Edney, a daughter of John M. Edney. Children by first marriage—

Alex B. Ray. Children by second marriage—Ida Louise Ray; T. M. Ray; and Gladstone Ray, of California.

Owens' Alabama, Vol. IV, page 1415.
Mountain Eagle, November 1, 1933.

REID, ABSALOM, entered government land in Section 35, Township 13, Range 5, on September 16, 1831.

Walker County Tract Record.

REID, JOHN, entered government land in Section 36, Township 13, Range 5, on December 19, 1832.

Walker County Tract Record.

REID, WILLIAM, entered government land in Section 36, Township 13, Range 5, on September 19, 1832. In 1857 he was elected Representative in the Legislature. A very plain farmer and quite modest, no man in the house was more respected. He was always courteous and obliging to all and everyone was his friend. He died shortly after his service in the Legislature.

Walker County Tract Record.
Mountain Eagle, January 5, 1887.

RHEA, WILLIAM, entered government land in Section 22, Township 17, Range 7, on January 31, 1837.

Walker County Tract Record.

RHEA, WILLIAM BARCLAY, was born October 27, 1842, on the Warrior River. On June 1, 1862, he enlisted as a private in Company G, Fifty-sixth Alabama Infantry, under Captain Shepherd. He was furloughed after the Kentucky campaign and re-enlisted in Company B, Musgrove's Battalion, and later served in Company K, Forty-third Alabama Infantry. He died March 18, 1931, and is buried at Heard Shoals. He was married to Martha E. Thompson, a daughter of Fleming R. Thompson.

Census of Confederate Soldiers, 1907.

EARLY SETTLERS

RHODES, JACOB, entered government land in Section 10, Township 14, Range 4, on October 28, 1859.
Walker County Tract Record.

RICE, WILLIAM, entered government land in Section 9, Township 14, Range 8, on December 19, 1848.
Walker County Tract Record.

RICE, JAMES LAFAYETTE, was born December 19, 1838, at Talbot Station, Jefferson County, Tennessee. On June 24, 1861, he enlisted at Talbot Station as a private in Company I, Second Tennessee Cavalry, under Captain Branner, and served until the close of the war. He later moved to Walker County and lived at Carbon Hill.
Census of Confederate Soldiers, 1907.

RICHARDSON, JOSIAH, and his wife, Lucy, entered government land in Section 7, Township 14, Range 6, about three miles east of Jasper, on August 5, 1835.
Walker County Tract Record.

RICHARDSON, WILLIAM, entered government land in Section 1, Township 14, Range 9, on December 12, 1835.
Walker County Tract Record.

RICHARDSON, HIRAM, entered government land in Section 19, Township 17, Range 7, on November 14, 1836.
Walker County Tract Record.

RICHARDSON, JOBE, was born November 8, 1802. He entered government land in Section 24, Township 17, Range 7, on May 2, 1836, but in 1872 he was living on a farm six miles north of Jasper, on which the town of South Lowell was laid out. He died on October 7, 1873, and is buried at South Lowell. His wife, Rutha Richardson, was born July 16, 1831, and died January 12, 1894.
Walker County Tract Record.
Gravestones.

RICHARDSON, JOHN, was born September 14, 1839, near the forks of the Sipsey and Mulberry Rivers. On June 10, 1862, he enlisted as a corporal in Company K, Forty-third Alabama Infantry, under Captain Shepherd. He was captured at Hatcher's Run, Va., on March 25, 1865, and imprisoned at Point Lookout, Md., until discharged on June 17, 1865. He died at Oakman and is buried in the Heard Shoals Graveyard. His wife, Susan Richardson, was born August 14, 1839, and died February 28, 1920.

Census of Confederate Soldiers, 1907.
Gravestones.

RICHARDSON, WILLIAM, was born September 16, 1840, six miles south of Jasper. In September, 1861, he enlisted at Jasper as a private in Company K, Fiftieth Alabama Infantry, under Captain Hutto, and served until the close of the war. He was wounded at Atlanta.

Census of Confederate Soldiers, 1907.

RICHARDSON, JOHN, was born November 11, 1842, six miles south of Jasper. In February, 1863, he enlisted as a private in Company K, Fiftieth Alabama Infantry, under Captain Hutto. He was wounded at Atlanta on July 28, 1864, and sent to a hospital at Barnesville, Ga., until April 1, 1865, when he was sent home. He died on June 21, 1918, and is buried at Pleasantfield. His wife, Mary Richardson, was born February 14, 1845, and died August 9, 1911.

Census of Confederate Soldiers, 1907.
Gravestones.

RICHEY, WILLIAM M., entered government land in Section 24, Township 13, Range 10, near Carbon Hill, on February 19, 1821. His son, Alexander Richey, entered land in the same locality on September 10, 1830. Another son, Joseph Richey, is mentioned as a class leader in the Methodist Church in 1833.

Walker County Tract Record.
West's History of Methodism, page 549.

ROBERTS, ABRAHAM M., entered government land in Section 9, Township 13, Range 5, on September 16, 1851.
Walker County Tract Record.

ROBERTS, GEORGE A., entered government land in Section 10, Township 14, Range 5, on April 23, 1856.
Walker County Tract Record.

ROBERTS, HENRY ALFORD, was born in 1858 at Greenville, South Carolina, but spent most of his life in Walker County. During 1906-07 he served for one term as County Commissioner from the first district. He died on June 25, 1933, and is buried in the Coal City Cemetery. He was the father of seven children—Davis Roberts, Floyd Roberts, Amos Roberts, Bama Roberts, Mrs. Maude Key, Mrs. Winnie Sherer, and Mrs. Pearl Richardson.
Mountain Eagle, June 28, 1933.

ROBERTSON, JAMES, entered government land in Section 28, Township 14, Range 5, on March 6, 1856.
Walker County Tract Record.

ROBINS, LEVI WILSON, entered government land in Section 36, Township 14, Range 7, on October 4, 1832.
Walker County Tract Record.

ROBINS, JOHN B., entered government land in Section 1, Township 15, Range 7, on November 18, 1833. He was married to Nancy Barton, a daughter of Moses Barton I. He later moved to Texas.
Walker County Tract Record.

ROBINS, WILLIAM A., entered government land in Section 10, Township 14, Range 5, on April 15, 1834. He was elected Tax Collector in 1844 and moved to Jasper, where he remained until the end of his term in 1848. He then returned to his farm, where he died a few months later.
Walker County Tract Record.
Mountain Eagle, May 9, 1917.

ROBINS, IRA, a son of William A. Robins, was born December 16, 1836, on his father's farm in the eastern part of Walker County. His mother died when he was seven years of age, and he was left a full orphan at the age of thirteen, and placed under the guardianship of William Stovall. He was educated at old Elyton College, where he graduated with first honors and where he taught until 1859, when he returned to Walker County as assistant principal of the Jasper Academy, under Prof. Hodgson, principal. He remained with the Jasper Academy until the outbreak of the Civil War when he enlisted as first sergeant in Company I, Fifty-sixth Alabama Regiment, under Captain Lacy. He served under General Forrest in East Tennessee, under General Joseph E. Johnstone in the Georgia campaign, and came near losing his life at the battle of Kennesaw Mountain. After the close of the war he returned to Jasper and organized a new Jasper Academy, where he remained until 1883, when he began to teach at other places. He died on December 20, 1904.

Mountain Eagle, May 9, 1917.

ROBINS, JESSE, entered government land in Section 10, Township 14, Range 5, on December 21, 1835.

Walker County Tract Record.

RODGERS, WILLIAM B., entered government land in Section 4, Township 14, Range 5, on October 9, 1832.

Walker County Tract Record.

ROGERS, EMERY W., entered government land in Section 21, Township 14, Range 7, south of Jasper, on February 8, 1834.

Walker County Tract Record.

ROGERS, JAMES, entered government land in Section 9, Township 13, Range 8, on November 17, 1836.

Walker County Tract Record.

ROGERS, REV. J. W., was born January 13, 1840, at New

Lexington, Tuscaloosa County. In the spring of 1862 he enlisted at Fayette Courthouse as a private in Company I, Thirty-second Alabama Infantry, under Captain Wiley Thompson. He was captured near Nashville, was exchanged; captured again at Resaca, Georgia, and was imprisoned at Camp Morton, Indiana, until the close of the war. He died on February 8, 1916, and is buried at Eldridge. His wife, Ellen E. Rogers, was born May 3, 1853, and died May 12, 1919.

Census of Confederate Soldiers, 1907.
Gravestones.

ROLLINS, REUBEN, entered government land in Section 5, Township 13, Range 5, on July 10, 1855.

Walker County Tract Record.

ROMINE, JOHN B., entered government land in Section 9, Township 14, Range 9, on October 13, 1836. He was married to Nancy Birdwell in 1812. She was born in Sullivan County, Tennessee, on November 3, 1795, and died near Holly Grove on June 20, 1885.

Walker County Tract Record.
Mountain Eagle, July 29, 1885.

ROSAMOND, WILLIAM CAPERS, was born in Lawrence District, South Carolina, on August 24, 1833, a son of Nathaniel J. and Amy (Powell) Rosamond, the former of French Huguenot origin, his ancestors coming to Virginia about 1600. His mother, Amy (Powell) Rosamond, was born in Kentucky; was taken by her parents to South Carolina, where she married. William Capers Rosamond worked on a farm until about nineteen years of age, when he began the study of medicine at Northport and was licensed to practice at Tuscaloosa. He came to Jasper in 1856 and soon attained an extensive practice. In 1862 he enlisted as a private in the Confederate Army, but was soon appointed assistant surgeon in General Ferguson's brigade, and saw service in Tennessee, Louisiana, Mississippi and Alabama.

In 1866 he returned to Jasper and practiced medicine until 1878 when he retired on account of his health. Soon after this he was elected to the State Senate from the senatorial district composed of Walker, Jefferson and Shelby Counties and served during the sessions of 1878-79. In 1878 he entered the drug business with John H. Cranford, and in 1883 sold out his interest to Mr. Cranford. He was superintendent of the Methodist Sunday School at Jasper for twenty-five years. He died on May 28, 1904, and is buried at Oak Hill Cemetery at Jasper. In 1866 he was married to Madorah F. Freeman, a daughter of Rev. James H. and Martha B. (Cole) Freeman. She died on November 15, 1882. On December 6, 1883, he married Henrietta Dinsmore, a daughter of David F. Dinsmore, of Laudersville. Children by first wife—Edward Powell Rosamond, who married Willie E. Owen, a daughter of William Marmaduke and Nancy L. (McAdory) Owen; William L. Rosamond, who married Ozella Frances Appling, a daughter of Joseph F. and Matilda Ann (Johns) Appling; Ethbert C. Rosamond, who married Susie K. Bouldin, a daughter of Wiley F. and Laura (Foote) Bouldin; Franklin K. Rosamond, who married Maude Shields, a daughter of Judge John B. and Carolyn (Long) Shields; Hester May Rosamond, who married Charles Millard Mills; Amy Lee Rosamond, who married Franklin D. McArthur, a son of William Franklin and Lilly F. (Connerly) McArthur. No children by second marriage.

Owens' Alabama, Vol. IV, page 1856.
Northern Alabama, page 176.
Armes' Story of Coal and Iron.

ROSS, HUGH P., entered government land in Section 24, Township 14, Range 9, on October 20, 1835.

Walker County Tract Record.

RUPELL, THOMAS J., entered government land in Section 11, Township 14, Range 7, on August 10, 1859.

Walker County Tract Record.

RUSSELL, ANDERSON, entered government land in Section 17, Township 15, Range 6, on August 20, 1836.
Walker County Tract Record.

RUSSELL, GEORGE, entered government land in Section 36, Township 14, Range 7, on February 14, 1837.
Walker County Tract Record.

RUTLEDGE, EDWARD, who, according to family tradition, was a descendant of Edward Rutledge, a signer of the Declaration of Independence, came to Walker County from Cumberland County, Kentucky, about 1835, accompanied by his wife and one child and his two brothers, Jack Rutledge and William Rutledge; the long trip having been made on pack horses. He settled on a farm near Pleasant Grove Church and was one of the charter members of that church when it was founded in 1842. He was married in Kentucky to Elizabeth Logan, of Cumberland County. Children—James Rutledge, who married Elizabeth Sides; Alfred King Rutledge, who married Eliza Sides; David Rutledge, who married Minerva Jeffries; Joseph Rutledge, who never married; Julia Rutledge, who married Samuel O'Rear; Polly Ann Rutledge, who married Vincent Ivey; Ollie Rutledge, who married Wid Swindle; and Elizabeth Rutledge, who married a Mr. Bolton.
Rutledge Family Records.

RUTLEDGE, WILLIAM, a brother to Edward Rutledge, came to Walker County about 1835 from Cumberland County, Kentucky. He settled on a farm near Pleasant Grove Church, and was married to Nancy Lawson, of Walker County. Children—John J. Rutledge, Dock Rutledge, Christopher Rutledge, and William Rutledge.
Rutledge Family Records.

RUTLEDGE, JAMES, a son of Edward and Elizabeth (Logan) Rutledge, was born in Cumberland County, Kentucky, on November 4, 1832. When but two years of age he was brought to Walker County by his parents. On February 1, 1862, he enlisted at Jasper as a private in Company E, Twenty-eighth Alabama Infantry, but in July, 1863, he was detailed to recruiting service under Major F. A. Musgrove, and was on this service in Walker County for the balance of the war. He died on May 25, 1918, and is buried in the Sides Graveyard. He was married to Elizabeth A. Sides, a daughter of William Sides. She was born October 8, 1839, and died November 11, 1905. Children—William Taylor Rutledge, who married Mary Key, a daughter of Thomas Key; Andrew A. Rutledge, who married Minerva Key, a daughter of John and Charity Elizabeth (Wood) Key; Mary Ann Rutledge, who married Robert Powers Key, a son of John and Charity Elizabeth (Wood) Key; Martha Frances Rutledge, who married, first, Doran Kilgore and, second, William Root; Sarah Rutledge, who married James Mulligan; James M. Rutledge, who married, first, Maggie Wright and, second, Fannie Pearson; John R. Rutledge, who married Mary Nix; Charles Rutledge, who married Alice Wade; George Houston Rutledge, who married Mollie Crump; Annie Rutledge, who married James A. Ward; and Etta Rutledge, who died in her youth.

Census of Confederate Soldiers, 1907.
Rutledge Family Records.

RUTLEDGE, DAVID, was born July 14, 1839, a son of Edward and Elizabeth (Logan) Rutledge. In August, 1862, he enlisted at Jasper as a private in Company G, Fifty-sixth Alabama Cavalry. He was married to Minerva Jeffries.

Census of Confederate Soldiers, 1907.

RUTLEDGE, JAMES DANIEL, was born near Pleasant Grove Church on February 12, 1846. In March, 1863, he enlisted at Jasper as a private in Company B, Tenth Alabama

Cavalry, under Captain Whatley, and served until the close of the war. He died February 12, 1922.

Census of Confederate Soldiers, 1907.
Gravestone.

RYAN, JOHN, and his wife, Susan Ryan, Irish immigrants, came to Walker County from Greene County about 1835, and, along with James Camak, operated the first hotel in Jasper, known as the Camak-Ryan Hotel. Children—Isaac, John B., Joseph, James, George, Thomas, William I., Patsy Martha, Betsie Elizabeth, Polly Mary.

Ryan Family Records.

RYAN, ISAAC, a son of John and Susan Ryan, was born in Edgefield District, South Carolina, October 9, 1801. He moved to Greene County, Alabama, and about 1835 he came to Jasper and built the first sawmill there on Town Creek. He was killed in an accident at this sawmill on February 8, 1845. About 1833, in Greene County, he was married to Mary Camak, a daughter of James and Nancy (Hutchinson) Camak, who was born in Fairfield District, South Carolina, on May 15, 1807, and died December 13, 1876. Children—Margaret Ryan, born January 29, 1834, and died May 30, 1843; Susan Ryan, born February 13, 1837, and died December 22, 1888, who married William Oliver Owen; John Camak Ryan; Martha E. Ryan, born October 9, 1843, and died April 26, 1910, who married Dock Robertson; James G. Ryan.

Ryan Family Records.

RYAN, JOHN CAMAK, was born in Jasper January 27, 1839, a son of Isaac and Mary (Camak) Ryan. On September 6, 1862, he enlisted at Jasper as a private in Company G, Fifty-sixth Alabama Cavalry, under Captain Shepherd, and served until the close of the war. He died on November 11, 1922. He was married to Sarah E. Lamkin, a daughter of Griffin and Sarah (Thacker) Lamkin. Children—Mary Ryan, Alice Ryan,

Isaac Ryan, James Thomas Ryan, William Ryan, John Ryan, Sally Ryan.

Census of Confederate Soldiers, 1907.
Ryan Family Records.

SANDERS, WILLIAM R., entered government land in Section 31, Township 13, Range 10, on September 18, 1835.

Walker County Tract Record.

SANDERS, JAMES, entered government land in Section 18, Township 13, Range 7, on June 9, 1846.

Walker County Tract Record.

SANDERS, NATHANIEL, entered government land in Section 2, Township 14, Range 6, on December 3, 1855.

Walker County Tract Record.

SANDERS, SAMUEL MONROE, was born in September, 1826, in Blount County, Alabama, a son of John and Lucy (Millsaps) Sanders—the former being one of seven brothers who came to Alabama from Tennessee in the early history of the state. Samuel Monroe Sanders came to Walker County in the 1840's and became identified with the early mining of coal in the vicinity of Cordova. During the Civil War he served as Orderly Sergeant in Company G, Eighth Alabama Cavalry. He died in 1901. On September 10, 1848, he was married to Nancy Cain, who was born July 27, 1830, a daughter of James Oscar and Elizabeth (McAuley) Cain. Children—James Sanders, who was killed in a steamboat explosion at Paducah, Ky., in 1872; Adkin Sanders, who married a Miss King; Venila Lucretia Sanders, who was born January 24, 1858, married to George D. O'Rear on January 18, 1880, and died March 16, 1934; Belle Sanders, who married William Files Kitchens; Lucie Sanders, who married John Catchings, of San Antonio, Texas; Catherine Lavonia Sanders, who married S. B. Smith; Nevada Hale

EARLY SETTLERS 327

Sanders, who married Chas. L. Rosser; and Samuel Monroe Sanders, Jr., who married Tinie Sturgis.

Sanders Family Records.

SANDLIN, DANIEL, entered government land in Section 1, Township 13, Range 5, on November 15, 1844.

Walker County Tract Record.

SARGENT, WILLIAM PENN, was born February 19, 1840, at Wetumpka, Elmore County, Alabama. On June 4, 1861, he enlisted at Asheville, Alabama, as a private in Company A, Tenth Alabama Cavalry, and later served with the St. Clair Sharpshooters and with Company A, First Kentucky Cavalry. He was with the party that escorted President Jefferson Davis from Smithfield, N. C., to the Savannah River. He died November 8, 1908, and is buried at Dora.

Census of Confederate Soldiers, 1907.
Gravestone.

SARTAIN, WILLIAM TURNER, a son of Jacob Sartain, was born September 13, 1803, near Charleston, South Carolina, but was brought to Tuscaloosa County by his father about 1817. He was reared in Tuscaloosa County, but in 1845 he moved his family to Walker County and settled on a farm near Providence, where he died in 1879. On January 12, 1832, he was married in Tuscaloosa County to Mary Summers Rammage, who was born September 19, 1813, and died in Walker County February 10, 1849. On November 1, 1860, he was married to Mary Taylor, who was born August 29, 1839. Children by first marriage—James Rufus Sartain, who was born November 24, 1832, who never married, and died a soldier in the Civil War; Sarah Susannah Sartain, who was born May 12, 1834, and was married to Frank Oxford, of Tuscaloosa County; Mary Ann Sartain, who was born March 6, 1836, and was married to a Mr. Blocker, of Tuscaloosa County; William Turner Sartain, Jr., who was born November 13, 1837, who never married, and died a soldier in the Civil War; Gerusha Teena Sartain, who was born October 4, 1839, and was married to William (Dock) Odom, a son of Jacob Odom; John Rammage Sartain, who was born December 31, 1841, and was married to Mary Jane Phifer; Zeruah Amanda Sartain, who was born December 12, 1843, and was married to Manly Sides; Peninnah Elizabeth Sartain, who was born April 18, 1846, and was married to John Sides. Children by the second marriage—Martha Jane Sartain, who was born December 30, 1861, and was married to Reece Courington; Isaac Lee Sartain, who was born November 29, 1863, and was married to Medda Sumner; Jacob Manly Sartain, who was born January 16, 1866, and was married to Bama Walton; George Washington Sartain, who was born May 17, 1867, and was married to Martha Sides; Eliza Frances Sartain, who was born August 17, 1869, and was married to William Courington; Minty Arletha Sartain, who was born July 30, 1874, and was married to Major Blanton; Roxanna Josephine Sartain, who was born December 11, 1876, and was married to Samuel Hinton, of Tuscaloosa.

Moore's Alabama, Vol. II, page 104.
Sartain Family Records.

SARTAIN, JOHN RAMMAGE, a son of William Turner and Mary Summers (Rammage) Sartain, was born December 31, 1841, near Hull, Tuscaloosa County, but was brought to Walker County by his parents while still a small child. He was reared on his father's farm near Providence, and received his education from the county schools. He followed farming all of his life, but was also a minister in the Missionary Baptist Church. On September 15, 1861, he enlisted at Jasper as a private in Company K, Fiftieth Alabama Infantry, under Captain Hutto, and served until the close of the war. He died on January 8, 1923. He was married to Mary Jane Phifer, a daughter of William

Phifer, who was born at Providence in 1844 and died there in 1914. Children—

John William Sartain, who married Martha Courington, a daughter of Robert Courington, and was County Farm Agent for more than twenty years.

James Rufus Sartain, who was born near Tuscaloosa in 1866, but was reared on his father's farm near Providence. He was a farmer all of his life, and a deeply religious man who early joined the Missionary Baptist Church and served as its Sunday School Superintendent for many years. He died in June, 1898. He was married to Rhoda M. Courington, a daughter of Randolph Courington, who was born near Providence in 1870. Children —James Virgil Sartain, born October 6, 1889, married on June 14, 1916, to Gertrude Riddlesperger, a daughter of Augustus C. and Savannah (Cole) Riddlesperger, Tax Collector of Walker County, 1921-27, and later postmaster at Jasper; Vada Sartain, who married Avery Odom, of Parrish; Vonie Sartain, who married William C. Jones, of Wyatt; Velma Sartain, who married Fred E. Bynum, of Oklahoma City, Oklahoma.

Charles Manual Sartain, who was Probate Judge of Walker County, 1913-18, and who was married to Alice Courington, a daughter of Randolph Courington.

Samuel Robert Sartain, who was born in 1872 and died June 19, 1935. He was married to Sallie Davidson, a daughter of Reuben Davidson. Children—Bertie Sartain, who married a Mr. Earnest; Claud Sartain; Zora Sartain, who married John Ritter; Mary Sartain, who married Wayne Campbell; Ward Sartain; Leon Sartain; and John Sartain.

Hosie Sartain, who married Thomas King.

Mary Laura Virginia Sartain, who married Sampson Morris.

Virgin Harbin Sartain, who died at the age of eighteen, unmarried.

Francis Marion Sartain, who married Rachel Inman, a daughter of Samuel Inman. Children—Frances Sartain, Jo Anna Sartain, and Mary Catherine Sartain.

Moore's Alabama, Vol. II, page 104.
Census of Confederate Soldiers, 1907.
Sartain Family Records.

SAVAGE, JAMES, was a prominent merchant in Jasper, and a charter member of the Masonic Lodge in 1854.

Campbell's Southern Business Directory.

SAVAGE, JAMES W., was born July 23, 1844, near Northport, Tuscaloosa County. In November, 1861, he enlisted at Tuscaloosa as a private in Fowler's Battery, and served in Phelan's Company, Alabama Light Artillery, during the entire period of the war. He is buried at Liberty Hill.

Census of Confederate Soldiers, 1907.
Gravestone.

SCOTT, CARTER, entered government land in Section 30, Township 13, Range 8, on March 4, 1847.

Walker County Tract Record.

SELF, JESSE, entered government land in Section 30, Township 13, Range 5, on September 17, 1833.

Walker County Tract Record.

SHAW, JAMES MARION, was born October 17, 1837, at Goodwater, Coosa County, Alabama. On August 13, 1862, he enlisted in Tallapoosa County as First Corporal in Company G, Fourteenth Alabama Infantry, and served until the close of the war. He was residing in Walker County in 1895.

Census of Confederate Soldiers, 1907.

SHAW, SEBORN JACKSON, was born May 12, 1837, at Madison, Morgan County, Georgia. In September, 1862, he enlisted at Covington, Georgia, as a private in Company F, Forty-second Georgia Infantry, and served until January, 1864, when he was discharged on account of physical disability.

Census of Confederate Soldiers, 1907.

SHEPHERD, JEREMIAH, was born in 1799. He came to Walker County in 1832, and entered government land in Section 32, Township 15, Range 5, on January 19 of that year. He died on January 27, 1869, and is buried at Wyatt. His wife, Kesiah Shepherd, born May 4, 1799, died December 29, 1874.
Walker County Tract Record.

SHEPHERD, JAMES, entered government land in Section 13, Township 15, Range 6, on February 24, 1834.
Walker County Tract Record.

SHEPHERD, ISAAC, entered government land in Section 21, Township 15, Range 5, on February 17, 1836.
Walker County Tract Record.

SHEPHERD, STEPHEN, entered government land in Section 19, Township 15, Range 5, on November 4, 1836.
Walker County Tract Record.

SHEPHERD, TINSON, born in the Abbeville District, South Carolina, in 1808, moved to Walker County about 1827, and on April 19, 1834, entered government land in Section 5, Township 16, Range 8, south of Oakman. He spent his entire life on the farm and died there in 1879, being buried at Liberty Hill. He was married to Minerva Raburn, who was born in Tennessee in 1814 and died near Oakman in 1879. Children—John B. Shepherd, who died in the Confederate service at Atlanta; Elizabeth Shepherd, who married Major John C. Hutto; Wilson Shepherd, who was born May 2, 1840, and on September 21, 1861, he enlisted at York Post Office as a sergeant in Company K, Fiftieth Alabama Infantry, under Captain Hutto, and served until severely wounded at Resaca, Georgia; Nancy A. Shepherd, who married Wilson W. Worthington, of Jasper; James Wiley Shepherd; and Tinson Shepherd, Jr.
Moore's Alabama, Vol. II, page 504.
Gravestones.

SHEPHERD, JAMES WILEY, a son of Tinson and Minerva (Raburn) Shepherd, was born on his father's farm near Oakman on December 24, 1850. Educated in the public schools of the county, he grew up on the farm. He spent three years teaching in rural schools, and twelve years farming near Oakman and Corona. In 1881 he was elected County Superintendent of Education, and served until 1887, when he was elected Sheriff. He served as Sheriff until 1892, and was then elected Probate Judge, which office he filled until 1912. After retiring from the office of Probate Judge, he entered the mercantile business in Jasper, and operated the same until his death on November 7, 1925. On September 18, 1877, he was married to Eustatia Palmer, a daughter of Robert T. and Elizabeth Ann (White) Palmer, who was born near Corona on January 12, 1859, and died in Jasper February 5, 1929. Children—Willie Lee Shepherd, who married James S. Freeman; Zack Palmer Shepherd, who married Ruby Sanford, a daughter of William A. and Willie (Sanders) Sanford, of Sheffield; John Carlisle Shepherd, a lawyer of Jasper, who served as Representative in the Legislature, 1931-34; Robert Herbert Shepherd, a physician at Townley; Annie Lou Shepherd, who married McDavid McPoland, of Jasper; and James Wiley Shepherd, Jr., a merchant at Jasper.

>Moore's Alabama, Vol. II, page 504.
>Memorial Record of Alabama, Vol. II, page 1025.
>Gravestones.

SHEPHERD, JACOB ROBERT, entered government land in Section 3, Township 15, Range 7, southeast of Jasper, on April 19, 1859. He recruited and was elected captain of Company G, Fifty-sixth Alabama Cavalry, and served throughout the war. At the close of the war he returned to Walker County, and was elected and served as Probate Judge from 1874 until his death on

April 29, 1877. He was married to Frances Gilcrease, a daughter of Edmund Gilcrease.
>Walker County Tract Record.
>Census of Confederate Soldiers, 1907.

SHERER, WILLIAM, born November 19, 1790, and who located at York, South Carolina, in the early 1800's, was a descendant of John Christopher Sherer, the founder of the family, who came to America October 13, 1709, from Hundsruck, on the west bank of the Rhine River. When but eighteen years of age John Christopher Sherer left home on the ship "Minerva," commanded by Captain Arnold. He settled in Reading, Pennsylvania, where he married Julianna Phillipi, the first female child born in that place. A sergeant in the Revolutionary Army, he was wounded at the battle of the Brandywine, and was one of the immortal eleven hundred who crossed the Delaware River with General Washington, and on the following morning fought the battle of Trenton Heights. His two sons were John and Jonathan. William Sherer was reared and educated in South Carolina, and on July 27, 1813, in York District, he was married to Martha Minter, who was born May 20, 1793, a daughter of William and Martha (Hillhouse) Minter, and granddaughter of John and Francis Minter. The Minter family are of Scotch-Welsh origin. The first representatives in America settled in James City County, Virginia, in 1635. In 1775 members of the family moved from Bedford County, Virginia, to Chatham County, North Carolina, and in this state John Minter served in the war of the Revolution. About 1855 William Sherer came to Walker County and settled near Jasper, where he died a number of years later. He was accompanied by seven sons, who brought with them their wives and children.
>Owens' Alabama, Vol. IV, page 1544.
>Moore's Alabama, Vol. II, page 139.
>Sherer Family Records.

SHERER, JAMES G., a son of William and Martha (Minter)

Sherer, was born in York District, South Carolina, on May 16, 1814. He came to Walker County about 1855 and settled near Jasper, where he operated a farm for the balance of his life. He died October 21, 1892, and is buried at Samaria. He was married in South Carolina to Mary A. Kirkpatrick, a daughter of J. and E. Kirkpatrick, who was born September 15, 1820, and died December 1, 1900. Children—

John Minter Sherer, who was born near Bullock Creek Church, York District, South Carolina, on December 20, 1841. In July, 1861, he enlisted at Courtland, Alabama, in Company B, Sixteenth Alabama Infantry, and served until the close of the war. He was married in Walker County to Samariamus Jones, a daughter of William Wallace and Artimissa (Garrison) Jones.

J. Taylor Sherer, who was born December 11, 1846, in York District, South Carolina. In June, 1864, he enlisted at Jasper as a private in Company K, Fourth Alabama Cavalry. He served until April, 1865, when he was captured at Selma and paroled. He died December 6, 1931, and is buried at Samaria. He was married twice—first, to Martha Hutto and, second, to a Miss Roberts.

Census of Confederate Soldiers, 1907.
Sherer Family Records.
Gravestones.

SHERER, JOHN T., a son of William and Martha (Minter) Sherer, was born in York District, South Carolina, on September 6, 1815. He came to Walker County, and entered government land in Section 15, Township 14, Range 7, near Jasper, on September 23, 1857. He was a farmer on this site until he died. His death occurred on November 7, 1899, and he is buried at New Prospect. Among his children were—Lohamie C. Sherer, who married Ensley Lightle Brown; J. Brawley Sherer, who married Mary Stephenson, a daughter of John and Catherine (Files) Stephenson; Jefferson Davis Sherer, who married Grisella

Stephenson, a daughter of John and Catherine (Files) Stephenson; Oat Sherer, who married Jake W. O'Rear; Martha Sherer, who married a Mr. McDonald; another daughter who married James Gabbert; and William Thomas Sherer, who was born January 20, 1847, in York District, South Carolina. On June 18, 1864, he enlisted at Jasper as a private in Company K, Fourth Alabama Cavalry, and served until the close of the war. He died on March 23, 1921, and is buried at Samaria. He was married to Laura M. Croswell, who was born June 10, 1857, and died January 5, 1929.

Census of Confederate Soldiers, 1907.
Sherer Family Records.
Gravestones.

SHERER, ABSALOM, a son of William and Martha (Minter) Sherer, was born in York District, South Carolina, on March 12, 1819. He came to Walker County and entered government land in Section 17, Township 14, Range 7, near Jasper, on March 6, 1857, and conducted a farm on this site for the balance of his life. He died on January 10, 1893, and is buried at New Prospect. He was married twice—first, to Raney Kirkpatrick, a daughter of J. and E. Kirkpatrick, and, second, to Sarah Gabbert, of Walker County.

Walker County Tract Record.
Sherer Family Records.
Gravestones.

SHERER, ELISHA A., a son of William and Martha (Minter) Sherer, was born in York District, South Carolina, on January 25, 1821. He came to Walker County and entered government land in Section 6, Township 14, Range 7, near Jasper, on January 1, 1859. At the outbreak of the Civil War he enlisted in Company K, Fourth Alabama Cavalry, was promoted to Lieutenant, and served throughout the war. Returning to Walker County, he operated his farm until his death. He died on February 3, 1907, and is buried at New Prospect. On December 16, 1844, he was married to Elizabeth Kirkpatrick, who was born in South Carolina on November 25, 1821, a daughter of J. and E. Kirkpatrick. She died on January 12, 1902, and is buried at New Prospect. Children—Amzi Sherer, who married Dorenda Kilgore, a daughter of Wiley and Nancy Caroline (Sides) Kilgore; James Sherer, who married Mattie Lollar; Harriett Sherer, who married George Stewart; Maliva Sherer, who married Benjamin Stewart; Dorenda Sherer, who married Thomas Hudson; and Nada Sherer, who married Robert Cain.

Walker County Tract Record.
Gravestones.
Sherer Family Records.

SHERER, MADISON, a son of William and Martha (Minter) Sherer, was born in York District, South Carolina, on October 26, 1822. Along with his uncle, Thomas Sherer, he came to Walker County, and entered government land in Section 8, Township 14, Range 7, near Jasper, on December 11, 1855, where he operated a farm until his death. He died on February 13, 1884, and is buried at New Prospect. He was married in Walker County to Sarah E. Kitchens, a daughter of John Kitchens, and who was born March 6, 1841, and died August 7, 1886. Children—Vera Sherer, who married William Thomas; John M. Sherer, who married Mary Sides; Mary Sherer, who married a Mr. Lavan; Sallie Sherer, who married David Cooner; Jane Sherer, who married Arthur Posey; Crissy Sherer, who married Silas Posey; and George Sherer.

Walker County Tract Record.
Gravestones.
Sherer Family Records.

SHERER, WILLIAM MINTER, a son of William and Martha (Minter) Sherer, was born in York District, South Carolina, on January 22, 1826. About 1855 he came to Walker County and settled on a farm near Jasper, where he remained for the balance of his life. He died on October 2, 1903, and is buried at New Prospect. He was married three times; first, in South Carolina to a Miss Goode; second, in Walker County to Caroline Jones, a daughter of Wallace and Susan (Beavert) Jones; and, third, to Sarah E. Love, who was born December 3, 1831, and died January 18, 1897. Children by first marriage—William J. Sherer, who married, first, a Miss Gilpin, and, second, Alice Rogers, of Mississippi; Sarah Jane Sherer, who married A. J. Copeland; Sallie Sherer, who married, first, William Randolph, and, second, James Copeland, a brother of A. J. Copeland. Children by the second marriage—Fen Sherer, who married Noland Hudson. Children by the third marriage—Thomas N. Sherer, who married Fannie Files, a daughter of R. M. Files; William Minter Sherer, Jr., who married Lura Moss, of Mississippi; Joseph Robert Sherer, who married Minnie Day, a daughter of C. H. Day; and Richard Abner Sherer, who married Hamie Anderson.

Sherer Family Records.
Gravestones.

SHERER, JEFFERSON NEELY, a son of William and Martha (Minter) Sherer, was born in York District, South Carolina, on May 3, 1828. He came to Walker County and entered government land in Section 5, Township 14, Range 7, near Jasper, on July 23, 1856, where he operated a farm until his death. He died on March 12, 1896, and is buried at New Prospect. He was married to Harriett Kirkpatrick, a daughter of J. and E. Kirkpatrick, who was born in South Carolina on September 24, 1829, and died in Walker County on March 25, 1909. Children—Joseph Sherer, who married Frances Thomas; William Sherer, who married Eliza Glover; Mollie Sherer, who married Robert Kilgore; Mandy Sherer, who married W. H. Lollar; Docena Sherer, who married W. H. Lollar after the death of her sister Mandy; and Madison Monroe (Bud) Sherer, who married Martha Kilgore, a daughter of Wiley and Caroline (Sides) Kilgore, and who was bailiff of the Walker County grand jury for more than thirty-five years. His children were: Etta Sherer, who married Robert Snoddy; Fannie Sherer, who married Samuel Houston Brown; Jessie, who married Luther Huss Brown; Benjamin B. Sherer, who married Clara McCrary; Hugh Sherer, who married Olla McCrary; Ruth Sherer; Gay Sherer, who married R. Jess Wilson; Maude Sherer, who married James Burton; and Mary Sherer, who married Robert Kilgore.

Walker County Tract Record.
Sherer Family Records.
Gravestones.

SHERER, THOMAS, was born in York District, South Carolina, on November 20, 1808, a son of William Sherer, who located in York, South Carolina, about 1800; and a brother to William Sherer, whose sketch is given herein. Thomas Sherer was reared on his father's plantation at York, South Carolina, and was educated in the district schools. He came to Walker County and entered government land in Section 8, Township 14, Range 7, on December 11, 1855. He operated this farm, near Jasper, until 1884, when he moved to Dry Creek, Fayette County, but shortly thereafter he moved to Jasper, where he died on September 15, 1888. In 1836 Thomas Sherer was married to Jane ————, who was born in South Carolina on August 12, 1811, and died in Jasper on September 26, 1886. Among their children were—

Jonathan D. Sherer, who was born in York District, South Corolina, and who came to Walker County with his parents about 1855. Sometime before the Civil War he moved to Dry Creek, Fayette County, and was one of the first nine men in that county to offer service to the Confederate cause. He walked from Jasper to Moulton to join the army. He was captured at

Franklin, Tennessee, and was imprisoned at Rock Island, Illinois, until the close of the war, when he returned to Fayette County to spend the balance of his days. He was married to Mary Eason, a daughter of Harrison and Mary Eason, of Dry Creek.

Joseph Thomas Sherer, who was born at Bullock Creek Church, York District, South Carolina, on April 8, 1848, and came to Walker County with his parents about 1855. In May, 1864, he enlisted at Eldridge as a private in Company K, Fourth Alabama Cavalry, under Captain Kelly. He was captured between Montevallo and Randolph Station, Alabama, about March 1, 1865, by Captain Dodd's Company of the Fourth Michigan Cavalry, and was kept in a stockade at Selma for about fifteen days, when he was carried to Montgomery and paroled.

Caroline Sherer, who married Christopher Scott.

Owens' Alabama, Vol. IV, page 1544.
Mountain Eagle, September 26, 1888.
Gravestones.
Sherer Family Tradition.

SHERER, JOHN MADISON, a son of Jonathan D. and Mary (Eason) Sherer, was born at Dry Creek, Fayette County, on June 7, 1874. He was educated in the public schools, which were often taught in log cabins and churches, attended the Fayette High School, and studied law at the University of Alabama. He was admitted to the bar in 1896, practiced at Gainesville for two years, removed to Ensley in 1899, and to Jasper in 1900. He served as Solicitor of Walker County in 1904-05, and as City Attorney of Jasper during 1906. On May 11, 1898, he was married at Gainesville to Lucy Reaves Jackson.

Owens' Alabama, Vol. IV, page 1544.

SHIELDS, JOHN BRABSON, was born at Marshall's Ferry, Grainger County, Tennessee, on August 25, 1840, a son of Dr. Milton and Priscilla (Brabson) Shields; a grandson of James Shields, who was a soldier in the Revolutionary War; a great-grandson of William Shields, who was born in the County Armagh, Ireland, on July 14, 1728, and who, when but nine years of age, embarked on a sloop commanded by Captain Alex Smith, bound for America, on February 26, 1737. His father, Robert Shields, died on the voyage, and the young orphan settled in Maryland. John Brabson Shields was educated in the old field schools of his neighborhood until fifteen years of age, when he was sent to Greenville College for two years. Medical studies were brought to a close by the outbreak of the Civil War. In February, 1862, he enlisted at Bean Station, Grainger County, Tennessee, as Second Lieutenant in Company I, Fifty-ninth Tennessee Infantry. He was captured and paroled at Vicksburg on July 4, 1863, but was exchanged on September 13, 1863, and went back to his old command as First Lieutenant. He was engaged in the battles of Grand Gulf, Baker's Creek, Piedmont, Morristown, Bull's Gap, Monocacy Junction, and Winchester. He was captured and paroled at Athens, Georgia, on May 4, 1865. After the close of the war he was a merchant at Newnan, Georgia, for eighteen months, and then returned to his old home in Tennessee, which was in ruins. After rebuilding the old homestead he became a clerk at Morristown, Tennessee. In 1868 he became a merchant and railroad station agent at Wolf Creek, Tennessee, and in 1872 moved to Carroll County, Georgia, to be superintendent of a paper manufacturing company. In 1873 he moved to Walker County, where he refitted Long's Mill, on Blackwater Creek, and became a merchant and miller. After three years he sold out to B. M. Long and moved to the then thriving town of South Lowell, where he operated a steam saw and planing mill. In 1884 he was elected to the Legislature on an independent ticket and served during the sessions of 1884-85. In 1886 he was elected Judge of Probate and was re-elected for successive terms until 1912, when he was succeeded by Judge Chas. M. Sartain. However, he continued to be one of the civic leaders of Jasper until his death on March 13, 1930. On September 19, 1866, he was married at Carrollton, Carroll County, Georgia, to Carrie Eliza Long, who was born June 29, 1845, and died March 27, 1933. She was a sister to Benjamin M. Long, who became one of Walker County's most prominent citizens, and a daughter of Judge John and Nancy (Davis) Long, the former a native of Tennessee who settled in Carroll County, Georgia, in 1826, and there served as judge, legislator, and in other offices for more than twenty-five years. Children —

Nanette P. Shields, who married Ezra Wilson Coleman, a son of Judge Thomas Wilkes and Frances Jane (Wilson) Coleman, of Eutaw, Alabama; Carrie May Shields; Maud Shields; and John B. Shields.

Northern Alabama, page 175.
Owens' Alabama, Vol. IV, page 1223.
Owens' Alabama, Vol. IV, page 1549.
Owens' Alabama, Vol. III, page 374.
Census of Confederate Soldiers, 1907.

SHORT, JAMES, a noted river pilot, entered government land in Section 17, Township 16, Range 6, on November 19, 1834.

Walker County Tract Record.

SHORT, LOUIS, entered government land in Section 17, Township 16, Range 6, on November 19, 1834.

Walker County Tract Record.

SHORT, WILLIAM, entered government land in Section 17, Township 16, Range 6, on February 22, 1836.

Walker County Tract Record.

SHORT, DANIEL, was born February 20, 1846, near the mouth of Baker Creek on the Warrior River. On January 20, 1864, he enlisted as a private in Company I, Fiftieth Alabama Infantry, and served until the close of the war.

Census of Confederate Soldiers, 1907.

SIDES, HENRY, born in 1734, was of a Holland Dutch family that immigrated to America shortly before the Revolutionary War, and family tradition states that Henry Sides served with distinction during that war. About 1818, while Alabama was still a territory, Henry Sides, then of advanced age, came to Walker County with several married sons and their families, among these sons being Henry, William, Levi, John, and Moses. He made his home with his son, William, who settled south of Pleasant Grove, and when he died he was buried in the Sides Graveyard on the old home place.

Sides Family Tradition.
Gravestone.

SIDES, HENRY II, a son of Henry Sides, was born January 9, 1779. With his wife, Susan, who was born January 6, 1789, and died September 26, 1874, he came to Walker County about 1818, along with his father and brothers. He settled northwest of Jasper, near Old Zion, where he died on January 15, 1867. Among his children was Elijah Sides, who was born January 4, 1825, and died March 28, 1900. On February 3, 1843, Elijah Sides was married to Nancy Brown, who was born in Morgan County February 2, 1820, and died in Walker County, near Lucky, April 12, 1886, a daughter of John and Hannah Brown.

True Citizen, April 22, 1886.
Gravestones.

SIDES, LEVI, a son of Henry Sides, came to Walker County with his father and brothers about 1818, and settled north of Jasper. He was a farmer and blacksmith, and also for years served as a Judge of the County Court. Col. Powell states that "Levi Sides died some years after the Civil War, without a personal enemy. Plain in manner and dress, universally kind, but he allowed no discount on the dignity of his court." His daughter, Nancy Caroline, married Wiley Kilgore, a son of Elzie and

Nancy (Larrimore) Kilgore. A son, Dock Sides, married Mary Kilgore.

Powell's Fifty-five Years in West Alabama.

SIDES, WILLIAM, a son of Henry Sides, was born in 1795. He came to Walker County with his father and brothers about 1818, and settled south of Pleasant Grove. He was the first clerk of the Pleasant Grove Missionary Baptist Church, when that church was constituted in 1842. He died on December 2, 1868, and is buried in the old Sides Graveyard. William Sides was married three times—first, in the old settlement; second, to Cerepta Dill, of Walker County; and, third, to Miss Myers. Children—

Hugh R. Sides, who was born July 22, 1819, and died December 30, 1855. He was the father of Richard Sides, and Eliza Jane Sides, who married John Kitchens.

Jonathan D. Sides, who was born in 1820 and died September 30, 1885. He was married to Frankie Hendon, but there were no children.

Harrison Sides, who married Polly Cooner, a daughter of James P. Cooner. Children—James M. Sides; John Sides, who was killed in the Civil War; Sarah Sides, who married Wm. Davidson; and Martha Jane Sides, who married N. J. Johnson.

Children by second marriage—

Cole Sides, who married a Miss Whatley and moved to Mississippi.

William F. Sides, who married, first, a Miss Dewese, and, second, a widow, Mrs. Martha (Kitchens) Stagg, a daughter of John Kitchens. Children by first marriage—Henry Coleman Sides, who married, first, Nannie Key, a daughter of Tom Key; and, second, Carrie Nix. Children by second marriage—Emily Sides, who married C. A. Wood; and Etta Sides, who married Wilson Odom.

Andy Allen Sides, who was born July 17, 1827. In the

early part of the Civil War he was enrolled and mustered into service by Captain Goodwin at Jasper, and was detailed as blacksmith for Walker County. He was elected Lieutenant of the Walker County Home Guard Company under Dr. L. C. Miller, its captain, and served until the close of the war. He died on August 31, 1912, and is buried at Liberty Grove. He was married to Mary Malone Staggs. Children—Henry Sides, who married Sarah Pike; Martha Sides, who married Joseph C. Pike; Jonathan M. Sides, who married Malinda Keeton; James M. Sides, who married Margaret Ellis; William L. Sides, who married Margaret Smith; Joseph V. Sides, who married Martha Faught; Nancy Sides, who married James Latham; Elizabeth Sides, who married William V. Keeton; Mary Ann Sides, who married Reuben F. Keeton; and Eliza Jane Sides, who married William Keeton.

Francis Sides, who was killed at the battle of Shiloh.

George Franklin Sides, who was born April 30, 1830, and died April 16, 1863, a member of Company G, Thirteenth Alabama Cavalry. He was married to Elizabeth Cooner, a daughter of James P. Cooner. Children—Manly Lee Sides, who married Zeruah Amanda Sartain, a daughter of William Turner and Mary Summers (Rammage) Sartain; James Harrison Sides, who was born June 7, 1852, became a prominent deputy sheriff of the county for a number of years, and died in 1933. In October, 1870, he was married to Martha Odom, who was born in 1848 and died June 9, 1933; William Lafayette Sides, who was born December 30, 1847; became a merchant in South Lowell and later in Jasper, and died October 1, 1930. He was married to Martha Elizabeth Staggs; Mary Elizabeth Sides, who married George Kilgore.

Frank Sides, who married Frances Kitchens, a daughter of John Kitchens. Children—Benjamin Franklin Sides, who was born November 27, 1856; and died August 20, 1930. He was married to Jane Minor, who was born August 10, 1859, and died June 13, 1920; John Sides, who married Carrie Wright; and Mary Sides, who married John Gray.

John B. Sides, who married, first, Peninnah Elizabeth Sartain, a daughter of William Turner and Mary Summers (Rammage) Sartain, and, second, a Miss Busby. Children by first marriage—Mary Ann Sides, who never married; Etta Sides, who married Samuel T. Brown; William Luther Sides, who married Lila Keene; John N. Sides, who married Ella Thompson; Fannie Sides, who married George L. Wakefield; Frank B. Sides, who moved to Mississippi. Children by second marriage—Johnnie B. Sides, a daughter, who married in Illinois; and Eugene Sides, who married a Miss Wright.

Sides Family Tradition.
Gravestones.
Census of Confederate Soldiers, 1907.
Mountain Eagle, June 14, 1933.
Mountain Eagle, September 5, 1934.

SIMPSON, WILT, entered government land in Section 20, Township 15, Range 9, on December 10, 1825.

Walker County Tract Record.

SIMPSON, JAMES, entered government land in Section 30, Township 13, Range 9, on November 20, 1837.

Walker County Tract Record.

SIMPSON, SAMUEL H., was born in South Carolina, a descendant of Scotch-Irish ancestors, who came to the Carolinas during the Colonial epoch. At a very early age he came to Walker County and settled just South of Oakman, where he engaged in farming for the balance of his life. He was married to Sarah Worthington, who was born in South Carolina in 1826, and died in Walker County at more than one hundred years of age. Among their children was—

William Thomas Simpson, who was born in Walker County June 10, 1849. He was educated at the University of Alabama, and spent his life as a school teacher and farmer. In 1874 he moved to Berry, in Fayette County, where he died on March 9, 1917. He was married in 1872 to Susan Gurganus, who was born in Walker County in 1853. Children—John Wesley Simpson, a physician in Parrish, who was born April 20, 1872, and married in 1894 to Emma Harbin, of Berry, and, after her death in 1902, he married Vada Sumner, a daughter of John H. and Elizabeth (Lollar) Sumner; Statie Simpson, who married William B. Cornelius, of Berry; Samuel H. Simpson; Zorilda Simpson, who married Rufus V. Jenkins, of Berry; James H. Simpson; Exer Simpson; Ando Simpson; Uriah Simpson; Mayrtie Simpson, who married Harry Kimbrell, of Berry; Ozella Simpson, who married Lester Wright, of Berry; and Grace Simpson, who married Alonzo Bennett, of Detroit, Michigan.

Moore's Alabama, Vol. II, page 191.
Mountain Eagle, September 12, 1917.

SINGLETON, EDMUND, was born in London, England, in 1856. He was educated at Edinburg, Scotland, and completed his musical studies in Paris. He served for a time with the British Army in Egypt and other colonies of the Crown, and his career was one of honor and distinction. About 1890 he went to Canada and lived there for a time, as well as in some of our Northern States. In 1895 he came to Dora, where he died on February 10, 1935. He was married in Dora to Matilda Davis, a descendant of James M. Davis, one of the pioneer settlers of Dora. Children—Edmund Singleton, James Singleton, Louise Singleton, Elizabeth Singleton, and Margaret Singleton.

Mountain Eagle, February 20, 1935.

SKELTON, NELSON, entered government land in Section 36, Township 16, Range 6, on August 10, 1847.

Walker County Tract Record.

SLOAN, STERLING W., entered government land in Section 36, Township 14, Range 4, on September 19, 1855.
Walker County Tract Record.

SLOAN, GEORGE A., entered government land in Section 9, Township 14, Range 4, on January 5, 1855.
Walker County Tract Record.

SLOAN, SIMPSON S., entered government land in Section 10, Township 14, Range 4, on March 11, 1856.
Walker County Tract Record.

SMITH, WILLIAM, entered government land in Section 27, Township 14, Range 8, on Lost Creek, south of Hilliard, on November 24, 1824.
Walker County Tract Record.

SMITH, JOHN, Jr., entered government land in Section 22, Township 17, Range 7, near Heard Shoals, on Warrior River, on July 2, 1840.
Walker County Tract Record.

SMITH, BENJAMIN J., entered government land in Section 20, Township 15, Range 8, northwest of Oakman, on March 16, 1848.
Walker County Tract Record.

SMITH, JESSE, entered government land in Section 5, Township 13, Range 7, on December 16, 1854.
Walker County Tract Record.

SMITH, EPHRAIM, entered government land in Section 35, Township 13, Range 7, on December 17, 1858.
Walker County Tract Record.

SMITH, ALVIN A., was born March 9, 1832, at Raleigh, Wake County, North Carolina. In January, 1862, he enlisted at Carbon Hill as a private in Company A, Forty-third Alabama Infantry, and served until the close of the war.
Census of Confederate Soldiers, 1907.

SMITH, LEONIDAS KIRKSEY, was born April 8, 1838, at Spartanburg, South Carolina. In September, 1862, he enlisted at Jasper as a private in Company H, Fifty-sixth Alabama Cavalry, under Captain Johnson, and served until the close of the war.

Census of Confederate Soldiers, 1907.

SMITH, REV. ALLEN, a native of North Carolina, moved from North Carolina to Tennessee about 1830, and from there to Walker County about 1835 or 1836. In 1826 he was married in North Carolina to Patsy A. ———, who was born July 4, 1807, and died in Walker County June 29, 1895.

Mountain Eagle, July 10, 1895.

SMITH, RICHARD H., a native of South Carolina, was born February 17, 1846. He came to Walker County when still a young man, and lived here until his death on April 3, 1917. He was married to Rebecca J. Cranford, who was born August 1, 1850, and died September 25, 1915. Children—H. Cam Smith, L. M. Smith, B. B. Smith, Richard H. Smith, Jr., Laura Smith, Mrs. Bell Cunningham, Mrs. Ida Childres, Mrs. Floyd McKessick.

Mountain Eagle, April 4, 1917.

SNODDY, JOHN, and his wife, Matilda, natives of Chester District, South Carolina, entered government land in Section 32, Township 13, Range 7, north of Jasper, on December 18, 1858.

Walker County Tract Record.

SNODDY, SAMUEL, a son of John and Matilda Snoddy, was born November 21, 1844, at Lowrysville, Chester District, South Carolina. In 1858, when but fourteen years of age, he was brought to Walker County by his parents. On October 10, 1863, he enlisted at Holly Grove as a sergeant in Company B, Tenth Alabama Cavalry, under Captain Whatley, and served until the close of the war. He died on July 19, 1930, and is buried at New Prospect. His wife, Mary C. Snoddy, was born September 15, 1851, and died September 25, 1916.

Census of Confederate Soldiers, 1907.
Gravestones.

SNOW, WILLIAM HENRY, a physician and Methodist minister, was born in Virginia on January 22, 1814, a son of Thomas Snow, who moved to Walker County and entered government land in Section 5, Township 16, Range 7, near the confluence of Lost and Cane Creeks, south of Parrish, on February 28, 1825; and, according to family tradition, a grandson of Dr. Peter and Elizabeth (Adams) Snow, who practiced medicine at Fitchburg, Massachusetts, for thirty-four years; great-grandson of Peter Snow and wife, a Miss Godfrey, and of Rev. Zabdiel and Elizabeth (Stearns) Adams, of Lunenburg, Massachusetts, double first cousin of John Quincy Adams. The American founder of the family was William Snow, who came from England in 1637, settled in Duxbury, Massachusetts, in 1645 and later was one of the first settlers in Bridgewater, Massachusetts, in 1657. William Henry Snow, who was but eleven years of age when brought to Walker County, received most of his education in the county schools and studied medicine under his uncles, Drs. Charles Snow, Henry Adams Snow, and Z. B. Snow, in Tuscaloosa. Early in life he became identified with the Methodist Church, and took an active part in the establishment of that church in Walker County, and at one time served as Presiding Elder. There was not much of an organization and very few churches, but Dr. Snow rode his circuit, preached in homes, held weekly prayer meetings, and did what he could for sick souls as well as sick bodies. He died on September 17, 1883, as the result of injuries received from being thrown from a mule. He is buried in the old Thompson Graveyard, near Snow Ferry, on the Warrior River. About 1832 he was married to Matilda

Ann Chilton, a daughter of Richard and Nancy (Key) Chilton. Children—

Richard Jackson Snow, who was born February 7, 1834.

Nancy Snow, who was born December 24, 1835, and was married, first, to Jack Davis, and, second, to Robert Waldrop.

Thomas J. Snow, who was born January 24, 1838, and was killed in the Civil War.

Zilphey Snow, who was born March 4, 1839, and was married to E. B. Cannon.

Malinda Snow, who was born February 3, 1841, and was married to Rev. Austin White, a Baptist minister, who was born May 5, 1844.

Robert Snow, who was born January 22, 1843.

Sarah Snow, who was born March 1, 1845, and was married to James Davis.

Francis Asbury Snow, who was born February 23, 1846. On May 1, 1864, he enlisted at Jasper as a private in Company G, Fifty-sixth Alabama Cavalry, under Captain Shepherd, and served until the close of the war. He died on June 11, 1915, and is buried at Lamon's Chapel, near Manchester. He was married to Eliza Franklin.

William Henry Snow, who was born June 12, 1851.

John W. Snow, who was born in 1853.

James Monroe (Jimroe) Snow.

Jesse Snow.

Elizabeth Snow, who married Francis Payne.

> Owens' Alabama, Vol. IV, pages 1601-02.
> Family Bible, William Henry Snow.
> Census of Confederate Soldiers, 1907.
> Gravestones.
> Snow Family Tradition.

SOWELL, THOMAS LAMAR, was born February 24, 1858, at Claiborne, Monroe County, Alabama, a son of William Calvin and Isabella (Roberts) Sowell, the former a native of Lancaster, South Carolina, who removed to Monroe County in 1847; grandson of James Lawrence and Mary (Hunley) Sowell; great-grandson of Captain James and Ann (Cook) Sowell, the former a native of Sumter District, South Carolina, and removed to Monroe County about 1817 or 1818. Thomas Lamar Sowell was educated in the common schools of Monroe County and studied law in the office of Hon. Charles J. Torrey, at Monroeville. He was admitted to the bar in January, 1879, and practiced in Monroe County until 1887, when he came to Jasper. He was Walker County's Representative in the Legislature in 1892; Solicitor of the county, 1895-1900; State Auditor, 1900-1905; was appointed Judge of the Walker County Law and Equity Court and served until that court was abolished; and was elected Circuit Judge of the Fourteenth Judicial Circuit. On January 17, 1894, he was married at Jasper to Margaret Eleanor Lollar, a daughter of John B. and Harriet T. (Taylor) Lollar.

Owens' Alabama, Vol. IV, page 1603.

SPAULDING, EPHRAIM, entered government land in Section 31, Township 15, Range 5, on December 5, 1854.
Walker County Tract Record.

SPAULDING, JOHN P., entered government land in Section 31, Township 15, Range 5, on February 21, 1855.
Walker County Tract Record.

SPEAR, GEORGE, entered government land in Section 36, Township 14, Range 4, on August 8, 1820.
Walker County Tract Record.

SPEAR, BENJAMIN, entered government land in Section 28, Township 14, Range 8, near Pleasant Grove, on January 6, 1825.
Walker County Tract Record.

SPEAR, JOHN, was born February 12, 1831, at Anderson, South Carolina. On July 22, 1861, he enlisted at McMinnville,

Tennessee, as a private in Company A, Ninth Tennessee Infantry, and served throughout the war. He came to Jasper about 1877, and at various times was a cattle dealer, a merchant, and marshal of Jasper. His wife, Ardena Spear, was born in 1833 and died December 17, 1908. A son, Richard, moved to West Virginia and one daughter married W. R. Richardson.

Census of Confederate Soldiers, 1907.
Mountain Eagle, December 26, 1917.
Gravestones.

SPRINGFIELD, ROBERT T., was born February 1, 1832, on the Ocmulgee River, Butts County, Georgia. In September, 1862, he enlisted at Jasper as a private in Company G, Fifty-sixth Alabama Cavalry, under Captain Shepherd, and served until the close of the war.

Census of Confederate Soldiers, 1907.

STACKS, JOHN MORGAN, was born September 29, 1842, near Atlanta, Georgia. In September, 1863, he enlisted at Jasper as a private in Company B, Tenth Alabama Cavalry, and served until the close of the war.

Census of Confederate Soldiers, 1907.

STAGGS, JOHN, entered government land in Section 32, Township 14, Range 8, on March 24, 1836.

Walker County Tract Record.

STANLEY, W. L., a pioneer of Jasper and Treasurer of Walker County before and during the Civil War, was born December 20, 1816, and, according to family tradition, a son of Samuel and Martha (Hendricks) Stanley, of Columbia, South Carolina, the former's father having come from England between 1740 and 1750, and settled in Virginia. It is thought that he came to Walker County about 1833, and in 1859 he was postmaster at Jasper, when the town had only two mails a week, one from Decatur and one from Tuscaloosa. At this time he also operated a store, in which the post office was located. He died on June 20, 1883, and is buried in the old cemetery at Jasper. His daughter, Alice C. Stanley, was married to George H. Guttery. A brother, J. M. Stanley, born June 11, 1818, died April 11, 1873, and is buried in one of two graves on the top of Hayes Hill, on the highway between Oakman and Patton Junction.

Owens' Alabama, Vol. IV, page 1612.
Gravestones.

STEEDMAN, JOHN BENJAMIN, was born January 12, 1835, at Rock Hill, South Carolina. In September, 1862, he enlisted at Holly Grove as a private in Company B, Fifty-sixth Alabama Cavalry, under Captain Guttery, and served until the close of the war.

Census of Confederate Soldiers, 1907.

STEPHENSON, SAMUEL M., born in North Carolina on September 22, 1825, came to Fayette County, Alabama, in early manhood, and in 1860 moved to Walker County and settled on a farm two miles south of Providence, on Cane Creek. He died on July 30, 1861, shortly after coming to the county, and is buried at Providence, as is also his second wife, Mary M. Stephenson, who died October 18, 1865. He was married twice and was the father of ten children—

Lisha Stephenson, who married Miles Whitson.

Mary Ann Stephenson, who married James Thompson.

John H. Stephenson, who married Jencie Ann Kirkpatrick, a daughter of William R. and Permelia H. (Meek) Kirkpatrick.

Tillian Stephenson, who died in young manhood.

Mose M. Stephenson, who married Mary A. Tierce, a daughter of Elliott C. Tierce.

Rachel Stephenson, who married Robert Taylor.

Ramsay Stephenson, who married Sallie King.

Doshie Stephenson, who married Green Covin.

Samuel Stephenson, who never married.

Stephenson Family Records.

STEPHENSON, MOSES MARION, a son of Samuel Stephenson, was born in Fayette County, Alabama, May 13, 1853. He was brought to Walker County by his parents in 1860, when his father settled on a farm two miles south of Providence. His father dying the following year, Mr. Stephenson suffered the many hardships of an orphan in a new country. After living at various places in the county, he moved to a farm near the present site of Corona, where he was married to Mary A. Tierce, a daughter of Elliott Tierce, on April 5, 1877. In 1880 he acquired a farm about two miles west of Parrish, on the old Jasper Taylor's Ferry Road, where he died on April 5, 1935. Mr. Stephenson was a devoted member of the Methodist Church, having his membership originally at old Antioch, on Key's Hill. However, shortly after moving near Parrish, his home was made a regular preaching place for the Methodist circuit rider until the establishment of the Parrish Methodist Church, which was organized in January, 1892, with six charter members, including Mr. Stephenson and his wife. He was the father of eight children—Elliott Stephenson, who married a Miss Lollar; John Stephenson, who married Ada Robinson; Ada Stephenson, who married Gilman Jones; Vada Stephenson, who married Fayette Blanton; Flossie Stephenson, who married Wm. Pate; Dessie Stephenson, who married Joe Legar; Lilly Stephenson, who married, first, Leo Brown, and, second, John Phillips; and Andrew Stephenson.

Stephenson Family Records.
Mountain Eagle, April 11, 1935.

STEPHENSON, JOHN E., a brother to Samuel M. Stephenson, entered government land in Section 28, Township 14, Range 7, near Calumet, on July 29, 1857. He was married to Catherine Files, a daughter of Richard and Mary (Lindsay) Files. Children—Miranda Stephenson, who married a Mr. Copeland; Mary Stephenson, who married J. Brawley Sherer; Grisella

Stephenson, who married Jefferson D. Sherer; and George Stephenson.

Stephenson Family Records.

STEPHENSON, HUGH WATSON, was born December 24, 1854, at St. Charles, Arkansas; a son of Hugh Stewart and Jane (Morrow) Stephenson, of St. Charles, Arkansas; a grandson of William Watson and Melinda (Johnson) Stephenson, the former, who lived in Columbia, Tennessee, in 1812-14, enlisted in General Jackson's Army and was in the battle of Horseshoe Bend and other battles with the Creek Indians, and in 1819 settled in Lawrence County; and of Molita Morrow, of Morgan County; a great-grandson of Hugh W. Stephenson; and a great-great-grandson of William Stephenson, a Scotch Irishman, who immigrated to Rock Creek, Chester District, South Carolina, and served in the Revolutionary War. Hugh Watson Stephenson graduated from the medical department of the University of Alabama, at Mobile, in 1880, with the degree of Doctor of Medicine, and immediately established himself in the practice of medicine in Lawrence County, until 1884, when he took post graduate work at Tulane University, New Orleans, Louisiana. In 1887 Dr. Stephenson moved to Oakman and started the practice of medicine. He served on the city council of Oakman several times and represented Walker County in the Legislature in 1915. During the World War he was a member of the Medical Reserve Corps. On December 24, 1884, Dr. Stephenson was married to Sallie Masterson, a daughter of James Newton Masterson, of Lawrence County. Children—Roscoe O. Stephenson, who never married; Claud M. Stephenson, who married Lacy Rutledge; Irene Stephenson, who married Harvey Ward; Pearl Stephenson, who married Warren S. Fleming; and Paul Stephenson, who married Mary King.

Owens' Alabama, Vol. IV, page 1620.
Moore's Alabama, Vol. II, page 459.

STEVENS, ABRAHAM, entered government land in Section 10, Township 15, Range 5, on November 15, 1854.
Walker County Tract Record.

STEVENS, ADAM J., entered government land in Section 9, Township 15, Range 5, on August 16, 1855.
Walker County Tract Record.

STEWART, WILLIAM, entered government land in Section 33, Township 13, Range 5, on January 22, 1822.
Walker County Tract Record.

STEWART, SAMUEL, was born near Jasper on December 28, 1832. On September 13, 1862, he enlisted at Jasper as a private in Company F, Fifty-sixth Alabama Cavalry, under Captain Rice, and served until the close of the war.
Census of Confederate Soldiers, 1907.

STOCKRIDGE, ANDREW, entered government land in Section 24, Township 14, Range 6, near the mouth of Blackwater Creek, on September 18, 1821.
Walker County Tract Record.

STOVALL, WILLIAM POOL, was born in South Carolina on December 11, 1797. He lived for a time in St. Clair and Jefferson Counties, Alabama, and finally came to Walker County, where he entered government land in Section 33, Township 13, Range 5, on July 16, 1832. He died in Jasper on September 10, 1862.
Owens' Alabama, Vol. IV, page 1631.
Gravestone.

STOVALL, DAVIS LEWIS, a son of William Pool Stovall, was born in Jefferson County, Alabama, and came to Walker County with his parents in 1832. He spent his entire life in Jasper, and was Clerk of the Circuit Court of Walker County for twenty-two years. He was married to Mary McLeese, and was the father of several children, among them being Dr. Andrew McAdams Stovall, who was born December 14, 1857, and was married in 1889 to Nancy Dodson, a daughter of Ezekiel Dodson; A. B. Stovall, born in 1864 and died October 2, 1917, and who was married in 1900 to Mary Propst, of Millport; James Stovall; and Eula Stovall.

Owens' Alabama, Vol. IV, page 1631.
Mountain Eagle, October 3, 1917.

STUBBLEFIELD, WILLIAM THOMAS, a son of John and Nancy (Wooten) Stubblefield, was born at Washington, Wilkes County, Georgia. He was reared in Georgia and in Talladega County, Alabama, and acquired an excellent education. During the war with Mexico he served as first sergeant in Company E, First Alabama Volunteer Regiment. About 1849 he moved to Coosa County, where he engaged in merchandising and farming, and where he served for a number of years as Clerk of the Circuit Court at Rockford, which position he was holding at the outbreak of the Civil War. He made up a company for service in the Confederate Army, was elected captain, and later went to the front as Major, in command of the Second Battalion of Hilliard's Legion. He served through two years of the war and then returned to his old office of Clerk of the Court at Rockford. About 1865 he moved to Walker County and settled on Wolf Creek, near Eldridge. In 1868 he was elected Representative in the State Legislature and served during the sessions from 1868 to 1870. He farmed until 1879, when he moved to Montgomery as Deputy Clerk of the Circuit Court of Montgomery County. He died and was buried at Montgomery. In 1849 he was married in Coosa County to Elizabeth Kelley, a daughter of John and Martha (Franklin) Kelley, who was born at Sylacauga, Alabama, in 1833, and died at Eldridge. Children— Mary Stubblefield, who married Robert Cutts, of Guin, Alabama; Nancy Graham Stubblefield; Martha Stubblefield; John Stubblefield; H. Eugene Stubblefield; Charles Wooten Stubblefield, who married Ida Emily Blanton, a daughter of Elijah Blanton; Talbot Kelley Stubblefield; and William F. Stubblefield.

Owens' Alabama, Vol. IV, page 1636.
Moore's Alabama, Vol. III, page 601.

STURGIS, JOSHUA FRANKLIN, was born at Rock Hill, South Carolina, December 30, 1840. On August 1, 1862, he enlisted at Jasper as a private in Company L, Fifty-sixth Alabama Cavalry, under Captain Guttery, and served until the close of the war.

Census of Confederate Soldiers, 1907.

SUMNER, FRANKLIN REUBEN, was born in Cherokee County, Georgia, November 30, 1845. On March 28, 1862, he enlisted in Walker County as a private in Company E, Twenty-eighth Alabama Infantry, under Captain Lollar. He was captured at Missionary Ridge and imprisoned until the close of the war.

Census of Confederate Soldiers, 1907.

SUGG, HERBERT L., entered government land in Section 28, Township 14, Range 9, on January 14, 1833.

Walker County Tract Record.

SULLIVAN, WILLIAM P., entered government land in Section 28, Township 15, Range 8, on September 11, 1835.

Walker County Tract Record.

SUTHERLAND, JAMES, entered government land in Section 24, Township 15, Range 6, on March 16, 1836.

Walker County Tract Record.

SUTHERLAND, ADAM, entered government land in Section 24, Township 15, Range 6, on September 27, 1836.

Walker County Tract Record.

SUTTON, PHILLIP, entered government land in Section 5, Township 14, Range 4, on December 19, 1833.

Walker County Tract Record.

EARLY SETTLERS 359

SUTTON, JACOB, Sr., entered government land in Section 2, Township 15, Range 6, on November 14, 1835.
Walker County Tract Record.

SUTTON, WILLIAM, was born October 8, 1837, at Chilton's Mill, near the mouth of Blackwater Creek. In February, 1862, he enlisted as a private in Company E, Twenty-eighth Alabama Infantry, and served until the close of the war.
Census of Confederate Soldiers, 1907.

SWINDLE, JOHN, entered government land in Section 20, Township 15, Range 8, on February 17, 1836.
Walker County Tract Record.

SWINDLE, DANIEL, was born in South Corolina, and was brought to Tuscaloosa by his parents while still a child. Reared in Tuscaloosa, he came to Walker County after his marriage, and entered government land in Section 20, Township 15, Range 8, near Coal Valley, on January 29, 1845. He was the father of Dennis Swindle, who married Amanda Myers; and Bayliss Swindle, who married Susan Raburn.
Walker County Tract Record.
Swindle Family Tradition.

SWINDLE, WILLIAM, a brother of Daniel Swindle, was born in South Carolina September 16, 1811, and was brought to Tuscaloosa by his parents while still a child. Shortly after reaching manhood, he came to Walker County and settled on a farm near Coal Valley, where he died on November 13, 1893, and is buried in the Swindle Graveyard. He was married twice, first, to a Miss Busby, and, second, to Susan Hogue (or Hogg). Children by first marriage—James Swindle, who married a Miss Kilgore; John H. Swindle, who married Cynthia Grace; Wid Swindle; Elias Swindle; Elijah Swindle; Permelia D. Swindle, who married George T. Davidson; Mandy Swindle, who married a Mr. Wiggins; Sis Swindle, who married John Payne; and Vinie Swindle, who married Pen Williamson. Children by the second marriage—Lucious C. Swindle, who married, first, Martha Helen Myers, and, second, Jennie Whitson; George Swindle, who married Jane Davidson; Daniel D. Swindle, who married Liza Davidson; Etta Swindle, who married W. Lafayette Cranford; Lula Swindle, who married Ven Lawson; E. Darl Swindle, who married Winnie Cranford; D. V. (Dock) Swindle, who married Alice Cranford; Jalie Swindle, who married Charles Falls; and Genie Swindle, who married Polly Gurganus.

Swindle Family Tradition.

SWINDLE, JOHN HOLLY, a son of William Swindle, was born February 26, 1843, on Cane Creek, northwest of Oakman. In May, 1861, he enlisted at Watts' Mill, on Lost Creek, as a private in Company K, Fiftieth Alabama Cavalry, under Captain Hutto; was later transferred to Company K, Fourth Alabama Cavalry, under Captain Kelley, and later still, to Company B, Tenth Alabama Cavalry, where he served until the close of the war. He died on July 11, 1911, and is buried at New Hope. He was married to L. Cynthia Grace, who was born December 7, 1848, and died October 14, 1928.

Census of Confederate Soldiers, 1907.
Gravestones.

SWINDLE, JAMES WESLEY, a son of William Swindle, was born August 10, 1845, on Cane Creek, northwest of Oakman. In September, 1863, he enlisted at Holly Grove as a private in Company B, Tenth Alabama Cavalry, under Captain Whatley, and served until the close of the war. He died on March 2, 1912, and is buried at Jasper. He was married to a Miss Kilgore.

Census of Confederate Soldiers, 1907.
Gravestone.

SWINDLE, JESSE, entered government land in Section 18, Township 15, Range 7, on August 14, 1852.

Walker County Tract Record.

TANNER, MICHAEL, entered government land in Section 20, Township 15, Range 5, on November 28, 1836.
Walker County Tract Record.

TAYLOR, WADE B., an attorney in Jasper in 1845.
Alabama Roll of Attorneys.

TAYLOR, WILLIAM W., entered government land in Section 28, Township 12, Range 7, on January 3, 1853.
Walker County Tract Record.

TAYLOR, ROBERT, was born December 15, 1841, in Morgan County, Alabama. In March, 1862, he enlisted at Jasper as a private in Company L, Twenty-eighth Alabama Infantry, under Captain Musgrove, and served until the close of the war. He was married to Rachel Stephenson, a daughter of Samuel M. Stephenson. In 1892 Mr. Taylor and his wife were two of the six charter members that organized the Parrish Methodist Church.
Census of Confederate Soldiers, 1907.

THACKER, SAMUEL, entered government land in Section 28, Township 14, Range 9, on January 7, 1833.
Walker County Tract Record.

THOMAS, JAMES MADISON, entered government land in Section 7, Township 14, Range 5, on January 26, 1836.
Walker County Tract Record.

THOMAS, ANDREW JACKSON, was born October 15, 1838, five miles south of Blount Springs, Blount County, Alabama. On March 17, 1862, he enlisted at Jasper as a private in Company L, Twenty-eighth Alabama Infantry, under Captain Musgrove. He was captured at Orchard Knob, Missionary Ridge, and was imprisoned at Rock Island, Illinois, until the close of the war. He was married to Julia Brown.
Census of Confederate Soldiers, 1907.

THOMAS, BENJAMIN FRANKLIN, was born December

2, 1844, at the Steedman Place, on Lost Creek. In August, 1862, he enlisted at Jasper as a private in Company G, Fifty-sixth Alabama Cavalry, under Captain Shepherd, and served until the close of the war. He died on April 12, 1931, and is buried at Pleasant Grove. His wife, Mary Thomas, was born August 8, 1850, and died August 21, 1910.

Census of Confederate Soldiers, 1907.
Gravestones.

THOMPSON, FLEMING R., entered government land in Section 29, Township 16, Range 7, on November 9, 1835. However, it is believed that he was the son of Samuel Thompson, who came to Walker County and entered land in 1822. Fleming R. Thompson died on January 31, 1879. He and his wife, Margaret Elizabeth Thompson, were the parents of twelve children—

Caroline Paralee Thompson, who married James Ira Odom.

Martha Elizabeth Thompson, who married William Rhea.

Florida A. Thompson, who married Samuel Johnson.

Georgianna Thompson, who married Sampson Brown.

Samuel B. Thompson, who was the father of Elizabeth Thompson, who married John Knight, and Georgianna Thompson, who married Watson Rhea.

Maria Louisa Thompson, born November 23, 1836, died October 28, 1924. She was married to Allen H. Johnston.

J. B. (Joberry) Thompson, born March 20, 1833, died April 28, 1900.

Fleming Rudolph Thompson.

Sarah J. Thompson, who married George Turner and moved to Dallas, Lafayette County, Mississippi.

Evaline E. Thompson, who married G. W. L. Leith and moved to Fayette County, Alabama.

John L. Thompson.

William Alexander Thompson, born November 10, 1831, died February 8, 1918.
Walker County Tract Record.
Walker County Will Record.
Census of Confederate Soldiers, 1907.
Gravestones.

THOMPSON, SAMUEL, entered government land in Section 12, Township 17, Range 7, on March 6, 1822.
Walker County Tract Record.

THOMPSON, WILLIAM ALEXANDER, was born November 10, 1831, near the confluence of Lost and Wolf Creeks. In May, 1862, he enlisted as a private in Company K, Forty-third Alabama Infantry, under Captain Shepherd. He died on February 8, 1918, and is buried at Liberty Hill. His wife, Elizabeth Thompson, was born March 14, 1838, and died June 10, 1906.
Census of Confederate Soldiers, 1907.
Gravestones.

THOMPSON, J. B., a member of Company G, Fifty-sixth Alabama Partisan Rangers, was born March 20, 1833, and died April 28, 1900, and is buried at Fairview.
Gravestone.

TINGLE, BENJAMIN FRANKLIN, was born March 27, 1844, near Cedartown, Paulding County, Georgia. On August 25, 1862, he enlisted at Arkadelphia, Alabama, as a private, later promoted to orderly sergeant, in Company D, Twelfth Alabama Cavalry, and served until the close of the war. In 1882 he was elected to the Legislature as Representative and served during the sessions of 1882–83.
Census of Confederate Soldiers, 1907.

TOWNLEY, DANIEL, entered government land in Section 7, Township 14, Range 8, on January 15, 1822. The town of Townley grew up near this site and is named after his family.
Walker County Tract Record.

TOWNLEY, JOHN, entered government land in Section 27, Township 14, Range 8, on March 20, 1822.
Walker County Tract Record.

TOWNLEY, RICHMOND, entered government land in Section 18, Township 14, Range 8, on January 24, 1825. His daughter, Martha A. Townley, born February 14, 1828, and died February 8, 1894, was married to William P. Fike, and is buried in the Fike Graveyard.
Walker County Tract Record.
Gravestone.

TUBBS, DANIEL, of English ancestry and Carolina stock, served in the war of 1812, and was present in the final battle at New Orleans. He came to Walker County and entered government land in Section 2, Township 15, Range 8, about four miles northeast of Oakman, on November 5, 1835. He was married to Matilda Sanders, and was the father of several children, among them being William Tubbs; Polly Tubbs, who married William Wallace Jones; Samuel Tubbs; and Daniel Lee Tubbs.
Owens' Alabama, Vol. IV, page 1687.
Moore's Alabama, Vol. III, page 169.
Walker County Tract Record.

TUBBS, SAMUEL, a son of Daniel and Matilda (Sanders) Tubbs, was born in 1823, and was brought to Walker County by his parents in 1835, when twelve years of age. Reared and educated in the county, at the outbreak of the Civil War he became a member of the Fifth Alabama Cavalry. He was captured in 1864 and imprisoned at Rock Island, Illinois, until the close of the war. He died on September 27, 1902, and is buried in the Tubbs Graveyard. He was married to Malinda E. Cranford, a daughter of John and Elizabeth (Wilkes) Cranford, who was born April 15, 1825, and died July 27, 1897. He was the father of James Madison Tubbs, a native of Oakman and a physician in Bessemer, who married Dorothy Hamilton, a daughter of Elbert and Susan (Vanselt) Hamilton, who was born in Walker County in 1858.

Owens' Alabama, Vol. IV, page 1687.
Moore's Alabama, Vol. III, page 169.
Gravestones.

TUBBS, DANIEL LEE, a son of Daniel and Matilda (Sanders) Tubbs, was born October 7, 1827, and was brought to Walker County by his parents while still a child. He spent his entire life in the county, where he died on November 5, 1859, and was buried in the Morris Graveyard. He was married to Nancy Emily Cranford, a daughter of John and Elizabeth (Wilkes) Cranford, who was born October 27, 1827, and died September 20, 1919. Children—Mary Ann (Polly) Tubbs, who was born May 13, 1846, and married Phillip Jefferson Myers; Matilda Jane Tubbs, who was born January 22, 1848, and was married to Robert William Johnson; Samuel Sanders Tubbs, who was born March 28, 1849, and died June 5, 1910; Dolly Dartha Tubbs, who was born March 26, 1851; Malinda Carlery Tubbs, who was born May 25, 1853; King David Tubbs, who was born October 7, 1855, and was married to Martha Hamilton; Daniel Lee Tubbs, Jr., who was born February 5, 1858, and was married to Julia Ann Phifer, a daughter of John and Mary Phifer.

Tubbs Family Records.

TUCKER, SAMUEL, entered government land in Section 27, Township 13, Range 10, on August 31, 1835.

Walker County Tract Record.

TUGGLE, JAMES B., entered government land in Section 12, Township 16, Range 6, on November 15, 1853. He became a noted river pilot.

Walker County Tract Record.

TUGGLE, EDWARD HARRISON, was born July 19, 1842, at Lawrenceville, Georgia. On August 1, 1862, he enlisted at

Jasper as a private in Company G, Fifty-sixth Alabama Cavalry, and served until the close of the war.
Census of Confederate Soldiers, 1907.

TURNER, MATHIAS, one of General Jackson's Tennessee Volunteers, was mustered out of service at Fort Jackson immediately after the treaty of peace was signed with the Creek Indians on August 19, 1814. While making his way back to his home in Tennessee he came up into what is now Walker County. A typical woodsman, he preferred to make his living through the trapping and hunting of wild animals, whose skins and furs had a ready sale. Attracted by the abundance of game along a creek in the southern part of Walker County, he settled there and followed his chosen calling, becoming noted far and wide as a hunter and trapper of game. Because of the number of wolves trapped and killed along this creek, it became known as Wolf Creek. He was the father of at least two sons—

John H. Turner, who entered government land in Section 23, Township 16, Range 7, on September 5, 1832, and as early as 1833 was prominently identified with the Methodist Church, being a local preacher at that time.

James T. Turner, who entered government land in Section 23, Township 16, Range 7, on September 5, 1832. He became associated with Major F. A. Musgrove in the coal business and for many years was his business manager.
Armes' Story of Coal and Iron.
West's History of Methodism, page 549.

TURNER, ELIHU, was born May 5, 1831, in York District, South Carolina. In August, 1862, he enlisted at Tuscaloosa as a private in Company D, Thirty-sixth Alabama Infantry, under Captain Woodruff. He was captured at Missionary Ridge and was imprisoned at Rock Island, Illinois, until the close of the war.
Census of Confederate Soldiers, 1907.

TURNER, JOHN OLIVER, was born January 9, 1845, at Conyers, Newton County, Georgia. His parents later moved to Rome, Georgia, where, on November 10, 1863, he enlisted as a private in Company G, Third Georgia Infantry, under Captain Richardson, and served until the close of the war. Some years after the war he moved to Walker County and in 1894 he was appointed State Superintendent of Education. He died in Walker County, and is buried at Union Chapel. His wife, G. A. Turner, was born January 1, 1847, and died March 16, 1919.

Census of Confederate Soldiers, 1907.
Mountain Eagle, June 26, 1895.
Gravestones.

TUTTLE, ROBERT G., entered government land in Section 9, Township 13, Range 5, on December 20, 1832.

Walker County Tract Record.

TYREE, JESSE, entered government land in Section 13, Township 14, Range 8, at Townley, on October 1, 1823. He became rather well-to-do in life, though, while always having plenty, he lived in plain style. He was about six feet four inches tall, very spare, but straight as an arrow.

Walker County Tract Record.
Mountain Eagle, October 19, 1887.

TYREE, JOSEPH, entered government land in Section 10, Township 15, Range 9, on June 27, 1823.

Walker County Tract Record.

UPTAIN, JOHN, a member of Fowler's Light Artillery, C. S. A., is buried at Fairview.

Gravestone.

USREY, JAMES WILLIAM, was born March 8, 1824, in Montgomery County, North Carolina. He served as a private in the Confederate Army under Captain Walthall. He died August 10, 1913, and is buried at Old Zion. His wife, Mary

M. Usrey, was born April 10, 1822, and died March 26, 1902.
Census of Confederate Soldiers, 1907.
Gravestones.

VANDEVEER, THOMAS, entered government land in Section 6, Township 16, Range 5, on July 3, 1855.
Walker County Tract Record.

VAN HOOSE, JESSE, originally came with his parents from New York, and settled in a colony established by Major William Russell in a part of the Chickasaw country, now known as Russellville, Franklin County, about 1815. In 1821 young Van Hoose became the first Clerk of the Circuit Court of Franklin County, but shortly afterwards he went on a trading trip to Fayette County and decided to stay there, being the second man to settle in that region. In 1826 he was elected to the State Senate from the senatorial district that included Walker County. He acquired coal lands in Walker County, and was associated with James Cain in the early development of the coal industry in Walker County.
Armes' Story of Coal and Iron.

VAN HORN, ANDREW J., a corporal in Company A, Forty-eighth Alabama Infantry, C. S. A., is buried at Dora.
Gravestone.

VICKORY, WILLIAM, entered government land in Section 14, Township 15, Range 6, on the Warrior River, on August 26, 1824.
Walker County Tract Record.

WADE, JOHN LANDON, was born August 17, 1846, on Indian Creek, near Fairview Church, Walker County. On October 1, 1863, he enlisted at Jasper as a private in Company K, Eighth Alabama Cavalry, under Captain Wharton, and served until the close of the war. At his death he was buried in the Providence Graveyard. He was married to Sarah Ann Blanton.
Census of Confederate Soldiers, 1907.

WAKEFIELD, JAMES MONROE, was born April 12, 1846, at Wetumpka, Coosa County, Alabama. In October, 1863, he enlisted in Fayette County in Company K, Fourth Alabama Cavalry, under Captain Kelley, and served until the close of the war.

Census of Confederate Soldiers, 1907.

WAKEFIELD, JOHN WESLEY, a member of Company C, First Alabama Cavalry, C. S. A., was born September 28, 1844, and died November 26, 1888, and is buried in the Guttery Graveyard at Townley. His wife, Malissa O. Wakefield, was born February 14, 1845, and died January 12, 1923, and is also buried at Townley.

Gravestones.

WALKER, SAMUEL, a native of County Durham, England, was born in the early 1790's. He came to America when quite a young man, and eventually settled in Georgia, where he met and married Nancy Taylor Brackett, who was born October 2, 1796, a cousin of Zachary Taylor, the twelfth President of the United States. Shortly after, the young couple moved into Alabama and, it is thought, settled in the Tennessee Valley, probably in Madison County, in or near Huntsville. In later years he removed to Walker County, probably during the 1840's, and settled near Dora, where most of his children married into the old pioneer families of that section. It is not known when or where Samuel Walker died, but his wife, Nancy, died near Dora on August 16, 1870, and is buried in the Friendship Graveyard. Children—Thomas Walker, who moved west before the Civil War; Amos B. Walker; William F. Walker; Samuel Walker; James R. Walker; Martha Walker, who married, first, Peter A. Morgan, and, second, James Bryant; Julia Walker, who married, first, William Legrand, and, second, William Simms; and Mary Walker, who died a spinster.

Walker Family Records.

WALKER, AMOS B., a son of Samuel and Nancy (Brackett) Walker, enlisted in the Confederate Army on October 7, 1863. He was captured at Missionary Ridge on November 25, 1863, taken to Louisville and later sent to Rock Island, Illinois, where he died on March 14, 1864. He was married to Eliza J. Morgan, a daughter of Ezekiel and Linnie (Brantley) Morgan, who was born January 28, 1832, and died October 24, 1886. Children—Samuel E. Walker; George Walker; Walter Walker; Samantha J. Walker, who married A. E. Morgan; Elizabeth Walker, who married H. Franklin Peterson; and Sarah F. Walker, who married Dr. C. B. Jackson, of Jasper.

Walker Family Records.

WALKER, WILLIAM F., a son of Samuel and Nancy (Brackett) Walker, was born January 8, 1832. He was connected with the operating department of the Memphis and Charleston Railroad before the Civil War, and also with Mississippi River traffic. After coming to Walker County he, at one time, together with his brother, Amos, was engaged in mining and boating coal from near Cordova to Mobile. On August 15, 1861, he enlisted at Moscow (now Vernon) as a private in Company K, Sixteenth Alabama Infantry. On September 16, 1862, he enlisted at Jasper as a corporal in Company B, Thirteenth Battalion, Partisan Rangers, which was later consolidated with the Fifteenth Battalion to form the Fifty-sixth Regiment Partisan Rangers, and served until the close of the war. He died on March 4, 1889, and is buried at Friendship. He was married, first, to a widow, a Mrs. Short, and, second, to the widow of his brother, Amos, Mrs. Eliza J. Walker. Children by first marriage—Samuel G. Walker, James R. Walker, and William Francis Walker, Jr. Children by second marriage—Jacob D. Walker; Abraham Walker, who died when ten years of age; and Isaac Walker.

Walker Family Records.

EARLY SETTLERS 371

WALKER, SAMUEL, a son of Samuel and Nancy (Brackett) Walker, enlisted as a private in Company K, Fiftieth Alabama Infantry, and was subsequently in Company G, Eighth Alabama Infantry; Company D, Seventeenth Alabama Infantry, and Company E, Twenty-fifth Alabama Infantry. He served until the close of the war. He never married, and died shortly after the war ended.
Walker Family Records.

WALKER, JAMES R., a son of Samuel and Nancy (Brackett) Walker, was born August 29, 1837. He served with Company E, Twenty-fifth Alabama Infantry, C. S. A., until discharged at Corinth, Mississippi, on June 20, 1862, on account of physical disability. He never recovered from this disability and died on June 26, 1862, and was buried at Friendship. He never married.
Walker Family Records.

WALKER, THADDEUS MONROE, was born August 22, 1836, three miles from Eldridge, on New River, in Fayette County. On June 1, 1861, he enlisted at Columbus, Mississippi, as a private in Company K, Fourth Mississippi Cavalry, and on August 31, 1862, he was transferred to Company K, Fourth Alabama Cavalry, under Captain Kelley, where he served until the close of the war.
Census of Confederate Soldiers, 1907.

WALL, A. A., was born in the Hartselle community, Morgan County, about 1850. After reaching manhood he moved to Vernon, Alabama, where he published a newspaper for a number of years. About 1895 he moved to Oakman, where he established a newspaper and conducted a hotel, and where he served as mayor of the town. About 1914 he moved to Jasper, and in 1932 he was elected judge of the city court of Jasper, which office he was filling at the time of his death on January

24, 1934. In 1879 he was married to Mary Agnes Summer, of Vernon, Alabama. Children—none.
Mountain Eagle, January 31, 1934.

WALLACE, JESSE B., entered government land in Section 15, Township 15, Range 8, on May 24, 1836.
Walker County Tract Record.

WALLING, DAVID, a Revolutionary War soldier, resided in Walker County on June 1, 1840.
Census of Pensioners, June 1, 1840.

WALTON, SAMUEL, a son of Samuel and Julia Walton, was born in Tuscaloosa on April 13, 1813. He came to Walker County about 1859 and settled near Providence, where he died on October 22, 1893. Among his children was Samuel Walton, who married Harriet Phifer, a daughter of John and Mary E. (Cook) Phifer. She was born in Tuscaloosa about 1840 and died at Providence about 1934. Children—John Walton; Thomas Walton; J. B. Walton; Bama Walton; America Walton; and Samuel Walton, who married Martha Beasley.
Moore's Alabama, Vol. III, page 622.
Gravestones.

WARD, MARTIN, entered government land in Section 34, Township 14, Range 8, on July 22, 1822.
Walker County Tract Record.

WASHBURN, RICHARD S., entered government land in Section 30, Township 14, Range 8, on November 16, 1835.
Walker County Tract Record.

WATSON, JESSE, entered government land in Section 28, Township 12, Range 9, on October 28, 1836.
Walker County Tract Record.

WATTS, Rev. JAMES J., was born near Taylorsville, Alexander County, North Carolina, on April 7, 1822. He moved to South Carolina and about 1856 moved to Walker County and settled near Providence, where he was pastor of the Providence Missionary Baptist Church for a number of years. He was also a farmer and in addition operated a grain mill and cotton gin in that vicinity. He died on July 28, 1876, and is buried at Providence. Children—

William Martin Watts, who was born near Taylorsville, Alexander County, North Carolina, on July 1, 1840. He came to Walker County about 1856, and on September 1, 1861, he enlisted at Jasper as a private in Company A, Twenty-second Alabama Infantry, and served until the close of the war. He died on June 20, 1922, and is buried at Providence.

J. S. Watts, who, for a number of years, was clerk of the North River Baptist Association.

Mollie Watts, who was born in South Carolina. She was married to Hugh Beaver, of Oakman, and died there in 1886.

Moore's Alabama, Vol. III, page 639.
Census of Confederate Soldiers, 1907.
Gravestone.

WEBB, EDWARD B., entered government land in Section 29, Township 15, Range 7, on March 4, 1836. His wife, Melvina Webb, was born January 7, 1816, and died May 29, 1866, and is buried at Carbon Hill.

Walker County Tract Record.
Gravestone.

WEDGEWORTH, RICHARD, entered government land in Section 31, Township 15, Range 9, on March 4, 1837.

Walker County Tract Record.

WELLS, WILEY, entered government land in Section 21, Township 13, Range 8, on April 21, 1848.

Walker County Tract Record.

WELLS, JAMES, entered government land in Section 4, Township 14, Range 4, on December 21, 1854.

Walker County Tract Record.

WHATLEY, DANIEL H., a farmer living east of Jasper, served as Sheriff of Walker County in 1861 and 1862. After the expiration of his term of office as sheriff he organized Company B, Tenth Alabama Cavalry, and served as its captain until the close of the war. After the war he moved to Siloam, Clay County, Mississippi. In 1856 he was married to Martha Elizabeth Leith, a daughter of George and Elizabeth (Branner) Leith, who was born July 16, 1842, and died about 1900. Children—none.

Genealogy of the Branner Family.

WHITE, JEPTHA, entered government land in Section 25, Township 13, Range 10, on February 23, 1826.

Walker County Tract Record.

WHITFIELD, Dr. B. W., was born in Lenoir County, North Carolina, March 27, 1828. He was brought to Alabama while still a child and was reared in Marengo County. He graduated from the University of North Carolina in 1849, and later studied medicine at the University of Pennsylvania, where he graduated in 1853. On June 7, 1855, he was married to Mary A. Fortescue, of Marengo County, and later moved to Walker County. Children—Dr. James B. Whitfield, Jesse George Whitfield, Augustus F. Whitfield, Bryan W. Whitfield, Jr., and Nathan B. Whitfield.

Memorial Record of Alabama, Vol. II, page 1026.

WHITSON, THOMAS J., entered government land in Section 20, Township 15, Range 9, on February 19, 1830. Mr. Whitson was a prominent member of the Methodist Church and had much to do with the establishment of that church in Walker County. On December 17, 1826, he was ordained deacon at Tuscaloosa, and on December 23, 1835, at the same place, he was ordained an elder. He was a local Methodist preacher prior to 1837.

Walker County Tract Record.
West's History of Methodism.

EARLY SETTLERS 375

WHITSON, ALBERT G., was born July 6, 1816. He entered government land in Section 21, Township 15, Range 9, on December 10, 1832. He died on April 22, 1890, and is buried at Oakman.

                                           Walker County Tract Record.
                                           Gravestone.

WHITSON, SAMUEL, entered government land in Section 34, Township 15, Range 9, on March 30, 1837.

                                           Walker County Tract Record.

WHITTEN, SPENCER, entered government land in Section 27, Township 14, Range 7, on February 10, 1830.

                                           Walker County Tract Record.

WHITTEN, GEORGE W., entered government land in Section 2, Township 15, Range 7, on November 27, 1834.

                                           Walker County Tract Record.

WILLIAMS, ROBERT, was born in the state of Georgia in the late 1700's, came to Walker County in the early 1800's and settled on government land about one and one-half miles east of Holly Grove. He was a local preacher of the Methodist Church and had much to do with the establishment of that church in Walker County. His daughter, Sarah Ann Williams, born May 8, 1804, was married to Robert Guttery on November 11, 1821. She died on February 8, 1881.

                                           Williams Family Record.
                                           Guttery Family Record.
                                           West's History of Methodism.

WILLIAMS, JOHN H., born about 1800, entered government land in Section 36, Township 12, Range 5, on August 19, 1852. He died in March, 1891.

                                           Walker County Tract Record.
                                           Headlight, March, 1891.

WILLIAMS, JOHN RANDALL, born in Wake County, North Carolina, on September 16, 1808, came to Alabama in

1837, but did not move to Walker County until 1842, when he settled on Lost Creek, south of the present site of Parrish. He was a hard working, industrious farmer, an honest and upright citizen, a clever neighbor and a kind husband and father. He died on February 21, 1886, and is buried in the Gray Graveyard, south of Parrish.

True Citizen, March 18, 1886.

WILLIAMS, WASH, was born March 7, 1816, and died May 23, 1903, and is buried in the Cooner Graveyard. He joined the Primitive Baptist Church at Bethel (Holly Grove) in 1840, and on January 16, 1843, he was married to Gemine Adeline Beckerstaff, who was born March 1, 1827, and died October 14, 1893.

Gravestones.

WILLIAMS, AUGUSTUS ALEXANDER, a son of August Williams and a grandson of Robert Williams, was born October 14, 1842, at Holly Grove. In September, 1862, he enlisted at Jasper as a private in Company L, Fifty-sixth Alabama Cavalry, under Captain Guttery, and served until the close of the war. He died on July 14, 1911, and is buried in the Cooner Graveyard. His wife, Rebecca Williams, a daughter of Harvey W. and Mary (Kitchens) Hamilton, was born May 15, 1840, and died January 8, 1908. A daughter, Mary Williams, was married to Benjamin Banks.

Census of Confederate Soldiers, 1907.
Headlight, November 18, 1890.

WILLIAMS, JAMES PERRY, was born April 22, 1830, in Pickens District, South Carolina. He came to Walker County and entered government land in Section 28, Township 15, Range 5, on July 24, 1848. In September, 1862, he enlisted at Jasper as a private in Company F, Fifty-sixth Alabama Cavalry, under Captain Rice, and served until the close of the war.

Census of Confederate Soldiers, 1907.
Walker County Tract Record.

WILLIAMS, LEROY, was born May 25, 1832, at Raleigh, North Carolina. On August 30, 1862, he enlisted at Tuscaloosa as a private in Company G, Thirty-eighth Tennessee Infantry, and served until the close of the war. He died September 11, 1908, and is buried at Boldo. His wife, Elizabeth Williams, was born about 1835 and died July 22, 1924.

Census of Confederate Soldiers, 1907.
Gravestones.

WILLIAMS, NAPOLEON BONAPARTE, was born May 12, 1844, at Fayetteville, Fayette County, Georgia. On July 28, 1861, he enlisted in Carroll County, Georgia, as a private in Company B, of Cobb's Legion, and served until the close of the war.

Census of Confederate Soldiers, 1907.

WILSON, THOMAS, entered government land in Section 32, Township 13, Range 5, on November 16, 1832.

Walker County Tract Record.

WILSON, WASHINGTON, was born in Anderson, South Carolina, a son of William and Sarah (Hawthorne) Wilson. After reaching manhood he came to Walker County, and on October 27, 1835, he entered government land in Section 18, Township 14, Range 5. For a time he served as County Commissioner. He was married to Margaret Taylor Gamble, a daughter of the Rev. John R. and Jane (Mills) Gamble, and a granddaughter of Robert Gamble and James Mills, both of whom were soldiers in the Revolutionary War.

Owens' Alabama, Vol. IV, page 1764.

WILSON, WILLIAM WALLACE, was born in Gwinnett County, Georgia, in 1834, a son of Young M. Wilson, a pioneer minister of the Methodist Church, who preached in Georgia and later died of yellow fever in New Orleans. William Wallace Wilson served in the Twenty-seventh Alabama Infantry throughout the Civil War, and shortly after the war was over he settled in Walker County. He was a carpenter by trade and erected many homes in Jasper. He died in 1906. He was married to Sarah M. Myrick, who was born in Pike County, Georgia.

Moore's Alabama, Vol. III, page 124.

WILSON, ROBERT L., a son of William Wallace and Sarah (Myrick) Wilson, was born near Montgomery, Alabama, on October 17, 1865, but was brought to Walker County by his parents at an early age. Reared and educated in the county, he farmed until 1920, when he retired and moved to Jasper. He served as farm land appraiser and constable. He was married to Martha J. Robinson, who was born in Georgia, October 23, 1865. Children—B. Grady Wilson, who married Alma Cowart, of Double Springs, Winston County; Birdie Wilson, who married Charlie Anderson, of Dora; Robert Jesse Wilson; William M. Wilson; Rufus Wilson; Coleman Wilson; and Lacy Wilson.

Moore's Alabama, Vol. III, page 124.

WINCHESTER, WILLOUGHBY, entered government land in Section 30, Township 14, Range 5, on October 27, 1835.

Walker County Tract Record.

WINCHESTER, J. V., entered government land in Section 29, Township 13, Range 5, on November 4, 1836.

Walker County Tract Record.

WINDHAM, JAMES EDWARD, was born July 24, 1831, at Independence, Montgomery County, Alabama. On September 6, 1862, he enlisted at Holly Grove as a private in Company L, Fifty-sixth Alabama Cavalry, under Captain Guttery, and served until the close of the war. He died on August 28, 1918, and is buried in the Fike Graveyard. His wife, Sarah Windham, was born November 12, 1838, and died January 29, 1911. She was a daughter of William James Myers.

Census of Confederate Soldiers, 1907.
Gravestones.

WINN, JOHN, was born near Edingburgh, Scotland, on April 15, 1854. His parents later moved to England, and in 1874 John Winn came to the United States to practice his profession of mining engineer. He opened coal mines in Pennsylvania, Texas, and Alabama. In 1908 he settled permanently in Walker County, near Good Springs, where he married. Children—R. T. Winn; Dennis T. Winn; William M. Winn; Giles T. Winn; Daisy Winn, who married C. A. Custard; Mamie Winn, who married L. H. Odom; and Mrs. W. E. Vines. He died June 15, 1933.

Mountain Eagle, June 28, 1933.

WINTER, SAMUEL F., entered government land in Section 10, Township 14, Range 7, on January 25, 1859.

Walker County Tract Record.

WOLF, DAVID, entered government land in Section 6, Township 13, Range 6, on July 12, 1836.

Walker County Tract Record.

WOOD, JOHN, entered government land in Section 15, Township 16, Range 7, near the confluence of Lost and Wolf Creeks, on September 27, 1821; and also in Section 22, Township 16, Range 7, on October 1, 1821, the latter tract, according to old deeds, being sold to Samuel Thompson on March 21, 1828. John Wood served as State Senator from the senatorial district which included Walker County during the sessions of 1828 and 1829.

Walker County Tract Record.

WOOD, EDWARD THOMAS, thought to have been a son of John Wood, was born in Walker County about 1817. He was married to Minerva Woods, a daughter of Samuel Woods.

Children—Lon Wood, who married Whitty Courington; Charity Elizabeth Wood, who married John Key, Curle Wood, who never married; Prudy Wood, who married James Davis; Commodore Wood, who married Zellie Nelson; Edward Wood, who never married; C. A. (Dock) Wood, who married, first, a daughter of Thomas Key, and, second, Emily Sides, a daughter of William Sides; Irene Wood, who married William Odom; and Phoebe Wood, who married Sherman Cranford. He died April 29, 1887.

Family Records.

WOODS, SAMUEL, a pioneer settler of Walker County, was the father of six children—Minerva Woods, who married Edward Thomas Wood; Lucy Allen Woods, who married John Martin Key; Nancy Woods, who married William Courington; David Woods, who married Betty Staggs; John Hop Woods, who married Lucinda Wilson; and Allie Woods, who married James Wood, a brother to Edward Thomas Wood.

Family Records.

WOOD, JOSEPH ARCHIBALD, was born October 12, 1840, on Cane Creek, near Oakman. In September, 1862, he enlisted at Jasper as a private in Company L, Fifty-sixth Alabama Cavalry, under Captain Guttery, and served until the close of the war.

Census of Confederate Soldiers, 1907.

WOODSON, WILLIAM A., entered government land in Section 26, Township 13, Range 5, on November 19, 1854.

Walker County Tract Record.

WORTHINGTON, WILLIAM WESLEY, or Wethington, as it was sometimes spelled, was born June 10, 1842, at Liberty Hill. On April 14, 1862, he enlisted at Cedar Creek Church, Walker County, as a private in Company L, Twenty-eighth Alabama Infantry, under Captain Musgrove, and served until the close of the war. He died June 7, 1916, and is buried at Liberty

·Hill. His wife, Elizabeth Worthington, was born August 1, 1847, and died December 13, 1895.

Census of Confederate Soldiers, 1907.
Gravestones.

WORTHINGTON, WILSON W., was born March 24, 1835, at the Gilcrease Place, nine miles south of Oakman; a descendant of John Worthington, who was born in England in 1650 and at the age of twenty-five emigrated to America and settled at Pendennis, Maryland, where he married Sarah Howard in 1689. On April 14, 1862, Wilson W. Worthington enlisted at Fairview Church as a sergeant in Company L, Twenty-eighth Alabama Infantry, under Captain Musgrove. He was captured at Orchard Knob on November 23, 1863, and imprisoned at Rock Island, Illinois, until the close of the war. On February 21, 1867, he was married to Nancy A. Shepherd, a daughter of Tinson and Minerva (Raburn) Shepherd.

Census of Confederate Soldiers, 1907.
Mountain Eagle, April 4, 1917.

WRIGHT, THOMAS I., entered government land in Section 10, Township 15, Range 6, near Benoit, on November 17, 1836.

Walker County Tract Record.

WRIGHT, WILLIAM FRANKLIN, was born May 30, 1832, near Arkadelphia, in Walker County. In the spring of 1863 he enlisted at Arkadelphia as a private in Company G, Eighth Alabama Cavalry, under Captain Wharton, and served until the close of the war.

Census of Confederate Soldiers, 1907.

WRIGHT, JOHN LANIER, was born October 4, 1841, at Holly Grove. On September 6, 1862, he enlisted at Jasper as a sergeant in Company G, Fifty-sixth Alabama Cavalry, and served until the close of the war. He died on August 3, 1924, and is buried at Pleasant Hill.

Census of Confederate Soldiers, 1907.

YARBROUGH, JOSHUA, entered government land in Section 6, Township 14, Range 7, on May 25, 1860.
Walker County Tract Record.

YORK, THOMAS F. S., a native of Georgia, came to Walker County in 1855 and settled near Empire. He served with the Confederate Army until the close of the war, when he returned to Walker County and remained until 1880, when he moved to Cullman County to spend the balance of his days. He was married to Martha Carr, who was born in Georgia and died in Cullman County.
Moore's Alabama, Vol. II, page 125.

YORK, AARON G. M., a son of Thomas F. S. and Martha (Carr) York, was born in Georgia on February 7, 1852. When but three years of age his parents brought him to Walker County, where he spent his entire life, about three miles northeast of Empire, a well-to-do farmer and a respected citizen. He died on September 5, 1914. He was married to Eliza Patterson, who was born in Pike County, Georgia, on February 26, 1851, and died at Empire in February, 1904. Children—Louise York, who married Dr. Edward D. Ward, of Hillsboro, Texas; Edward York, who died at the age of twenty-three; Aaron A. York, a physician, who married Ophelia Attaway, of Jefferson County; Emma York, who married David M. Sellers, of Jefferson County; Dora York, who died at the age of sixteen; and Melvin York.
Moore's Alabama, Vol. II, page 125.

YOUNG, ANDERSON, of South Walker, made application in September, 1885, for a pension on account of disability incurred during the Mexican War in 1846, when he was disabled in making his escape from a wrecked vessel.
Mountain Eagle, September 30, 1885.

History of Walker County, Alabama

AARON, BRACK	118	. WARREN	297	. WALLER	122
. CHARLES	117	ADGERTON, JAMES P.	119	. WILILAM B.	122
. COY RICHARD	118	ADKINS, WILLIAM	119	. WILLIAM	122
. DEWEY HOBSON	118	AKINS, JOHN CALVIN	119	. WILLIAM B.	107, 121
. FRANCIS MARION	117-118	. SARAH	119	. WILLIAM J.	122
. GRACIE	118	ALDRICH, JAMES	120	AREY, CHRISTINA	268
. IRA	117	ALDRIDGE, ABNER B.	120	ARGO, FANNIE GUNTER	209
. JAMES	117-118	. ALFRED	119	. H.S.	209
. JOHN	117-118	. ANNIE M. BURTON	120	ARMES,	155
. JOSEPH	117	. ASHBY	31	. ETHEL	14, 23, 75
. LEROY	118	. ASHLEY	119	ARNOLD,	333
. LUVENA	118	. ETTA S. PHARR	120	ASHCRAFT, MARTHA	204
. MARY MAYBERRY	117-118	. ISHAM	119	. MARY L. APPERSON	123
. MONROE	118	. JAMES	120	. SALLY M.	256
. NORA REID	118	. PRINCE W.	119	. THOMAS	123, 256
. NOVELLA	118	ALEXANDER,	299	ATKINS, BUD	310
. SALLIE CHAMBERS	117	. JASON C.	83, 121	. MODINE POSEY	310
. SYBIL	118	. JEREMIAH	120	. WILLIAM COLUMBUS	123
. WILLIAM	117	ALLEN, ASA	121	ATTAWAY, OPHELIA	382
. WILLIAM JEAN	118	. JOHN	121	ATWOOD,	71, 103
. WINNIE TUBB	117	. JOSEPH	121	AVERY,	303
ABBOTT, ANN RAINES	118	. MARIA	260	. A.W.	123
. ASENETH A.	118	ALLISON,		BACHELOR, ELISHA	123
. BASHEBA	118	. ZACHARIAH DEASON	121	BAGBY,	278
. CYNTHIA A.	245	ANDERSON, ADA GRACE	207	. JOAB	123
. DORA MYERS	118	. BIRDIE WILSON	378	BAILEY, BOICE	260
. ELIZABETH C.	118	. CHARLIE	378	. EDNA	238
. HILL	118, 246	. EDITH	200	. FRANKIE	246-247
. HILL COPLAND	118	. HAMIE	337	. LOUISE LACY	260
. IRA	118	. JOHN F.	83	. SARAH JANE HOLDEN	248
. JAMES	118	. JOHN T.	63	. WILLIAM	248
. JAMES STANLEY	118	. MARTHA A.	166	BAKER,	294-295
. JANE MILLS KEY	118, 246	. SALETA	128	. ALVIN	123, 256-257
. JOHN WESLEY	118	ANDLETON,		. ANNIE	124
. MALINDA J.	118	. CATHERINE FILES	190	. BETHEL	125
. MARY P. NELSON	118	ANDREWS, D.W.	38	. DARLING P.	124
. META SANDLIN	118	. RICHARD HARRISON	121	. DEMPSEY D.	125
. PILGRAM	118	APPERSON, MARY L.	123	. ELIJAH	125, 154
. REBECCA BLEVINS	118	APPLING, EDMUND W.	122	. ELIJAH P.	124
. SARAH ANN LAY	118	. ELIZABETH C.	122	. GEORGE H.	124
. SHERAN	118	. ETTA	122	. GILES	205
. SOPHRONIA	118	. JAILY W. EMBRY	122	. GUINEA	125-126
. WILLIAM WASHINGTON	118	. JAMES C.	122	. JAMES A.	124
ABLES, JAMES	119	. JOSEPH F.	122, 322	. JOHN D.	124
ACUFF, J.D.	77	. MARTHA ANN	122	. L.W.	47
. JAMES	253	. MARTHA L.	122	. LAMBERT J.	92
. SUSAN	39	. MATILDA ANN JOHNS	322	. LAMBERT W.	40, 126
ADAMS, ELIZABETH	349	. MATTIE J.	122	. LOUISA	124
. ELZIABETH STEARNS	349	. MATTIE W. CUMMINS	122	. M.C. WATTS	124
. JOHN QUINCY	349	. MYRA	122	. MARY	125
. ZABDIEL	349	. NEWBERN	122	. MARY ANN CAIN	125, 154
ADCOCK, ELIZABETH	297	. OZELLA F.	322	. MARY CAROLINE	124, 256
. HONOR ODOM	297	. RICHARD	122	. MINNIE	124
. LUCY ODOM	297	. SALINA S.	122	. NATHAN	125
. MARY	204-205	. W.B.	61, 71, 94, 109	. OBID	125

. PETER	22,123	. WILL	204	. SALLIE BROCK	132
. SARAH L.	124	. WILLIAM	129	. SARAH	132
. SUSAN J.	124	BARBEE, JAMES	83,129	. SARAH WILLIS	131
. SUSAN KITCHENS	124,257	BARNES, ALEXANDER H.	129	. SUSAN KEYS	130
. SUSAN KNIGHT	205	. THOMAS	38	. TANEY	132
. VIRGINIA	124	BARRENTINE, LEWIS	94,297	. THOMAS	129
. WILLIAM	125	. NANCY ODOM	297	. WASHINGTON	132,287
. WILLIE	124	BARRINGTON, IDA OWEN	301	. WILLIAM	131
. WILLIS	126	. W.L.	301	. WILLIAM WALLACE	133
BALL,	196	BARTON,	180	BATES, CANASDA ODOM	296
BALLEGER, LUDA	84	. ABRAHAM	129	. JAMES	133
BALLENGER, JOHN	25	. ABSALOM	132	. JOHN	134,296
. SARAH A.	284	. BARBARA KING	132	. LEVI	133
. WILLIAM	126	. DAVID	129-130	BAYES, JOHN	134
BALLINGER, LUDA	65	. DELLA	132	BAYLOR, WALKER K.	32
BANKHEAD,	69,128	. DOVIE MORROW	132	BEAN,	105
. ADELAIDE E. SLEDGE	128	. ELIAS	133	BEASLEY, C.A.	74
. ELIZABETH BLACK	126	. ELIZABETH A.	156	. ELIJAH	134
. ELIZABETH STANLEY	127	. EPHRAIM	132	. ELIZABETH	134
. EMELIL CRUMPTON	128	. FELIX	132	. JESSE	134
. EVELYN EUGENIA	128	. FRANCES	130,287	. MARTHA	293,372
. FLORENCE McGUIRE	128	. HENRY	131	BEAVER, HUGH	373
. GEORGE	126	. HIRAM	130-132,218	. MOLLIE WATTS	373
. HENRY M.	127	. HUGH	132	BEAVERT, SUSAN	235-238
. JAMES	126-127	. IRENA	132	.	337
. JAMES GREER	126	. IRENA STOVAL	132	BECK, LUCETA	142
. JANE GREER	126	. JAMES	131	BECKERSTAFF,	
. JOHN H.	73,78,167	. JAMES A.	130	. GERMINE A.	376
. JOHN HOLLIS	69,126-128	. JAMES ALLEN	133	. GERMINE ADELIA	134
. LOUISE	127-128	. JAMES H.	132,257	. JOHNSON	134
. MARIE S.	127	. JOHN M.	38-39,132,254	. M.	134
. MARION	128	. JOHN MACE	130	BEDDINGFIELD, W.H.	134
. MUSA HARKINS	128	. JOSHUA	130	BELL, ANTHONY	134
. SUSAN F. HOLLIS	126	. LEE	132	. ELIZ. WOMMACK	237
. TULLULAH BROCKMAN	128	. LIDIA	130,287	. PRUDY KEY	247
. TULLULAH J.		. LIZE	131	. RUFUS	247
.	BROCKMAN 127	. LOUISA	130	BENNETT, ALONZO	346
. WILLIAM B.	73,128	. MARGARET	132	. ELLEN ELIZA	186
. WILLIAM BROCKMAN	127	. MARGARET A.	131	. GRACE SIMPSON	346
.	128	. MARTHA	132,253	. JESSIE LIVINGSTON	134
. WILLIAM WALTER	128	. MARTHA J. KITCHENS	132	. JOSEPHINE L. JONES	135
BANKS, ANNE	255	. MARTHA JANE		. MARY ANN	169,258
. ANNIE	240	.	KITCHENS 257	. MICHAEL	186
. BENJAMIN	314,376	. MARTY	191	. PHOEBE LIVINGSTON	186
. ELIZABETH	129	. MARY A.	130	BENSON, W.H.	135
. MARGARET GRACE	204	. MARY WILSON	131	. WILLIAM	25
. MARTHA	204	. MILLEY	130	BESS, JOHN	25
. MARTHA JANE GRACE	204	. MOLLIE MORROW	132,287	BESTOR, JULIET	166
. MARY WILLIAMS	376	. MOSES	22,129-132,287	BEVILL,	245
. NOAH	204	.	318	BIBB,	162,232
. P.L.	129	. NANCY	130,318	. JAMES	161
. SALLIE	129	. NANCY K.	132	. MARY ANN CHILTON	161
. SANFORD W.	129	. NATHANIEL	130-132	BICKNELL, JAMES	163
. SUSAN	204	. RACHEL DANIEL	132	BIDDY, EDWARD	135
. TIMIE RANDOLPH	314	. REBECCA	130	BILLINGSLEY, JEPTHA	135

History of Walker County, Alabama

. JESSE	135
. SAMUEL	135
. THOMAS	135
. W.M.	135
BIOCHI,BELLE FILES	192
BIRDWELL,JOHN	135
. NANCY	321
BLACK,	132
. ARCHIBALD	135
. ELIZABETH	126
. ENOCH MILLER	77
. HUGH	135
. JOHN	90
. MARGARET	287
. SAMUEL	135
BLACKBURN,JOHN	136
BLACKSTON,JAMES	136
BLACKWELL,	
. ALEXANDER HENRY	136
. DAVIDSON	136,177
. J.F.	136
. JAMES M.	136
. LAVILLA	137
. McKINLEY	137
. ROBERT	137
. WILLIAM RALEIGH	136
. ZACH	137
BLACKWOOD,ELIZA	253
. SUSAN JONES	240
. WILLIAM	137,240
BLANKENSHIP,AUGUSTUS	137
. CULLEN	137
BLANTON,	37
. AARON	137
. ALTON MAURICE	139
. BENJAMIN	138
. DAVID	30-31,104,137
. E.M.	138
. ELIJAH	104,138-139,358
. ELSA	139
. FANNIE M. SARTAIN	139
. FAYETTE	354
. IDA E.	358
. IDA EMILY	138
. ISAAC	138-139
. JAMES	137
. JOHN	137
. MAJOR	328
. MARTHA	138
. MARVIN	138
. MARY A. ISBELL	139
. MARY ISBELL	138
. MARY M. GIBSON	139
. MILLIE CHEEK	138-139
. MINTY A. SARTAIN	328
. PERRINE	139
. R.L.	138
. ROBERT L.	138
. ROBERT LEE	139
. ROBERT QUINTON	139
. SARAH ANN	248,368
. VADA STEPHENSON	354
BLEVINS,ARM	173
. CELIA CRANFORD	173
. JOHN	139
. REBECCA	118
BLOCKER,	
. MARY ANN SARTAIN	326
BLYTHE,JAMES	139
BOATNER,JOHN R.	140
BOLDING,MARVID	140
BOLTON, ELIZABETH RUTLEDGE	323
BONNER,BELLE GRACE	204
. GEORGE M.	140
. JAMES	205
. MISSOURI O.	205
. NANCY GRACE	204
. ROBERT	204
BOONE,DANIEL	129
BORDEN,HAWKINS	84
BOSHELL,	112,204,213-214
. ADA	191
. CORNELIA	191
. EDGAR	191
. FRANCES FILES	191
. GUINEA BAKER	126
. HODIE	279
. ISOM	191
. J.B.	256
. LOUISA C. SPARKS	256
. M.C.	140
. MAE	191
. MARTHA KING	279
. McMINTER	140
. NICHOLAS	140
. ROBERT	140
. W.R.	279
BOTELER,BENJAMIN	43,92
. JAMES	93
. WILLIAM A.	140
BOUCHELLE,	140
. FRANCES FILES	191
. ISOM	191
BOULDIN,LAURA FOOTE	322
. SUSIE K.	322
. WILEY F.	322
BOX,JOHN	141
BOYD,HANNAH	141
. JAMES LEE	141
BOYLE,ARMANDA CAIN	154
BRABSON,PRISCILLA	217
.	339
BRACKETT,NANCY	370-371
. NANCY T.	284,369
BRADLEY,FRANCES M.	141
. JOHN	141
. LOUIS W.	141
. THOMAS	141
BRAGG,	198
BRAKE,JOHN	141
BRAKEFIELD,DAVID A.	141
. GEORGE	141
BRANNER,	182,317
. CARL	269
. CATHERINE	269
. CHRISTINA AREY	268
. ELIZABETH	264-266,268
.	281,286,298,374
. J. MICHAEL	268
BRANTLEY,LINNIE	283,370
. RILEY	283
BRASFIELD,J.B.	83
BRAZEAL,GEORGE	83
. MORGAN	83,142
BRECKENRIDGE,	224
. RICHARD	14
BREWSTER,	
. MALINDA WORTHAM	258
. MARTHA	258
. SHERIFF	258
BRIGGS,VESTA	300
BRITTON,	71,103
. BURWELL	142
. LIDA SELLERS	142
. LLOYD C.	142
. LUCETA BECK	142
. WILLIAM	142
. WILLIAM HENRY	142
BROCK,SALLIE	132
BROCKMAN,TULLULAH	128
. TULLULAH J.	127
BROOKS,	
. BASHEBA ABBOTT	118
. ELEANOR	310
. MARY A.	236
. SAMUEL	118
BROTHERTON,CLYDA	203
. CLYDE B.	203
. LIMA PATTERSON	203
BROWN,A.H.	143,194
. ADELE	300
. ADIS WALTON	144
. BELL ROBINSON	144
. BERRY BARNEY	77

History of Walker County, Alabama

. BETTIE	144	. NANCY	146,342	. ROBERT	148	
. CALLIE	145	. NOLAND	144	. SARAH M.	151	
. CAROLINE	266,298	. QUEENIE	144	. T.C.	71,101	
. CARRIE REEVES	144	. RICHARD LEE	144	BUSBY,	345,359	
. DAVID	112,145	. SALLIE	142-143,218,313	. AUTRESS	150	
. DAVID LIGHTLE	145	. SALLY	124,254	. DEMP	109	
. DELLA	144	. SAMUEL	145	. ELIAS DEMSON	149	
. EARLY A.	145	. SAMUEL HOUSTON	145,338	. ELIZABETH	149	
. EBENEZER	146	. SAMUEL T.	345	. ELIZABETH KEY	246	
. ELEANOR	143,256	. SARAH ANN	144,215	. ERNEST	150	
. ELIZABETH	143	. SUSAN M.	143	. ESTELLE	150	
. EMMA SNODDY	145	. THOMAS	39,142-144,254	. IRVIN	150	
. ENSLEY LIGHTLE	144,334		256,313	. JALIE	149	
. ETTA SIDES	345	. W.K.	95	. JAMES MADISON	149	
. FANNIE SHERER	145,338	. WILLIAM	112,146	. JOHN T.	149	
. FRANCES	142	. WILLIAM FRANK	143	. KENNIE SNOW	150	
. FRANCIS	254,313-314	BRUCE,JOHN	146	. LUANNA	149	
. GEORGE	145	BRYAN,JAMES	146	. MARTHA J.	149	
. HANNAH	146,342	. WILLIAM	146	. MATILDA	249	
. HOLMAN	145	. WILLIAM J.	92,146	. NANCY A.M. IRELAND	149	
. I.B.	143	BRYANT,J. THOMAS	147	. S. LEVIN	149	
. ISAAC	83,104,143,145	. JAMES	146,369	. STEPHEN	149,152	
. JACK	256	. LURANIA	147	. STEPHEN SAMPSON	149	
. JAMES G.	142	. MARTHA W. MORGAN	147	. VANCE W.	150	
. JAMES W.	142	. MARTHA WALKER	147,369	. WILLIAM	246	
. JANSIE ELKINS	145	. MARY	147	BUSH,JOE	106	
. JESSIE SHERER	145,338	. NANCY	147	BUTCHER,HENRY P.	151	
. JOHN	32,53,143-144,146	. SUTTANIA	147	BUTT,		
	215,256,342	BRYSON,	273	. WASHINGTON		
. JOHN HARVEY	144	. DUNLOP	147	.	McDONALD	150
. JOHN M.	145	. JOSEPH T.	147	. WILLIAM	15,90,150	
. JOSEPH	145	. ROBERT	147	BUZBEE,BERMA ARMASIA	151	
. JULIA	144,361	BURDEN,HAWKINS	84	. CORA DREW MORROW	151	
. L.C. GABBERT	143,194	BURDIN,	35	. CORA ORLANE	151	
. LEO	354	. HAWKINS	22,147	. EVERETT ORVILLE	151	
. LILLY STEPHENSON	354	BURGER,DOROTHY	257	. HUBERT HUDSON	151	
. LILY L.	145	BURKE,W.H.	147	. HUDSON HALL	151	
. LOHAMIE C. SHERER	144	BURKETT,		. JOHN EVERETT	151	
.	334	. BENJAMIN FRANKLIN	147	. JOSHUA QUINTON	151	
. LOVEY	39,142-143,256	. DANIEL	147	. ROBERT BUELL	151	
. LUCINDA A.	143	BURNUM,JOEL	148	. SAMUEL SEBASTIAN	151	
. LUCY	145	BURRELL,ASA	148	. SARAH M. BURTON	151	
. LUTHER HUSS	145,338	. WILLIAM RICHARD	148	. SARAH STEPHENS	151	
. MABEL CRUMP	144	BURT,C.	189	. WILLIAM	151	
. MARGARET LOLLAR	143	BURTON,	35,85,245	BYLER,	20	
. MARTHA CLACK	215	. ANNIE M.	120	. JOHN	19	
. MARTHA E.	228	. C.L.	71,101	BYNUM,FRED E.	329	
. MARTHA E. CLACK	144	. CALLER	148	. VELMA SARTAIN	329	
. MARTHA JANE	143	. DIANA H.	169	CAIN,	153	
. MARY	143	. FANNIE	148	. ADKIN	154	
. MARY DUTTON	143	. J.R.	71,101	. ARKANSAS R. WOOD	154	
. MARY F.	143	. JAMES	338	. ARMANDA	154	
. MARY SUSAN	144	. JOHN	148	. BATHSHEBA	238	
. MATILDA KITCHENS	143	. LAVINA	148	. BLANCHE GRACE	205	
.	256	. MAUDE SHERER	338	. CHARLOTTE	154,312	

History of Walker County, Alabama

. ELIZABETH 154,290	. NANCY HUTCHINSON 155	. LAURA V. 158
. ELIZABETH McAULEY 154	. 156,325	. LAURA V. CARTER 158
. 290,326	. NEWTON 271	CATCHINGS,JOHN 326
. GEORGIA A. SIMPSON 154	. SARAH J. 156	LUCIE SANDERS 326
. JAMES 22,25,32-35	. THOMAS 155	CATES,ELIZA ANN 311
. 39-40,125-126,149,152	. W.H. 156	. EMILY LOVETT 311
. 154,160-161,210,276	CAMP, 71,103	. W.E. 311
. 290,312	. DAVID 157	CHAMBERLAIN,J.B. 99
. JAMES F. 154	CAMPBELL, 92,120,293	CHAMBERLIN,J.B. 65
. JAMES O. 90	. ADAM 157	CHAMBERS,SALLIE 117
. JAMES OSCAR 152,326	. ALEXANDER 157	CHAMBLEE,ALEX 63,86
. JOANNE KING 152	. MARY SARTAIN 329	CHANCE,GEORGE S. 159
. JOYCE B. 154,161	. WAYNE 329	CHANDLER,HIRAM B. 256
. LAURA 260	CANNON,E.B. 350	. MACK 299
. LUCINDA 154	. ELISHA BARTON 157	. SALLY M. KITCHENS 256
. MARY ANN 125,154	. MELVIN F. 168	CHAPPELL,BASIL 296
. NADA SHERER 336	. VERA 168	. CATHERINE ODOM 296
. NANCY 154,300,326	. ZILPHEY SNOW 350	. IRENE WOODS 296
. RANDOLPH P. 155	. ZYLPHA SNOW 157	. JAMES 296
. RENIE 154	CARAWAY,JOHN 157	. JENNIE ANN LOVE 296
. ROBERT 154,210,336	CARELTONS,JOHN S. 158	. JOHN 296
. WILLIAM 154	CARMACK,C.L. 63,86	. JOHN J. 296
CALDWELL,MARY POLLY 204	CARMICHAEL, 42,92	. JULIA JONES 296
. 205	. A.L. 158	. MARY 296
CALHOUN, 278	. A.R. 93	. NANCY WILSON 296
CALLAHAN,ED 77	. ABNER 256	. THOMAS 296
. JOSHUA 155	. CECILA JONES 238	CHEATHAM, 40,112
CALVERT, 144	. DORA 158	. JAMES 159
. GEORGE F. 155	. EDWARD 158	. JAMES WYATT 159
CAMAK, 61,91	. F.M. 93	. JONATHAN EVANS 159
. ALICE R. 156	. FANNIE 158	. LOUIS E. 159
. AMANDA H. 156	. FRANCIS M. 158,218	CHEEK,MILLIE 138-139
. ANNA MAE 157	. FRANK 158	CHILDERS,
. BURWELL L. 157	. JAMES 172	. ANNIE C. KEMP 160
. CARRIE G. LONG 271	. JAMES TAYLOR 158,218	. BLANCHE 160
. CHARLES M. 157	. JULY A.R. 218	. DORIS JUANITA 160
. D.H. 281	. LOUISA 184,218	. EDWARD 160
. DAISY KILGORE 157	. MATILDA KITCHENS 256	. IDA 160
. DAVID 155	. RADIE COURINGTON 172	. JOHN C. 160
. DAVID H. 156	. RICHARD 238	. LEVI 159
. ELIZABETH A.	. SARAH HAMILTON 158,218	. MAGGIE ETTA
BARTON 156	. THOMAS 158	MASTERS 160
. FRADONIA ELLIOTT 156	. V.H. 158	. MILDRED KEMP 160
. FRED L. 157	CARPENTER,MAUDE 205	. NANCY JACKSON 232
. J. NEWTON 157	CARR,HINTON E. 64,98	. THOMAS 93,159,232
. JAMES 155-156,325	. MARGARET A. 191	. THOMAS H. 160
. JAMES N. 156	. MARTHA 382	. WILL AB 159
. JULIA A. 156	CARRINGTON,JOHN B. 199	. WILLIAM SAMUEL 160
. LAVONIA C. MILLER 156	. LEILA K. GAMBLE 199	CHILDRES,IDA SMITH 348
. 157,281	CARROLL, 69	CHILDRESS,JACK 173
. MARGARET 155	. JAMES 306	. JOHN 160
. MARTHA 156	. MOSES 158	. MINERVA CRANFORD 173
. MARY 155,301,325	. SALLY PHIFER 306	CHILTON,BELINDA 161
. MOSES 35,53,155-156	CARTER,D.K. 65,99	. D.H. 76
. NANCY 156	. J.W. 158	. DARLE 161

History of Walker County, Alabama

. DAVID HOUSTON	161,197	. HARDY	163	. COLEMAN	341
. JAMES	161	. HATTIE	248	. FRANCES J. WILSON	166
. JAMES K. POLK	161	. JOSEPH B.	164	.	341
. JOYCE B. CAIN	154,161	. JOSEPH H.	164	. FRANCIS JANE	
. KATHLEEN	161	. LAVADA JONES	164	. WILSON	167
. LULA MAY GAINES	161	. LOUISA C. CHISM	164	. JAMES	166
.	197	. MADIE GABBERT	164	. JAMES COBB	166
. MARY ANN	161	. MARTHA HARGROVE	164	. JOHN	166
. MATILDA	161	. MARY SUSAN PHIFER	164	. JOHN S.	167
. MATILDA ANN	157,180	.	307	. JULIET BESTOR	166
.	350	. MIDDLETON	164	. MARTHA A. ANDERSON	166
. NANCY KEY	161,246,266	. MIDDLETON C.	164	. MARY	164
.	350	. SHALIE	164	. MARY ROUNDTREE	166
. RICHARD	33,35,152,161	. SYLVESTER H.	109	. NANETTE P. SHIELDS	341
.	246,266,350	. SYLVESTER HOUSTON	164	. NANETTE SHIELDS	167
. RICHARD L.	160	. THOMAS	164	. RHODA COBB	166
. SALLY	161	. VICTOR A.	164	. THOMAS WILKES	166-167
. SICILINE E.	265-266	. WILLIAM O.	164	.	341
. SYLVESTER JOHN	154,161	CLEVELAND,ORLENA A.	260	COLLINS,BESSIE MAE	168
. WILIAM	161	CLIFTON,LOUIS	164	. DORA RENFRO	168
CHISM,JAMES M.	205	COBB,	377	. JAMES B.	167
. LOUISA C.	164	. DAVID	165	. LULA	168
. MARY A. GRACE	205	. LUCINDA	165	. PAULINE	168
CHRISTIAN,JOHN	161	. O.F.	73,101	. RICHARD DEAN	168
. THOMAS ANTHONY	161	. RHODA	166	. VERA C. JONES	168
. TOM	107,109	. STANCIL	165	. VERA CANNON	168
CLACK,MARTHA	215	. STANCILL	90	. WILLIAM D.	167
. MARTHA E.	144	. WILLIAM	104,165	COLLISON,L.W.	143
CLANCY,JOHN E.	40,92,162	COFFEE,JOHN	14	. MARY F. BROWN	143
CLARK,BETSY	261	COKER,L.H.	165	CONLEY,JOHN	168
. CLYDE EDWARD	163	COLBERT,JAMES	165	CONN,JAMES	249
. EDWARD	163	COLE,	37	. MAHULA	249
. IRA L.	163	. ARTHUR T.	240	. NANCY ANN	249
. IRA LOUIE	163	. BYRD GARLAND	165,246	CONNERLY,LILLY F.	322
. JAMES	261	. CARISSA	166	CONWAY,GEORGE	168
. JAMES ALLEN	162	. DORCIA	246	CONWELL,THOMAS	70,106
. JOHN	163	. JAMES RICHARD	166	COOK,ANN	351
. JOSEPH M.	163	. JOSEPH MARION	166	. J.E.	105
. MARY KING	163	. MARTHA B.	193,322	. JOHN	168
. MATTIE PALMER	163	. NANCY LOUISE	165	. MARY E.	306,372
. ROBERT	163	.	246-247	. RUTH	139
. RUFUS	162	. RACHEL	165,246	COONER,	112,195,234,314
. SUSANNA	261	. SAVANNAH	329	.	376
. WILLIAM	163	. TEMPERANCE E.		. ANICE LOLLAR	169
. WILLIAM RICHARD	162	. JONES	240	. ANNIE PIERCE	169
. WYATT	163	. WILLIAM	31,165	. CALLIE BROWN	145
CLAY,	278	COLEMAN,	69,128	. DAVID	336
CLEBURN,PAT	209	. A.A.	289	. DIANA H. BURTON	169
CLEMENTS,		. CAROLINE	167	. ELIZABETH	344
. ALICE MANUEL	164	. CHARLES	166	. FRANCIS MARION	169
. BELL HAMILTON	164	. E.W.	73	. ISABELLA ODOM	169
. BENJAMIN F.	164,307	. ELLEN	167	. ISABELLE ODOM	296
. CORA PAYNE	164	. EZRA W.	166-167	. JAMES CARROLL	168
. ELIZABETH FERGUSON	164	. EZRA WILSON		. JAMES P.	168-169,343
. FANNIE	164,245,247			. JOHN E.	296

History of Walker County, Alabama

. JOHN ELLISON 169
. LUSINDA DILL 169
. LUSINDA E. 169
. MARTHA JANE 169
. MARY ANN BENNETT 169
. POLLY 168,343
. ROXEY ANN RANDOLPH 169
. SALLIE SHERER 336
. SAMUEL ELLISON 168
. SAMUEL GREEN 169
. SARAH MARGARET 169
. WESLEY C. 145
. WESLEY CARROLL 169
. WILLIAM JAMES 169
COOPER,MARY C. 301
. MINERVA 208
COPELAND,A.J. 337
. ANICE ELLEN POSEY 311
. JAMES 337
. JOHN 311
. MARTHA ANN JONES 240
. MARTHA R. ROBINSON 256
. MIRANDA STEPHENSON 354
. NORA KIRKPATRICK 253
. S.W. 256
. SALLIE SHERER 337
. SARAH JANE SHERER 337
. WASH 169
. WILLIAM 253
CORLEY,CLEMENT 170
CORNELIUS,ABNER 170
. BRADFORD 170
. McPHERSON 66
. STATIE SIMPSON 346
. WILLIAM B. 346
CORNETT,LIZZIE 269
CORNWELL,MATILDA H. 184
CORONA, 59
CORRY,EDITHA I. 170,179
. ELIZABETH M.
. McGARNES 170
. J.M. 70,106,179
. JAMES 106
. JOSEPH MORTIMER 170
. L.J. 70,106
. MARTHA A. GUTTERY 170
. MORTIMER 104
COURINGTON, 245
. AB 172
. ALICE 329
. BELLE 171
. CAROLINE SUMNER 172
. ELIZA F. SARTAIN 328
. ELLA KIMBALL 171
. EMILY 171,306

. G.A. 172
. JAMES 171
. JAMES BENJAMIN 172
. JAMES REUBEN 172
. JANE 172
. JOHN 171
. JOHN D. 171
. JOSEPHINE 171
. KATIE SAVAGE 171
. LEITHIE 172
. LESTER 171
. MARGARET 171
. MARTHA 171-172,329
. MARTHA JANE
    SARTAIN 328
. MARY SUMNER 171
. MAUD EARNEST 171
. MORRIS LUTHER 171
. NANCY WOODS 380
. NEDIE GRAY 172
. RADIE 172
. RANDOLPH 171,329
. REASON 90,104,170-171
. REECE 328
. RHODA M. 329
. ROBERT 171,306,329
. RUFUS M. 171
. SUSIE 170
. VERA M. 315
. WHITTY 380
. WILLIAM 328,380
COVIN,DAISY E. 173
. DOSHIE STEPHENSON 353
. EVALINE 238
. GREEN 353
. JAMES WALTER 173
. L.V. 108
. LAZARUS 172
. LEWIS VANN 172-173
. LOUIS EMMETT 173
. MARIAH A. PLYLAR 173
. MARIE ANNIE LEROY 172
. MARY E. MORRIS 172
. ROSE LEE 173
. SCOTTY KILGORE 172
. SIMEON S. 172
COVINGTON, 71,103
COWART,ALMA 378
COX,J.E. 56,94,278
    SARAH MANASCO 278
CRAIG,ALICE R. CAMAK 156
. J.L. 156
CRANFORD,ABNER 173
. ALICE 360
. ANNIS E. LYON 175

. CELIA 173
. CHARLOT 173
. CHESLEY HARDY 173-174
. E. 70,106
. ELIZABETH WILKES 173
    174,364
. ELMARTHA MORRIS 174
. ETTA SWINDLE 174,360
. H.W. 73,101
. J.H. 65,74,99-101,105
. J.M. 269
. JACK 96,174
. JOHN 173-174,364
. JOHN E. 173
. JOHN H. 71,78,322
. JOHN HARVEY 174
. LYDIA 173
. MALINDA 173
. MALINDA E. 364
. MARY ANN JONES 238
. META J. LOLLAR 269
. MINERVA 173
. NANCY E. 173,364
. NANCY EMILY 292
. PATSY 173
. PHOEBE WOOD 380
. REBECCA J. 348
. SADIE 310
. SHERMAN 380
. W. LAFAYETTE 174,360
. WILLIAM 173,238
. WINNIE 173,360
CRICKET,MAHALEY 253
CROCKER,J.W. 76
. MOSES 175
CROFT,JAMES 175
CROSWELL,LAURA M. 335
CROWNOVER,ANNIE 176
. BELMA WRIGHT 176
. J. FILES 176
. JOSEPH B. 176
. JOSEPH BERRY 176
. LILA 176
. S.C. 176
. ULESS A. 176
. URSULA A. POOL 176
. WILLIAM F. 175-176
CROWSON,RICHARD T. 176
. THOMAS 176
. WILLIAM 176
CRUMP,HENRY 144
. HENRY C. 310
. HENRY CLAY 176
. MABEL 144
. MISSOURI POSEY 177,310

History of Walker County, Alabama

. MOLLIE	324	. J.M.	90	DELOACH,J.E.		197
. WILLIAM	31	. J.T.	180	. SUSAN FRANCES		
CRUMPTON,EMELIL	128	. JACK	350	.	GAINES	197
CULPEPPER,HANNAH	204	. JAMES	35,87,350,380	DERRICK,TESSIE		241
CUMMINGS,JOHN M.	177	. JAMES M.	179,346	DESKIN,I.G.		30,182
CUMMINS,MATTIE W.	122	. JAMES WESLEY	180	DICKENSON,ANTHONY S.		30
CUNNINGHAM,		. JANE D.	178	DICKERSON,THOMAS		183
. BELL SMITH	348	. JEFFERSON	46,162,179	DICKINSON,ROBERT		183
. C.J.	61	.	326	DILL,ABNER		183
. C.J.L.	64,178	. JESSE TYRA	179	. CEREPTA		343
. ELIAS	177	. JOHN	181	. ENOCH		183
. JOHN	177,293	. LUSINDA E. COONER	169	. EZEKIEL		183
. MARGARET LEONARD	177	. LYDIA	179	. HANCY		39
. SALLY KING	252	. MALISSA MORGAN	180,285	. LIDIA ODOM		297
. W.M.	61,161,177	. MARD ELIZ. GRAY	181	. LUSINDA		169
. WILLIAM CARTER	177	. MARTHA	178	. VIRGIL ENOCH		77
CURTIS,J.J.	181	. MATILDA	346	. WILLIAM		183
CUSTARD,C.A.	379	. NANCY	341	DINSMORE,DAVID F.		322
. DAISY WINN	379	. NANCY SNOW	350	. HENRIETTA		322
DAILEY,		. NARCISSUS MORGAN	180	DITTO,		12
. BARBARA RATCLIFFE	310	.	285	DOBBS,		
. EFFIE	177	. NEWTON	180	. NANCY J. ROBINSON		256
. EMILY E.	310	. PATSIE	180	. W.F.		256
. GEORGE	310	. PRUDY WOOD	380	DOCKINS,WINIFRED		261
DALTON,CORA GARRISON	200	. ROBERT	31,92,178	DODD,		339
. W.M.	200	. SAMUEL McGEE	181	. J.W.		69
DANIEL,JAMES	93,178	. SARAH E. SNOW	180	. LULU		300
. RACHEL	132	. SARAH SNOW	350	DODSON,E.K.		183
DAVID,ROBERT	43	. THOMAS	103,179	. EZEKIEL		357
DAVIDSON,	120	. THOMAS W.	180,285	. NANCY		357
. GEORGE T.	359	. W.G.	65,99	DOUGLAS,GEORGE		183
. HASSIE	205	. WILEY	170,179	SARAH		257
. JANE	360	. WILLIAM	178,180	DOWDY,WILLIAM		183
. JOHN	240,311	. WILLIAM C.	181	DOWNEY,		
. LIZA	360	. WILLIAM COLUMBUS	181	. THOMAS JOHNSON		184
. MARTHA HELEN POSEY	311	. WILLIAM LEAS	181	DOWNS,ISAAC		118
. PERMELIA SWINDLE	359	. WILLIAM T.	169	. LUVENA AARON		118
. PERNIE JONES	240	. ZILPHA	178	DOYLE,SIMON C.		184
. REUBEN	329	DAY,	60,226	DRENNEN,CHARLES		184
. SALLIE	329	. BERT W.	144	. MATILDA H.		
. SARAH SIDES	343	. C.H.	337	.	CORNWELL	184
. WILLIAM	343	. CALLIE	196	. WALTER B.		184
DAVIS,	22,67,245,247,297	. DAVID MARION	306	DREWRY,HOWARD P.		139
. BENJAMIN	180	. DELLA BROWN	144	. PERRINE BLANTON		139
. CARL	102	. MINNIE	337	DUNCAN,WILLIAM D.		184
. DANIEL	180	. NANCY	182	DUNKIN,MARY		94
. EDITH CORRY GAINES	179	. SARAH ANN PHIFER	306	DUNN,		59
. EDITHA I. CORRY	170	. WILLIAM BYRD	104,182	. EVANS J.		60
.	179	DEASON,ABSALOM	182	. NATHANIEL O.		184
. ELIZABETH	179	. DOLLY	240	. T.J.		105
. ELIZABETH GRAY	181	. MERRICK M.	182	. WILLIAM		20,90,184
. ELLEN GRACE	204	. PATILLO	257	DUPREY,JOHN M.		184
. EMILY J. LACY	181	. REBECCA	182	DUPUY,JOHN M.		32
. GEORGE H.	102	. SARAH ANN KITCHENS	257	DUSKIN,		
. ISAAC	204	DEES,J.A.	182	. ELIZABETH C.		

History of Walker County, Alabama

. ABBOTT 118	EASON,HARRISON 339	FALLS,CHARLES 360
. JAMES 118	. MARY 339	. JALIE SWINDLE 360
DUTTON, 148,158,232	. SADIE 302	FAUGHT,ELIZABETH 188
. ALEX 256	EDGIL,MALINDA 189	. JOSEPH INMAN 187
. ALVIN H. 184	EDNEY,ELLA E. 315	. MARTHA 344
. ANNIE CROWNOVER 176	. JOHN M. 315	FAVER,WILLIAM 188
. CORDELIA WILLIAMS 219	EDWARDS,LEO 266	FELKINS,BURL 287
. DOLLIE 184	. WILLIE LEITH 266	. CATHERINE MORROW 287
. ELIJAH 219	ELDRIDGE, 144	FELTMAN,SARAH M. 299
. ELIZABETH A. 184,219	ELKINS,JANSIE 145	FERGUSON, 321
. ELIZABETH KITCHENS 256	ELLIOTT,FRADONIA 156	. ALBERT 189
. FRANCES 256	. JAMES 15,186	. EDWARD H. 189
. G.W. 143	. JOHN JOSEPH 77	. ELIJAH A. 189
. GEORGE 47	. MARTHA CAMAK 156	. ELIZABETH 164
. GEORGE W. 184	. THOMAS 156	. ERNEST 189
. GRAFTON 176	ELLIS,BERTIE 271	. FANNIE C. 245,247
. JAMES 184,218-219	. BETTY 186	. FANNIE CLEMENTS 164
. JAMES H. 256	. CHRISTIANA H. 186	. HENRY 83,188
. JAMES M. 218	. ELLEN ELIZA	. JOHNSON 189
. JOHN 184	BENNETT 186	. JOSEPH 112,188-189
. JOHN F. 256	. EMMA JANE 186	. JOSEPH WALSTON 189
. JOSEPH 218	. G.T. 256	. LURANIA WALSTON 188
. JOSEPHINE 218	. GEORGE 186,294	. 189
. LOUISA CARMICHAEL 184	. GEORGE WASHINGTON 186	. MALINDA EDGIL 189
218	. JOHN LEMUEL 186	. MINNIE B. POSEY 311
. LUVINA T. 256	. LEONIA 186	. MUD 247
. MALTA 218	. LUCY 163	. PAUL 189
. MARY 143	. MARGARET 344	. PEARL 189
. MARY BROWN 143	. MARTHA A. WILLIAMS 187	. PORTER 311
. MARY F. 256	. MARY ELLEN	. RUTH WOODS 188
. MARY F. DUTTON 256	KITCHENS 256	. SUSAN KEY 247
. MARY JANE 184	. MARY SUSAN 186	. WALTER 189
. PETER 184	. PEGGY NELSON 186,294	FETERSON,JAMES M. 189
. QUEEN 218	. RICHARD 186	FIELDS,
. REUBEN 204	. RICHARD MARTIN 187	. ANNA MAE CAMAK 157
. ROSA GRACE 204	ELMORE,GEORGIANNA 284	. ELIZABETH 307
. S.M. 184	. SOPHRONIA C. 285	. HAMILTON 190
. SARAH J. 218,256	EMBRY,ANDREW H. 187	. J. LEON 157
. SARAH JANE 204	. JAILY W. 122	FIKE, 267,294
. STEPHEN T. 256	ENSLEY, 88	. MARTHA A. TOWNLEY 190
. THOMAS F. 184,218	. ENOCH 75	. 364
. TONEY 184	ESTES,ASA MARTIN 77	. SARAH J. 190
. W.C. 256	. MARY SUSAN ELLIS 186	. W.A. 190
. WILLIAM 184,218	. THOMAS G. 186	. WILLIAM P. 190,364
DUVALL,ALEXANDER C. 184	EVANS,BENJAMIN LONG 298	FIKES,EULA ANN POSEY 311
. ELISHA 184	. HENRY 238	. J.C. 311
EARNEST,	. JOHN W. 187	FILES, 96,237,261
. BERTIE SARTAIN 329	. JONATHAN 187	. ABNER 190
. MAUD 171	. MARGARET BARTON 132	. ANGELINE STANLEY 191
. RICHARD 184	. MASSIE ANN 187	. BELLE 191-192
. ROBERT 186	. MASSIE ANN EVANS 187	. CATHERINE 190,334-335
. SARAH 210	. PEARL ODOM 298	. 354
EASLEY,ALBERT G. 186	. SALLY JONES 238	. CORNELIA 190-191
JOSIAH M. 41,186	. THOMAS 132	. DAVID JASPER 191
EASMAN,JANE 296	. THOMAS HAMPTON 187	. DONIE 192

History of Walker County, Alabama

. ELIZA	239	. LUCIUS G.	193	. MARY	196
. FANNIE	192,337	. MADORAH F.	193,322	. MATTIE	196
. FLORENCE	191	. MARTHA B. COLE	193,322	. NANCY	195-196,201
. FRANCES	191	. WILLIE LEE		. SUSAN	196
. J.F.	66	. SHEPHERD	332	. SUSAN FRANCES	197
. J.M.	247	FRIERSON,GIDEON	153	. WILLIAM M.	195
. JOHN W.	190	. GORDON	34,153	. WILLIAM R.	196
. LORA	192	. JOE	34,153	GAINEY,LUKE R.	197
. LOU	190	FROST,C.S.	194	GALLAGHER,DAVID E.	197
. MACK	190	. EDWARD	193-194	. JOHN BERNARD	77
. MARGARET A. CARR	191	. EDWARD BENTON	193	. JOHN L.	244
. MARTHA	190	. M.V.	193	. JOHN WRIGHT	197
. MARTY BARTON	191	. STEPHEN ORR	194	. MATTIE L. KELLEY	244
. MARY	190-191	FULTON,HORATIO S.	194	GALLOWAY,	62
. MARY D.	255	GABBERT,	42,92	GAMBLE,	55,58,61,68,166
. MARY LINDSAY	221,255	. BENJAMIN	249	.	184,223,285,314
.	354	. JAMES	335	. F.A.	41,54,57,64-66,75
. MARY LINDSEY	190-191	. L.C.	143,194	.	93-94,96,98-99,110
. MILDRED	191,221,260	. LOUISA JANE	195	.	193,198
. OLIVER	190	. MADIE	164	. FOSTER K.	199
. R.M.	337	. N.P.	94	. FRANK	199
. RICHARD	190-191,221	. NANCY KILGORE	249	. FRANKLIN ASBURY	198
.	354	. SARAH	335	. J.W.	198
. RICHARD MANLY	191,255	. T.M.	93	. JANE MILLS	198,377
. SUSAN KEY	247	. THOMAS L.	194	. JERUSHA A. FREEMAN	193
. THOMAS	191-192	. THOMAS LEANDER	194	.	199
FINDLE,JAMES	291	. THOMAS M.	41,43,92,194	. JOHN R	198
. JANE MYERS	291	. THOMAS N.	211	. JOHN R.	31,91,197,377
FITE,BELVA	241	. VIOLA A. GURGANUS	211	. LEILA K.	199
FLEMING,		GAINES,ANN McDOWELL	196	. MARGARET	197
. PEARL STEPHENSON	355	. ANN TIERCE	196	. MARGARET T.	377
. WARREN S.	355	. BARTLEY	196	. MARY A. OWEN	199
FONDREN,JAMES N.	43,92	. CALLIE DAY	196	. ROBERT	197,377
FOOTE,LAURA	322	. DICK	196	. THOMAS OWEN	199
FORD,JAMES	192	. EDITH CORRY	179	GAMMONS,REUBEN	77
. JOHN L.	192	. EDITHA I. CORRY	170	GARNER,	246
FOREST,J.S.D.	192	. EDMOND THOMAS	196	. CARRIE G. LONG	271
FORREST,	320	. ELIZA	196	. FRANK	190
FORTESCUE,MARY A.	374	. ELIZABETH	196-197	. H. POLLY	249
FOSTER,W.S.	64	. EUGENE PENDLETON	197	. LARANDY	190
FOWLER,	274,330,367	. EUGENIE	196	. LERO	271
. JAMES B.	192	. FRANCES JONES	196	. MARTHA FILES	190
. MARTHA K.	207-208	. GEORGE S.	75	. MILLIE	238
FRANKLIN,ELIZA	150,350	. GEORGE SHIP	195-196	. POLLY	246
. JOHN GURGANUS	192	. H.A.	71	. ROBERT	190
. LOTT M.	192	. H.P.	195-196	. THOMAS	190
. MARTHA	243-244,357	. HENRY P.	195	. WASH	190
FREEMAN,BIRDA G.	193	. JAMES P.	195-196	GARRETT,	155
. FATIMA STANLEY	193	. JENNIE SWINDLE	196	. EDWARD	200
. JAMES	102	. JOHN S.	196	. WILLIAM	153-154
. JAMES H.	31,192-193	. JOHN STROTHER	161,196	GARRISON,	
.	199,322	. LAVINA J.	196	. ALABAMA GUTTERY	215
. JAMES S.	193,332	. LEWIS	196	. ARTAMISSA	239
. JERUSHA A.	193,199	. LULA MAY	161,197	. ARTIMISSA	334
. JESSE	31	. MARGARET ANN	196	. CORA	200

History of Walker County, Alabama

. DAVID		200	GILLEN,SUSAN	143,268-269	. LUCINDA		204
. DAVID WILLIAM		200	GILPIN,		337	. MALISSA		205
. EDITH		239-240	GLAZE,WILLIAM		203	. MANELLE		205
. EDITH ANDERSON		200	GLENN,ANN MARIA		260	. MARGARET		204
. JACOB		200	. JOHN BOWLES		260	. MARTHA ASHCRAFT		204
. LLOYD		200	. MARIA ALLEN		260	. MARTHA BANKS		204
. MARGARET		200	GLOVER,ELIZA		337	. MARTHA E.		205
. MARGARET SIDES		200	. LOUIS A.		203	. MARTHA E. RANDOLPH	205
. MARTHA C. ROBISON	200	GODFREY,		349	. MARTHA ELLEN		314
. SALLIE		200	GOINES,			. MARTHA JANE		204
. SARAH LOLLAR		200	. MELISSA JOHNSTON	235	. MARTHA RANDOLPH		205
. SILAS		200	GOODE,		337	. MARY A.		205
. STEPHEN		200	GOODWIN,		344	. MARY ADCOCK	204-205
. W.H.		215	. WILLIAM H.		203	. MARY JANE		205
GARTH,EVELYN E.		128	GORD,WILLIAM A.		203	. MARY POLLY		
GASH,LEANDER		200	GORDOZ,		97	.	CALDWELL	204
GIBSON,ANN		201	GORE,GEORGE W.		203	.		205
. CHARLOT CRANFORD	173	GOYNE,HARRISON W.	32	. MATTIE MINOR		205
. DANIEL		196	GRACE,			. MAUDE		205
. DANIEL JAMES		201	. ABAGAIL KITCHENS	204	. MAUDE CARPENTER		205
. GEORGE W.		201	.		256	. MENTA WETHINGTON		205
. H.P.		75,201	. ADA		207	. MINNIE		205
. ISHAM P.		139	. ALZAH ROBERTS		205	. MISSOURI O. BONNER	205
. JACK		196	. ANNIE SPARKS	204,207	. MISSOURI ODOM		205
. JACOB	35,85,201	. BELLE		204	. MOLLIE		204
. JOHN A.		201	. BLANCHE		205	. NANCY		204
. MARY GAINES		196	. CHESTER VICTOR		205	. NATHAN	204-205
. MARY M.		139	. CYNTHIA		359	. NATHAN A.		205
. NANCY GAINES	196,201	. DANIEL		204	. NATHAN PENNINGTON	205
. SARAH ELIZABETH	139	. ELIZABETH	204-205	. PHOEBA JANE		
. THOMAS		173	. ELLEN		204	.	HANDLEY	205
. W.N.		43,92	. EMILY ODOM	205,296,314	. REBECCA		204
GILBERT,L.E.		93	. EULA		207	. RONIE		205
GILCREASE,ADALINE	202	. FRED		207	. ROSA		204
. CLARINDA		202	. HANNAH		279	. SALINA	204-205
. EDMOND	201-202	. HANNAH CULPEPPER	204	. SALINA HILL		204
. EDMUND		333	. HASSIE DAVIDSON	205	. SARAH C.		205
. FRANCES	202,333	. JAMES A.	296,314	. SARAH J.	204,279
. JANE		202	. JAMES CAMPBELL	205	. SARAH J. DUTTON		218
. JOHN M.		202	. JAMES T.		205	. SARAH JANE DUTTON	204
. JULY		202	. JANE R. MYERS	204	. SUSAN BANKS		204
. MARTHA		202	. JANE RANDOLPH	204	. SUSAN MINOR		205
. MARY E.		202	. JESSE		207	. THOMAS		207
. MISSOURI B.		202	. JOHN	203-205,279	. VIOLA		205
. ROBERT		202	. JOHN E.		204	. VONIE		204
. SUSAN		202	. JOHN EDMOND		205	. WILLIAM	204-205
GILDER,BESSIE		203	. JOHN L.		205	. WILLIAM H.		205
. CHARLES HADDON	203	. JOHN T.		204	. YOUNG		204
. CLARENCE KELLEY	203	. JOSEPH J.	204,256	GRAHAM,DORA JONES	237
. CLYDA BROTHERTON	203	. JOSHUA	204,218	. WILLIAM A.		237
. EVERETTE		203	. JOSHUA B.	204-205	GRAVLEE,		
. GEORGE SUTTLE	202	. JULIA TUBB		205	. HARVEY JACKSON	207-208
. JAMES L.	83,202	. L. CYNTHIA		360	. HERBERT B.		308
. MARTHA C. KELLEY	203	. LAVINIA		238	. J.A.		65,99
. MARY ANN SUTTLE	202	. LEROY		205	. J.W.		105

History of Walker County, Alabama

. JOHN A. 207	. JOHN 30,104	. JOSEPH G. 215
. JOHN DAVID 207-208	. JOHN WASHINGTON 31	. L.J. 213
. JOSEPH M. 207	. 209-210	. LUCINDA KING 214
. LABAM 207	. JOSEPH 211	. LUCIUS CURTIS 215
. MARIETTA PHILLIPS 308	. MARTHA FRANCES 211	. MAE 215
. MARTHA K. FOWLER 207	. MELISSA WALLER 210	. MARTHA A. 170
. 208	. POLLY 360	. MARTHA ANN 213
. NANNIE M. 262	. ROBERT 211	. MARTIN VAN BUREN 215
. SARAH A.E. ROBERTS 207	. SARAH 210	. MARY E. 215
. W.C. 97	. SARAH EARNEST 210	. MARY LULA 215
. W.G. 75	. SUSAN 346	. MARY WILSON 214
. W.L. 207	. SUSAN I. WHITNEY 211	. NANCY ROMINE 213
. WALTER F. 207	. VIOLA A. 211	. NEWTON W. 214
. WALTER G. 207	. WILLIAM 211	. PEARL 217
. WILLIAM 35,84-85,90	. WINDHAM 211	. ROBERT 14,29,38,42
. 207-208	GURLEY,J. 158	. 45-46,90,112-113,212
GRAY, 376	. NATHANIEL W. 211	. 213,215,218,254,277
. ALANSON J. 181	GUTHERIE, 188	. 375
. AMELIA WISE 208	. A.J. 47	. ROBERT M. 214
. ELIZABETH J.	GUTHRIE,A.J. 281	. SARAH 214
. NETHERY 181	. ARAMINTA ANN	. SARAH ANN BROWN 144
. HESTER 241	. MILLER 281	. 215
. JANE 238	. CLELIA 266	. SARAH ANN WILLIAMS 213
. JOHN 345	. ELIZA JANE MORRIS 286	. 215,375
. JOHN P. 108	. JOHN K. 266	. SARAH ELIZABETH 215
. MARD ELIZ. 181	. JOHN M. 286	. WALTER L. 79,110
. MARY SIDES 345	. MARY JOHNSON 266	. WILLIAM 14,90,112
. MERRIL 208	GUTTERY, 136,181,242,252	. 211-214
. MINERVA COOPER 208	. 295,353,358,369,376	GUY,R.M. 71
. NEDIE 172	. 378,380	HALE,STEPHEN F. 167
. WILSON ALEXANDER 73	. A.J. 213,215	HALEY,CURTIS B. 217
. 208	. ALABAMA 215	. ELIZABETH M. 217
GREEN,BENJAMIN M. 208	. ALICA AURORA 215	. FRANCES JONES 217
GREER,JANE 126	. ALICE C. STANLEY 217	. J.F. 95
GREGG,JAMES 93	. 353	. JAMES FRANKLIN 217
GREGORY,SAMUEL S. 208	. ARAMINTA A. MILLER 213	. JOEL 217
GRIFFIN,R.P. 61	. 215	. PAUL S. 217
GRINDLE,JAMES 25	. B.F. 213	. PRISCILLA J.
GROTE,C.A. 76	. CATHERINE 213	. SHIELDS 217
GUIN,WILLIAM C. 208	. CLAUD 217	HALL,ED 71,103
GUNTER,FANNIE 209	. ELIZABETH 213	HAMILTON,ANDREW J. 218
. HATTON 209,299	. G.H. 97-98	. BARTON 218
. J.R. 209	. GEORGE H. 64,353	. BELL 164
. P.B. 209	. GEORGE HOUSTON 214-215	. C.C. 184
. P.M. 209	. HANNAH 212,214	. CHRISTOPHER C. 219
. PERNIA 209	. ISHAM 14,90,112,213	. DOROTHY 364
. S.M. 61,299	. ISHAM P. 144	. ELBERT 364
. SAMUEL M. 209	. J. RUSSELL 213	. ELIZABETH A.
. W.W. 209	. JOHN 213	. DUTTON 184
GURGANAS,	. JOHN McQUEEN 217	. 219
. JOHN WASHINGTON 104	. JOHN T. MORGAN 215	. FRANCES A. 219
GURGANUS,ELIZABETH 211	. JOHN W. 69,113	. HARRY P. 219
. ISAAC 211	. JOHN WILLIS 215	. HARVEY W. 39,47,169
. JAMES F. 211	. JOHNSON 14,90,112	. 218-219,254,376
. JANE 211	. 214-215	. HENRY 218

History of Walker County, Alabama

. ISAAC 219
. JACOB 169
. JACOB B. 219
. JAMES B. 219
. JAMES J. 218
. JOHN B. 217
. JOHN T. 218
. MARTHA 364
. MARTHA JANE COONER 169
. MARY B. 218
. MARY KITCHENS 376
. MARY POLLY 39
. MARY POLLY
. KITCHENS 218
. MARY S.P. KITCHENS 254
. MAY E. 219
. MAY S. 218
. NANCY J. KEY 246
. REBECCA 219,376
. SARAH 158,218
. SARAH E. 218
. SUSAN M. 219
. SUSAN VANSELT 364
. WILLIAM 219
. WILLIAM P. 219
HANCOCK, JAMES 35,87
. JAMES R. 220
HANDLEY,
. ELIZABETH BUSBY 149
. JOHN 248
. PHOEBA JANE 205
. SARAH KILGORE 248
. WILLIAM 149
HARBIN, EMMA 346
. JAMES LOUIS 220
. JESSE 30,220
. L.B. 220
HARGROVE, DUDLEY 164
. MARTHA 164
. MARY COLEMAN 164
HARKINS, LULA HARRIS 128
. MUSA 128
. WALTER WORTH 128
HARRIS, ALLEN 118
. LULA 128
. NOVELLA AARON 118
. PHILLIP ARCHIBALD 220
HARRISON, BENJAMIN 68
HAUSMAN, FRANK 122
. MYRA APPLING 122
HAWES, AYLETTE 295
. CLARA 295
HAWKINS, JOSIAH 220
HAWTHORNE, SARAH 377
HAYES, 261

. ALMA 221,260
. EDGAR 221
. J. HENRY 191
. J.J. 75
. JEREMIAH M. 221
. JHN S. 221
. JOHN HENRY 221,260
. JOHN S. 220
. MILDRED FILES 191,221
. 260
. MOLLIE L. 221,260
. OSCAR 221
. ROSEANA 221
. SARAH G. PETERSON 306
. W.J. 99
HAYGOOD, 310
HAYNES, GREEN 189
. W.J. 65
HEARD, JOHN KEYS 221
. THOMAS 221
HELLAMS, JOHN 22
. WILLIAM 22,221
HELLUMS, JOHN 222
HELMS, IRA 79,110
HENDERSON, 121,177,219
HENDON, FRANKIE 343
. JAMES A. 222
. JAMES HARVEY 222
. JAMES R. 222
. JOHNSON 222
. PERDIE L. 222
. SALLIE R. 222
. T.S. 62,75,113,222
HENDRICKS, MARTHA 352
HENDRIX, A.B. 223
. MARTIN T. 108
. THOMAS MARTIN 223
HENLEY, DONIE FILES 192
. ODESSA 300
HENSON, 307
. ELI 223
. JOHN 223
HERRING, ELIZABETH 246
HERRON, AARON 223
. HENRY KELLEY 77
. JOSEPH 224
. WILLIAM 224
HERZBERG, ALMA LACY 260
. CLIFF 260
HESTER, CHAPMAN 224
HEWLETT, 47,136,150,188
. 215,224-225
. WILLIAM 35
. WILLIAM A. 41,43,46,92
. 224

HICKS, DANIEL 225
HILL, JACOB 225
. JAMES 70,106
. JAMES A. 225
. LARKIN 225
. SALINA 204
. SILAS W. 225
. WILLIAM L. 225
HILLHOUSE, MARTHA 333
HILLIARD, 52,357
HILTON, 108
HINSON, JOHN 226
. JOSHUA 226
HINTON, MELISSA C. 271
. ROXANNA J. SARTAIN 328
. SAMUEL 328
HITCHCOCK, ABNER 54,110
. 198
HOCUTT,
. MARY C. KITCHENS 255
. WILLIAM J. 255
HOGAN, JAMES 42,83
. JAMES A. 256
. LUVINA T. DUTTON 256
HOGG, SUSAN 359
HOGUE, SUSAN 292,359
HOLBROOK, FATIMA E. 226
. JACOB 226
. JACOB ELIJAH 226
HOLDEN, SARAH JANE 248
HOLDERNESS,
. ADA CLARE LONG 271
. SIDNEY 271
HOLLAND, HENRY 226
. JAMES B. 227
HOLLEY, MARTHA 284
HOLLIDAY, OTIS 298
HOLLIS, J.D. 74
. JOHN 126
. SUSAN F. 126
HOLLOWAY,
. ARMISTEAD M. 227
HOLLY, BENJAMIN 227
. DAVID 227
. JOHN C. 227
HOLT, A.J. 227
. JULIA ANN 227
HOLTZCLAW, 138
HOOD,
. ANDREW JACKSON
. WILLIS 227
. DAVID 227
. WILLIAM P. 227
HOOKER, DORA 65,84
. JOHN E. 205

History of Walker County, Alabama

. MARY JANE GRACE 205
. R.R. 65,84
HOPKINS,ISAAC F. 228
. ROBERT 228
HOPSON,A. 228
HOTTO, 360
HOUSTON, 199
HOWELL,G.W. 93
HOYT,
. EVELYN E. BANKHEAD 128
. MORTON 128
HUBBARD, 71,103,265
. CATHERINE 174
. DANIEL G. 228
. DAVID 174,224,228
. ELIJAH H. 228
. LEONARD 228
. MARTHA E. BROWN 228
HUDSON,
. DORENDA SHERER 336
. FEN SHERER 337
. GARNIE 145
. LUCY BROWN 145
. NOLAND 337
. THOMAS 336
HUGGINS,BEN 77
. HOWARD H. 168
. PAULINE COLLINS 168
HUGHES, 229
. JOHN B. 64,98,228
HULSEY,JOHN BAYLESS 229
HUMBER,
. JANE GILCREASE 202
. JOHN 202
HUSLEY,JOHN B. 94
HUTCHINSON,NANCY 155-156
. 325
HUTTO, 171,195,210,224
. 249,286,318,328,331
. AMANDA McDUFF 230
. CHARLES 230
. ELIZABETH GURGANUS 211
. ELIZABETH SHEPHERD 230
. 331
. ERASTUS 211
. JOHN C. 47,57,229,331
. LOUISE 230
. MARTHA 334
. NANCY 249
. RICHARD 230
HUTTON,WILEY W. 105
HYATT,DAVID 315
. FANNIE RANDOLPH 315
HYCHE, 240
. ELI 253

. HARMON LIPSCOMB 231
. JACKSON ELI 231
. JOSEPH CLAYTON 230
. LUCINDA
.   KIRKPATRICK 253
. N.L. 231
. THOMAS BAYNES 230
HYCHLIN,RACHEL 289
INGLE,ANDREW L. 231
INGRAM,HENRY 231
. SOLOMON 231
INMAN,CLINTON 255
. IDA M. KITCHENS 255
. RACHEL 329
. SAMUEL 330
IRELAND,NANCY A.M. 149
IRWIN,JOHN 41,231
ISBEL,GODFREY 139
. RUTH COOK 139
ISBELL,MARY 138
. MARY A. 139
IVEY,LARANDY GARNER 190
. POLLY ANN RUTLEDGE 323
. VINCENT 323
IVY,WARREN HILL 232
. YOUNG MARION 232
JACKSON, 12,14,276,310
.   355,366
. ALBERT C. 102
. ANDREW 32,39,197,233
.   251,276,278
. BUD 192
. C.B. 370
. COLIE 233
. CORDELIA ANN 240
. ELIZABETH 233
. ELIZABETH M. 208
. ETTA 233
. FRANCES A.
.   HAMILTON 219
. GERTRUDE 303
. JOSEPHINE THOMAS 233
. LORA FILES 192
. LUCY REAVES 339
. MAGDELINE 233
. MARY B. HAMILTON 218
. MATTIE NELSON 233
. MELADINE 233
. MOLLIE SIDES 233
. NANCY 232
. NEWBERN J. 233
. ROBERT 233
. SAMUEL 159,232-233
. SAMUEL WALTER 233
. SARAH F. WALKER 370

. TEMPIE 233
. W.A. 232
. WILLIS M. 218
JACOBS,DAVID 233
JAMES,FRANK 314
. NANCY RANDOLPH 314
. SARAH 291
. WILLIAM 233
JANES,SARAH 311
JASPER, 23
JEEMS,SARAH 291
JEFFRIES,ANN GIBSON 201
. B.F. 201
. MINERVA 323-324
JELTON,EPHRAIM 233
. JOSEPH SYLVESTER 233
JENKINS,EMMA 247
. J.R. 286
. RUFUS HENRY 234
. RUFUS V. 346
. WILLIAM 233
. ZORILDA SIMPSON 346
JOHNS,MATILDA ANN 322
JOHNSON, 119,149,215,242
.   262,348
. FLORIDA A.
.   THOMPSON 362
. HOLLY 247
. J.A. 97
. JAMES ALLEN 234
. JULIA OWEN 301
. LULA KEY 247
. MANDY 292
. MARTHA JANE SIDES 343
. MARY 266
. MATILDA J. TUBBS 364
. MELINDA 355
. MOSES 234
. N.J. 343
. NEHEMIAH 234
. PATTIE 292
. ROBERT 301
. ROBERT WILLIAM 364
. SAMUEL 362
. TIBE 86
. WILLIAM B. 234
JOHNSTON,ALLEN H. 235
. 362
. ARCHEVI 235
. BARBARA 235
. BARBARA LECRONE 234
. FLEMING A. 235
. HEWITT 235
. IRA J. 235
. JESSE 234-235

History of Walker County, Alabama

. JOSEPH F.	98	. HENRY	236	.	337
. MANLY H.	235	. HESTER GRAY	241	. TARLEY W.	237
. MARIA L. THOMPSON	362	. IDA	237	. TEMPERANCE E.	240
. MARY L. THOMPSON	235	. IDA J.	315	. TESSIE DERRICK	241
. MELISSA	235	. J.A.	60,86	. THOMAS	204,241
. NOAH A.	235	. JACOB	239	. THOMAS A.	238
. POWELL	235	. JACOB A.	240	. THOMAS G.	71
JOHNSTONE,JOSEPH E.	320	. JAMES	239,296	. THOMAS L.	71
JONES,	108-109,246	. JAMES AUSBORN	236,238	. TOBE	236
. ABNER	237	. JAMES J.	237	. TRAM	107,240
. ADA STEPHENSON	354	. JAMES W.	237	. TUDGE	239-240
. AMANDA ETHEL	241	. JANE GRAY	238	. VADA	240
. AMANDA ROBINSON	240	. JASPER RILEY	237	. VERA C.	168
. ANNETTE ODOM	296	. JEPTHA C.	241	. VICTORIA LAWSON	240
. ANNIE BANKS	240	. JOHN J.	238	. VIRGIL	296
. ARTAMISSA GARRISON	239	. JOSEPHINE L.	135	. VONIE GRACE	204
. ARTHUR CECIL	241	. JULIA	296	. VONIE SARTAIN	329
. ARTIMISSA GARRISON	334	. KIRG	239	. W.R.	164
. AUSBORN	239	. LAVADA	164	. W.W.	93
. BATHSHEBA CAIN	238	. LAVINIA GRACE	238	. WALLACE	14,235-238,337
. BELVA FITE	241	. LEIGHTON TRAMUEL	240	. WARREN	236
. BENJAMIN	31	. LEONARD	196	. WILLIAM	20,90,104
. BENJAMIN GILES	237	. LEROY	241	. WILLIAM C.	329
. BESSIE	239	. MARIN	236	. WILLIAM H.	241
. BISS	240	. MARTHA ANN	240	. WILLIAM JEFFERSON	239
. BUD	60,240	. MARY A. BROOKS	236	.	240
. CANASDA ODOM	296	. MARY ANN	238	. WILLIAM LLOYD	109
. CAROLINE	238,337	. MARY E.		. WILLIAM LOYD	241
. CECILA	238	. KIRKPATRICK	239	. WILLIAM R.	239-240
. CORDELIA ANN		. MARY KIRKPATRICK	253	. WILLIAM RUFUS	68,107
. JACKSON	240	. MATTIE ZULA	241	.	109
. DANIEL LEE	238	. MILLIE GARNER	238	. WILLIAM W.	236
. DOLLY DEASON	240	. MINERVA	236	. WILLIAM WALLACE	236
. DORA	237	. NEWTON EVERETT	241	.	237,334,364
. DORENDA	239	. OLLA	306	. WILLIAM WARREN	237
. EADDIE	246	. PAUL PINKSTON	238	. WILMETTA	237
. EADY	239	. PERNIE	240	JORDAN,LUCY	251
. EDITH GARRISON	239-240	. POLLY TUBB	237	JORDON,MATTHEW M.	241
. EDNA BAILEY	238	. POLLY TUBBS	364	JUMPER,ELIZABETH	291
. EGBERT FERDINAND	241	. RAS	236	KARRH,SAMUEL A.	241
. ELIAS A.	241	. RILLA LIVINGSTON	241	KEENE,LILA	345
. ELIZ. WOMMACK BELL	237	. ROBERT LEWIS	241	KEETON,	112
. ELIZA FILES	239	. ROSE LEE COVIN	173	. CATHERINE	242
. ELIZABETH GAINES	196	. RUFUS	107,240,253,289	. EARL	315
. ELIZABETH WOMMACK	237	. RUFUS FRED	241	. ELIZA JANE SIDES	344
. ELZIA	239	. RUFUS LOYD	239	. ELIZABETH SIDES	344
. EVALINE COVIN	238	. SALLY	238	. JOHN	242
. FAYETTE	173	. SAMANTHIA ODOM	237	. MALINDA	344
. FRANCES	196,217	. SAMARIAMUS	239,334	. MARY JANE	242
. G.C.	43,92	. SAMUEL C.	241	. MARY JANE DUTTON	184
. GILES	236	. SAMUEL H.	238	. QUEENIE RANDOLPH	315
. GILES C.	236	. SARAH	239	. REUBEN	184,242
. GILES O.	238	. SARAH D.	239	. WILLIAM	242,344
. GILES W.	240	. SUSAN	240	. WILLIAM V.	344
. GILMAN	240,354	. SUSAN BEAVERT	235-238	KELLEY,	144,234,264,360

History of Walker County, Alabama

.	369,371
. ANNE	255
. BARNEY	242
. BENJAMIN D.	243-244
. C.C.	75
. D.M.	244
. E.D.	197
. ELIZABETH	243,357
. ESOM D.	47,56,243
. GUSSIE	243
. JAMES A.	244
. JOHN	243-244,357
. JOHN T.	244
. MARTHA C.	203
. MARTHA E. WALKER	243
. MARTHA FRANKLIN	243
.	244,357
. MATTIE L.	244
. WILSON	244
KELLY,	339
. SAVANNAH	160
KEMP, ANNIE C.	160
. JAMES	244
. PRESLEY	244
. SAVANNAH KELLY	160
. THOMAS P.	160
KENNEDY, JAMES	244
KERR, JOHN B.	244
KEY,	118,170,179,296
. ADA	247
. AILEEN	248
. ANNIE	247
. AUBREY	247
. BEDFORD THOMAS	247
. BELINDA	118,165,245
. BELINDA MILSTEAD	161
.	245,247
. BENJAMIN	247
. BERTHA	245
. BERTHINA NELSON	247
. BESSIE	247
. BUCK	246
. BYRD GARLAND	246
. CHARITY E. WOOD	245
.	380
. CHARITY ELIZ. WOOD	247
.	324
. CHARLES RICE	246
. CLARA ANN	248
. CLAUDINE	248
. CYNTHIA A. ABBOTT	245
. DOCK CLIFTON	165
.	246-247
. DONIE	248
. DORCIA COLE	246
. EADDIE JONES	246
. EDWARD THOMAS	247
. ELIZA	247
. ELIZABETH	245-246
. ELIZABETH HERRING	246
. EMMA JENKINS	247
. ETHEL	307
. FANNIE C. FERGUSON	245
.	247
. FANNIE CLEMENTS	164
.	245,247
. FLETCHER	248
. FLOYD G.	248
. FRANKIE	248
. FRANKIE BAILEY	246-247
. FRONIE	248
. GABRIEL	161
. HENRY	149
. HENRY GRADY	247
. HOWELL	245
. IDA KILGORE	247
. JACOB CLIFTON	248
. JALIE BUSBY	149
. JAMES	245
. JAMES BUCHANAN	246
. JAMES D.	247
. JAMES HEZEKIAH	246
. JANE MILLS	118,246
. JENNINGS B.	109
. JENNINGS D.	247
. JOHN	22,30,90,104,118
	161,165,244-247,324
.	380
. JOHN BYRD	246
. JOHN CLIFTON	246
. JOHN MARTIN	245-247
.	380
. JOHN R.	247
. JOSEPH	165
. JOSEPH GARLAND	246
. JOSEPH MARTIN	246,248
. JULIA	246
. JULIA KEY	246
. JULIUS LORENZA	248
. LINDSAY	246
. LINDY	245
. LIZA JANE	246
. LUCY	245
. LUCY ALLEN WOODS	245
.	380
. LUCY B.	292
. LULA	247
. MAMIE IRENE	248
. MANDY VERLIN	248
. MARVIN SCOTT	248
. MARY	246-247,324
. MARY ANN RUTLEDGE	247
.	324
. MARY KEY	246
. MARY POLLY	245
. MARY POLLY KEY	245
. MARY SNOW	245-246
. MAUDE ROBERTS	318
. MINERVA	247,324
. MINNIE SIDES	247
. MINTER SWINDLE	247
. MINTIE ANN WADE	248
. MITA	247
. NANCY	161,245-246,248
.	266,350
. NANCY J.	246
. NANCY LOUISE COLE	165
.	246-247
. NANNIE	343
. NEWTON EDWARD	248
. NICHOLAS RICE	246-247
. OCTAVIUS WINIFRED	248
. PAUL LANDON	248
. POLKA WILLIAMS	246
. POLLY GARNER	246
. PRUDY	247
. RACHEL COLE	165,246
. REBECCA WINTERS	246
. RHODA	248
. RICE	245
. ROBERT	246
. ROBERT CLARENCE	248
. ROBERT POWERS	247,324
. SALLY CHILTON	161
. SAMANTHIA WILLIAMS	246
. SAMUEL	245
. SAMUEL L.	247
. SARAH BELINDA	246
. SHAY BENJAMIN	248
. SUSAN	247
. T.D.	307
. TALMAGE D.	247
. THOMAS	245,324,380
. TOM	343
. WASHINGTON	245
. WILLIAM	245-246
. WILLIAM S.	
.	WASHINGTON 245
. ZILPHIA	246
KEYS, JOHN	130
SUSAN	130
KILGORE,	245,359-360
. ADELINE WADE	249
. CAROLINE SIDES	338
. CHARLES C.	249

History of Walker County, Alabama

. CHARLES E.	249	. WILEY L.	249	. MARY E.	239
. DAISY	157	. WILLIAM	248	. MONRE	253
. DIDA DAVID	248	. WILLIAM D.	249	. MOSES M.	253,257
. DORAN	324	. WILLIAM PARKER	251	. NARCISSA	253
. DORENDA	251,336	KIMBALL,ELLA	171	. NORA	253
. ELZIE	249,342	KIMBRELL,HARRY	346	. PERMELIA E. MEEK	253
. ETTA	219	. MAYRTIE SIMPSON	346	. PERMELIA H. MEEK	353
. GEORGE	248,344	KING,	326	. RANEY	335
. H. POLLY GARNER	249	. BARBARA	132	. ROSCOE	253
. HATTIE CLEMENTS	248	. ELIZABETH WILSON	252	. S.J.	132
. HEWITT	233	. EMMA JANE ELLIS	186	. SIS STEPHENSON	253
. IDA	247	. GEORGE	186	. WILLIAM R.	252,353
. IRA	249	. HOSIE SARTAIN	329	KIRKWOOD,DAVID	59,75
. ISAAC	249	. JOANNE	152	KITCHENS,	194
. ISAAC K.	249	. JOHN 22,75,90,112,214		. ABAGAIL	204,256
. J. ROBERT	249		251-252	. ANNE BANKS	255
. J. THOMAS	249	. JOHN W.	252	. ANNE KELLEY	255
. JAMES	219,248-249	. LUCINDA	214	. BELLE SANDERS	255,326
. JAMES M.	249	. LUCY JORDAN	251	. BERTHA SMITH	257
. JOHN 71,103,219,249		. MARTHA	252,279	. BIRDIE POSEY	257
. JOHN M.	249	. MARY	163,252,355	. BUCK	254
. JOHN R.	249	. MARY WOODSON	251	. CHRISTOPHER C.	39
. JOSEPH O.	249	. SALLIE	353	. CHRISTOPHER	
. LILLY B.	249	. SALLY	252		COLUMBUS 254
. MAGDELINE JACKSON	233	. THOMAS	329	.	255,257
. MARTHA 145,249,251,338		. THOMAS JORDAN 251-252		. DOROTHY B. TANDY	257
. MARTHA F. RUTLEDGE 324		. WILLIAM	251	. DOROTHY BURGER	257
. MARY	249,343	. WILLIAM R. 251-252,279		. ELEANOR BROWN	143,256
. MARY ELIZ. SIDES	344	. WILLIAM RUFUS	251	. ELIZA JANE SIDES	258
. MARY POLLY KEY	245	KINGSLEY,		.	343
. MARY SHERER	251,338	. QUEENIE BROWN	144	. ELIZABETH	256
. MATILDA BUSBY	249	. ROME	144	. EMILY BIRDIE POSEY 311	
. MITCHELL	249	KINSEY,THOMAS	252	. ETTA A.	257
. MOLLIE SHERER	337	KIRKPATRICK,AUGUST	253	. FRANCES	124,254,256
. MOSELLA	219	. BENIE	253	.	258,344
. NANCY	249	. BESSIE	253	. GEORGE	253,258
. NANCY ANN CONN	249	. E.	334-337	. GILBERT LEE	255
. NANCY C. SIDES 249,336		. EARL	253	. HENRY	253
.	342	. ELIZA BLACKWOOD	253	. HUBERT TAYLOR	256
. NANCY HUTTO	249	. ELIZABETH	336	. IDA M.	255
. NANCY LARRIMORE	249	. EMILY McDUFF	253	. ISAAC STANLEY	255
.	343	. FANNIE	253	. JAMES	39,258
. ROBERT	248,337-338	. HARRIETT	337	. JAMES CHRISTOPHER	257
. ROBERT F.	249	. J.	334-337	. JAMES LAFAYETTE	254
. RODIE SMITH	249	. JACOB	253	. JAMES M.	38
. ROSS M.	249	. JENCIE	253,353	. JAMES MATLOCK	47-48
. RUTH	248	. JOSEPH	108,253	. 124,142-143,191,218	
. SAMUEL D.	248	. LUCINDA	253		253-254,257-258
. SARAH	248-249	. MAHALEY C.		. JESSE 47,143,255-256	
. SCOTTY	172		KITCHENS 253	. JESSE ANDREW	257
. SUSAN M. HAMILTON	219	. MAHALEY CRICKET	253	. JESSE SIMEON	132,253
. THOMAS	249	. MAHALY L. KITCHENS	257	.	255,257,296
. THOMAS ALLEN	249	. MARTHA BARTON	132,253	. JOHN 83,254,258,336	
. WILEY 249,336,338,342		. MARY	253	.	343-344
. WILEY E.	249	. MARY A.	334	. JOHN H.	258

History of Walker County, Alabama

. JOHN M.	254	. LILA	205	. VIRGINIA L. LAMAR	260
. JOHN MATLOCK	255	. MAE BOSHELL	191	. VIRGINIA	
. JOSEPH	258	. NANCY	258	. LONGSTREET	260
. MAHALEY C.	253	. NATHAN PENNINGTON	205	. WILLIAM H.	260
. MAHALY L.	257	. POLLY	205	. WILLIAM HARMONG	260
. MARTHA	254,258,343	. RICHARD TOWNLEY	258	LAMBERT,WASHINGTON	261
. MARTHA C. PHIFER	255	. SALINA GRACE	205	LAMKIN,BETSY CLARK	261
.	306	. SARAH KILGORE	249	. ELIZA BIBB	262
. MARTHA J.	132	. SUSAN	205	. GEORGE GRIFFIN	262
. MARTHA JANE	257	LACY,	71,76,320	. GRIFFIN	43,90,92
. MARY	376	. ABNER WISE	258	.	261-262,301,325
. MARY ANN BENNETT	258	. ALBERTA	260	. HANNAH	262,301
. MARY C.	255	. ALMA	260	. JOHN JAMES	261
. MARY D. FILES	255	. CECIL JUSTUS	258	. LUCY CLARK	262
. MARY ELIZABETH	255	. E.R.	74	. MARIAH JANE	262
. MARY ELLEN	256	. EARNEST	102	. MARTHA JANE	262
. MARY FILES	191	. EMILY J.	181	. MARY BOOKER	262
. MARY ODOM	255,257,296	. ERNEST RENFROE	258	. NANNIE M. GRAVLEE	262
. MARY POLLY	218	. GAYE MUSGROVE LONG	258	. PETER	261-262
. MARY S.P.	254	. JOHN E.	221,260	. PETER SHARP	261
. MARY SUSAN	257	. LORENE	258	. PETRONELLA	262
. MATILDA	143,256	. LOUISE	260	. PETRONILLA	262
. MATLOCK	47	. MARTHA BREWSTER	258	. SARAH E.	262,325
. NANCY	256	. MARY ELLA		. SARAH THACKER	261-262
. ROBERT F.	306	. McCOLLOUGH	258	.	301,325
. ROBERT FRANKLIN	255	. MARY WISE	258	. SUSANNA BIBB	261
. SALLIE BROWN	142-143	. MAUD	260	. THOMAS PETER	262
.	218,313	. MOLLIE L. HAYES	221	. THOMAS RICHARD	262
. SALLY BROWN	124,254	.	260	. WINIFRED DOCKINS	261
. SALLY M. ASHCRAFT	256	. PAULINE	258	LANDER,LUTHER	69
. SAMUEL	255	. RUTH	258,272	LANDERS,NATHANIEL	263
. SARAH	39	. SHERIFF	258	LANE,A.G.	43,92
. SARAH ANN	257	. WILLIAM	258	. ALFRED	30
. SARAH ANN TAYLOR	254	LAIRD,JAMES I.	239	. ALFRED G.	31,263
. SARAH DOUGLAS	257	. SARAH D. JONES	239	. JOSEPH L.	263
. SARAH E.	258,336	LAMAR,ALMA	261	LANG,MARTHA KING	252
. SARAH J.	258	. ALMA HAYES	221,260	LANGLEY,NATHAN B.	263
. SAREH E.	254	. ANN MARIA GLENN	260	LARRIMORE,CORA POSEY	311
. SUSAN	124,257	. ANNIE	261	. GRADY	311
. W.C.	254	. CHARLES R.	260	. NANCY	249,343
. WILEY L.	311	. EDITH STONESTREET	261	LATHAM,ELIZABETH	310
. WILEY LEANDER	257	. GEORGE HOLT	261	. JAMES	344
. WILLIAM	39,255,258	. GLENN	261	. JAMES LEANDER	263
. WILLIAM CALVIN	256	. GLENNIE C.	260	. NANCY SIDES	263,344
. WILLIAM FILES	255,326	. HENRY	261	. THOMAS MARION	263
. WILLIAM HENRY	257	. HOWARD	221,260-261	LAVAN,MARY SHERER	336
. WILLIAM TAYLOR	254	. LAURA CAIN	260	LAWHORN,NEAL	299
KNIGHT,	205	. MARTHA ANNE YOUNG	260	LAWRENCE,	136,274
. ABNER	258	. MILDRED	261	. BENJAMIN	264
. ELIZA	205	. ORLENA A.		. W.H.	197
. ELIZABETH THOMPSON	362	. CLEVELAND	260	LAWSON,	112
. EMILY	205	. THEODORE JEMISON	260	. ALBERT GALLATIN	264
. JAMES ANDREW	205	. THOMAS	260	. SALLIE	291
. JOHN	205,362	. VIRGINIA L.	260	. VICTORIA	240
. JOHN R.	249			LAY,SARAH ANN	118

LAYMON,		263	. CAROLINE BROWN	266,298	. ELIZABETH	346
. JAMES WASHINGTON		262	. DAVID	177,266	. ELIZABETH TAYLOR	269
. NANCY E.		262	. JAMES LEWIS	298	. ERASTUS	205
LEAKE,W.E.		59	. JAMES LOUIS	266	. FANNIE E.	269
LECRONE,BARBARA		234	. MARGARET	177	. H.G.	93
LEE,	50,71,103,219		. MARTELIA	266,298	. HARRIET TAYLOR	351
. ROBERT E.		270	LEROY,MARIE ANNIE	172	. HUGH	22-23,47,90,104
LEECH,ELBERT C.		295	LESLIE,AARON	267	.	147,200,246,268
. MARY		295	LESTER,JAMES	267	. HUGH GAUNT	268-269
LEEPER,ISABEL		270	. LUCINDA	204	. ISAAC H.	269
LEGAR,			LINCOLN,	45,224	. JOHN	90
. DESSIE STEPHENSON		354	LINDSAY,		. JOHN A.	143,268-269
. JOE		354	. FRANCES KITCHENS	254	. JOHN B.	351
LEGRAND,JULIA WALKER		369	. HELEN	311	. JOHN BERRY	269
. WILLIAM		369	. J.D.	254	. JOSEPH	269
LEITH,ALICE		298	. MARTHA KITCHENS	254	. LIZZIE CORNETT	269
. CLELIA GUTHRIE		266	. MARY	221,255,354	. LUCIUS R.	269
. CORTEZ		264	LINDSEY,MARY	190-191	. MANDY SHERER	337
. EBENEZER	264,268		. WILLIAM	267	. MARGARET	143
. ELIZABETH	65,84		LINN,DORA KATE	302	. MARGARET E.	269,351
. ELIZABETH BRANNER		264	LITTLE,E.T.	281	. MATITE	336
.	265-266,268,281,286		. J.M.	190	. META J.	269
.	298,374		. JAMES	22,267	. PEARL	306
. EVALINE E.			. JAMES POLK	302	. QUEEN VICTORIA	269
.	THOMPSON	362	. LOU FILES	190	. SARAH	200
. F.M.		298	. LOVENIA PALMER	302	. SARAH C. GRACE	205
. FRANCIS MARION		264	. PETER	267	. SARAH CATHERINE	
. G.W.L.		362	LITTLETON,		.	LEITH 268
. GEORGE	112,264-266,268		. BENIE KIRKPATRICK	253	.	269
.	281,286,298,374		. SOLOMON	253	. SEBASTIAN NAPOLEON	269
. JANE LYLE		265	LIVINGSTON,JESSE	267	. SUSAN GILLEN	143
. JOHN	65,84		. PHOEBE	186	.	268-269
. M.L.		74	. RILLA	241	. W.H.	337
. M.P.	65,84		LOCKART,FRANK	149	. WILLIAM R.	269
. MARGARET C.		286	. MARTHA J. BUSBY	149	. ZEPHRONIA E.	269
. MARTHA E.		374	LOCKHART,		. ZILPHIA KEY	246
. MARTIN LUTHER		266	. CHARLES LOCKHART	267	LONG,	60,97,166,205,229
. MARY JANE	156-157,215		. DORA CARMICHAEL	158	.	231,282,300,308-309
.		281	. DORCAS	267	. A.C.	94
. MITCHELL PORTER		265	. DORCAS LOCKHART	267	. ADA CLARE	271
.		266	. S.M.	267	. AMANDA	63,86
. QUINNIE		266	. SAMUEL	267	. AMANDA C. WOOTEN	271
. SARAH CATHERINE		268	. THOMAS	267	. AUGUSTA M. SPROTT	271
.		269	LOGAN,	245	. B.M.	47,50,63,66,70-71
. SARAH F. WHITSON		298	. ELIZABETH	323-324	.	75,86-87,132,157,162
. SARAH WHITSON		265	LOGGAMS,JOHN C.	268	.	175,180,191,297,340
. SICILINE E.			LOLAR,HUGH GAUNT	255	. BENJAMIN M.	42,85,270
.	CHILTON	265	. MARY E. KITCHENS	255	.	341
.		266	LOLLAR,	286,354,358	. BENJAMIN McFARLAND	269
. VERA		266	. A.T.	93	. BERTIE ELLIS	271
. WILLIE		266	. ANDREW J.	269	. CARRIE	167,271
LELIEVERE,L.F.		176	. ANICE	169	. CARRIE E.	341
. LILA CROWNOVER		176	. CICERO	269	. CARRIE G.	271
LEMONS,NORA		301	. DOCENA SHERER	337	. E.W.	78,102
LEONARD,			. E.H.	94	. EDGAR WILLIAM	271

History of Walker County, Alabama

. FRED	271	MAGBY,ROBERT	275	. PERMELIA H.	353
. GAYE MUSGROVE	258	. VARDRY	275	. ROBERT B.	143
. H.S.	76	MALLARD,	276	MEHARG,LEWIS	280
. HENRY M.	271	. ELDRIDGE	32-33,39,275	MERRELL,F.A.	73,101
. HENRY WHITFIELD	271	MALONE,		METZER,J.	71
. IDA	271	. EVERETTE GILDER	203	METZGER,J.	103
. ISABEL LEEPER	270	. J. MORGAN	145	MILES,W.L.	108
. JAMES	270	. JOHN M.	203	MILLER,ARAMINTA A.	213
. JANE WALKER	270	. LILY L. BROWN	145	.	215
. JESSE ORVILLE	271	MANASCO,	41,57,232	. ARAMINTA ANN	281
. JOHN	269,341	.	277-278	. B.M.	181
. JOHN B.	258,290	. CARLTON W.	278	. E.W.	61
. JOHN BENJAMIN	271	. CARTER	279	. ELLEN A. KINSEY	
. KATHLEEN PHIFER	272	. CHRISTINE	279	.	MYERS 292
. LOU	271	. DAVID	92,278	. ERASTUS WASHINGTON	281
. LULA MANDEVILLE	271	. HODIE BOSHELL	279	. ETTA JACKSON	233
. MISSOURI K.		. JAMES K. POLK	278	. IDA LONG	271
.	MUSGROVE 271	. JASPER	137	. JOE	137
.	290	. JEREMIAH	276,278	. JOHN DUDLEY	281
. NANCY DAVID	269	. JOHN	39-41,51,56,61	. JOHN M.	271
. NANCY DAVID LONG	269	.	112,153,186,204,231	. L.C.	49,56,112,213,265
. NANCY DAVIS	341	.	276,279	.	344
. NONA BELL SPROTT	271	. JOHN C.	279	. LAVATOR	292
. POPE McFARLAND	271	. LUCILE	279	. LAVONIA C.	156-157,281
. R.L.Y.	94	. LUCINDA LESTER	204	. LUCIUS C.	156-157,215
. ROBERT	269	. LUCINDA LUSTER	278	. LUCIUS CARL	280
. RUTH LACY	272	. ORIZABA	279	. MARY JANE LEITH	156
. RUTH LACY LONG	272	. SARAH	278	.	157,215,281
. T.L.	65,99	. SARAH J. GRACE	204,279	. O.C.	205
. THOMAS L.	73	. VICY ODUM	276	. POLLY KNIGHT	205
. THOMAS LEEPER	271	MANDEVILLE,LULA	271	. VIRGIL MARONIS	281
. ZOU MUSGROVE	258	MANUEL,ALICE	164	. WILLIAM	233
LONGSTREET,VIRGINIA	260	MARTIN,	278	MILLS,	
LOONEY,ANNIE LIZA	272	. CAUDACE	315	. CHARLES MILLARD	322
. MADISON W.	272	. CHARLES R.	279	. HESTER M. ROSAMOND	322
LOVE,JENNIE ANN	296	. JAMES B.	279	. JAMES	198,377
. SARAH E.	337	. JOHN	279	. JANE	198,377
LOVELADY,SARAH M.	305	MASON,	133,187,287	. MARGARET	198
LOVETT,EMILY	311	. JOHN D.	266	MILNER,HENRY W.	75
LOWERMORE,SAMUEL	272	MASTERS,MAGGIE ETTA	160	MILSTEAD,BELINDA	161,245
LOWERY,	97	MASTERSON,		.	247
LUCY,	61	. JAMES NEWTON	279-280	MINOR,JANE	344
LUMDEN,	122	.	355	. MARTHA KILGORE	249
LUND,ANDREW J.	127	. MAHALA	280	. MATTIE	205
. LOUISE BANKHEAD	127	. SALLIE	280,355	. ROLAND W.	282
LUNN,J.W.	196	. THOMAS	279	. SUSAN	205
. LAVINA J. GAINES	196	. W.R.	280	. TOBE	249
LUSTER,LUCINDA	278	MATTINGLY,	71,103	MINTER,FRANCIS	333
LYLE,JANE	265	MAY,WILLIAM	280	. JOHN	333
LYON,ANNIS E.	175	MAYBERRY,MARY	117-118	. MARTHA	333-337
. ELIZABETH MORRIS	175	MAYFIELD,P.P.	237	. MARTHA HILLHOUSE	333
. JOHN	175	. WILMETTA JONES	237	. WILLIAM	333
MACDONALD,JOHN	247	MEEK,		. WILLIAM E.	282
. MITA KEY	247	. LUCINDA A. BROWN	143	MONROE,	18
MACKEREL,JAMES	275	. PERMELIA E.	253	MONTEITH,J.E.	189

History of Walker County, Alabama

MONTGOMERY,	120	. PETER A.	147,284,369	MORTON,P.G.	65,98
. DAVID	156	. RACHEL	284	MOSGROVE,	208
. JULIA A. CAMAK	156	. REUBAN	284	MOSS,LURA	337
MOODY,JONATHAN P.	282	. REUBEN	35,87,283	MOTES,JAMES	118
. THEOPHILUS	30	. REUBEN MARDIS	285	. MALINDA J. ABBOTT	118
MOON,MOSES	282	. ROBERT J.	284	MULFORD,MARY KING	252
MOONEY,ANNIE C.	282	. ROBERT JASPER	284	MULLENS,BURGESA	130
. JONATHAN PAUL	282	. ROSA	284	. REBECCA BARTON	130
MOORE,	45-46	. SAMANTHA J. WALKER	370	MULLIGAN,JAMES	324
. ALBERT BURTON	15	. SARAH A. BALLENGER	284	. SARAH RUTLEDGE	324
. DAVID ERSKIN	266	. SARAH ANN	284	MULLINAX,RICHARD	287
. ELIZABETH M. HALEY	217	. SARAH BARTON	132	. S.A.	235
. FLORENCE FILES	191	. SOPHRONIA C.		MULLINS,BUDDY E.	287
. J. ALEX	102,217	. ELMORE	285	MURPH,MALISSA GRACE	205
. JAMES	24	. WILLIAM	283	MURPHEE,DAVID	288
. SAMUEL H.	282	. WILLIAM R.	284	. MARTIN	288
. VERA LEITH	266	MORRIS,	104	MURPHREE,DAVID	15
. W.H.	191	. CATHERINE HUBBARD	174	MURPHY,HARVEY	181
. WALTER	63,75,88	. DAVID	286	MURRAY,B.	90
MORGAN,A.E.	370	. ELIZA JANE	286	. BENJAMIN	22,288
. AUGUSTUS	285	. ELIZABETH	175,286	. RICHARD HENRY	288
. BABE	284	. ELMARTHA	174	MUSGROVE,	23-24,61,90-91
. BAMA	285	. JAMES HARVEY	286	.	96,133,150,187,192
. BOSS	284	. JAMES LARRY	286	.	238,246,266,281,287
. CORNELIA BOSHELL	191	. JOHN H.	285	.	305,316,361,380-381
. DELLA	284	. JOHN HARVEY	174	. CALPERNIA RACHEL	290
. DOCK	284	. LAVONIA A.	286	. COLEMAN	290
. DOLLY	284	. LOUISA VIRGINIA	286	. E.G.	92
. ELIZA	284	. MARGARET C. LEITH	286	. EDWARD G.	22,30,89,289
. ELIZA J.	370	. MARY E.	172	. EDWARD GORDON	288
. ETTA	284	. MARY LAURA SARTAIN	329	. ELIZABETH CAIN	154,290
. EZEKIEL	87,90,180	. ROBERT	285	. F.A.	42,92-93,271,324
.	282-283,370	. SAMPSON	329	.	366
. GEORGIANNA ELMORE	284	. SARAH ELIZ.	286	. FRANCES A.	41
. HENRY	132,285	. SEBASTIAN N.	286	. FRANCES ASBURY	289-290
. HENRY TERRELL	285	. WILLIAM A.	182,285	. FRANCIS A.	47,154
. HULDA	284	MORRISON,NANCY	303	. J.C.	64,75,98
. IDA	284	MORROW,ALTA DEASON	287	. JOHN WILLIAM	288
. JAMES I.	284	. ARCHIBALD	287	. L.	121
. JOHN	283	. CATHERINE	287	. L.B.	58-59,61,64-65,67
. JOHN PERRY	284	. CORA DREW	151	.	75,77,95,98-99,209
. JOHN R.	284	. DOVIE	132	. LYCURGUS	
. LINNIE BRANTLEY	283	. FRANCES BARTON	130,287	. BRECKENBRIDGE	290
.	370	. HUGH	287	. MISSOURI K.	271,290
. LOUISE	285	. JAMES	130,287	. NANCY TATE	288
. MALISSA	180,285	. JANE	355	. RACHEL HYCHLIN	289
. MARTHA	284	. JOHN QUINCY	287	. SUSAN F. NEAL	290
. MARTHA HOLLEY	284	. LIDIA BARTON	130,287	. ZOU	258
. MARTHA W.	147	. MARGARET BLACK	287	MYERS,	343
. MARTHA WALKER	284,369	. MARTHA SANDERS	151	. ABRAHAM	83
. MARY	284	. MARY ANN SANDERS	287	. AMANDA	359
. MATSON C.	284	. MOLITA	355	. AMANDA S.	292
. MELVIN W.	285	. MOLLIE	132,287	. DORA	118
. NARCISSUS	180,285	. SAMUEL	130,287	. ELIZA KEY	247
. OCTAVIA	284	. THOMAS B.	151	. ELIZABETH JUMPER	291

History of Walker County, Alabama

. ELLEN A. KINSEY	292
. GEORGE A.	291
. GEORGE H.	247
. HOWELL ARNOLD	292
. JACOB	291
. JAMES AUGUSTUS	292
. JANE	291
. JANE R.	204
. JANE RANDOLPH	291
. JOHN HENRY	291
. JOHN JAMES	291
. JOHN W.	204
. JOSEPHINE	292
. LUCY B. KEY	292
. MANDY JOHNSON	292
. MARTHA H.	360
. MARTHA HELEN	292
. MARY ANN TUBBS	292,364
. MEHALEY C. SWINDLE	292
. NAN	291
. PATTIE JOHNSON	292
. PHILLIP JEFFERSON	292
.	364
. POLLY TUBBS	364
. RICHARD	205
. RUDOLPH	291
. SALINA GRACE	204
. SALLIE LAWSON	291
. SARAH	291,378
. SARAH JAMES	291
. SARAH JANES	311
. SARAH JEEMS	291
. SUSAN F.	311
. SUSAN FRANCIS	292
. WAKE ASBURY	292
. WILLIAM DICKSON	291
. WILLIAM J.	311
. WILLIAM JAMES	291,379
MYRICK,SARAH M.	378
McADORY,NANCY L.	322
McARTHUR,	
. AMY LEE ROSAMOND	322
. FRANKLIN D.	322
. LILLY F. CONNERLY	322
. WILLIAM FRANKLIN	322
McAULEY,ELIZABETH	154
.	290,326
McCLAIN,ELIZA	272
. GEORGE W.	272
. JOHN M.	272
. MARY KEY	247
. W.H.	247
McCOLLOUGH,	
. JOHN MARTIN	258
. MARY ELLA	258
. RUTH SKINNER	258
McCOLLUM,JOSEPH	272
. LULA COLLINS	168
. TRAVIS	168
McCONNELL,	31,91
McCORMACK,W.J.	273
McCRARY,CLARA	338
. JAMES I.	218
. MAY S. HAMILTON	218
. OLLA	338
McCRORY,HUGH H.	273
McCULLAR,	
. ANDREW MARBELL	273
. WILLIAM H.H.	273
McDANIEL,BENJAMIN B.	273
McDONALD,A.	75
. ALEX	83
. GEORGE W.	273
. JAMES	83
. MARTHA SHERER	335
. WILLIAM K.	273
McDOWELL,ANN	196
McDUFF,AMANDA	230
. ELIZABETH	230
. EMILY	253
. ISAAC	274
. RICHARD	230
McELROY,JOHN	274
McFALL,	
. FANNIE E. LOLLAR	269
. G.W.	269
McFINN,JAMES	274
. JOHN	274
McGARNES,	
. ELIZABETH M.	170
McGLATHERY,BONAPARTE	154
. RENIE CAIN	154
McGLATHNEY,DAVID	274
McGOUGH,JOHN	274
McGREGOR,	
. BIRDA G. FREEMAN	193
. D.A.	193
McGUIRE,FLORENCE	128
. JOSEPH H.	128
. SALETA ANDERSON	128
McKENZIE,G.D.	172
. LEITHIE COURINGTON	172
McKESSICK,FLOYD	348
McKEY,WILLIAM A.	274
McKITTERICK,JOHN	293
McLAIN,GEORGE	205
. JAMES	218
. JULY A.R.	
. CARMICHAEL	218
. LILA KNIGHT	205
McLEESE,MARY	356
McMAHAN,ALPHA ODOM	298
. MINTER	298
McMILLAN,ALLEN	274
. FRANK MARION	274
. JOSEPHINE	
. COURINGTON	171
. SARAH A. WHITSON	275
. SID	171
McMURRAY,ANDREW J.	275
McNEAL,GEORGE V.	118
. MALINDA J. ABBOTT	118
McNEER,DANIEL	275
McNEIL,MICHAEL	275
McNUTT,JAMES	275
McPOLAND,	
. ANNIE LOU SHEPHERD	332
. McDAVID	332
McQUEEN,JOHN	61
NATION,HENRY	63,86
NATIONS,BAILES	22,293
. FRANCIS E.	293
. JOSEPH	22,85,292-293
. MARY A. BARTON	130
. MARY SUSAN	
. KITCHENS	257
. ROBBIN	257
NEAL,SAMUEL	293
. SUSAN F.	290
NEIL,	120
NELSON,	297
. ANDREW	186,293-294
. ANDREW JACKSON	294
. BERTHINA	247
. CATHERINE	294
. JOHN MARTIN	294
. JOHN N.	294
. L.S.	294
. LAURA A.	295
. LEWIS H.	241
. MARY P.	118
. MATTIE	233
. MATTIE ZULA JONES	241
. PEGGY	186,294
. ZELLIE	380
NESMITH,	
. CHRISTOPHER	
. COLUMBUS	73
NETHERY,ELIZABETH J.	181
NICHOLSON,	
. MARY S. ROBINSON	256
. T.J.	256
NIX,CARRIE	343
. MARY	324
. TROY	137

History of Walker County, Alabama

NOBLE,DELLA POSEY 311	. JAMES IVAN 297	. GUNTER 299
. JAMES 311	. JANE EASMAN 296	. GUY V. 249,300
NOLES,JOSEPH 295	. JANE PLYLAR 296	. HANNAH 94
NORRIS,	. JANSIE 296-298	. HANNAH LAMKIN 262,301
. JOSEPH ZACHARIAH 295	. JEREMIAH NEWTON 297	. HATTON GUNTER 209,299
. YOUNG 22,295	298	. J.D. 209
NORVELL,CLARA DAVIS 295	. JOHN BERRY 297	. JAKE W. 335
. CLARA HAWES 295	. L.H. 379	. JAMES 49,93
. KATHLEEN 295	. LEWIS 298	. JEFFERSON 299
. LUCIEN BONAPARTE 295	. LIDIA 297	. JEFFERSON D. 299
. MARY HAWES 295	. LUCY 297	. JEREMIAH 299
. MARY LEECH 295	. MAHALEY E. PLYLER 257	. JESSE 93
. PAYTON 295	. MAHALEY ELINOR	. JOHN 300-301
. PEYTON 295	PLYLAN 296	. JOSEPH 299
. SALLY NELSON 296	. MAMIE WINN 379	. JUDSON 300
ODOM,ALICE LEITH 298	. MARTELIA LEONARD 266	. JULIA RUTLEDGE 323
. ALLAN THURMAN 298	298	. JUSDON 77
. ALPHA 297-298	. MARTHA 344	. LULU DODD 300
. ANNETTE 296	. MARY 255,257,296	. MABEL 300
. ASBURY 296	. MARY E. 205,296	. MARTIN 209,298-300
. AUGUSTUS ADOLPHUS 297	. MARY E. ODOM 205	. MAYNARD 300
. AVERY 329	. MINARD 298	. OAT SHERER 335
. BELLE 306	. MISSOURI 205	. ODESSA HENLEY 300
. CANASDA 296	. NANCY 297	. PERNIA GUNTER 209
. CAROLINE P.	. NANCY KILGORE 249	. R.A. 76
THOMPSON 297	. NOAH 297	. RUFUS A. 73
. CAROLINE THOMPSON 362	. OLIVER 296	. RUFUS ALLEN 300
. CATHERINE 296	. PARALEE THOMPSON 296	. SAMUEL 299,323
. CATHERINE SANFORD 296	298	. SARAH M. FELTMAN 299
. CORELY 298	. PEARL 298	. VENILA L. SANDERS 300
. DALTON 296,307	. SAMANTHIA 237	326
. DAVID 297	. SAMUEL 296	. VESTA BRIGGS 300
. DOCK 297,328	. TENNA SARTAIN 328	. WILLIAM 298
. ELIZABETH ADCOCK 297	. THOMAS 296	. WILLIAM B. 262,299
. ELIZABETH SEDBERRY 296	. VADE SARTAIN 329	. WILLIAM BYRD 300
. ELSIE RUTH 298	. WILLIAM 249,296-298	. WILLIAM J. 299
. ELVIN RAY 297	328,380	ORR,JONATHAN 22,301
. EMILY 205,296,314	. WILSON 343	OWEN,CHARLES C.P. 301
. ETTA SIDES 343	ODUM,ABRAHAM 276	. CHARLES C.P. 301
. GAYE WALTON 298	. VICY 276	. DOLLY WILLIAMS 199
. GERUSHA T. SARTAIN 297	OLIVER,WILLIAM 269	. ELIZABETH 301
. GRAHAM N. 298	. ZEPHRONIA E.	. ELLA 301
. HENRY G. 298	LOLLAR 269	. HUBERT CARLOS 302
. HONOR 297	OREAR,ADELE BROWN 300	. IDA 301
. HUBERT 298	. ANDERSON 299,301	. ISAAC 302
. HUGH DAVID 298	. CAINE 300	. JULIA 301
. IRENE WOOD 380	. DANIEL 299	. MARIE S. BANKHEAD 127
. ISABELLA 169	. EDWARD 299	. MARY A. 199
. ISABELLE 296	. ELIJAH 94,97,299	. MARY C. COOPER 301
. J. AVERY 298	. ETHEL 300	. NANCY L. McADORY 322
. J. NEWTON 266	. FIELDS 300	. NORA LEMONS 301
. JACOB 297,328	. G.D. 94	. RUFUS 301
. JAMES 205,257,296-297	. GEORGE 96	. SADIE EASON 302
. JAMES I. 105	. GEORGE D. 326	. SUSAN RYAN 325
. JAMES IRA 296-298,362	. GEORGE DANIEL 299	. SUSANNA RYAN 301

History of Walker County, Alabama

. THOMAS	199
. THOMAS McADORY	127
. WILLIAM MARMADUKE	322
. WILLIAM	
. MONTREVILLE	301
. WILLIAM OLIVER	325
. WILLIE E.	322
OWENS,	122
OXFORD, FRANK	326
. SARAH S. SARTAIN	326
PALMER, ASBURY THOMAS	302
. DORA KATE LINN	302
. EDNA	303
. ELIZABETH ANN WHITE	302
.	332
. EUSTATIA	302,332
. GERTRUDE JACKSON	303
. JESSE	302
. JESSE DAWSON	303
. JOSEPH HENRY	303
. LINN	303
. LOVENIA	302
. LUCY ELLIS	163
. MATTIE	163
. R.H.	88
. ROBERT	75
. ROBERT HENRY	302
. ROBERT T.	104,302-303
.	332
. RUTH	303
. THOMAS A.	163
PARKER,	97
. ELLA OWEN	301
. PETER	91
. WILLIAM	301,303
PARNELL, JAMES ALLEN	303
PARSONS,	50
. THOMAS	303
PARVIN, J.L.	303
PATE,	
. FLOSSIE STEPHENSON	354
. ISHAM	303
. WILLIAM	354
. WILLIAM H.	83
PATTERSON,	382
. GEORGE W.	303
. JOHN	303
. LIMA	203
. NANCY MORRISON	303
. SAMUEL B.	303
. WILLIAM B.	303
PATTON,	59
. DORAN	305
. GEORGE W.	303

. JAMES	25
. JAMES M.	30-31,303
. SAMUEL	90
. SAMUEL B.	32
. W.B.	235
. WILLIAM	305
PAYNE, CORA	164
. DAVID	15,305
. ELIZABETH SNOW	350
. FRANCIS	350
. JOHN	359
. MATHEY	305
. SIS SWINDLE	359
. WILLIAM	15,25,305
PEAKE, DANIEL B.	305
PEARSON, FANNIE	324
PENDLEY, WILLIAM M.	305
PENNINGTON, J.M.	78
PERRY,	
. LOUISE BANKHEAD	127
. MARGARET ANN GAINES	196
. WILLIAM	196
. WILLIAM HAYNE	127
PERSINGER, ANTHONY	55,94
. WINFIELD	55,94
PETERSON,	
. ELIZABETH WALKER	370
. H. FRANKLIN	370
. SARAH G.	306
. SARAH M. LOVELADY	305
. W.F.	305
. W.H.	306
PEYTON, WILLIAM	295
PHARR, ETTA S.	120
PHELAN,	330
PHIFER, BELLE ODOM	306
. BERTIE SWINDLE	307
. CARL	306
. CLAYTON O.	307
. CLYDE	306
. EMILY COURINGTON	171
.	306
. ETHEL KEY	307
. HARRIET	372
. HARRIETT	306
. HENRY	306
. IDA	306
. J.J.	105
. JAMES J.	171,306
. JOHN	255,306,364,372
. JOHN WORTH	306
. JULIA	306
. JULIA ANN	364
. KATHLEEN	272

. LOYD	307
. MARTHA C.	255,306
. MARTHA ROSE	306
. MARTIN	306
. MARY	364
. MARY E. COOK	306,372
. MARY JANE	307,328
. MARY SUSAN	164,307
. OLLA JONES	306
. OSTREA SIMPSON	306
. PEARL LOLLAR	306
. QUEENIS	306
. REBECCA	306
. SALLY	306
. SARAH ANN	306
. STALIE	306
. THENIA	306
. WILLIAM	307,329
PHILLIPI, JULIANNA	333
PHILLIPS, ALFORD BYRD	307
. ELIZABETH FIELDS	307
. ELMER ANTHONY	77
. GEORGE W.	307
. GLENNIE C. LAMAR	260
. J.M.	76
. JACOB	35,85,90,307
. JEFFERSON	307
. JEFFERSON L.	308
. JOHN	83,307,354
. JOHN B.	308
. JOHN WASHINGTON	308
. LAVONIA A. MORRIS	286
. LILLY STEPHENSON	354
. MARGARET TERRY	307
. MARIETTA	308
. MARTIN MARION	307
. PRESTON B.	83
. ROBERT	307
. T.S.	260
. W.L.	286
. WILLIAM	308
PIERCE,	251
. ANNIE	169
PIKE,	112
. GRACE	311
. JOSEPH	308
. JOSEPH C.	344
. JOSEPH CARROLL	309
. MARTHA SIDES	309,344
. PHILLIP	308
. REUBEN	309
. SARAH	344
. WILLIAM	309
PITT, WILLIAM	309

History of Walker County, Alabama

PITTMAN,DANIEL W.	77	. N.B.	177	. FRANCIS BROWN	254
PLYLAN,		. NAPOLEON BONAPART	292	.	313-314
. MAHALEY ELINOR	296	. NAPOLEON BONAPARTE	309	. GEORGE S.	205,314
PLYLAR,JAMES B.	173	.	310	. HEWITT CLAY	314
. JAMES BURTON	309	. NAPOLEON COLORADO	292	. J.D.	254
. JANE	296	.	311	. JAMES	314
. MARIAH A.	173	. RUFUS	311	. JAMES DAVID	314
PLYLER,MAHALEY E.	257	. SADIE CRANFORD	310	. JANE	204,291
POE,	314	. SEBURN	311	. JEREMIAH	313
POLK,JAMES K.	278	. SILAS	336	. JOHN B.	94
PONDER,JAMES N.	309	. SQUIRE	311	. JOHN D.	39,142,313-314
POOL,JAMES H.	309	. SUSAN F. MYERS	311	. JOHN F.	205
. MARY A.	309	. SUSAN FRANCIS		. LORENZO D.	313
. URSULA A.	176	. MYERS	292	. LYDIA CRANFORD	173
POOLE,JAMES A.	176	. TRISSEY	310	. MALISSA	314
POPE,JOHN	51	. WASHINGTON	310	. MARTHA	205
POSEY,ADOLPHUS	310	POWELL,	342	. MARTHA E.	205
. ANICE ELLEN	311	. AMY	321	. MARTHA E. GRACE	205
. ARTHUR	336	. E.A.	212	. MARTHA ELLEN GRACE	314
. AUGUSTUS	311	PRATT,	83,88	. MATTIE	173
. BARBARA	311	PRESCOTT,JOHN	312	. MINNIE GRACE	205
. BARBARA POSEY	311	PRESTON,S.R.	78	. NANCY	314
. BIRDIE	257	PRICE,CHARLOTTE CAIN	154	. QUEENIE	315
. CLINTON	311	.	312	. ROXEY ANN	169
. COLUMBUS	310	. DANIEL	253	. ROXIE	314
. CORA	311	. JAMES MONROE	312	. SALLIE SHERER	337
. CRISSY SHERER	336	. NARCISSA		. SALLY WILLIAMS	314
. DELLA	311	. KIRKPATRICK	253	. SUSAN JANE	314
. EFFIE	311	. THOMAS W.	154,312	. THOMAS	314
. EFFIE DAILEY	177	PROPST,MARY	357	. THOMAS BROWN	314
. ELEANOR BROOKS	310	PRUITT,MAJOR	312	. TILLMAN	314
. ELIZA ANN CATES	311	QUEEN,HIRAM	312	. TIMIE	314
. ELIZABETH LATHAM	310	RABURN,F.G.	313	. VERA M. COURINGTON	315
. EMILY BIRDIE	311	. FRANK	144	. WILEY GRIFFIN	315
. EMILY E. DAILEY	310	. JOHN B.	312	. WILLIAM	314,337
. EULA ANN	311	. MARY SUSAN BROWN	144	RATCLIFFE,BARBARA	310
. FRANCIS MARION	311	. MINERVA	230,331-332	RAY,ALEX B.	316
. GEORGE WASHINGTON	311	.	381	. ALFRED	315
. GILBERT	311	. SUSAN	359	. CAUDACE MARTIN	315
. GRACE PIKE	311	RAINES,ANN	118	. ELIJAH	315
. HELEN LINDSAY	311	. ASENETH A. ABBOTT	118	. ELLA E. EDNEY	315
. JANE SHERER	336	. HIRAM	118	. GLADSTONE	316
. JESSE N.	310	. MILLEY BARTON	130	. IDA J. JONES	315
. JOSEPH H.	310	RAINS,JAMES	313	. IDA JONES	237
. LARUA ELLEN	311	. ROBERT	313	. IDA LOUISE	316
. LARUA ELLEN POSEY	311	RAMMAGE,MARY S.	326,328	. JAMES J.	237
. LEWIS HOLMES	311	.	344-345	. JAMES JASPER	315
. LOUIS	311	RANDOLPH,		. LUCY ANN WRIGHT	315
. MARTHA E.	312	. ADA WILLIAMS	314	. SILAS B.	315
. MARTHA HELEN	311	. ELISHA	313	. T.M.	316
. MARY SWINDLE	311	. ELLEN	314	. W.W.	315
. MINNIE B.	311	. FANNIE	315	READ,WILLIAM	41
. MINNIE SHERER	311	. FLOSSIE RUSSELL	315	REED,	208
. MISSOURI	177,310	. FRANCES	39	. BELLE COURINGTON	171
. MODINE	310	. FRANCES BROWN	142	. DALLAS	236

History of Walker County, Alabama

. ELLEN RANDOLPH	314	. PETRONILLA LAMKIN	262	ROBISON,MARTHA C.	200
. F.P.	171	RITTER,JOHN	329	RODDY,	265
. JOSEPH	314	. ZORA SARTAIN	329	RODGERS,WILLIAM B.	320
. LEVI	25	ROBBINS,IRA	95	ROGERS,	283
. MINERVA JONES	236	. JOHN	130	. ALICE	337
. PIERCE	236	. NANCY BARTON	130	. ELLEN E.	321
. POLK	236	ROBERTS,	334	. EMERY W.	320
. REUBEN	236	. ABRAHAM	318	. J.W.	320
. THOMAS	236	. ABRAHAM M.	207	. JAMES	320
REEVES,CARRIE	144	. ALZAH	205	ROLLINS,REUBEN	321
REID,ABSALOM	316	. AMOS	318	ROMINE,	112
. JOHN	316	. BAMA	318	. ELIZABETH ROBINSON	256
. NORA	118	. DAVIS	318	. JOHN B.	321
. WILLIAM	118,316	. FLOYD	318	. MACK	219
RENFRO,DORA	168	. GEORGE A.	318	. N.R.	256
RHEA,		. HENRY ALFORD	318	. NANCY	213
. GEORGIANNA		. IRENA BARTON	132	. NANCY BIRDWELL	321
. THOMPSON	362	. ISAAC	257	. ROBERT	219
. MARTHA E. THOMPSON	316	. ISABELLA	351	. SUSAN M. HAMILTON	219
.	362	. JOHN	132	ROOSEVELT,FRANKLIN D.	80
. WATSON	362	. MAUDE	318	ROOT,M.W.	63,86
. WILLIAM	316,362	. NATHAN	38	. MARTHA F. RUTLEDGE	324
. WILLIAM BARCLAY	316	. PEARL	318	. QUINNIE LEITH	266
RHODES,JACOB	317	. RUTHA SPARKS	257	. RALPH	266
RICE,	223,228,232	. SARAH A.E.	207	. WILLIAM	324
.	284-285,308,356,377	. WINNIE	318	ROPER,JOHN	268
. CORNELIA FILES	191	ROBERTSON,DALTON	301	ROSAMOND,	97
. E.J.	162	. DOCK	325	. AMY LEE	322
. GREEN P.	32	. ELIZABETH OWEN	301	. AMY POWELL	321
. JAMES LAFAYETTE	317	. JAMES	318	. EDWARD POWELL	322
. MANLY	191	. MARTHA E. RYAN	325	. ETHBERT C.	322
. WILLIAM	317	. WILLIAM	35,87	. FRANKLIN K.	322
RICHARDSON,	367	ROBINS,IRA	320	. HENRIETTA DINSMORE	322
. HIRAM	317	. JESSE	320	. HESTER M.	322
. JAMES W.	94,97	. JOHN B.	318	. MADORAH F. FREEMAN	193
. JOBE	54,110,198,317	. LEVI WILSON	318	.	322
. JOHN	97,318	. NANCY BARTON	318	. MAUDE SHIELDS	322
. JOSIAH	317	. WILLIAM A.	318,320	. NATHANIEL J.	321
. LUCY	317	ROBINSON,ADA	354	. OZELLA F. APPLING	322
. MARY	318	. AMANDA	240	. SUSIE K. BOULDIN	322
. PEARL ROBERTS	318	. BELL	144	. W.C.	65,75,93,99,105
. RUTHA	317	. BUD	172	.	175,193,229
. SUSAN	318	. ELIZABETH	256	. WILLIAM CAPERS	321
. W.R.	352	. JAMES F.	256	. WILLIAM L.	322
. WILLIAM	317-318	. JANE COURINGTON	172	. WILLIE E. OWEN	322
RICHEY,ALEX	83	. JOHN H.	108	ROSE,J.T.	70,106
. ALEXANDER	318	. MARGARET	108	. JULY GILCREASE	202
. JOSEPH	30-31,318	. MARTHA J.	378	. NEWTON	306
. WILLIAM M.	22,31,83	. MARTHA R.	256	. THOMAS N.	202
.	318	. MARY S.	256	ROSENWALD,	102
RIDDLESPERGER,		. NANCY J.	256	ROSS,HUGH P.	322
. AUGUSTUS C.	329	. NANCY KITCHENS	256	ROSSER,CHARLES L.	326
. GERTRUDE	329	. ROBERT	158	ROUNDTREE,MARY	166
. SAVANNAH COLE	329	. TEMPIE JACKSON	233	RUPELL,THOMAS J.	322
RIGHT,ELIAS	262	. WILLIAM	233	RUSSELL,	71,103

. ANDERSON	323	. JOHN B.	325	SAPP,	263		
. FLOSSIE	315	. JOHN C.	262	SARGENT,WILLIAM PENN	326		
. GEORGE	323	. JOHN CAMAK	325	SARTAIN,			
. WILLIAM	24,368	. JOSEPH	325	. ALICE COURINGTON	329		
RUST,RACHEL	142	. MARGARET	325	. BAMA WALTON	328		
RUTHERFORD,JOSEPH	33	. MARTHA E.	325	. BERTIE	329		
RUTLEDGE,	112	. MARY	325	. CHARLES M.	340		
. A.A.	247	. MARY CAMAK	155,301,325	. CHARLES MANUEL	329		
. ALFRED KING	323	. PATSY MARTHA	325	. CLAUD	329		
. ALICE WADE	324	. POLLY MARY	325	. ELIZA F.	328		
. ANDREW A.	324	. SALLY	326	. FANNIE M.	139		
. ANNIE	324	. SARAH E. LAMKIN	262	. FRANCES	330		
. CHARLES	324	.	325	. FRANCIS MARION	329		
. DAVID	323-324	. SUSAN	325	. GEORGE WASHINGTON	328		
. EDWARD	323-324	. SUSANNA	301	. GERTRUDE			
. ELIZA SIDES	323	. THOMAS	325	. RIDDLESPERGER	329		
. ELIZABETH	323	. WILLIAM	326	. GERUSHA T.	297		
. ELIZABETH A. SIDES	324	. WILLIAM I.	325	. HOSIE	329		
. ELIZABETH LOGAN	323	SAFFORD,ELI	38-39	. ISAAC LEE	328		
.	324	SALLADE,	71,103	. J.R.	108		
. ELIZABETH SIDES	323	SANDERS,	35,85,285	. JACOB	326		
. ETTA	324	. ADKIN	326	. JACOB MANLY	328		
. FANNIE PEARSON	324	. BELLE	255,326	. JAMES RUFUS	326,329		
. GEORGE HOUSTON	324	. CATHERINE L.	326	. JAMES VIRGIL	329		
. JACK	323	. CHARLES L. ROSSER	326	. JOANNA	330		
. JAMES	247,323	. JAMES	326	. JOHN	329		
. JAMES DANIEL	324	. LOUISA BARTON	130	. JOHN R.	307		
. JAMES M.	324	. LUCIE	326	. JOHN RAMMAGE	328		
. JOHN R.	324	. MARTHA	151	. JOHN WILLIAM	329		
. JOSEPH	323	. MARY ANN	287	. LEON	329		
. JULIA	323	. MATILDA	364	. MARTHA COURINGTON	171		
. LACY	355	. NANCY CAIN	154,326	.	329		
. MAGGIE WRIGHT	324	. NATHANIEL	326	. MARTHA JANE	328		
. MARTHA F.	324	. NEVADA HALE	326	. MARTHA SIDES	328		
. MARY ANN	247,324	. SAMUEL MONROE	154,326	. MARY	329		
. MARY KEY	324	. TINIE STURGIS	326	. MARY ANN	326		
. MARY NIX	324	. VENILA L.	300,326	. MARY CATHERINE	330		
. MINERVA JEFFRIES	323	. WILLIAM R.	326	. MARY JANE PHIFER	307		
.	324	. WILLIE	332	.	328		
. MINERVA KEY	247,324	SANDES,NANCY CAIN	300	. MARY LAURA	329		
. MOLLIE CRUMP	324	. SAMUEL MONROE	300	. MARY S. RAMMAGE	326		
. OLLIE	323	SANDLIN,DANIEL	326	.	328,344-345		
. POLLY ANN	323	. JOHN	118	. MARY TAYLOR	326		
. SARAH	324	. META	118	. MEDDA SUMNER	328		
. WILLIAM	323	. SOPHRONIA ABBOTT	118	. MINTY A.	328		
. WILLIAM TAYLOR	324	SANFORD,	296	. PENINNAH E.	328,345		
RYAN,ALICE	325	. CATHERINE	296	. RACHEL INMAN	329		
. BETSIE ELIZABETH	325	. G. RILEY	108	. RADIE COURINGTON	172		
. GEORGE	325	. JOHN W.	149	. RHODA M.			
. ISAAC	91,155,301	. LUANNA BUSBY	149	. COURINGTON	329		
.	325-326	. RUBY	332	. ROXANNA J.	328		
. JAMES	325	. WES	109	. RUFUS	172		
. JAMES G.	325	. WILLIAM A.	332	. SALLIE DAVIDSON	329		
. JAMES THOMAS	326	. WILLIE SANDERS	332	. SAMUEL ROBERT	329		
. JOHN	75,155,325-326	SANKEY,H.J.	76	. SARAH S.	326		

History of Walker County, Alabama

. TENNA	328	. JAMES	331	. KIRKPATRICK	337	
. VADE	329	. JAMES W.	75	. HUGH	338	
. VELMA	329	. JAMES WILEY	331-332	. J. BRAWLEY	334,354	
. VIRGIN HARBIN	329	. JEREMIAH	331	. J. TAYLOR	334	
. VONIE	329	. JOHN B.	47,331	. J.T.	65,98	
. WARD	329	. JOHN CARLISLE	332	. JAMES	336	
. WILLIAM	171	. KESIAH	331	. JAMES G.	333	
. WILLIAM TURNER	326,328	. MINERVA RABURN	230	. JANE	336,338	
.	344-345	.	331-332,381	. JEFFERSON D.	355	
. ZERUAH A.	328,344	. NANCY A.	331,381	. JEFFERSON DAVIS	334	
. ZORA	329	. ROBERT HERBERT	332	. JEFFERSON NEELY	337	
SAVAGE,BUD	171	. RUBY SANFORD	332	. JESSIE	145,338	
. JAMES	42-43,61,92-93	. SARAH ELIZ. MORRIS	286	. JOHN	333	
.	96,330	. SARAH J. CAMAK	156	. JOHN CHRISTOPHER	333	
. JAMES W.	330	. STEPHEN	331	. JOHN M.	336	
. KATIE	171	. TINSON	103,230,331-332	. JOHN MADISON	339	
. MARGARET		.	381	. JOHN MINTER	238-239	
. COURINGTON	171	. W.H.	171	.	334	
SCOTT,		. WILLIE LEE	332	. JOHN T.	144,334	
. CAROLINE SHERER	339	. WILSON	156,331	. JONATHAN	333	
. CARTER	177,330	. ZACK PALMER	332	. JONATHAN D.	338	
. CHRISTOPHER	339	SHERER,ABSALOM	335	. JOSEPH	306,337	
. SALLIE R. HENDON	222	. ALICE ROGERS	337	. JOSEPH ROBERT	337	
. THOMAS J.	222	. AMSI	251	. JOSEPH THOMAS	339	
SEDBERRY,ELIZABETH	296	. AMZI	336	. JULIANNA PHILLIPI	333	
SELF,JESSE	330	. BENJAMIN B.	338	. LAURA M. CROSWELL	335	
SELLERS,DAVID M.	382	. BUD	338	. LOHAMIE C.	144,334	
. EMMA YORK	382	. CAROLINE	339	. LUCY REAVES		
. HENRY	142	. CAROLINE JONES	238,337	. JACKSON	339	
. LIDA	142	. CLARA McCRARY	338	. LURA MOSS	337	
. RACHEL RUST	142	. CRISSY	336	. MADISON	258,336	
SHAW,ARTHUR	172	. DOCENA	337	. MADISON MONROE	145,251	
. JAMES MARION	330	. DORENDA	336	.	338	
. LEITHIE COURINGTON	172	. DORENDA KILGORE	251	. MALIVA	336	
. SEBORN JACKSON	330	.	336	. MANDY	337	
SHEFFIELD,	303	. ELISHA A.	335	. MARTHA	335	
SHEPHERD,	146,169,179	. ELIZA GLOVER	337	. MARTHA HUTTO	334	
.	229-230,233,238,264	. ELIZABETH		. MARTHA KILGORE	145,251	
.	269,278,286,293,316	. KIRKPATRICK	336	.	338	
.	318,325,350,352,362	. ETTA	338	. MARTHA MINTER	333-337	
.	363	. FANNIE	145,338	. MARY	251,336,338	
. ALBERTA LACY	260	. FANNIE CARMICHAEL	158	. MARY A.		
. ANNIE LOU	332	. FANNIE FILES	192,337	. KIRKPATRICK	334	
. COLEMAN	260	. FEN	337	. MARY EASON	339	
. E.W.	286	. FRANCES THOMAS	337	. MARY SIDES	336	
. EDWARD W.	108	. GAY	338	. MARY STEPHENSON	334	
. ELIZABETH	230,331	. GEORGE	336	.	354	
. EUSTATIA PALMER	302	. GRISELLA		. MATITE LOLLAR	336	
.	332	. STEPHENSON	334	. MAUDE	338	
. FRANCES GILCREASE	202	. GRISILLA		. MINNIE	311	
.	333	. STEPHENSON	355	. MINNIE DAY	337	
. ISAAC	331	. HAMIE ANDERSON	337	. MOLLIE	337	
. J.W.	302	. HARRIETT	336	. NADA	336	
. JACOB R.	199,202	. HARRIETT		. OAT	335	
. JACOB ROBERT	57,332			. OLLA McCRARY	338	

History of Walker County, Alabama

. RANEY KIRKPATRICK 335
. RICHARD ABNER 337
. RUTH 338
. SALLIE 336-337
. SAMARIAMUS JONES 239
. 334
. SARAH E. KITCHENS 258
. 336
. SARAH E. LOVE 337
. SARAH GABBERT 335
. SARAH JANE 337
. STALIE PHIFER 306
. THOMAS 192,336,338
. THOMAS N. 337
. VERA 336
. WILLIAM 333-338
. WILLIAM J. 337
. WILLIAM MINTER 336-337
. WILLIAM THOMAS 335
. WINNIE ROBERTS 318
SHIELDS, 61
. CARRIE E. LONG 341
. CARRIE LONG 167
. CARRIE MAY 341
. J.B. 65,75,99
. JOHN B. 57-58,66,78
. 167,341
. JOHN BRABSON 217
. 339-340
. MAUD 341
. MAUDE 322
. MILTON 217,339
. NANETTE 167
. NANETTE P. 341
. PRISCILLA BRABSON 217
. 339
. PRISCILLA J. 217
. WILLIAM 340
SHIRLEY,ABNER 177
. JONATHAN 31
SHORT, 370
. DANIEL 341
. G.W. 200
. JAMES 25,341
. LOUIS 341
. MARGARET GARRISON 200
. WILLIAM 341
SHORTERIDGE,
. GEORGE B. 172
SIDES, 97
. ANDY ALLEN 263,309,343
. BENJAMIN FRANKLIN 344
. CAROLINE 338
. CARRIE NIX 343
. CARRIE WRIGHT 345
. CEREPTA DILL 343
. COLE 343
. DAVID 200
. DOCK 249,343
. ELIJAH 146,342
. ELIZA 323
. ELIZA JANE 258,343-344
. ELIZABETH 323,344
. ELIZABETH A. 324
. ELIZABETH COONER 344
. ELLA THOMPSON 345
. EMILY 343,380
. ETTA 343,345
. EUGENE 345
. FANNIE 345
. FRANCES KITCHENS 258
. 344
. FRANCIS 344
. FRANK 258,344
. FRANK B. 345
. FRANKIE HENDON 343
. GEORGE FRANKLIN 344
. HARRISON 168,343
. HENRY 14,90,112,146
. 342-344
. HENRY COLEMAN 343
. HUGH R. 343
. HUGH ROBERT 258
. JAMES HARRISON 344
. JAMES M. 343-344
. JANE MINOR 344
. JOHN 328,342-343,345
. JOHN B. 345
. JOHN N. 345
. JOHNNIE B. 345
. JONATHAN D. 343
. JONATHAN M. 344
. JOSEPH V. 344
. LEVI 249,342
. LILA KEENE 345
. MALINDA KEETON 344
. MANLY 328
. MANLY LEE 344
. MARGARET 200
. MARGARET ELLIS 344
. MARGARET SMITH 344
. MARTHA 309,328,344
. MARTHA E. STAGGS 344
. MARTHA FAUGHT 344
. MARTHA JANE 343
. MARTHA JANE LAMKIN 262
. MARTHA K. STAGG 343
. MARTHA KITCHENS 258
. 343
. MARTHA ODOM 344
. MARY 336,345
. MARY ANN 345
. MARY ELIZ. 344
. MARY KILGORE 249,343
. MARY M. STAGGS 344
. MARY STAGGS 263,309
. MINNIE 247
. MOLLIE 233
. MOSES 342
. NANCY 263,344
. NANCY BROWN 146,342
. NANCY C. 249,336,342
. NANNIE KEY 343
. PENINNAH E.
. SARTAIN 328
. 345
. POLLY COONER 168,343
. RICHARD 343
. SARAH 343
. SARAH PIKE 344
. W.L. 262
. WILLIAM 90,258,324
. 342-343,380
. WILLIAM F. 258,343
. WILLIAM L. 344
. WILLIAM LAFAYETTE 344
. WILLIAM LUTHER 345
. ZERUAH A. SARTAIN 328
. 344
SIMMS,JULIA WALKER 369
. WILLIALM 369
SIMPSON,ANDO 346
. EMMA HARBIN 346
. EXER 346
. GEORGIA A. 154
. GRACE 346
. JAMES 83,345
. JAMES H. 346
. JOHN WESLEY 346
. MAYRTIE 346
. OSTREA 306
. OZELLA 346
. SAMUEL H. 104,345-346
. SARAH WORTHINGTON 345
. STATIE 346
. SUSAN GURGANUS 346
. URIAH 346
. VADA SUMNER 346
. WILLIAM THOMAS 345
. WILT 345
. ZORILDA 346
SINGLETON,EDMUND 346
. ELIZABETH 346
. JAMES 346
. LOUISEE 346

History of Walker County, Alabama

. MARGARET	346	. ELIZA FRANKLIN	150,350	. JOHN W.	257
. MATILDA DAVIS	346	. ELIZABETH	350	. LOUISA C.	256
SIVELY,		. ELIZABETH ADAMS	349	. MARY CAROLINE	
. AMANDA H. CAMAK	156	. ELIZABETH KEY	245	BAKER	124
. W.L.	156	. FRANCIS A.	150	.	256
SKELTON,NELSON	346	. FRANCIS ASBURY	350	. RICHARD THOMAS	256
. ROBERT	77	. HENRY ADAMS	349	. RUTH SUSAN	124
SKINNER,RUTH	258	. JAMES MONROE	350	. RUTHA	257
SLEDGE,ADELAIDE E.	128	. JIMROE	350	. SAMUEL E.	257
. EVELYN E. GARTH	128	. JOHN W.	350	. THOMAS E.	124
. J. THOMAS	128	. KENNIE	150	SPAULDING,EPHRAIM	351
SLOAN,GEORGE A.	347	. MALINDA	350	JOHN P.	351
. SIMPSON S.	347	. MARY	245-246	SPEAGLE,DAVID	173
. STERLIN W.	347	. MATILDA ANN		. PATSY CRANFORD	173
SMITH,ALEX	340		CHILTON 157	. WINNIE CRANFORD	173
. ALLEN	348		180,350	SPEAR,ARDENA	352
. ALVIN A.	347	. MATILDA CHILTON	161	. BENJAMIN	351
. B.B.	348	. NANCY	350	. GEORGE	351
. BELL	348	. PETER	349	. JOHN	351
. BENJAMIN J.	347	. SARAH	350	. RICHARD	352
. BERTHA	257	. SARAH E.	180	SPEARS,JOHN	96
. CATHERINE L.		. THOMAS	349	SPINKS,ELSA BLANTON	139
SANDERS	326	. THOMAS J.	350	. JAMES S.	139
. EPHRAIM	347	. W.W.	245	SPRINGFIELD,	
. EUGENE A.	58	. WILLIAM	349	. ROBERT T.	352
. H. CAM	348	. WILLIAM HENRY	157,161	SPROTT,AUGUSTA M.	271
. IDA	348		180,349-350	. NONA BELL	271
. JESSE	347	. Z.B.	349	SRYGLEY,F.D.	70,100
. JOHN	347	. ZILPHEY	350	STACKS,JOHN MORGAN	352
. KATHLEEN CHILTON	161	. ZYLPHA	157	STAGG,MARTHA K.	343
. L.M.	348	SOWELL,ANN COOK	351	. MARTHA KITCHENS	258
. LAURA	348	. ISABELLA ROBERTS	351	. W.W.	63,86
. LEONDIAS KIRKSEY	348	. J.L.	76	. WILLOBY	63,86
. MARGARET	344	. JAMES L.	102	STAGGS,BETTY	380
. PATSY A.	348	. JAMES LAWRENCE	351	. JOHN	352
. R.H.	97	. MARGARET E. LOLLAR	269	. MARTHA E.	344
. REBECCA J.		.	351	. MARY	263,309
CRANFORD	348	. T.L.	71,269	. MARY M.	344
. RICHARD	348	. THOMAS L.	167,266	STANFORD,	
. RICHARD H.	348	. THOMAS LAMAR	350-351	. IDA CHILDERS	160
. S.B.	326	. WILLIAM CALVIN	350	. JAMES T.	160
. S.P.	61	SPARKS,ALVIN R.	125	STANLEY,	42,92-93
. SAM P.	97	. ALVIN S.	124	. ALICE C.	217,353
. SUSAN GAINES	196	. ANNIE	204,207	. ANGELINE	191
. WALTER KELLOGG	161	. ELI	124,256	. BENJAMIN F.	352
. WILLIAM	347	. ELI A.	124-125,256	. ELIZA GAINES	196
SNODDY,EMMA	145	. ELIJAH	143	. ELIZABETH	127
. ETTA SHERER	338	. ELIZABETH	257	. FATIMA	193
. JOHN	348	. ELIZABETH BROWN	143	. FRANK	196
. MARY C.	349	. EMILY KNIGHT	205	. J.M.	353
. MATILDA	348	. FRANCES KITCHENS	124	. MARTHA HENDRICKS	352
. ROBERT	338	.	256	. MARY P.	217
. SAMUEL	49,348	. JAMES E.	205	. NANCY THOMAS	352
SNOW,	37,303	. JAMES M.	257	. SAMUEL	352
. CHARLES	349	. JOHN E.	124	. W.L.	92-93,217,352

History of Walker County, Alabama

STEADMAN,	124	. SALLIE MASTERSON	280	. WILLIAM THOMAS	52,243
. EULA GRACE	207	.	355	.	357
. JAMES F.	124	. SAMUEL	353-354	STURGIS,	
. ROBERT	207	. SAMUEL M.	353-354,361	. JOSHUA FRANKLIN	358
. SARAH L. BAKER	124	. SIS	253	. TINIE	326
STEARNS,ELZIABETH	349	. TILLIAN	353	SUGG,HERBERT L.	358
STEEDMAN,	272,294	. VADA	354	SULLIVAN,JOHN	35,87
. JOHN BENJAMIN	353	. WILLIAM	355	. WILLIAM P.	358
STENSON,	279	. WILLIAM WATSON	355	SUMMER,MARY AGNES	372
STEPHENS,SARAH	151	STEVENS,ABRAHAM	356	. NEIL	306
STEPHENSON,ADA	354	. ADAM J.	356	. REBECCA PHIFER	306
. ADA ROBINSON	354	STEWART,BENJAMIN	336	SUMMEY,	
. ANDREW	354	. C. HARVEY	271	. MARGARET CAMAK	155
. CATHERINE FILES	190	. G.W.	97	. PETER	155
.	334-335,354	. GEORGE	336	SUMNER,CAROLINE	172
. CLAUD M.	355	. HARRIETT SHERER	336	. DELLA BARTON	132
. DESSIE	354	. JOHN	95	. ELIZABETH LOLLAR	346
. DOSHIE	353	. LOU LONG	271	. FRANKLIN REUBEN	358
. ELLIOTT	354	. MALIVA SHERER	336	. JAMES	132
. FLOSSIE	354	. SAMUEL	356	. JOHN B.	307
. GEORGE	355	. WILLIAM	22,356	. JOHN H.	346
. GRISELLA	334	STOCKRIDGE,ANDREW	22,90	. MARY	171
. GRISILLA	355	.	356	. MEDDA	328
. H.W.	280	STOCKS,EFFIE POSEY	311	. VADA	346
. HUGH STEWART	355	. ELLEN RANDOLPH	314	SUTHERLAND,ADAM	358
. HUGH W.	355	. W. HOUSTON	311	. JAMES	358
. HUGH WATSON	355	STONESTREET,EDITH	261	SUTTLE,ISAAC W.	202
. IRENE	355	STOVAL,IRENA	132	. MARY ANN	202
. JANE MORROW	355	STOVALL,	237	SUTTON,JACOB	359
. JENCIE KIRKPATRICK	253	. A.B.	357	. PHILLIP	358
.	353	. A.M.	61	. WILLIAM	359
. JOHN	190,334-335,354	. ANDREW McADAMS	357	SWANSON,	
. JOHN E.	354	. D.L.	43,64,92-93,96	. ELIZABETH GRACE	205
. JOHN H.	108,253,353	. DAVIS LEWIS	356	SWINDLE,	241,297
. LACY RUTLEDGE	355	. EULA	357	. ALICE CRANFORD	360
. LILLY	354	. JAMES	357	. AMANDA MYERS	359
. LISHA	353	. LEWIS	43,92	. AMANDA S. MYERS	292
. MARY	334,354	. MARY McLEESE	356	. BAYLISS	359
. MARY A. TIERCE	108	. MARY PROPST	357	. BERTIE	307
.	353-354	. NANCY DODSON	357	. CHRISTIANA H.	
. MARY ANN	353	. WILLIAM	320	.	ELLIS 186
. MARY KING	355	. WILLIAM POOL	356	. CYNTHIA GRACE	359
. MARY M.	353	STUBBLEFIELD,C.W.	138	. D.V.	360
. MELINDA JOHNSON	355	. CHARLES WOOTEN	357	. DANIEL	292,359
. MIRANDA	354	. ELIZABETH KELLEY	243	. DANIEL D.	360
. MOLITA MORROW	355	.	357	. DENNIS	292,359
. MOSE M.	353	. H. EUGENE	357	. DOCK	360
. MOSES MARION	354	. IDA E. BLANTON	358	. E. DARL	360
. MOSES N.	108	. IDA EMILY BLANTON	138	. ELIAS	359
. PAUL	355	. JOHN	357	. ELIJAH	359
. PEARL	355	. MARTHA	357	. ETTA	174,360
. RACHEL	108,361	. NANCY GRAHAM	357	. FELIX	172
. RAMSAY	353	. NANCY WOOTEN	357	. GENIE	360
. ROSCOE O.	355	. TALBOT KELLEY	358	. GEORGE	70,106,360
. SALLIE KING	353	. WILLIAM F.	358	. JALIE	360

. JAMES	359	
. JAMES WESLEY	360	
. JANE DAVIDSON	360	
. JENNIE	196	
. JENNIE WHITSON	360	
. JESSE	360	
. JOHN	359	
. JOHN H.	204,359	
. JOHN HOLLY	360	
. L. CYNTHIA GRACE	360	
. LIZA DAVIDSON	360	
. LUCINDA GRACE	204	
. LUCIOUS C.	360	
. LUCIUS C.	292	
. MANDY	359	
. MARTHA COURINGTON	172	
. MARTHA H. MYERS	360	
. MARTHA HELEN MYERS	292	
. MARY	311	
. MEHALEY C.	292	
. MINTER	247	
. OLLIE RUTLEDGE	323	
. PEN WILLIAMSON	359	
. PERMELIA	359	
. POLLY GURGANUS	360	
. SIS	359	
. SUSAN HOGG	359	
. SUSAN HOGUE	292,359	
. SUSAN RABURN	359	
. VINIE	359	
. W.M.	186	
. WID	323,359	
. WILLIAM	104,292	
	359-360	
. WINNIE CRANFORD	360	
TALBOT,	317	
TANDY,DOROTHY B.	257	
TANNER,MICHAEL	361	
TATE,JAMES	293	
. NANCY	288	
TAYLOR,ELIZABETH	269	
. HARRIET	351	
. ISAAC	269	
. JASPER	354	
. MARY	326	
. RACHEL STEPHENSON	108	
	353,361	
. ROBERT	108,353,361	
. SARAH ANN	254	
. WADE B.	92,361	
. WILLIAM W.	361	
. ZACHARY	369	
TERRY,	278	
. BESSIE GILDER	203	
. LUCIUS L.	203	
. MARGARET	307
THACKER,B.	210
. SALLY	261
. SAMUEL	261,361
. SARAH	261-262,301,325
. SARAH GURGANUS	210
THIRSK,RUSSELL A.	77
THOMAS,	
. ANDREW JACKSON	144,361
. BELLE COURINGTON	171
. BENJAMIN FRANKLIN	361
. DAVID	205
. ELIZA KNIGHT	205
. FRANCES	337
. JAMES MADISON	361
. JOSEPHINE	233
. JULIA BROWN	144,361
. MARY	362
. NANCY	352
. SIM	171
. VERA SHERER	336
. WILLIAM	336
THOMPSON,	349
. CAROLINE	362
. CAROLINE P.	297
. CAROLINE PARALEE	297
. ELIZABETH	362
. ELLA	345
. ETTA A. KITCHENS	257
. EVALINE E.	362
. FLEMING R.	297,316,362
. FLEMING RUDOLPH	362
. FLORIDA A.	362
. GEORGIANNA	362
. J.B.	362-363
. JAMES	353
. JOBERRY	362
. JOHN L.	362
. MARGARET ELIZABETH	362
. MARIA L.	362
. MARTHA E.	316,362
. MARY ANN STEPHENSON	353
. MARY L.	235
. MATTIE GAINES	196
. PARALEE	296,298
. SAMUEL	22,362-363,379
. SAMUEL B.	362
. SARAH J.	362
. SYLVESTER	257
. WILEY	321
. WILLIAM ALEXANDER	363
TIERCE,	146,210,249,286
. ANN	196
. ELLIOTT	354
. ELLIOTT C.	108
. FRANCIS	108
. L.A.	222
. MARY A.	108,353-354
. PERDIE L. HENDON	222
TINGLE,B.F.	66
. BENJAMIN FRANKLIN	363
. J.D.	189
TOMPSON,	285
TORREY,CHARLES J.	351
TOWNLEY,BOB	62
. DANIEL	22,90,112,363
. JOHN	22,364
. LOUISA BAKER	124
. MARTHA A.	190,364
. POLLY COONER	168
. RICHMOND	364
TOWNSLEY,ROBERT	113
TUBB,	37,123,204-205
. DANIEL	237
. DANIEL LEE	306
. J.A.	200
. JULIA	205
. JULIA PHIFER	306
. POLLY	237
. SALLIE GARRISON	200
. SAMUEL	104
. THENIA PHIFER	306
. WINNIE	117
TUBBS,DANIEL	364
. DANIEL LEE	173,292,364
. DOLLY DARTHA	364
. DOROTHY HAMILTON	364
. JAMES MADISON	364
. JULIA ANN PHIFER	364
. KING DAVID	364
. MALINDA CARLERY	364
. MALINDA CRANFORD	173
. MALINDA E. CRANFORD	364
. MARCUS LESTER	77
. MARTHA HAMILTON	364
. MARY ANN	292,364
. MATILDA J.	364
. MATILDA SANDERS	364
. NANCY E. CRANFORD	173
	364
. NANCY EMILY CRANFORD	292
. POLLY	364
. SAMUEL	173,364
. SAMUEL SANDERS	364
. WILLIAM	364
TUCKER,SAMUEL	364
TUGGLE,	

History of Walker County, Alabama

. EDWARD HARRISON 364	WALDROP,A.P. 235	. HARRIETT PHIFER 306
. JAMES 25	. MATTIE 109	. J.B. 372
. JAMES B. 364	. NANCY SNOW 350	. JOHN 372
TURNER, 37,42,92	. ROBERT 109,350	. JULIA 372
. ELIHU 366	. ROBERT G. 109	. MARTHA BEASLEY 298,372
. G.A. 367	WALKER,ABRAHAM 370	. SAMUEL 298,306,372
. GEORGE 362	. AMOS 370	. THOMAS 372
. JAMES T. 366	. AMOS B. 284,369-370	WARD,ANNIE RUTLEDGE 324
. JOHN 30-31	. ANDERSON 284	. D.W. 63,86
. JOHN H. 366	. DAISY E. COVIN 173	. EDWARD D. 382
. JOHN OLIVER 367	. ELIZA J. 370	. HARVEY 355
. MATHIAS 14,31,366	. ELIZA J. MORGAN 370	. IRENE STEPHENSON 355
. SARAH J. THOMPSON 362	. ELIZA MORGAN 284	. JAMES A. 324
TURRENTINE,	. ELIZABETH 370	. LOUISE YORK 382
. SARAH J. DUTTON 256	. EZEKIEL 284	. MARTIN 22,372
TUTTLE,ROBERT G. 367	. GEORGE 370	WARE,MAE 95
TYREE,JESSE 112,367	. ISAAC 370	WARRANFELDT,J.J. 65,84
. JOSEPH 367	. JACOB D. 370	WARREN, 133
UNDERWOOD,IDA PHIFER 306	. JAMES R. 369-371	. JOHN W. 43,92
. J.W. 306	. JANE 270	WASHBURN,RICHARD S. 372
UPCHURCH,	. JOHN W. 18,23	WASHINGTON, 333
. BESSIE MAE COLLINS 168	. JULIA 369	. GEORGE 129
. PHILIP R. 168	. LEROY P. 278	WATHALL, 367
UPTAIN,JOHN 367	. MARTHA 147,284,369	WATSON,A.B. 43,92
USREY,JAMES WILLIAM 367	. MARTHA E. 243	. JESSE 372
. MARY M. 367	. MARY 369	WATTS, 360
UTLEY,W.H. 298	. NANCY BRACKETT 370-371	. J.J. 124
VANBUREN, 278	. NANCY T. BRACKETT 284	. J.S. 373
VANDEVEER,THOMAS 368	. 369	. JAMES J. 372
VANHOOSE,JESSE 24,34,152	. RILEY 284	. JAMES S. 105
. 368	. S. RAYMOND 173	. M.C. 124
VANHORN,ANDREW J. 368	. SAMANTHA J. 370	. MOLLIE 373
VANSELT,SUSAN 364	. SAMUEL 284,369-371	. WILLIAM MARTIN 373
VICKORY,WILLIAM 368	. SAMUEL E. 370	WEBB,EDWARD B. 373
VINCENT,JAMES 310	. SAMUEL G. 370	. MAUD LACY 260
. TRISSEY POSEY 310	. SARAH F. 370	. MELVINA 373
VINES,ALPHA ODOM 297	. THADDEUS MONROE 371	. MELVINA WEBB 373
. CLARENCE 297	. THOMAS 369	. W.E. 88
. W.E. 379	. WALTER 370	WEDGEWORTH,RICHARD 373
VOYLES,BERTHA KEY 245	. WILLIAM F. 369-370	WEEMBS,JOSEPH 246
. JASPER 245	. WILLIAM FRANCIS 370	. NANCY KEY 246
. LINDY KEY 245	WALL,A.A. 371	WELCH,CALLIE 65,84
. LUCY KEY 245	. MARY AGNES SUMMER 372	WELLS,JAMES 373
WADE,ADELINE 249	WALLACE,JESSE B. 372	. WILEY 373
. ALICE 324	. LUCINDA CAIN 154	WEST, 119,137
. JOHN LANDON 248,368	. RANSOM 154	. EMMA 65,84
. MINTIE ANN 248	WALLER,MELISSA 210	. GUSSIE KELLEY 243
. SARAH ANN BLANTON 248	WALLING,DAVID 372	. J.W. 65,84
. 368	WALLIS,W.L. 64,98	. JAMES R. 243
WAKEFIELD,	WALSTON,LURANIA 188-189	. MATTIE 189
. FANNIE SIDES 345	WALTON,ADIS 144	WETHINGTON,MENTA 205
. GEORGE L. 345	. AMERICA 372	WHARTON, 138,284,368,381
. JAMES MONROE 369	. BAMA 328,372	. J.M.C. 56
. JOHN WESLEY 369	. GAYE 298	. JOHN 157
. MALISSA O. 369	. HARRIET PHIFER 372	WHATLEY, 123,205,258,265

History of Walker County, Alabama

.	292,294-295,300-301
.	325,343,348,360
. DANIEL H.	47,374
. MARTHA E. LEITH	374
WHITE,	71,103
. A.J.	108
. AUSTIN	350
. CLAYTON	246
. ELIZABETH ANN	302,332
. JEPTHA	83,374
. MALINDA SNOW	350
. SARAH BELINDA KEY	246
. T.J.	184,205
. ZACK	302
WHITFIELD,	
. AUGUSTUS F.	374
. B.W.	374
. BRYAN	75
. BRYAN W.	374
. GUS	75
. JAMES B.	374
. JESSE GEORGE	374
. MARY A. FORTESCUE	374
. NATHAN B.	374
WHITNEY,AMELIA	211
. MARION	236
. MINERVA JONES	236
. SUSAN I.	211
. SUSANNA	236
. TONEY	236
. WILLIAM T.	211
WHITSITT,	120
WHITSON,ALBERT G.	375
. JENNIE	360
. LISHA STEPHENSON	353
. MILES	353
. SAMUEL	375
. SARAH	265
. SARAH A.	275
. SARAH F.	298
. THOMAS	31
. THOMAS J.	374
. WILLIAM	34
WHITTEN,GEORGE W.	375
. SPENCER	375
WIGGINS,CHARLES R.	296
. MANDY SWINDLE	359
. SALLY N. NORVELL	296
WILES,THOMAS	262
WILKES,ELIZABETH	173-174
.	364
WILLCUTT,JOHN	248
. RUTH KILGORE	248
WILLIAMS,	37,118,246
. A.	42

. ADA	314
. AUGUST	376
. AUGUSTUS ALEXANDER	219
.	376
. BELINDA CHILTON	161
. CORDELIA	219
. DOLLY	199
. ELIZABETH	377
. GERMINE A.	
. BECKERSTAFF	376
. GERMINE	
. BECKERSTAFF	134
. IDA	219
. JAMES	124
. JAMES PERRY	376
. JOHN A.	219
. JOHN H.	375
. JOHN RANDALL	375
. LEE	105,161
. LEROY	377
. LOUISA BAKER	124
. MARTHA A.	187
. MARY	376
. MAY E. HAMILTON	219
. MELTON	291
. NAN MYERS	291
. NAPOLEON BONAPARTE	377
. POLKA	246
. REBECCA HAMILTON	219
.	376
. ROBERT	30-31,213
.	375-376
. ROBERT G.	218
. SALLY	314
. SAMANTHIA	246
. SARAH	219
. SARAH ANN	213,215,375
. SARAH E. HAMILTON	218
. WASH	376
. WASHINGTON	134
WILLIAMSON,PEN	359
. VINIE SWINDLE	359
WILLIS,SARAH	131
WILSON,	50,93,220,233
.	284,294,301
. ALMA COWART	378
. B. GRADY	378
. BIRDIE	378
. COLEMAN	378
. ELIZABETH	252
. FRANCES J.	166,341
. FRANCIS JANE	167
. GAY SHERER	338
. J.H.	49
. JAMES	167

. LACY	378
. LUCINDA	380
. MARGARET T. GAMBLE	377
. MARTHA J. ROBINSON	378
. MARY	131,214
. MARY ANN BENNETT	169
. NANCY	296
. R. JESS	338
. ROBERT	167
. ROBERT JESSE	378
. ROBERT L.	378
. RUFUS	378
. SARAH HAWTHORNE	377
. SARAH M. MYRICK	378
. THOMAS	377
. WASHINGTON	377
. WILLIAM	377
. WILLIAM M.	378
. WILLIAM WALLACE	377
.	378
. YOUNG M.	377
WINCHESTER,J.V.	378
. WILLOUGHBY	378
WINDHAM,JAMES EDWARD	291
.	378
. SARAH MYERS	291,378
WINKLE,	296
WINN,DAISY	379
. DENNIS FRANKLIN	77
. DENNIS T.	379
. GILES T.	379
. JOHN	379
. MAMIE	379
. R.T.	379
. WILLIAM M.	379
WINTER,SAMUEL F.	379
WINTERS,REBECCA	246
WISE,AMELIA	208
. ELIZABETH M.	
. JACKSON	208
. JOHN	208
. MARY	258
WOLF,DAVID	379
WOMMACK,ELIZABETH	237
WOOD,ALLIE WOODS	380
. C.A.	343,380
. CHARITY E.	245,380
. CHARITY ELIZ.	247,324
. COMMODORE	380
. CURLE	380
. DOCK	380
. EDWARD	380
. EDWARD THOMAS	247
.	379-380
. EMILY SIDES	343,380

History of Walker County, Alabama

. ETHEL OREAR	300	
. IRENE	380	
. JAMES	380	
. JOHN	22,24,90,379	
. JOSEPH ARCHIBALD	380	
. LON	380	
. MINERVA	247	
. MINERVA WOODS	379-380	
. PHOEBE	380	
. PRUDY	380	
. WHITTY COURINGTON	380	
. WILLIAM W.	300	
. ZELLIE NELSON	380	
WOODFIN,		
. AMANDA ETHEL JONES	241	
. IRVIN	241	
WOODRUFF,	366	
WOODS, ALLIE	380	
. BETTY STAGGS	380	
. DAVID	380	
. IRENE	296	
. JOHN HOP	380	
. LUCINDA WILSON	380	
. LUCY ALLEN	245,380	
. MINERVA	379-380	
. NANCY	380	
. RUTH	188	
. SAMUEL	245,379-380	
WOODSON, MARY	251	
. WILLIAM A.	380	
WOOTEN, AMANDA C.	271	
. HENRY POPE	271	
. MELISSA C. HINTON	271	
. NANCY	357	
WORTHAM, MALINDA	258	
WORTHINGTON,		
. ELIZABETH	381	
. JOHN	381	
. NANCY A. SHEPHERD	331	
.	381	
. SARAH	345	
. WILLIAM WESLEY	380	
. WILSON W.	331,381	
WRIGHT,	112,345	
. ADA BOSHELL	191	
. BASCOM	191	
. BELMA	176	
. CARRIE	345	
. ELIZABETH	315	
. JESSE	315	
. JOHN LANIER	381	
. LESTER	346	
. LUCY ANN	315	
. MAGGIE	324	
. OZELLA SIMPSON	346	
. THOMAS J.	381	
. WILLIAM FRANKLIN	381	
. WILLIAM M.	176	
YANCY,	278	
YARBROUGH,	131	
. JOSHUA	382	
YORK, AARON A.	382	
. AARON G.M.	382	
. DORA	382	
. EDWARD	382	
. ELIZA PATTERSON	382	
. EMMA	382	
. LOUISE	382	
. MARTHA CARR	382	
. MELVIN	382	
. OPHELIA ATTAWAY	382	
. THOMAS F.S.	382	
YOUNG, ANDERSON	382	
. MARTHA ANNE	260	

www.ingramcontent.com/pod-product-compliance
Lightning Source LLC
Chambersburg PA
CBHW070058020526
44112CB00034B/1438